VALUATION AND EXPLOITATION OF INTELLECTUAL PROPERTY AND INTANGIBLE ASSETS

John Sykes, Solicitor
Partner, Lupton Fawcett

Kelvin King,
Partner, Valuation Consulting

© emis professional publishing and the Authors 2003

Published by
emis professional publishing ltd
31–33 Stonehills House
Welwyn Garden City
Hertfordshire
AL8 6PU

ISBN 1 85811 281 8

Typeset by Jane Conway

Cover design by Jane Conway
Cover photography by Jon Adams

Printed in Great Britain by Antony Rowe

Dedicated to

John Sykes: Siobhan, William, John and Maeve

Kelvin King: for Gill, Anna and Dominique

Acknowledgements

We are very grateful to Paul Strzelecki, Tim Hill and Phil Sykes for taking the time in their busy lives to read drafts of the book and for making helpful and always constructive comments.

We are also very grateful to Gary Salt who collaborated on the chapter about securitisation.

THE AUTHORS

John Sykes

John Sykes has a degree in business administration, is a qualified UK lawyer, and trained as a patent attorney. In the early 1990s, he was instrumental in setting up and working in the first multidisciplinary practice of lawyers and patent attornies in the UK. He is currently a partner in the professional services firm Lupton Fawcett (www.luptonfawcett.com).

He has over the last almost twenty years handled many leading intellectual property disputes reported as precedent cases. The first two in the early 1980s, one involving patents and the other copyright. The most recent cases in 2002, one involving design rights and the other the right to own an alphanumeric famous brand. There were many in between including in 1989 the landmark Improver patent infringement case.

John Sykes has advised in all types of transactions involving intellectual property both in his home country and internationally, often leading teams working on major transactions. These have involved due diligence in M & A and corporate finance work, infringement due diligence, the assignment and licensing of intellectual property, and the use of intellectual property as security for business finance. He has in recent years been asked by companies and investors to advise on and implement strategies and process about the management, exploitation, and valuation of intellectual property. He has lectured extensively on all aspects of intellectual property.

Kelvin King

Kelvin King is a valuer with involvement in private equity most of his working life. After working on the UK Government's Shares Valuation, he established a valuation unit for a large accountancy practice and was the MD of a specialist valuation company within a major Swiss bank. The founder of Valuation Consulting (www.valuation-consulting.co.uk) and the Society of Shares and Business Valuers he is a lecturer and a contributor to many books, journals, television and radio.

He has been one of two separately listed Expert Witnesses in the areas of intellectual property and intangible asset valuation and one of the five separately listed Unquoted Company experts in the *Law Society Directory of Expert Witnesses* (1996–2003). He is a founding expert of Lord Woolf's Expert Witness Institute, member of the Licensing Executives Society, Chartered Institute of Patent Agents (Associate) and the International Association of Consultants, Valuers and Analysts.

CONTENTS

Chapters

CHAPTER 1
INTRODUCTION

Most people do not have the most basic understanding of IP. Ask even the largest company CEOs the difference between "patentability" and "freedom to use" and probably 95% of them, and 100% of their shareholders, would not know the answer to this most basic of questions. Yet technology, creative works, brands and so much else that is intangible – a business's *intellectual capital* – makes up an increasing percentage of shareholder value.

Ian Harvey, C.E.O., BTG Group plc

Price WaterhouseCooper/Landwell's UK Intellectual Property 2002 survey provide some interesting trends, in particular:

- the role of IP in the business is often insufficiently understood;

- IP is probably undervalued;

- IP is often either under-managed or under-exploited; and

- there is little co-ordination between the different professionals dealing with the organisation's IP.

With the onset of major changes in the IP environment, many of the risks associated with this are largely ignored.

The importance of IP should not be under-estimated. It is a key factor in the worth of a company and is increasingly given a substantial value in acquisitions, disposals, securitisations, and in enforcement litigation. It also needs to be identified and managed if companies are to maximise shareholder value.

Given that IP can be so fundamentally linked to the underlying value of a company and its operations, our survey was designed to assess whether businesses truly understand the issues surrounding IP, and whether they are aware of the associated risks and sensitivities. The survey also investigated whether organisations have put in place procedures to protect, manage and exploit their IP rights.

As far as we are aware, this is the first formal survey to consider the full range of IP issues.[1]

---

1. *Publisher's note*: we are grateful for permission to reproduce this and other extracts. The report can be obtained via www.pwcglobal.com.

Why read this book?

There are four good reasons.

1. Intellectual property is a vital asset for business, governments and for academic and research organisations.

2. You are likely to come across intellectual property and other "intellectual capital" in your work or study.

3. You probably need to have a better understanding about intellectual capital and its ownership, acquisition and use.

4. You need a practical source of knowledge and guidance about intellectual property and other intellectual capital in a commercial context.

You might be a chief executive of an intellectual capital-dependent company or a brand based business (or both). You might be a manager of such a business or a research director or academic. Maybe you are a student on a management programme or an accountant, a corporate finance professional, investor or a venture capitalist. You may have an MBA that probably taught you about finance, marketing, production management, and about dealing effectively with people in the business and outside. Intellectual capital was not a core subject.

Whatever the reason, you need to understand intellectual capital, especially intellectual property, to do your job better or to be more successful in your career. Patents, brands, copyright, know how, and product designs are familiar to you. You may know the importance of R&D and of intellectual property in business. But you also know the high costs that are involved and that many R&D projects will fail to be successfully commercialised.

You are also aware that intellectual capital is both important and complex. It tends to involve substantial costs. It can be very valuable. You think of the Dyson vacuum cleaner, the Apple "one click" patent for e-commerce, and the Coca Cola brand.

Have you heard these?

These are some of the critical questions and statements you might hear from anyone dealing with intellectual capital:

1. "We must innovate and have new products to succeed. Or we must maintain the power of our brands. The intellectual property rights are important. But doing the R&D, supporting the brand, and protecting the intellectual capital is costing a fortune. How can we maximise the return on all the capital tied up and demonstrate increased shareholder value?"

2. "Somebody senior needs to have a good understanding of intellectual capital and get a grip of it. We need a Board Director solely responsible for intellectual capital exploitation."

3. "What do we own, what is its value and what can we do with it? We don't seem to be using it."

4. "Do we need all the intellectual property – can we sell it or licence it? Should we simply get rid of some it? Do we need to protect our complete patent and trade mark portfolio."

5. "If we are going to acquire this intellectual capital or the business that owns it, how do we know if the legal rights are any good? How do we manage this risk?"

6. "How do we know how much to pay (capital sum or royalty) or if we are over paying? Is this guess work and more gambling?"

7. "How do we know if we might get caught infringing the rights of someone else? I have heard of companies paying large damages claims. How do we manage this or is it just a gamble? Can we use due diligence to manage the risk?"

8. "If we are going to sell or licence some of our intellectual capital, how do we know what it is worth? If it has a value, we might be criticised for giving some of it away or for not achieving a return associated with what it is worth to a purchaser or licensee."

9. "We might save R & D cost or be faster to market using someone else's intellectual capital. But we come back to doing due

diligence on what they have – do they own it and how strong are their rights?"

10. "Can we use what we need of this intellectual capital without paying – i.e. can we get round their rights? What is the infringement risk if we do this?"

This book has been written specifically to answer these questions and more. It gives those running businesses and other organisations – and their advisors – sufficient information to be able to manage intellectual capital effectively: to value it *and* to exploit its value better. Confidence in dealing with specialist advisors in the field of intellectual capital such as intellectual property lawyers, patent attornies, and valuers of intellectual capital will follow.

The effective management of intellectual capital means that those leading an organization such as chief executives, research directors, lenders and venture capital investors can be confident that processes are in place to ensure that the questions mentioned above and others about intellectual capital in a specific context have been properly addressed.

The future winners will be those who own and effectively manage intellectual capital

The efficient exploitation of the intellectual capital they use must be a key objective for business enterprises. Those that are able to manage these assets properly are poised to take commanding positions of economic power. It is no longer an exaggeration to say that the business world is dividing between those companies and corporations that possess intellectual capital and effectively exploit it and those who do not. The have-nots will tend to diminish in status and importance, unless they can gain access to items of intellectual capital such as patents or well regarded trademarks and manage them. Diagram 1 reflects these trends.

Those companies that have developed clear strategies, based on accurate appraisals of the strength and value of intellectual capital are out in the market place enhancing their earning power, productivity and market-share, harnessing home-developed as well as acquired intellectual capital in their expansion.

> "The process is very simple but extremely powerful. It allows the analysis of where Dow and key competitors are in the market place and in the innovation race, and allows decisions on research direction and intangible asset protection to be made in a reasoned and structured manner"
>
> Gordon McConnachie,
> Intellectual Asset Manager Dow Chemical Company.

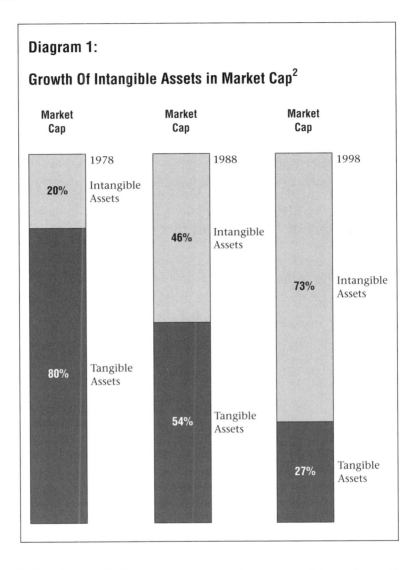

Diagram 1:

Growth Of Intangible Assets in Market Cap[2]

Industrial muscle is no longer enough to ensure a future of growth and profitability. At the extreme a manufacturing company lacking intellectual capital has two choices: manufacturing for other corporations in a sub-contract relationship; or the mass production of a commodity. In either case the likely result is poor growth and profits. This, coupled with the increasingly global nature of the marketplace, is leading to a new form of international commercial

2.   Source: Brookings Institute.

activity, transaction-based, and involving the transfer, in one form or another, of intellectual capital rather than the goods or services that the property supports. This commercial activity, whether taking the form of outright sale, joint ventures or licensing has changed the face of international business.

This has led to a window of opportunity to obtain intellectual capital at bargain prices or low royalty rates, due to the current inefficient market in which intellectual property rights are bought, sold and licensed, and the fact that accurate economic values are not being attributed to these valuable assets.

The meaning of "valuing" in this book

The simple expression "valuing" alludes to two concepts. First, valuing in the narrow sense of a financial valuation. This is dealt with extensively in Chapter Four concerning valuing intellectual capital. Secondly, valuing in a broader sense of understanding intellectual property, knowing the importance of it in a particular business, and managing the acquisition and exploitation of intellectual property effectively. This is covered in the Chapter Two on management, in Chapter Three and the Appendix on understanding intellectual property, in Chapter Five on due diligence and, to the extent that it affects financial valuation, in the valuation chapter too.

The meaning of the collective term "intellectual capital" in this book

Intellectual capital is used as a collective term to refer to a broad range of intangible assets. The range includes intellectual property rights in an organisation such as patents, know how, trademarks, brands, as well as rights given by agreements such as licensing or franchise agreements. But it also includes workforce and other "knowledge": often difficult to identify but which contribute to its success, continued operation, and even growth.

In some places in the book, the expressions "intellectual property" and "other intangible assets" are used when the collective "intellectual capital" is not appropriate. For example, in the chapters on understanding intellectual property rights using the collective intellectual capital would be inappropriate because the chapter deals with protectable rights commonly called intellectual property.

Yet accounting commonly refers to "intangible assets" meaning both intellectual property and assets such as brands that typically encompass a number of these assets. Intellectual capital in the valuation section applies to all types of intangible asset (including people) making use of the collective term appropriate.

Intellectual capital as used in this book will comprise a series of valuable assets which earn enhanced *revenue and profits* for businesses. Some of these assets such as patents and brands may be included as assets on the balance sheet. Many of these assets now attract valuable tax reliefs.

Principles of Value

The value of any intellectual property is broadly dependent on three principles. First, that legal rights actually exist to prevent other businesses gaining access to or using the assets and in which countries. Secondly, that ownership of those legal rights can be proven so that the rights can be enforced if necessary to prevent others infringing the rights or gaining access to the intellectual capital. Thirdly, that the legal rights relate to some product or services or a business as a whole which produces an income stream.

However, the value of many intangible assets is not so dependent on legal principles, for example secrets, knowledge generally, customer relationships, market entry, people in the business and brands. Here value is less based on restricted legal rights to an income source, but on having something scarce – a source of income or potential income that is distinctively yours, but not protectably yours in a legal sense.

The importance of intellectual capital

Intellectual capital is coming into its own. It is increasingly being recognised as an asset, the possession of which confers major economic benefits. Companies are licensing, selling and trading intellectual capital around the world, and it provides one of the foundations of the global economy. The question of worldwide intellectual property rights was one of the key issues under discussion in the GATT talks. Intellectual capital is big business. It can cost many hundreds of millions of pounds to create. Once firmly established, the many different forms of intellectual capital are unique assets which have no substitute. Taking the UK as an example, in 1990, copyrights alone accounted for more £4bn worth of exports and 2.6% of the Gross National Product. Today the figure is unknown but patent applications rose significantly (by 6%) in 1999 and moderated to a 3% increase in 2000.

Much has been made of the progress of Japan and it is salutary to reflect upon the words of Korekiyo Takahasti, a Japanese official sent to the USA at the turn of the 20th century, who is reported to have said

> "we have looked about to see what nations are the greatest, so we can be like them. We asked ourselves what is it that makes America such a great nation, and we investigated and found it was patents, and we will have patents".

And indeed they do. As long ago as 1989 357,464 patent applications were filed in Japan. This compared with 161,660 in the USA, 90,234 in the UK, 74,942 in France and 114,474 in Germany (made up as to 12,047 in the then GDR, and 102,427 in West Germany). Whilst applications from Japan remain steady, those from the USA rose by 11% from 1999 to 2000. Diagram 2 illustrates this point.

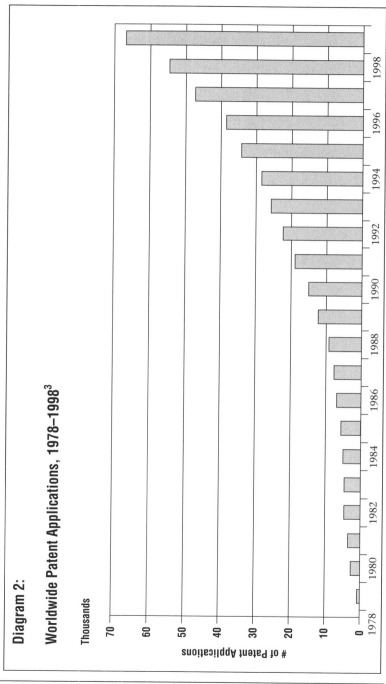

Diagram 2:

Worldwide Patent Applications, 1978–1998[3]

The number of designs registered in the UK increased in 1999 by 13% and trademark applications by 11%. March 2000 broke Patent Office records and was responsible for more trademark applications than had previously been received in one month of their history.

The correlation between industrial and economic performance, innovation and intellectual capital seems to be a fact of life. When Pope John Paul II wrote in his encyclical of a new important form of ownership, "the possession of know-how, technology and skill", he was acknowledging that intellectual capital is increasingly being recognised as the most important asset of many of the world's largest and most powerful companies. Intellectual capital is the foundation for the market dominance and continuing profitability of many leading corporations and is often the key objective in mergers and acquisition.

The need to understand intellectual capital

Many individuals in business life now have to make decisions involving intellectual capital and the legal rights which protect that capital or property. Chief executives, managers, research directors, those trying to "spin out" academic research into businesses, accountants, venture capitalists, and bankers all need to understand the nature of intellectual capital, how the different types of legal rights in intellectual property can be acquired, and the extent of the legal rights given by the different types of intellectual property.

Any person making decisions, advising about developing products or services, or seeking to invest in intellectual capital either by taking a licence or by acquiring the intellectual property or some part of it, will want to undertake a due diligence investigation into the ownership and strength of the intellectual property available. Ensuring a good ownership to the intellectual property is desirable and, for protected intellectual property often essential before it is exploited or attempts are made to enforce any legal rights protecting it.

The unique attribute protected by, or contained in, the intellectual capital may give enhanced value. Whether it does or not will depend both on the legal protection of the unique attribute and the market demand for the products and services produced or provided using the intellectual capital. No matter how strong the protection given by the legal rights in the particular intellectual capital, if nobody wants or is likely to want the product or service then the intellectual capital may have no external value unless it can be used in a "blocking" way to give enhanced value through restriction of a competitor. But if there is a demand for the product or service, the protection given by intellectual capital may allow above normal revenue to be earned because the legal rights in the intellectual capital effectively limit the availability of the product or service to competitors.

But some intellectual property will have legal rights which give a more limiting effect than others on the supply of a competing product or service. Limited supply often will mean enhanced value. Chapter Three is therefore an important precursor to the reader's understanding of valuation: a useful overview that is explored further in the Appendix for those who require it. The effect of intellectual capital on revenue generation will vary. The need to undertake due diligence of the *strength* of the intellectual property is little appreciated. Most due diligence looks simply at ownership and not strength. Chapter Five provides tools and methods to understanding.

The concept of value

The concept of value is very broad. We are not concerned with ethical values in this book. We are concerned with value to be placed on assets and how that value might be acknowledged and assessed with as much accuracy as possible.

The value placed on something is often essentially a subjective judgement. A family hierloom may to one person be a priceless object but to another a worthless piece of junk. If sentiment is involved, estimating value with confidence will be almost impossible. A single Georgian candlestick will be enhanced by its pair.

If speculation is involved, the effect is the same as that caused by sentiment. If the asset is thought to have potential, especially huge potential, then anybody acquiring the asset may pay a price to have access to the gamble represented by the speculation. It is not easy to predict the value that such speculation and sentiment might give to an asset. In recent years the very high value put on the shares of biotechnology businesses and their patented technologies or on the dotcom businesses, because of the growth expected by using the internet, are good examples. It is a question of timing and of judging the cycle.

Many of these businesses run at a loss for many years and have many obstacles to success to overcome including complex regulatory requirements to overcome. Some of these businesses are the most valuable in the world, however no one would back such businesses as sure winners at any early stage yet they are (or were) highly valued. It is the speculation in the gamble of huge profits if the technology and associated intellectual capital is successful which leads to the value. However, the slightest sign of failure can cause the value to fall fast. The value is, therefore, at times highly volatile.

But if the thing is in the nature of a commodity, its price (really the cost of acquiring it) will be determined by the market. The price will change with the rise and fall of the market. The commodity could be a stock market quoted share or fish in a wholesale market. Assessing the price is a matter of investigating the market.

The valuation of intellectual capital requires a professional skilled approach and experience to reach a value. It will use market based prices and royalty rates based on available market information and some assumptions (tending to have a subjective element), as well other methods.

The New Zealand case of *Wham-O Manufacturing Co* v *Lincoln Industries Limited* is an example of an engraving given copyright protection by the courts. This concerned the mould from which "frizbees" were made.[4] The value of one "frizbee" as a collectable item would be almost nothing. Whereas at the height of the popularity of playing with them, the value of the copyright to prevent others copying the particular popular design would have been high. Nevertheless, the value would have been linked to the likely period for which large sales volumes would be achieved and the likely size of the profits made.

---

4.   [1985] RPC 127(New Zealand CA).

Valuing intellectual capital

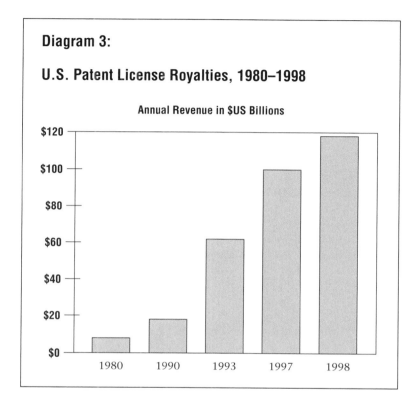

Diagram 3:

U.S. Patent License Royalties, 1980–1998

Annual Revenue in $US Billions

Knowledge is America's most valuable export. According to Thomas Stewart, *The Wealth of Knowledge* (Nicholas Brealey) three years ago it earned the country $37 billion (£26 billion) in licensing and royalties compared with $29 billion in aircraft sales. The shift towards the knowledge economy is well known but a few figures show just how dramatic the transformation has been.

Take the American giant General Electric. Under its former chief executive Jack Welch, it discovered that it could sell services as well as products. It could also package its expertise in aircraft engine repairs, the installation of magnetic resonance imaging machines and other operations. These activities accounted for $17 billion in revenues in 2000 compared with $8 billion 1995 when the initiative was launched.

"Knowledge is what we do," says Stewart. "Ideas, knowledge and information have always mattered but today they define our working life. This is unprecedented."

Few people will need persuading that the western world is now predominantly knowledge-based but the extent of the shift may be surprising. The US Commerce Department estimates that by 2006 almost half of the American workforce will be employed by industries that are either big producers or intensive users of information technology, leading to Stewart's conclusion: "I think, therefore I earn."

The Wealth of Knowledge is structured in a manner designed to show how good knowledge management can transform the operations of a company. Stewart describes how BP Amoco, in just one year, used shared knowledge to add $260m to the bottom line with another $400m in possible savings yet to be booked.

But it is not just global companies that can benefit. Stewart tells the story of a company that started out as a debt-collection agency chasing restaurants that owed money to fishermen before using the knowledge gained to transform itself into an online industry portal. This story is enticing enough to make a book in itself.

Stewart includes an excellent think piece on the short comings of accounting for intellectual capital. "Investors have been systematically misled," he contends, a claim that may have seemed controversial when he thought of including it but one that has proved to be prophetic for entirely different reasons.

Source: *The Sunday Times*, April 2002

In this new economy, wealth-creating assets are non-physical. They are capable of separate identification and valuation. As one of the most important advances in wealth creation for centuries, this magnifies risk and liability assessment. In most acquisitions intellectual capital – intellectual property and intangible assets – are likely to account for a large proportion of consideration. Every public and private business has these rights, even if they are only in the name under which it trades. Just as importantly, every business uses other people's intellectual capital. More often than not, the questions to be answered are:

- What is goodwill and what are the intellectual property rights used in the business or project;

- How do you obtain exclusive rights to them?

- How do you protect them against infringement – i.e. against use without permission?

- What is their value?

- How do we increase intangible value?

- How can it be transferred and exploited?

Investors look for the returns they hope to get either by way of income or by way of a future capital gain on realisation, or a combination of both. In arriving at the expected return they will have to consider a number of factors which will vary in their relative importance depending on the facts of the particular situation. Bearing in mind that no two, say, patents or trademarks are exactly alike, and that the circumstances at the date of valuation – assessing the return – may vary from case to case, it is essential to examine many factors.

Industries may show by their past history that trade is cyclical or even completely unpredictable. Political situations may have a vital bearing upon some sectors and this includes, naturally the stability or not, of an intellectual property legal regime in another part of the world.

The quality of the management is an important factor, particularly to the small private limited company whose prosperity often depends upon one or more individuals who may be difficult to replace. The larger the company the greater the opportunity for training future executives and managing knowledge.

> "Companies have to recognise that knowledge can be the most valuable of assets."
>
> Margareta Barchen, CEO, Celemi

Thus there are many situations when proprietors, directors and professionals will require an expert opinion as to the valuation and creation of value in respect of these unique intellectual capital assets. They may be considering insurance, lending, credit risk and recovery, a sale or purchase of the company or asset, assessing damages following infringement or for a variety of other reasons. These assets can be transferred to low tax jurisdictions and valuation for tax purposes will often be required. Licensing is a key tool for exploitation.

A company's published accounts are prepared for many good reasons but not for representing worth and value. A balance sheet sets out a series of facts. A statement of the assets and liabilities of the company at a given moment in time; but it does not purport to represent a valuation of the company as a going concern. To suggest that it should do so would make the already over-burdened accountant's life completely impossible. It is common practice to see regular re-valuations of real estate and plant and machinery.

Management and institutions have long since acknowledged that the most valuable assets of successful companies are not bricks and mortar but of an intangible nature. Management and institutions obviously need to know the value of what might be the single most valuable asset in the company and business managers need to know, or should know, the value of all assets under their stewardship and control. They cannot rely on their accounts: this book will help them achieve a sense of that value for themselves.

CHAPTER 2
THE MANAGEMENT OF
INTELLECTUAL CAPITAL

Contents

CHAPTER 2
THE MANAGEMENT OF
INTELLECTUAL CAPITAL

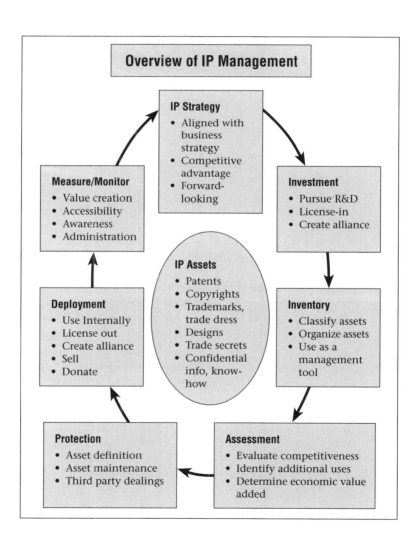

Overview of IP Management

IP Strategy
- Aligned with business strategy
- Competitive advantage
- Forward-looking

Investment
- Pursue R&D
- License-in
- Create alliance

Measure/Monitor
- Value creation
- Accessibility
- Awareness
- Administration

IP Assets
- Patents
- Copyrights
- Trademarks, trade dress
- Designs
- Trade secrets
- Confidential info, know-how

Inventory
- Classify assets
- Organize assets
- Use as a management tool

Deployment
- Use Internally
- License out
- Create alliance
- Sell
- Donate

Protection
- Asset definition
- Asset maintenance
- Third party dealings

Assessment
- Evaluate competitiveness
- Identify additional uses
- Determine economic value added

The Challenge for Business Executives

Understanding the Principles of Effective Management of Intellectual Capital

Intellectual property is a complex subject. The rights in intellectual property are an important, even vital, asset in many businesses. The modern business executive has a responsibility to manage these intellectual property assets just like any other asset in the business. The challenge to these executives is to understand the principles of effective management of intellectual capital and to become themselves effective managers of intellectual capital in business. They need to acquire sufficient knowledge about:

- intellectual property and the legal rights which protect the intellectual property;

- how intellectual property rights are created and obtained;

- the ways in which these rights can be lost;

- how intellectual property rights can be bought and sold, and used for loan security;

- The licensing of intellectual property rights and other intellectual capital;

- how to put a value on the intellectual capital in a business context.

A business executive who has acquired this knowledge will have the basic knowledge to be able then to develop and put in place an effective strategy and process for management of any intellectual property in the business for which the executive is responsible.

Most businesses do not manage their intellectual capital well. Intellectual capital management techniques will enable any person involved in business to understand the importance of intellectual capital – for their business *and* that of competitors. They can then use that understanding to meet the challenge of intellectual property successfully.

A management process will be implemented differently by each organisation which decides to embrace intellectual capital management. Several large organisation have put intellectual capital management into practice very successfully. These include The Dow Chemical Company, The Canadian Imperial Bank of Commerce, Scandia and AFS of Sweden.

The modern business executive is under pressure to manage intellectual property effectively from two directions. One essentially driven by the need for growth and to remain competitive. The other essentially defensive driven by the need to manage risk in any business and protect shareholder and investor value.

Prospecting for Intellectual Capital

The drive for growth and to remain competitive

The drive to be competitive in business is unrelenting. The need to maximise the return from capital assets employed in the business and the techniques for doing so are very well understood by successful business executives. More efficient machines, information technology, and people used more efficiently give a better gross margin at least. These successful companies have used information technology to enable the operation and management of the business to be carried out with less people. Again this has made them leaner yet still able to produce quality products and services and achieve high customer satisfaction.

Responsible business executives continue to look at ways to make the businesses which they run more efficient or to create greater revenues from existing operations and even additional revenue streams from their existing assets. The pressure is continually on the need to squeeze more value out of the assets of any businesses. Every business executive is hunting for growth. Striving to achieve the holy grail of proven additions to shareholder value. Combining businesses by acquisition is one traditional way of achieving this result.

However, many executives in recent years have been looking at all aspects of the businesses they run for ways to squeeze out more value. One aspect which in most businesses has *not* been given this intense scrutiny is intellectual capital including the knowledge used in the business. Intellectual capital, if managed properly, can produce added value to the business and better profit. It can give strategic advantage in two ways. First, by making a business able to beat the competition in the market or in financial performance or both. Secondly, by putting the competition at a strategic disadvantage as they have to find ways to avoid misusing the intellectual capital or have to pay to use it through licensing.

This, of course, assumes that having access to intellectual capital such as a strong reputation in a known brand or some new technology protected by patents *can* make a difference in a particular business sector. One essential strategic outcome of the process of intellectual capital management suggested in this book is that an objective assessment will be made of the importance of intellectual capital to the business generally and for specific intellectual capital. Intellectual property will be strategically important if it is giving the strategic advantage mentioned above or adding value to the business or enabling better profit to be made. The more so if the intellectual capital can do all these things. These advantages from the intellectual capital can be *owned* by a business because the intellectual property can be owned. Therefore, the competitive advantage is sustainable if all available legal rights have been obtained for the intellectual property.

This then is the importance of managing intellectual property. Some businesses have developed strategies and processes for managing this valuable or potentially valuable asset. The concept of *intellectual capital management* in business is developing. This concept has been adopted and applied seriously in some businesses and other organisations, particularly those which rely on innovation to remain competitive, for example, chemical and pharmaceutical companies.

The understanding and active management of intellectual capital has in too many businesses not been taken seriously enough. It should be an item for consideration at board level and should be at the forefront of every chief executive's strategic thinking.

Corporate Governance

Preserving shareholder value

Proper corporate governance is the responsibility of all senior executives of companies whose shares are quoted on any of the major stock exchanges. It is many cases a legal requirement. Directors and senior executives of these public companies can be made personally liable where corporate governance failings occur. The London Stock

Exchange has published a Combined Code on Corporate Governance. The Securities and Exchange Commission in New York has over recent years promoted the importance to capital markets of high standards of corporate governance. The collapse of Enron in the United States in 2001 and other scandals prompted a serious review how corporate governance is being achieved in businesses regulated in the United States.

The basic principle of corporate governance is succinctly put in the Combined Code, Principle D.2 which states:

"The Board should maintain a sound system of internal control to safeguard shareholders' investment and the company's assets."

Increasingly, one type of asset requiring to be managed in this way is intellectual property. Intellectual property, and its effective use, has become a significant or even vital part of value creation in many businesses. Improvements in earnings, and so returns on capital, can be achieved through:

- improving strategic use of existing intellectual property;

- improving future intellectual property development or acquisition, and its use;

- maximisation of revenue from intellectual capital generally when used in the business and through licensing its use, perhaps in non core markets

- alternatively accessing new markets and revenues by licensing the intellectual property of another business.

Directors of public companies will be expected to have put in place a strategy and management process to provide the sort of internal controls required to meet the corporate governance obligations in relation to intellectual property of the regulatory body for the exchange on which the shares are listed.

Private companies generally do not have the same degree of legal obligation to achieve corporate governance as do public companies. However, in practice investors in private companies such as venture capital companies and banks providing development capital will require high levels of corporate governance.

The old style of dealing with intellectual capital common in many businesses is no longer sufficient. This old style is characterised by a management which regards intellectual property as a purely legal problem dealt with by the company secretary (or by the legal department if one existed) and as only about obtaining legal rights. This management approach makes no proper attempt to link spending on intellectual capital, the market place and the obtaining of legal rights; and only sporadic attempts to find out what intellectual property is owned.

In contrast, the new style of successful businesses using intellectual capital is characterised by a management which understands concepts of intellectual property, knows the intellectual capital of the businesses, analyses the market and intellectual capital in relation to the market, links spending on intellectual property development and acquisition to measures of added value, and secures those legal rights necessary to sustain the market advantage derived form the intellectual capital.

A proper understanding of intellectual property and the principles of intellectual capital management are essential to achieving the level of internal control of the intellectual property in a business sufficient to demonstrate proper corporate governance.

Key Corporate Governance Questions

You should by now be considering the due diligence questions which ought to be posed and answered in relation to intellectual capital. These are the type of question which need to be answered:

1. Do you know the extent of the intellectual capital in your business? Meaning traditional intellectual property rights through to simple organisational/business know how. The deep knowledge buried in your business. Including the "ask Jim, he's been here for ages" type of information.

2. Have you assessed this intellectual capital and recorded or otherwise safeguarded it?

3. Do you have one person who has responsibility for this?

4. Do you evaluate the commercial need for and or value of this intellectual capital to your business? Do you make the most of these assets?

5. Do you have any registered intellectual property rights such as patents or trade marks? Do you manage the portfolio? Do you assess whether other rights by registration should be obtained as the business grows? Who does this?

6. Are the costs of having the intellectual property rights assessed and compared to the benefits?

7. Do you have any intellectual property which could be registered? E.g. the design element of your brands. Is anybody responsible for this?

8. Does any one check that intellectual property assets are being used correctly in the business? E.g. are trade marks being used properly? Are they in danger of becoming generic through inappropriate use?

9. Is your business likely to make innovations? Who is responsible for knowing about such innovations, evaluating them, and seeking intellectual property rights protection for them. Do you have a policy about this?

10. Do your employees have contracts of employment dealing with intellectual property ownership and confidentiality?

11. Do your contracts with sub-contractors and other third parties deal with intellectual property ownership and confidentiality?

12. Has your business acquired any intellectual property rights from a third party? Was a professional due diligence assessment made about title and ownership? Have all the appropriate steps been taken post acquisition, such as in relation to register entries?

13. Do you check for any likelihood of intellectual property rights infringement before launching new products or services? If not, why not?

14. Can the intellectual property of the business and intellectual property rights be licensed to anyone? Perhaps into non core

markets to generate revenue? Is any one responsible for managing this?

15. Has the validity of all registered intellectual property rights used in the business been professionally assessed?

If you can not answer these sorts of questions genuinely in a positive way and with confidence, then an ability to increase shareholder value exists in your business by adopting the practice of good intellectual property management.

The benefits of good Intellectual Capital Management

It is important to understand the important benefits that can be achieved through effective intellectual capital management. Not all of them will be goals or be achievable in every business. These benefits include:

- increased returns on capital invested in the business, particularly capital tied up in intellectual property;

- increased shareholder value;

- a proper understanding of the alignment of intellectual property development or acquisition and business strategic objectives;

- the ability to make informed decisions about intellectual property development or acquisition;

- the creation of new and diverse revenue streams from intellectual capital and especially from underused intellectual capital;

- the ability to know the valuable intellectual capital and so protect it fully, and the intellectual capital of no significant value which might be sold or abandoned;

- achieving lower overall costs associated with intellectual capital development or acquisition, protection, and utilisation;

- creating internal awareness of the importance of intellectual capital to success;

- the ability efficiently and successfully to absorb acquired intellectual capital into the operations of the business, particularly in relation to mergers and acquisitions.

The Principles of Intellectual Capital Management

Intellectual capital should be regarded as knowledge with value or potential value. As an asset which can create real value in a business. It is concerned with patents, designs, copyright, brands, and know how. Successful business executives of the future will be the ones which develop a strategy, and adopt management techniques, enabling intellectual capital created or acquired by their businesses to be identified, protected and exploited to the fullest extent possible. The strategy and management techniques will also enable them to establish if their business needs to acquire or develop specific intellectual capital to remain competitive.

The knowledge and understanding of the principles of effective intellectual capital management explained and illustrated in this book will enable those involved in business to face the intellectual capital challenge with confidence. They will understand how to develop a strategy for intellectual capital in their businesses and the management process required to manage intellectual capital effectively.

The same knowledge and understanding will enable those advising businesses such as accountants, bankers, and venture capital professionals to understand better the way that intellectual property can add real value to a business in its core markets. Sometimes, also, additional value through licensing into non core markets. An example is IBM which licensed some of its technology for hard disk drives for use in replacement heart valves.

The principles have been derived from the authors' understanding and study of the concept of intellectual capital as assets to be managed like any other so as to maximise return on the capital represented by that asset based on extensive due diligence work in relation to intellectual property, and from many years experience in the valuation of intellectual property.

The principles are the foundation of intellectual capital management. Adoption of the principles will lead to the management and measuring of the use and financial performance of specific intellectual property in business by rigorously identifying and linking specific intellectual property and financial results of the business or parts of it.

Principle One

Make intellectual capital a part of business strategic thinking and planning

This is the responsibility of the executive management of the business. The strategy will include some or all of the following:

- *Developing and implementing processes delivering risk control in relation to the intellectual capital of others*. Legal rights in this intellectual capital might threaten the continued profitability and growth of the business which they are managing.

- *Maximisation of value from any intellectual capital existing in the business by implementing appropriate management processes*.

- Being aware of emerging technologies in their own businesses and those being developed by others and assessing these as potential competitive threats.

- Seeking appropriate legal protection of home grown intellectual capital; and

- Being on the look out for intellectual property relating to important technical developments with good legal rights protection and assessing whether or not to acquired these intellectual property rights or at least the right to use them.

It will be immediately apparent that intellectual capital will be a peripheral concern to executive managers in some businesses. In others, intellectual capital will be one of the, if not the, most important asset of the business. The integration of intellectual capital in to strategic thinking and planning will be vary accordingly.

However, in each business a process of intellectual capital management needs to be followed. This may be a simple exercise in some businesses achieved without incurring huge cost either of management time or of money spent. For other businesses, it will be strategically vital, complex, and time consuming with significant costs associated with the process.

Following the principles of intellectual capital management set out here will help executive managers develop successful processes most suited to their business and to be confident they have been successful in addressing the intellectual capital challenge facing their business.

The starting point for executive managers is to acquire a good understanding of meaning of the different types of intellectual property rights, how these rights are acquired and owned, and what power each has in the market place.

Chapter three of this book provides all the information about intellectual property rights required by an executive manager to gain this understanding.

Principle Two

Understand the role of intellectual capital

This will involve assessing the importance of intellectual capital now and in the future to the market position and future success of the business.

Every person running a business should at least think about this. In many businesses intellectual capital will not be important to the current or future success of the business. This may even seem so obvious that a busy executive, in the high pressure atmosphere running a business, dismisses the whole process straightway. This may be the correct decision. But be wary of failing to appreciate the intellectual capital of any business. Most businesses have valuable know how often in the minds of employees. If the employee goes, does the know how go too? Important know how need not be the technical "rocket science" type. It is often the day to day knowledge, the "I don't know, ask Ron, he's been here for years" information which can be valuable. The smart businesses will have identified this as a potential weakness. They will have managed and protected this know how.

Most businesses at least have a trading name or style which they would not want competitors to use. Protection should be obtained for brands and the designs of trading styles.

Much depends on the sector. Anybody running a business in some sectors will know that intellectual property is important. These sectors, with no great surprises, are pharmaceutical, chemical, biotechnology, electronics, telecommunications, media, and consumer retailing and merchandising. Intellectual property and associated legal rights, if properly managed, will prevent or restrict competitors in their use of important technology.

In a business operating in a sector where having intellectual property is vital to success, the intellectual capital challenge is acute. A part of the difficult intellectual capital challenge facing the busy business executive is to identify in their business the good intellectual property from the bad. The valuable from the invaluable. They need to do this for all existing intellectual capital. Even more importantly, they need to identify for their business or sector the potentially good intellectual capital from the rest. The R & D function may be bristling with the next generation of intellectual capital. But realistically, this intellectual capital is just as likely to be in development by another business or research institution.

Another part of the intellectual capital challenge in some businesses is to identify the intellectual property of others and avoid infringing the associated legal rights. The worst nightmare of the ambitious executive is the launching a new product or opening a new processing plant with all the investment this will require, followed soon after by a legal battle over intellectual property rights infringement. Even if the battle is won, the cost in money and management time will have been high. If this is to happen, it should be planned and the anticipated legal battle needs to be part of the strategy and all the costs properly considered in making the decision.

The principles of intellectual capital management, if implemented carefully and thoughtfully for a particular business, will enable business executive to be successful in this process.

Principle Three

Be aware of competing intellectual capital

This will require the evaluation the capabilities, intellectual capital, and related business strategies of existing competitors, emerging businesses, and research institutions as far as possible on a regular basis.

An important element of an intellectual capital strategy is being aware of the intellectual property rights which may enable competitors to prevent your business from exploiting new products, processes, or services. Alternatively, those rights which prevent you from competing because a product, process, or service is in demand and protected by intellectual property rights. Your business is losing sales and these rights do not allow your business to offer the same thing or possibly even something similar.

Chapter five of this book is all about this aspect of intellectual property management: due diligence and intellectual capital. The assessment of the intellectual property rights of others is best described as "negative due diligence". The objective is to find out if any of the intellectual property rights of these others can *prevent* any commercial or research activity being carried out. Preferably before substantial investment has been made which would be wasted if the activity could not go ahead or had to be stopped.

Much depends on the competitor's intellectual property rights which are being assessed. Patent rights are for concepts. Designs and brands are for specific features or names and styles. Patents offer broader protection for an innovation than do designs and brands.

Principle Four

Know your own intellectual capital

This means employing a rigorous process to identify and evaluate the existing intellectual capital in the business, creating a comprehensive record of the results, and developing a process for identifying future intellectual property being developed. It might be termed "positive due diligence".

The intellectual property will range from the general know how of the business to the important technical developments. Each business will be different. For many businesses the intellectual capital will be simply the general know how and possibly the trading name. Perhaps there may be some product designs or software. For others, complex technologies will define the business. Intellectual property rights for these will be the life blood of the business. The rights protecting this intellectual property are likely to be international patents, strong brands, rights in designs, and copyright in software.

You will only have begun to apply principle four to your business if the intellectual capital management processes of principles one to three have established that intellectual capital is important for your business. Sufficiently so that a formal evaluation of the intellectual capital in the business should be carried out.

This process should be approached with an open mind and not be influenced or constrained, even prejudiced, by existing thinking in the business as to the intellectual capital which is important. It may be for this reason that an independent assessment is preferable. The important point is that *all* intellectual capital is identified, whether apparently trivial or relating to obsolete technology. Recently BT found, as part of review its patent portfolio, an older patent which appeared to cover the process of hyperlinking used over the internet. BT appointed independent advisors to see if this patent can be enforced in the sense of being used to generate substantial royalty payments. Though it now appears unlikely at the time of writing, the review could prove a classic and successful application of the principles of intellectual property management.

A first impression of the likely intellectual capital will be apparent from the type of business. The process will start with a first sweep, looking for the differing types of intellectual capital. Then further, more detailed investigations will be done. These will be repeated in more detail in relation to the intellectual capital as it is identified until a full picture of all the intellectual capital in the business has been identified and recorded.

The next stage is to classify it. This will be in three ways:

1. by reference to the associated legal rights such as patents, rights in designs or trade marks, copyright, and as confidential know how;

2. by reference as to whether the particular intellectual capital is owned out right or jointly, or whether licensed in or out;

3. by reference to how the intellectual capital is used in the business.

Properly applied, the result of the application of principle four of the intellectual capital management will be that the executive management of the business have a proper, and comprehensive understanding of the intellectual capital in their business, the associated legal rights, and precisely how this intellectual property is applied in the running and operation of the business. This knowledge is vital for proper intellectual capital management, which in itself is a vital part of risk management and delivering shareholder value.

A management process

The second part of the successful and proper application of principle four is the development of a management process to identify intellectual capital being created in the business. This process will identify it and categorise the identified intellectual capital by reference to the three categories mentioned above based on assumptions as to the potential of the intellectual capital.

The process must be carefully devised and implemented. The process will be a continual one but the intensity of the application will depend on the particular business. For some businesses, a quarterly review might be adequate, for others it might be annual. Yet in others a different process might be required – relying not on regular reviews but on a system of reporting of important technical innovations as they arise.

The process will need to be supported at main board level and will need an individual with sufficient authority in the business to promote and drive the process through the whole organisation.

Again, the knowledge in chapter five about due diligence in relation to intellectual property rights is important here. Executive managers will learn about effective due diligence in relation to intellectual property and the associated legal rights and their practical application. Effective methods are explained and illustrated with practical examples, as are the difficulties and limitations inherent in the practical application of the due diligence process.

Due diligence has been explained and illustrated for the two perspectives encountered by business in practice. The first is assessing the intellectual property rights of other businesses and organisations and covered by principle three. We have called this negative due diligence. The second relates to assessing the intellectual property rights available in the business under review. We have called this positive due diligence.

Principle Five

Know the cost and value of your intellectual capital

This is another rigorous assessment which will need to be carried out with two very important and clear objectives in mind. First, to know the cost of obtaining and maintaining each part of the intellectual capital in the business. Secondly, to know the value to each part of that intellectual capital.

With this knowledge, it is possible to formulate a strategy and action plan to maximise the value of the intellectual capital in line with the overall business strategy which may including selling, licensing or abandoning intellectual capital.

Investing in intellectual capital is only justified if it delivers a sufficient return on investment for a particular business or can be used to block a competitor. A particular investment decision will relate to one of three costs in relation to intellectual property. First, is the cost of obtaining the intellectual property and associated legal rights likely to be justified? Secondly, is the cost of continuing to maintain the intellectual property and the associated legal rights likely to be justified? Thirdly, is the likely high cost of enforcing rights in intellectual property likely to be justified?

Executive managers will need to make decisions which may depend in part on the assessed value of the particular intellectual capital. Such decisions might be about continuing an expensive research programme, building a new production facility, launching a product or service, or taking a licence of technology.

Chapter four is all about the valuation of intellectual capital. Executive managers will learn the fundamentals of effective valuation of intellectual capital and the associated legal rights and their practical application. The most effective methods are explained and illustrated with practical examples, as are the difficulties and limitations inherent in the valuation process.

Executive managers must understand these fundamentals of the valuation of intellectual capital to become effective managers of intellectual capital and understand the rates of return on one of the most valuable types of corporate asset. The correct application of principle four and principle five will deliver successful intellectual capital management, enable executive managers to meet the intellectual property challenge, achieve effective intellectual capital risk management, and maximise shareholder value.

The conclusion of the valuation of each part of the intellectual capital and the associated legal rights will lead on to decisions in relation to the intellectual capital which seek to maximise the value from the intellectual capital in the business. Intellectual property and the legal rights that go with it for core activities and likely future core activities need to be preserved, often exclusively for the business. But these rights might be licensed for uses outside the core activities of the business. Good examples have been bearing technology from hard disc drives licensed for use in heart valves or nappy lining technology licensed for use in protecting underwater cables.

The valuation process will identify the potential revenue available from licensing enabling managers of intellectual capital to devote time and resources to those areas likely to give the best returns either in revenue levels or deals that can be done quickly or at low cost.

The valuation process will also identify intellectual capital which is not being used or which is producing a low return. If strategies such as licensing to third parties cannot deliver or possibly even show potential for improved valuation in the future, the cost of keeping and maintaining the intellectual capital is not justified. Abandoning the intellectual capital may lead to substantial cost saving. But this strategy has the risk of abandoning intellectual property and associated legal rights which might become hot property later. This too is part of intellectual capital management: in this case as an aspect of risk management in the business.

The revenue from better use of intellectual capital in the business including licensing activity in non core areas and the costs saved by managed abandonment of intellectual capital will all lead to greater returns for the business. Greater returns lead to improved and sustained shareholder value. Maybe even to the triggering of bonus payments or the triggering of stock options!

Principle Six

Identify required intellectual capital

This is a process of forecasting future needs of the business. It will be a process under regular review over time since neither the market nor the business will be standing still. An assessment will be made, in line with the business strategy, of the intellectual capital likely to be needed to maintain market position and to grow.

The intellectual capital will be in the form of technologies, techniques, processes, products, and capabilities. This should be a part of the strategic thinking of those running the business.

Principle Seven

Acquire any required intellectual capital

This is a bold statement. The authors are acutely aware from years of experience of the difficulty, even impossibility, of achieving this goal. The intellectual capital management carried out so far has identified the likely future intellectual capital needs of the business. The objective must be to set out to obtain the identified intellectual capital. It would be wrong to set out aiming for second best. So the next step is to put in place a strategy for development in-house or acquisition of this intellectual capital.

The principles of intellectual capital management, if applied properly, will have identified for executive managers:

- the intellectual capital available to competitors and being developed by relevant research organisations;

- the extent of the intellectual capital available in their own business, and a valuation of it;

- the legal rights associated with all this intellectual capital and who owns or is likely to own these rights;

- the intellectual capital which the business is likely to require in the future but does not currently have in development itself or in collaboration.

It should be easier then to devise a strategy for the attempt to secure the intellectual capital necessary for future survival and prosperity of the business. The challenge is better put as an attempt to secure the required intellectual property rights *deliberately*. Identifying the intellectual capital needed in the context of a business is a big challenge and one addressed by the principles of intellectual capital management. *Securing* that intellectual capital and the associated legal rights is another big challenge. There is no guarantee of success either in developing the required intellectual capital alone or with others or in acquiring the intellectual capital through acquisition or licensing.

Principle Eight

Think tax and balance sheet

Intellectual capital is highly prized if it relates to products or services which generate strong revenues. The intellectual capital will then have a value. Alternatively, intellectual capital may be used to generate royalties or be used to raise finance. Again, this intellectual capital will have a value. Similarly if intellectual capital is sold or abandoned, a capital value may be obtained or a loss incurred. Costs may need to be written off.

The process of the management of intellectual capital should be undertaken with proper accounting and tax advice.

Principle Nine

Be ready to protect your rights

The importance of acquiring legal rights for intellectual property is that these rights can be used to stop others from using your intellectual property without permission. This is important for two reasons. First, the obvious one. Your business model will usually be based on having the exclusive right to the intellectual property. Secondly, because permission for others to use the intellectual property is usually linked to payment or other beneficial outcome. Without the legal rights, neither is possible.

But equally importantly, enforcing legal rights in intellectual property will involve incurring costs, sometimes substantial costs. If you have the rights, but no money to pay to enforce the rights, then the effect is often as if the rights did not exist because they are ignored. This is a risky strategy for the business or person ignoring the rights because the liability to pay compensation continues for several years. The owner of the rights may become successful, sue for infringement, be successful despite the best efforts of the "ignorer", and then substantial compensation will be payable.

In the 1840s Charles Goodyear perfected the vulcanisation of rubber after ten years of obsessive research into rubber. He made the breakthrough in the end totally by accident. He patented his innovation. Surely a fortune awaited him. Alas not. The process was easy to duplicate, competitors just stole it, and Goodyear did not have the money to enforce the patent against all the competitors who began to use his intellectual property. The Goodyear business which we know about was not connected with Charles Goodyear, the inventor.

This is a real problem for start up businesses without substantial investment funding available. Insurance might be available but tends to be expensive and have quite strict conditions attached. Cover for infringements in the United States is difficult to obtain. The alternative is to investigate if legal advice and assistance can be obtained on a "no win, no fee" basis.

The possible need to incur the cost of enforcement of rights in intellectual property is also an important point that investors in start up or early stage businesses must appreciate. The investment they have made may be put at risk by infringement of the very intellectual property which was a major reason for the investment. To protect the intellectual property, part of the investment already made or even a further investment might need to be spent on the costs of enforcing the rights in the intellectual property.

The boot, of course, may be on the other foot. The investment in a new product or service or a new brand may lead to allegations that the rights in the intellectual property of others has been or will be infringed. Chapter 5 on due diligence include a major section on the serious problems this may cause and how to reduce the risk of being caught in this way. This is a very important aspect of intellectual capital management.

Types of Infringement

There are broadly three types of business which or persons who infringe rights in intellectual property. First, the counterfeiters who know exactly what they are doing and deliberately try to make money on the back of the genuine product, service or brand. They are usually slippery and hard to stop. As a result limiting the activities of counterfeiters (stopping them being almost impossible) is a never ending task.

Secondly, the badly informed who have no idea that they are doing anything wrong until the nasty lawyer's letter lands on the chairman's desk or worse the court-ordered injunction is delivered to the door. Mostly, these can be resolved quickly and relatively inexpensively. The rest may result in a long court battle with all the associated costs.

In the 1990s Polaroid sued Kodak in the United States for patent infringement which resulted in a long court battle and huge damages awarded against Kodak which had the effect of almost putting Kodak out of business. The Polaroid patent related to the number and order of layers of chemical in a photographic film. It was claimed to be different to earlier types of film. The court held the patent to be valid and infringed by Kodak. Polaroid was the innovator in instant photography. Kodak wanted a share of that market. The major obstacle was the Polaroid patents. Kodak tried to emulate the technology but went too near to the patented technology. Kodak infringed and paid Polaroid damages said to be over $900 million. Kodak could have avoided infringement by using earlier public domain techniques!

Thirdly, the well informed who have assessed the legal rights in the intellectual property, have concluded that they are invalid or unenforceable, and start using the intellectual property fully prepared to defend themselves and gambling that they have made the correct judgement. Or rather that their advisors have done so. The resolution of these circumstances tend to polarise.

One possibility is that the businesses involved decide that large litigation costs should be avoided if possible. A mutually beneficial deal is done. If both parties have intellectual property and associated legal rights, the business alleged to be infringing may be in a good position to negotiate a better deal, assuming that its intellectual property is needed by the owner of the "infringed" rights.

A good example where a combination of this approach involved the Amazon patented "1-Click" system. Amazon sued Barnes and Noble in October 1999. Amazon argued that Barnes and Noble's web site used technology that Amazon alleged was too similar to Amazon's patented "1-Click" system. That system stores billing and shipping information so online customers do not have to re-enter data each time they buy. Barnes and Noble's online subsidiary, barnesandnoble.com, used a similar system, called "Express Lane". Amazon announced that it had settled the case in 2002. The terms of the settlement are confidential.

This was just one of several cases brought by Amazon seeking to enforce its rights in the patented "1-Click" system. But whilst these case were continuing, Apple agreed in 2001 to take a licence of the Amazon patented "1-Click" system. Again the terms are confidential but the payment of royalties are likely to be part of the deal.

The other possibility is that a massive court battle ensues with the court deciding if the gamble paid off. Substantial legal costs will be incurred. In January 2002 Pfizer's Viagra patent was confirmed as invalid on appeal in the courts in London. The case was brought by Pfizer's US competitor Eli Lilly seeking a ruling that the 1993 patent on the main ingredient of the drug was invalid. The judge ruled that the invention disclosed in the patent was based on information already in the public domain. Eli Lilly was trying to develop and sell an impotency drug of their own.

Your intellectual property will come to the attention of your competitors at some stage. Sooner if they too have an intellectual capital management discipline in place or later when they are suffering from your success. They will be concerned only if the success of your intellectual property impacts on their business. This could be directly because sales are lost or indirectly because the returns being achieved by your business are better than they can achieve as a result of the intellectual property.

The intellectual capital management adopted for a particular business must include a policy on dealing with infringers and plan for the costs of resolving disputes involving the intellectual property by negotiation of terms for its use, suing the infringer or using some form of alternative dispute resolution process.

Principle Ten

Measure improvements

It is an essential part of good intellectual capital management to develop measures of success of the management and evaluation of intellectual capital.

Several measures will be apparent. Some short term, others longer. Some objective, others subjective. The most important overall requirement is to measure the effectiveness of the intellectual capital management process. The best way to do this is to lay down some benchmarks before starting to implement an intellectual capital management process.

Appropriate benchmarks might be the cost of maintaining portfolios of intellectual property and the legal rights associated beforehand and a survey of the business assessing the level of knowledge and understanding of intellectual capital, awareness of the intellectual capital of the business and that of its rivals or being developed in research organisations, the costs of acquiring and owning intellectual capital, and the returns derived form it. The historical performance of the business could be used to assess the value of the intellectual capital as then managed in the business.

Completing the identification and recording of intellectual capital can be measured in the short term by the production of the record of all the intellectual capital and the associated legal rights. In the longer term, any intellectual capital missed may become apparent almost by accident or through the follow up process.

Cost savings can be compared to the benchmark costs. Improved revenues can be analysed for core and non core licensing activities. In each case looking for measurable improvements which can be put down to better intellectual capital management.

Principle Eleven

Spread the message

Just as important as measuring improvements is communicating the strategy and process. The strategy and intellectual capital management process must be explained to those working in the business, maintaining secrecy where required.

The Black Hole of Technology

Research and Development

The management of R&D merits a mention on its own in the context of intellectual capital management. Very many companies undertake R&D seeking innovations which will give them competitive advantage, allowing survival and prosperity in the future. Principles 4 and 7 lead to an assessment of the innovations being developed in a business and to the effective management of this aspect of the intellectual property being created in a business. The R&D may be in low technology areas or in seeking ground-breaking technologies for example in the biotechnology or telecommunications fields. The difficulty is to ensure that the R&D delivers competitive advantage more times than not and enables the business to make better profits or at least to sustain an acceptable level of return on capital employed.

The following quotes illustrate the dangers:

"a recent world wide survey of 284 companies by SRI INTERNATIONAL found no correlation between technology spending and financial performance."[1]

"a study by the Imperial College Management School for the UK Department of Trade and Industry found that financial

---

1. Reported in the *Financial Times* on 21st May 1996.

performance was not directly linked to R&D spending. It was the effectiveness with which the companies could convert the research into new products that added value and lead to better financial performance."[2]

Businesses investing in R&D need a crystal ball which would enable them to see which R&D will produce good innovations, leading to good intellectual property, with strong legal protection. Products and services based on such innovations if commercially successful will lead to enhanced profits as a result of higher margins or larger market share due to the legal rights in the intellectual property protecting them. This is successful innovation. If the intellectual property rights do not deliver these enhanced profits, principles 5 and 8 of intellectual capital management would dictate that this intellectual property might not be worth maintaining. The innovation might nevertheless still be commercially successful. It is just that the intellectual property is not adding anything or anything sufficient to justify continuing the cost of maintaining the intellectual property.

Of course, taking each research and development project through to a commercialised product or service is a very expensive and a scatter gun approach to finding successful innovations. Indeed, managing research and development necessarily involves having no real idea if any successful innovations will be developed. Still less if any of the developed innovations give the intellectual property required by the business for its future success.

The intellectual capital management principles will help to ensure that R&D is aligned with the corporate strategy of the organisation or more importantly with that of a particular business group in the organisation. Few commercial organisations can afford to engage in "blue sky" research and remain competitive. The executive management that can organise the R&D function so that it comes up more regularly with successful innovation and intellectual property will make their business at worst competitive and at best a world leader in its field.

So money invested in research and development will need to be justified at each stage of the project. Most large organisations have developed models to assist in this process. Using the principles of intellectual capital management and the appropriate valuation techniques which are the subject of chapter four, managers can make a reasoned prediction of the present values of cost and revenue and

reported in the *Financial Times* on 21st May 1996.

whether the project, the product or service based on the innovation being developed, and the intellectual property being created, meet organisation-specific targets. For example, the internal rate of return expected (see further, page 137).

If the project does not meet the criteria used to predict likely success, the project can be abandoned along with any legal rights which exist or are being acquired. No further costs are incurred. The skill in managing this process is for the business in question to set the criteria to reflect the risk-taking or innovative nature of the business. Being too cautious, risks missing or abandoning innovations which would have been successful. Being too gung ho, is almost certain to lead to investment or continued investment in high risk projects. Too many long shots!

The unpredictable nature of R&D and long development times make accurate prediction fraught with difficulty. Returns tend to be over the longer term. R&D can easily be seen as a black hole into which corporate money is poured for years with no return compared to an advertising campaign which can typically bring increased sales very quickly.

This quote will express a common feeling amongst those working in R&D:

> "R&D managers face an uphill struggle in justifying their expenditures. Strangely, too, it has been somewhat of a vogue in management literature to present technology transfer as inevitable (no transfer, no deal). R&D managers need every extra tool they can get to help show the value of R&D investment or the cost of not investing in R&D, and the price of handling over technology too easily."[3]

Faced with this problem some organisation have turned to option pricing theories (see further below) to determine whether or not a particular R&D project should go on. Many financial institutions rely on the advice of experts in theoretical statistics to evaluate the relative risk in different strategies. The same techniques are used in corporate finance in its widest sense to evaluate the risks associated with a particular acquisition or capital asset investment.

Some financial commentators now advocate the use of option pricing to assess the value of options about R&D. Put very simply if an organisation invests in a project, it retains the option to invest further in the project or to reap the rewards of a successful exploitation of a

---

3.   From article by Dr David Newton in Mastering Management series published by the *Financial Times*.

new technological development. Similarly at milestone points in the project, a further investment leads to a continuation or renewal of the option. If the investment at any stage is not made, then the opportunity to partake further in a project which may have value is lost. Consequently, the option to be bought with the initial investment and then renewed with each subsequent further investments must at each stage have a value.

Option pricing theory is a way of arriving at such a value. The expected net present value of the project can be likened to a share price. The decision whether or not to invest in an option to buy shares by paying for the option depends on the price of the share now and an assessment of the risk of an acceptable return not being delivered. The vagaries of the stock market, the performance of the company and general trade circumstances mean that the share price will fluctuate over time and the shares will have a particular price at the time the option can be exercised. Option pricing is used to put a value on the option at the outset.

Not Invented Here

The acquisition of technology

A powerful incentive to innovate is the need to survive. Developing or acquiring strategically important intellectual capital such as brands or a patentable innovation giving a step change in applied technology is important in many businesses sectors. Many businesses have recognised the need to seek strategic R&D collaboration arrangements with other organisations to develop new products or services quicker and at the same time share the risk of failure as well as the potential rewards.

Businesses, if they are to survive, have realised that they must collaborate or look for developed technologies in the face of:

- growing diversity and complexity of customer's requirement;
- increasing pace of change;
- shortening product life cycles;
- the cost of R&D increasing exponentially;
- pressure on margins.

The implementation of a structured intellectual capital management process is essential to managing the risks inherent in the acquisition or development of intellectual property.

The result of implementing the principles of intellectual capital management may be to identify a technology or intellectual property requirement for the future. This may be innovations to give products additional functionality, solve known problems, or the need for a new consumer brand. One solution would be to attempt to develop the required innovations to fill this requirement. If this technology gap has been revealed early in strategic terms, an attempt at developing the required innovations can be made. This may be the best way of filling this gap if the necessary R&D capacity is available.

But often the gap is revealed when strategically the need for the technology is imminent. Insufficient time is available to allow development of the solution. The technology must be found from outside the organisation if possible in the time available. This can typically be achieved in three ways or by a combination of the three ways. These are: licensing in the technology; by undertaking joint R&D with a specialist organisation; or through a joint venture with a partner.

If managing intellectual capital at a strategic level, the strategic analysis will have been done at both overall corporate level and at market sector level. The need to find technology will have been identified. For example the following case study is illustrative. A food company expanding into the Asian subcontinent identified that it needed to find an alternative to gelitin for use in products to be sold in India where the use of beef products in food was unacceptable. An alternative with similar characteristics was the goal. The food company considered licensing the technology once identified or entering a joint R&D project with another organisation. In fact it did both: the alternative was developed by a university and then licensed to the food company.

Identifying the need for certain intellectual property requires the type of sophisticated strategic intellectual capital management advocated here. Developing or locating the required intellectual property in relevant innovations requires further hard work in technical and legal due diligence. Also possibly in commissioning the development of the innovation and all the practical considerations and legal agreements which will be required to do this successfully. This might be briefing a design house about new packaging or an advertising business about a new brand. It might be working with a research organisation such as a university. Then there is doing the deal, if the innovations is not developed in house, to have access to the intellectual capital perhaps through ownership or by exclusive licence rights.

Once all this has been achieved successfully, the innovation and the intellectual capital will need to be accepted by the organisation which is going to develop and commercially exploit it. Those working in the business which has "brought in" the innovation may find the innovation accepted enthusiastically or may find resistance to adopting innovations not created by the in house team. Part of the management of intellectual capital is to be aware of this as a potential problem and then to plan and implement adoption of the innovations accordingly. Effective intellectual capital management can remove these prejudices by addressing the need to create value to the business from using the technology rather than on the need to justify the R&D function through the quality of its developed technology.

Letting the Cat out of the Bag

Pre-deal discussions

Any business considering entering a collaboration or licensing arrangement may have to disclose secret technical or other information to asses whether or not the technology fits. This means for the seeker of the technology whether it fills the gap identified by the intellectual property management review. Disclosing confidential information is by its very nature risky. In one famous UK case about the "Spycatcher" book, confidential information was likened to an ice cube taken out of the freezer and put into a drink. Once out the ice begins to melt, up to a certain point the ice cube can be put back in the freezer and it will return to the original shape. But if the ice cube melts too much, this cannot be done. The material (water/information) is the same but is in a different state with different attributes (properties/legal rights). Like many analogies it is not perfect but it does illustrate in everyday language a difficult legal concept and area of potential mishap.

The important point is that once confidential information is openly and freely disclosed it cannot be made secret again. More important still is to understand that the cumulative disclosure of small parts of a body of confidential information will, after a point, be sufficient to constitute a disclosure of the whole body of information. Once disclosed you cannot erase it from the memory of the individuals who will have had access to it. The human memory can not be erased like a computer memory.

You must carefully assess the risk. Consider the risk/benefit analysis. Is it marginal? Find out what you can about the other side. Have a good confidentiality agreement and implement it properly. Remember the problem of verbal exchanges. There should be a written record of the information disclosed so that later it is possible to show what is yours and what has been disclosed to you. Disclose only what is necessary and preferably begin with "old" technology until the relationship develops.

The sections on confidential information at page 256 deal with this in more detail in the due diligence chapter.

Spotting a Winner

Rigorous assessment and strategic investment

One of the purposes of intellectual capital management is to manage risk in innovation. Backing the wrong intellectual capital (whether in your own business or in that of your customers) or not having the right intellectual capital may mean disaster for the business and for the ambitious management team. In the UK the executive management of Marconi restructured the business and effectively bet the company on the roll out of broadband technology. They invested hugely to meet expected demand from customers operating in this sector. The intellectual property in the broadband technology in the hands of Marconi's customers did not generate sales as expected. Marconi effectively lost the bet. Its share price collapsed and executives lost their jobs in a high profile way.

The risks of failing the intellectual capital challenge will be reduced if you have assessed rigorously:

• what intellectual capital is likely to be required?

• what your competitors are up to?

- whether you have or are likely to have any required intellectual capital?

- If not, can you acquire it in the time required?

The nature of the challenge should not be exaggerated. The Marconi example is not an everyday example of the intellectual capital challenge. The challenge is not often about going effectively going bust if you fail. It is more about remaining competitive, stealing a march on rivals, having your own intellectual capital so that you can do deals with rivals perhaps to access their technology or intellectual capital or gain extra revenue.

Businesses must have a clear strategic understanding of what is likely to be required and be open-minded about the sources of the intellectual capital they seek. This will required removal of any tendency to prejudice based on the "not invented here" attitude. A good illustration of corporate arrogance is the development of the telephone. In 1876 Alexander Graham Bell made the breakthrough to achieve a working telephone. He took his new invention to Western Union, a large American corporation at the time. The reaction of the company executives was to refer to the invention as an interesting novelty and to conclude that it had no commercial possibilities. They described it as an electrical toy. Not deterred, Bell formed AT&T. In four years he had sold 60,000 telephones. Within 20 years he had sold 6,000,000 telephones at which point AT&T was the largest American corporation at the time.

A more up to date example is the bagless vacuum cleaner invented by James Dyson. He faced being rejected by existing manufacturers, unable to find substantial financial backing, with his patents challenged in court. After winning all these battles, the bagless vacuum cleaner is a massive commercial success.

However, businesses needed to be alive to the hopeless. A book published in the United Kingdom catalogues patent failures. It is called *Patent Nonsense – A Catalogue of Inventions that failed to change the World* by Clive Anderson, published by Michael Joseph in London. It illustrates many inventions which have crashed on to the commercial rocks. For example, an invention to use ice blocks as substitutes for vehicle wheels. This patent was filed in the British Patent Office in 1964. Another one related to a "pat on the back" apparatus: in this case a United States patent filed in 1986. The book contains many other amusing illustrations of inventions never likely to make their inventors a fortune. Yet substantial amounts of money will have been spent on obtaining the patent rights.

The serious point about these failed ideas is that a patent on its own is worth little if anything. If the product or service is commercially successful, having a patent is likely to *increase* the money to be made out of successfully selling the product or service, and possibly from allowing others to do so in return for some kind of payment. The substantial costs of obtaining intellectual property rights for the product or service such as patent, trade mark, and design registrations would be money well spent if the product or service is commercially successful but *wasted* if not. The intellectual capital challenge here is to manage this risk and to spend money on the winners and not waste money on the losers.

Intellectual capital management will be an essential part of this risk management process. Properly carried out, the risks of backing a loser can be reduced. The circumstances of the investment in intellectual capital will affect risk. Of course, investing in early stage research will always be more risky than in developed products or services. But through managing intellectual property, knowing what intellectual capital – technology, brand, or know how – is desired for the future, that once acquired the intellectual property is likely to enhance revenues and by how much, and that the intellectual property has good legal rights attached to it, will enable an informed decision to be taken.

At appropriate intervals that decision can be reviewed. The actual achievements and outcomes can be reviewed with a strong element of objectivity against the documented information on which the original decision was made and the expected progress. This is important because the continued investment in the intellectual capital can be reviewed and monitored at critical points, those points typically associated with further investment. Informed decisions can be taken about continuing to invest, the chances of success, the likely revenues. Lessons can then be learnt and improvements made. By repeating this process regularly, the risks of backing an intellectual property loser from initial decision to market failure should be almost eliminated.

The example based on the invention of the telephone and the examples from the Clive Anderson book illustrate a very important point which relates both to intellectual property management and valuation. In the early stages of a development, it is extremely difficult to be certain what will be successful and what not. Whilst it was perhaps obvious that the "ice block wheels" and "pat on the back device" were never going to be rip roaring commercial successes, other technology might not be so easy to predict.

In one case study, the innovation was based on a waste product from an existing manufacturing process. It had, when treated in a particular way, exciting and very surprising technical properties. These could be used in very different fields such as absorption of chemical spillages and exceptional fire retardant properties. There was no doubt that the technology worked. Graphic physical demonstrations could be given to potential investors or commercial partners. The results were very impressive. A patent had been filed for a number of particular applications. The difficulty was in assessing the commercial potential when a wide range of different applications were possible. For example, in one application the material gave a much better technical effect than existing technologies. However, to be used in practice, a number of expensive tests would have to have been carried out. The application would require regulatory approval which would again be expensive to achieve and maintain.

The end products in which the invention would be used were very price sensitive. Success was likely to be based on gaining and maintaining market share from existing players in the market with the new and better product rather than in obtaining a better margin. Competitors were bound to try to fight back. The cost of enforcing the patent rights looked a likely expense to be incurred early in the development of the business. A further concern was that since the product was a waste product there was a limited amount of the waste product available. Whilst cheap at the outset, if the innovation proved successful, the price of the waste product would undoubtedly increase.

All these indications made investors nervous of a substantial investment. At this stage, the opportunity was highly risky. But how to know? The only way is to have a planned investment programme based on the achievement of agreed milestones. The investment must be stopped if the criteria for continued support, such as the achievement of the next milestones, will not or have no prospects of being achieved.

This may require tough and unpopular decisions to be taken. The implementation of an intellectual capital management programme will make the implementation of these decision easier to manage.

Those involved will know that intellectual capital is managed like any other part of the business, that criteria for future investment have been set with objective measures which were realistic, and that investment in the continued development of the project whatever it may be is dependant on these criteria at least being substantially met. If they are not, it should be less of a surprise and easier to explain if the project is cancelled. It is not seen as an arbitrary decision of some person remote from the project who knows nothing about the development and prospects for success. Rather it is a properly managed process, with a reasonable chance of taking those involved along rather that risking a feeling of alienation.

CHAPTER 3
UNDERSTANDING INTELLECTUAL
PROPERTY RIGHTS

Contents

This chapter provides an overview of the legal protection available for intellectual capital – which can have a profound effect on value.

It is a summary: a more detailed explanation of Intellectual Property Rights can be found in the Appendix: More on Intellectual Property Rights.

CHAPTER 3
UNDERSTANDING INTELLECTUAL
PROPERTY RIGHTS

Introduction

The purpose of this chapter is to provide an overview of intellectual property rights: intellectual property being that part of intellectual capital that is legally protectable. It will give a basic understanding to those undertaking valuations and managing intellectual capital. Appendix 1 starting on page 373 contains a much more detailed explanation of the various types of intellectual property rights and will provide a deeper understanding of these various types of intellectual property rights.

Appendix 1 is also a practical reference source about intellectual property rights which can be consulted from time to time for a better understanding of the different intellectual property rights that are likely to be encountered by business executives, their accountants and their bankers, and by investors such a venture capital professionals.

Intellectual property is now the subject of due diligence investigations and valuations as a business asset in acquisitions, floatations, and when finance is being raised whether as a secured loan, a securitisation or provided by a venture capital investor. A good understanding of the legal rights and procedures relating to intellectual property is essential to appreciate the strengths and weakness of intellectual property and the associated rights in particular circumstances and how these relate to the value of the intellectual property.

The expression "intellectual property rights" is a general one, used as short hand for the many and complex rights which can arise in relation to work created by individuals. These rights are not abstract concepts. They are rights which relate closely to the outcome of work done by an individual or by a group of individuals and give legal protection to that outcome which can take many forms. Legal protection simply means that the intellectual property right can be owned, that the owner can prevent others using the right without permission and that these intangible rights can be the subject of agreements allowing use by someone not the owner or transferred to such a person. So patent rights would relate to the invention of a new product or process or copyright could relate to software that has been written.

The intellectual property in any particular outcome of work by the individual or group of individuals must have certain attributes which are essential if a particular intellectual property is to have any value and for that value to be assessed as part of a commercial venture. These essential attributes are that

- the product of the work be identifiable,
- it has protection by legal rights
- the ownership of those rights can be ascertained
- the extent of such rights can also be identified, and
- the rights can be transferred.

Intellectual property rights are often important assets in any commercial transaction or investment decision. Yet many of those in business, professional advisors, and finance professionals and bankers involved in such transactions or investment decisions have little or no understanding of even the basic concepts of intellectual property, the associated rights and procedures.

A better understanding of intellectual property must begin with an appreciation of a system of national legal rights and in some cases procedures relating to intellectual property. One of the essential features of potentially valuable intellectual property rights is that the rights give legal protection. Such legal protection will be given by national laws and not by a harmonised law applicable world wide and unitary in character. For example, the rights given to the owner of a trade mark will be broadly the same in the UK, the USA, and in Germany but the detail will be different. A further complication is that, in this example, the trade mark can be owned by different persons in different countries. The detail of ownership and extent of legal protection, however, could be important.

Staying with the trade mark example, the detail will determine whether and to what extent:

- a particular person has a proper and complete ownership of the trade mark;

- the rights in the trade mark give protection against others taking advantage of the asset without permission;

- any defects in ownership or protection can be cured.

A good example of this is the interpretation of the Improver patent in the UK and in Germany referred to later.[1] Here, a European Patent effective in many European countries was claimed to be infringed by a product. The courts in Germany concluded that there was an infringement. In England the courts came to the opposite conclusion, that there was no infringement. The case became more complicated later when an appeal in each country reversed the position. The dispute eventually settled out of court. A commercial assessment of the patent based on the legal protection in Germany would be different to that based on the legal protection in England.

Discussions and moves to harmonise laws protecting intellectual property rights began in the Nineteenth Century when global trade became more organised. These discussion continue almost all the time in international governmental trade meetings and within the European Union.

In the late Nineteenth Century a mood of international co-operation on trade enabled a convention to be called on aspects of intellectual property rights. The convention lead to an agreement being signed in Paris in 1883 called the Paris International Convention for the protection of Industrial Property. Industrial Property was the old terminology used to describe those rights which are now called intellectual property rights. It was last revised at Stockholm 1967. It is the first attempt at an international level to codify the law and procedures as to the protection of intellectual property rights. The aim which has been reasonably successful was to set out general rights which would be applicable in those countries which signed up to the Convention. It was left up to the individual countries to enact laws or procedures to give effect to the obligations imposed by the provisions of the Convention.

---

1.   At page 402.

Just over a hundred years later in 1994, the world trading community felt sufficient need to co-operate that again an agreement was concluded on aspects of intellectual property. This is known as the Agreement on Trade Related aspects of Intellectual Property Rights, including the trade in counterfeit goods or the TRIPS agreement for short. Other conventions were agreed after the Paris Convention and preceding the TRIPS agreement. These will still need to be considered as they still have important provisions governing intellectual property rights at the international level.

The Convention or Treaty provides general objectives to be achieved and each signatory country decides how its own law will put the general objectives into effect. The Convention is currently administered by the World Intellectual Property Organisation (WIPO) which is an arm of the United Nations and based in Geneva. Since the early 1950s, a number of other important international agreements have been reached within the framework of the Paris Convention. For example, in relation to patents, the Patent Co-operation Treaty signed in 1970 and the European Patent Convention signed in 1973.

The TRIPS agreement was concluded as part of the GATT agreement signed in Marrakech in April 1994 at a meeting of Trade Ministers. This was the conclusion of the long running and troublesome negotiations. At the meeting, an agreement was also reached and signed to set up the World Trade Organisation. The TRIPS agreement is an annexe to this GATT agreement.

The spur to reach the agreement was the growing world trade in counterfeit goods and the decision by the United States government to take retaliatory action against those states it believed where not giving adequate protection against the counterfeiting of goods in which intellectual property rights subsisted. The TRIPS agreement identifies internationally recognised intellectual property rights, the protection that signatory states must have in place or adopt in due course, and ensure reciprocity of protection. The types of intellectual property rights recognised in the TRIPS agreement are:

- copyright and related rights
- trade marks
- geographical indications
- industrial designs
- patents

- topographies of integrated circuits
- protection of undisclosed information

The TRIPS agreement, therefore, gives a powerful influence and legal requirement in world trade terms for the adoption of similar rights and procedures for the protection, ownership and acquisition of intellectual property world wide. TRIPS does not call for and is unlikely to lead to harmonisation of these rights and procedures world wide or to a global set of rights and procedures for intellectual property.

These conventions and agreements give some positive rights to persons in respect of intellectual property rights but in the main lay down minimum standards for the rights of intellectual property. In some the terms of the particular convention have effect as a local law once ratified. Others require local laws to be made. In the UK, for example, the provisions of a convention are not effective until implemented by suitable national legislation.

So in the last hundred years or so many countries (but importantly not all) have become signatories to these treaties. But those that have signed such treaties have not all signed all of them! By signing, countries commit to adapt or implement laws so that their laws are or will eventually be built on the same principles but differ in the detail.

As this book goes to press two developments in Europe have been announced. The most significant is the agreement for a Community Patent after 30 years of negotiation. This will allow one patent to be obtained for the whole of Europe. The second announcement is about the proposal for a European Directive to harmonise the enforcement of intellectual property rights across Europe.

These international aspects of intellectual property rights and procedures mean that the concepts of the legal rights and procedures relating to intellectual property are effectively the same world wide. The intellectual property law and procedures of the UK and at a European Union level illustrated in this chapter and in the Appendix are generally compliant with the requirements of TRIPS. Anyone understanding the concepts of intellectual property law and procedure of the UK and at the European level from this chapter and the Appendix will have a sufficiently detailed knowledge to give a good understanding of intellectual property in a global context.

This chapter and Appendix have not been written to provide a detailed understanding of the intellectual property laws and procedures of a particular country. They have not been written for the specialist in intellectual property.

Copyright

Introduction

In the UK, the need to prevent the unlawful copying of books lead to the laws which became known as copyright. The need became particularly acute after the printing process had been invented in the fifteenth century and developed. For the first time books could be duplicated quickly by the standards of the time. The need arose to prevent copying and the loss of business for early book makers. Copyright owners today have the same concerns as the early bookmakers all those hundreds of years ago. Lobbying of governments and interstate bodies to change or amend the law to protect the interests of copyright owners continues most recently in connection with the accessing and use of copyright work over the internet.

The protection against unlawful copying given by copyright has two broad aspects to it. First, the types of creative work qualifying for copyright. Copyright now covers such diverse subjects as sound recordings, works of sculpture, and computer programs. Secondly, the activities that constitute an infringement of the rights given by copyright.

Copyright is not a right arising out of registration. It is a right which arises out of the act of creating and recording in some way the thing created. In copyright parlance the thing is commonly referred to as " the work " or "the copyright work". A book is not the subject of copyright protection until it has been 'recorded', for example, on paper or on a computer. It may be confidential before being 'recorded' which would give the author rights in confidential information which are covered later. A key concept follows from this. Copyright does not protect ideas but the form in which those ideas have been expressed. This concept is interpreted differently by the courts of countries round the world.

EU Copyright Directive

The EU Directive (2001/29/EC) came into effect on 22nd May 2001. The EU states must implement the Directive by 22nd December 2001. The Directive seeks to harmonise aspects of copyright law across Europe with the aim of encouraging the development and exploitation of intellectual property.

EU Electronic Commerce Directive

This Directive clarifies and harmonises various legal issues relating to information society services including electronic commerce and provides a harmonized framework of principles and provisions relevant to important parts of the Copyright Directive.

These Directives and the national legislation that will follow have been designed specifically to address the concerns of rights holders in relation to copyright works which have arisen through the ease of access and copying of copyright works over the internet. The ease of access and copying has been of particular concern to businesses developing software, in the media and information industry, and those in the music business.

Copyright Works

Copyright works are defined in, for example, UK copyright law and include literary works, sound recordings, software, films, broadcasts, and databases. In each country local nuances will exist on what copyright can protect.

A work only becomes a copyright work if it meets certain qualifying conditions such as being original and when it has been recorded in writing or otherwise. The fundamental conditions are:

- whether the work qualifies for copyright by reference to the creator of the work or to its place of first publication; and

- whether the work has sufficient originality.

For example, a book is a literary work and any illustrations will be artistic works. A computer game or website will have software (a literary work), complex graphics (artistic works), animations (a film), and sounds (musical works and a sound recording).

Ownership

In UK law, ownership is determined by reference to the author. The author is the first owner of copyright in a work. This is subject to an exception. For a literary, dramatic, musical, or artistic work made by an employee during the course of employment, the employer is the first owner of the copyright in the work unless there is an agreement to the contrary. The author of a work is the person who creates it.

Works created by Employees?

A work created by an employee will in UK law be owned by the employer if the work was

- created by the employee;

- during the course of employment with the employer claiming ownership; and

- there is no agreement that some other person should own the copyright.

Any agreement about ownership?

The question of whether any agreement about ownership existed will again depend on the relevant facts. The existence of an agreement between an employer and employee is often a written agreement or clear from the circumstances and surrounding documents such a correspondence and usually does not cause a problem in practice.

The existence of an agreement about ownership of copyright outside the employment relationship can be more difficult to confirm. A clear written contract dealing with ownership may exist. But often the written agreement for the creation of a copyright work does not cover ownership or is unclear about it. Often the agreement is formed by a number of documents or from correspondence.

Transfer of copyright

By agreement

One way of removing doubts about the ownership of copyright is to confirm the ownership in one person by an agreement to which all the relevant persons are made party. It is perhaps a counsel of perfection but if the copyright is to form the basis of a substantial business investment, a risk free title should be the aim.

By operation of law

Copyright would form part of a person's estate. Therefore, it would pass by operation of law in the event of say death or bankruptcy.

Duration

The duration of copyright protection under UK law depends on the identity of the author of the work. Copyright in an original literary, dramatic, musical or artistic work will exist for 70 years after the end of the year in which the author dies. This is the case irrespective of ownership of the copyright. Where the author of the work is unknown, the copyright will expire 70 years after the end of the calendar year in which the work was first made available to the public. If authorship to the work is joint, this is often the case in copyright of computer cases, then providing all the authors are known, protection lasts until 70 years after the last surviving author dies. If all are not known, the right lasts for 70 years after the death of the last known author. The copyright in a typographical arrangements only exists for 25 years. A typographical arrangement is the layout of a page say of a newspaper ready for printing.

Infringement – rights to prevent unlawful copying

The right to prevent unlawful copying is really the fundamental point of copyright. The commercial value of the copyright derives from the ability to prevent others copying a commercially successful work without permission. It is only an infringement of copyright if copying has occurred without permission. This is straight forward with counterfeit goods. But can be more difficult where products are similar but not identical. The copyright owner must prove that copying has occurred to win a copyright case. If the original work and "copy" are closely similar, a court will often infer that copying took place and require an explanation from the person accused of copying. Such a person, to escape a finding of copying, will need to show a convincing defence of independent creation not copying. As always, the facts believed by the judge in a court will determine who succeeds.

The importance of the infringement rights to a commercial assessment or valuation of the copyright as a business asset are that they define the products that the copyright owner can prevent others copying and selling.

Legitimate Copying

It is not an infringement of copyright to copy a copyright work in certain limited circumstances. These are often referred to as permitted acts. These include so called "fair dealing" exceptions such as copying for private study or for criticism, review and news reporting. Others cover use in education and for libraries and archives.

Databases

Intellectual property rights of two kinds now potentially exist in a database under UK law. First, a database is now specifically categorised as a literary work in which copyright will subsist if the qualify conditions are met. Secondly, by an intellectual property right called a database right which is more limited than copyright.

Defining a database?

An understanding of UK law about databases will give a good indication of the protection of databases throughout the EU States because the UK law implements EC Directive 96/9 harmonising intellectual property rights for databases in Europe. In UK law (and under the Directive) a database means a collection of independent works, data or other materials which have two characteristics. First, they are arranged in a systematic or methodical way. Secondly, they are individually accessible by electronic or other means.

A database normally has a structural part and the part which forms the content of the database. Each of these can be protected by the intellectual property rights in databases either by the database right or by copyright.

Subsistence of copyright in a database

As with other copyright works, copyright will exist in a database if the database is original. There is an important difference from other copyright works. The standard of originality is much stricter for a database than with other copyright works. The stricter standard is that a database will only be original for copyright purposes if the database constitutes to the author's own intellectual creation by reason of the author's selection or arrangement of the contents of the database.

Ownership of copyright in a database

The author (for copyright purposes) of a database will be the person who creates it. In practice many databases are produced using computer systems. If this happens, the author will be the person by whom the arrangements, necessary for the creation of the work, are undertaken. Typically, this will be a business or corporate body rather than an individual.

As explained earlier, the key to establishing who owns the copyright in a database is knowing who is the author. The author will own the copyright unless that person is an employee creating the database during the course of employment duties or an agreement provides that someone else will own the copyright.

Subsistence of the database right

The first point to understand is that database rights can exist whether or not the database is a copyright work. The database right will exist if there has been a substantial investment in the obtaining, verifying, or presenting the contents of the database. Investment in this context includes any investment which is financial, human, or technical. The practical assessment of the database right as an intellectual property right will need careful application and evaluation.

Ownership of the database right

The maker of a database is the first owner of the database right in it. For these purposes, the maker of the database is the person who puts the effort into organising the information for the database, checking it, and investing in it. An employer will be the maker if the person who makes the database is an employee acting in the course of his employment.

Infringements of the database right

Broadly, a person infringes the database right if, without permission, that person extracts or re-utilises all or a substantial part of the contents of the database. Substantial will be considered taking into account quality and/or quantity. This pretty well speaks for itself. One point worth emphasising is that repeated and systematic extraction or re-utilisation of insubstantial parts of the contents of the database can amount to infringement.

Duration

The database right lasts for 15 years. The trigger point forming the start of that period needs care. The 15 year period can

- either start from the end of the calendar year in which the making of the database was completed; or

- 15 years from the end of the calendar year in which the database was first made available to the public provided this was done within 15 years from the end of the year in which the database was completed.

Author's Rights

These rights are separate from rights in copyright works but are related to them. They are sometimes referred to as related rights or, equally ambiguously, as author's rights or even moral rights. In UK law, these rights are known as moral rights and only exist in copyright works. In other words, no copyright, no related rights. The same applies generally in other jurisdictions.

A further complication may arise because the person having these individual rights might not be the person who is the owner of the copyright in the particular work. This has implications for anyone wishing to exploit the particular work commercially. The author's rights are often not assignable (depending on the jurisdiction) whereas the copyright in the particular work can be assigned. However, author's rights can sometimes but not always be waived again in respect of some countries.

Rights in Performances

Rights in performances are rights of individuals. They are distinct from the author's rights. The legal position is again complex. Performer's rights are primarily of concern in the entertainment industry involving the exploitation of recordings of music and literary works, films and making of broadcasts.

Recording Rights

These are rights accorded to any person having an exclusive recording contract with performers. Typically, record companies and broadcast organisations will have the benefit of exclusive recording contracts with performers. The recording rights exist for the benefit of the person having exclusivity in relation to the commercial exploitation of such recordings. They are clearly valuable rights. The usual remedies exist for the prevention of infringement of these rights.

Patents

Introduction

Patents can be obtained for inventions if certain criteria are met. There is no definition of an invention. There are requirements for a patentable invention. The general requirements for a patentable invention and for obtaining the grant of a patent are now applicable in most of the important countries in the world. This is the culmination of the effects of the various international conventions. The most important of the conventions in this respect is the Patent Co-operation Treaty. This usually referred to as the "PCT".

The exception is the United States. The basic concepts are the same as the rest of the world. However, there are important differences in law and procedure. A separate section giving an overview of the important conceptual differences appears later in this chapter and in the Appendix.

A patent is a nationally registered right. It is obtained by filing an application. The application is filed at a Patent Office where the administration of the patent granting process takes place. The application can be filed at a national or at a regional Patent Office. The national Patent Office could be that of the United Kingdom. The regional Patent Office might be the European Patent Office in Munich. An international patent application is filed at a national or regional Patent Office designated for that purpose. In the language of the patent world, you will come across expressions like "a national filing", "an international filing", "a PCT filing" used to describe a patent application as appropriate.

The application must comply with certain administrative formalities as well as meeting the requirements for a patentable invention. The administrative formalities are complex and must be met by the application if the application is to proceed through the process to a granted patent. More importantly, if these formalities have not been completed properly, they are difficult and often impossible to correct subsequently and particularly after the patent has been granted. The failure to meet properly these formalities can make the patent eventually granted invalid or to be not as strong as it could have been.

In any detailed due diligence investigation an assessment needs to be made as to whether these requirements have been met and, if not, what likely effect will the omission have on the validity and strength of the patent and can it be corrected.

Basic requirements for a Patent

There are four key legal, rather than administrative, requirements to be satisfied to conclude that a patentable invention exists and before a patent can be granted. An understanding of these is necessary for anyone attempting to understand patent rights and any due diligence investigation about patent rights which might be the subject of an investment decision or so as part of the evaluation of those rights so as to put a value on a patent. The key requirements are that the invention:

- must not be excluded by law from being patented;

- must be new. This is often referred to in patent parlance as "having novelty" or "being novel";

- must involve an inventive step meaning a technical advance over existing technological understanding which is not obvious. Again in patent parlance, this is often referred to by the shorthand expression "the invention is obvious" or "is not obvious" or "is inventive";

- must be capable of industrial application.

Essential patent terminology

Each of these key requirements is considered in more detail in the Appendix. These key requirements cannot be understood without first being aware of three other fundamental concepts in patent law. Each of these key concepts is also considered in more detail in the Appendix. These are the concepts of:

- the priority date of a patent;

- prior art; and

- the person skilled in the art, sometimes referred to as the "man skilled in the art" or simply as "the skilled man".

A knowledge of these concepts is necessary to understand the process by which patents are granted and to appreciate how a patent might be attacked as being invalid. The classic defence to a patent infringement claim is to show that the patent is invalid. If invalid, no patent. No patent, no infringement. Also without this understanding many of the due diligence points cannot be understood which are covered in Chapter Five.

Exclusions from patentability

Certain types of innovations are excluded and cannot be patented.

Validity and Revocation

The grant of a patent is not a guarantee that the patent will continue to be registered. This is often not understood and leads to a common misconception with registered intellectual property rights generally that once registered the rights given by the registration cannot be challenged.

The examination of the patent application by a Patent Office makes sure that the patent application and the invention disclosed in it meet all the administrative requirements for a patent to be granted. It also searches for prior art. Whilst this search is reasonably extensive, it will include mostly patents which have been granted and possibly other literature. If the invention is apparently valid compared to this prior art, the patent would be granted.

Many patents are challenged as being invalid and revocation sought as part of a defence to a patent infringement claim. It is common to see a defence to a patent infringement claim, a counterclaim to revoke a patent.

The patent application process

The process by which a patent is granted for an invention is now similar whichever Patent Office is handling it. The procedure if an international application is filed under the Patent Co operation Treaty is rather different.

The normal process may generally be described like this. The inventor files an application for the patent. This must comply with many administrative requirements. Most inventors would employ a patent agent to assist them to do this. A filing fee is payable. The application will be acknowledged. There are provisions in place to file a patent application by fax and e-mail.

The application will be examined to ensure that it meets all the administrative requirements. Once an application has met the administrative requirements, various events happen in accordance with a set timetable.

There are two key events in the application process. First, the patent application is examined after a request to do so by the applicant and the payment of a fee. The examination process scrutinises the patent application to ascertain whether it is a patentable invention. Secondly, the application is published in accordance with the procedures of the Patent Office undertaking the examination. Publication does not take place usually earlier than 18 months after the priority date of the application.

Once the application has passed these hurdles it can go forward to grant and the intention to grant the patent will in many Patent Offices be published in an official journal to allow any interested party to oppose the grant of the patent. Such a procedure exists under the European Patent Convention but does not exist in the United Kingdom.

Once the patent has been granted the applicant is sent a document which is the grant of the patent and appropriate entries are made on the register of patents. From the date of grant, the patent establishes legally enforceable rights which date back to the priority date of the application which became the granted patent.

The patent when granted consists of a specification and several claims at the end. The specification essentially describes the invention and the claims are a statement of the features of the invention which cannot be used without the permission of the owner of the patent.

World Wide and European patents

Framework

World wide or European patent rights can be obtained through procedures set up by agreement between countries. The agreement is then recorded in a treaty to which each country adheres. The treaty providing for an international patent application process is called the Patent Co-operation Treaty or PCT for short. There are two treaties for Europe. These are the European Patent Convention and the Community Patent Convention. Respectively shortened to EPC and CPC.

The CPC is not yet in force despite being agreed many years ago. When in force, the CPC will enable one patent to be obtained covering the whole of Europe. It is already possible to obtain a trade mark and design rights for the whole of Europe as well as separate national rights. Recently, discussions have begun to activate the CPC. It is likely that this will happen.

The framework provided by the PCT and the EPC are similar to process described above. The difference is that one patent application is filed for several countries. So a European patent application covers most, but importantly not all, European countries. This is because not all the countries of Europe have adhered to the EPC. An international patent application covers most, but again importantly not all, countires of the world. Not all the countires of the worlds have adhered to the PCT. An international patent application can include the United States.

Designating countries – every country or only some?

The countries for which a patent is required must be designated when the application is filed. It is important to do this correctly since the opportunities to add later are very limited. Countries can be deleted easily later up to a certain stage. This leads to many international applications designating all possible countries and deleting those not needed later. For those countries not covered by an international application, individual national applications must be filed.

The international and European patent application process

The process of scrutinising the application is carried out in a central patent office rather than in local national patent offices. The basics of the application through to grant are similar. Once the application has reached a certain stage – either after the international prior art search has been done or for some countries after both that and the international examination have been done – the application "cascades" to each designated country for translations to be filed and other formalities to be attended to. It is these national requirements which make obtaining world wide patent protection expensive.

Grace Periods

An invention if disclosed and made public, it is not new. If not new, a patent cannot be obtained for it. This is a trap for business people and others not familiar with the qualification requirements for obtaining a patent. The effect of falling into the trap will result in a good innovation being denied patent protection and can seem unfair. There are, however, good reasons in support of the strict qualification requirements based around certainty. It is not necessary to set them out here. Even if the innovation had been disclosed publicly but was still able to be regarded as new for patent purposes, allowing the inventor or owner of the invention to delay for a even a relatively short time before claiming the right to a patent could be unfair. Other people would now of the innovation but would not be sure of whether the innovation could be used or not. If eventually no patent was claimed, the innovation could have been used. But if a patent was claimed, it could not.

A way round this is to allow in certain limited circumstances a period from public disclosure during which a patent application can be filed. These are referred to as grace periods. There are two such circumstances. First, where disclosure has been in breach of confidence or otherwise as a result of being obtained unlawfully. Secondly, where disclosure is at an international exhibition defined by reference to the Convention on International Exhibitions. Effectively, only really large international exhibitions are likely to qualify.

Two recent developments in relation to grace periods should be noted. First, discussion have been taking place amongst interested parties and government bodies in Europe about the introduction of a general grace period into the Europe. Secondly, a grace period has been introduced in Australia covering disclosure within the 12 month period prior to the filing date of a complete patent application.

Overview of the US patent system

The basic concepts explained about the patenting of inventions, the application process, and the rights given by a granted patent apply in the United States. However, there are some conceptual differences in the law and procedure which it is important to understand if managing intellectual property.

The essential difference

The most significant difference between the United States patent system and the rest of the world relates to novelty. Novelty in the United States patent system is complex and is covered in the Appendix. The important point to keep in mind is that public disclosure of an invention before filing does not necessarily mean that no patent can be obtained for the United States.

Such a disclosure would effectively prevent a patent can being obtained for the publicly disclosed invention anywhere else in the world. This is not a categoric statement because it is just possible that under the local patent laws of a particular country a patent could be obtained despite the public disclosure. However, these countries will not be the main developed economies.

Types of patent

There are three types of patent in the United States patent law namely a utility patent, a plant patent, and a design patent.

Utility patents relate to the invention or discovery of any new and useful process, machine, article of manufacture, or compositions of matters, or any new useful improvement. Design are for inventions relating to new, original, and ornamental designs for an article of manufacture. Plant patents may be granted to anyone who invents or discovers and asexually reproduces any distinct and new variety of plants.

Utility

This is another difference of United States patent law compared to the rest of the world although it is akin to the need for industrial application referred to earlier. To be regarded has having "utility" the invention must be "useful." The term "useful" in this connection really means that the invention has a useful purpose and is effective in use. So that a machine which will not operate to perform the intended purpose would not be called useful, and therefore a patent could not be granted for it or if granted was liable to be rendered invalid.

The date of the invention

The date of the invention is not important in jurisdictions out side the US. It is the date of filing the patent or patent application or those on which the particular patent is based which is critical. This was explained further in the Appendix. This has the advantage of certainty and is comparatively easy to administer.

Not so in the United States where the date of the invention can be and often is critical. The date of the invention is the date when the inventor proves that the innovation was conceived by the inventor. The date of the conception of an invention is insufficient on its own to be effective in deciding questions about novelty and ownership. The date of conception will be effective if coupled to the date of reduction to practice by diligence on the part of the inventor. Such diligence must also be shown from the date of actual reduction of practice to the filing date of a patent application

Reduction to practice is a complex subject but basically has two meanings. Actual reduction to practice being the making some embodiment of the innovation to show that it works. Constructive reduction to practice being the filing of a patent application completely disclosing the invention.

Inventor must apply

In the United States only the inventor may apply for a patent, with certain exceptions. If a person who is not the inventor should apply for a patent, the patent, if it were obtained, would be invalid. The person applying in such a case who falsely states that he/she is the inventor would also be subject to criminal penalties.

If the invention is owned and so the patent is to be owned by some one else such as an employer of an employee inventor then an assignment of the invention and all rights in it is required and is usually filed with the patent application.

Ownership

The proprietor of a patent or patent application will be the person named on the relevant patent register unless the contrary is proved. A search of the relevant national registers will show who is the registered patent proprietor. The entry on such a register is not a guarantee that the person registered as the proprietor is in fact the true owner.

Three situations typically account for this. First, an assignment of the patent or the patent application from one person to another has not been recorded at the national Patent Office in question. This is usually easy to spot during due diligence. The recording of the relevant assignment will rectify the position unless an intervening transaction has occurred in good faith without any knowledge of the assignment. If this has occurred, the person to whom the patent was originally assigned and where the assignment was not registered might not have a good title. Secondly, an employee claims ownership against an employer who filed the patent application. Thirdly, where one party has filed a patent application for an invention claimed to be owned by another. For example, a collaboration partner.

Collaborations are usually regulated by a proper formal agreement which makes adequate provision for intellectual property rights ownership.

Infringement

The teeth of a patent are the rights to prevent others using the invention without permission. This is referred to as an infringement of the patent. The extent of the rights given by the patent are broadly similar from country to country, but the details vary. Typically, it is an infringement to do any of the following without the permission or licence of the patent owner:

- if the patent is for a product, making the product, keeping it or advertising, selling or otherwise disposing of it. Importing can be an infringement;

- if the invention protects the process, it would usually be an infringement to operate the process and to deal in products by advertising, selling or importing them which had been made by the use of the process.

These powers to prevent infringements, if necessary by taking court action against an infringer, give the patent its potential value. The patent gives in effect a monopoly as defined by the patent specification and the claims. The patent owner and in some circumstances an exclusive licensee has the right to prevent anyone else commercialising a product or a process which falls within the specification and those claims.

The interpretation by a national court of the specification and claims of a patent determine whether a particular activity or product is an infringement of the patent. The following case clearly illustrates this point. The courts in the United Kingdom and Germany took a different view as to whether the teeth would bite in the particular circumstances.

Infringement Case Study – Improver and Remmington

This case study is based on the reported patent case in the UK of *Improver Corporation* v *Remmington* and is in Appendix 1 at page 407.

Transactions in patents

Patents can be transferred by assignment or can be licensed. The licence can be exclusive or non exclusive. There are some technical requirements when making an assignment or granting a licence and these would need to be checked carefully in any due diligence investigation. It is important that assignments and licences and other dealings such as a charge over a patent are properly registered at the national Patent Offices.

Supplementary Protection Certificates

A supplementary protection certificate can be granted for a patented medicinal or plant protection product and is intended to compensate a patent owner for the loss of the opportunity to exploit the patent invention by the making and selling of a particular product during the period that regulatory approval to market such product was being obtained.

Trade Marks

Introduction

There is no scheme for obtaining a world wide trade mark registration by a single application for registration. Some international schemes do exist for the registration of trade marks. The Madrid Protocol relating to the International Registration of Trade Marks is one. Another arises in Europe only from a European Regulation on trade mark law.

At national level each country has its own requirements. Some of these are harmonised. For example, in Europe as a result of an EC Directive requiring countries in Europe to modify their laws relating to registered trade marks in European Member States.

This chapter and the Appendix will consider the registration of trade marks by reference to the law and procedures operating in Europe governed by a European Regulation since this illustrates the sort of considerations which will apply in Europe and generally in countries granting registered trade marks. The detail will vary in different countries and not all the aspects of registration will be relevant. However, the reader will have an understanding of the factors likely to be in issue when considering the registration and legal rights in a trade mark. These rights give the trade mark its market power which is closely related to the value of the trade mark. Weak legal rights will not enable exclusivity to be enforced easily or at all. Exclusivity is an important factor in building trade mark value.

Registration

General requirements

Any system for the registration of trade marks has to address some key concepts. These are common to many systems around the world. Each country will deal with them differently in the detail.

There are three key concepts. First, that the trade mark to be registered must be sufficiently distinctive and not descriptive. Descriptiveness should be seen as shorthand for several related grounds on which a trade mark could be refused registration. Secondly, the rights given to prevent the unlawful use of the trade mark or one similar to it. This unlawful activity constitutes an infringement of the rights given by the registration of the trade mark. Thirdly, the need to establish confusion between trade marks or at least the likelihood of such confusion for infringement.

The aim of any trade mark legal system is, therefore, to balance these competing interests. For registration, the balance is between distinctiveness and descriptiveness. For infringement, the balance is as to whether a rival trade mark is sufficiently similar to cause confusion or not. Both are difficult to achieve in practice.

An understanding of the legal rights and concepts in relation to trade marks explained here referring to the European Regulation will be applicable across Europe even if some detailed differences at national exist. Theses legal rights and concepts are also applicable in general terms in many countries across the world.

Community Trade Mark

What is a trade mark?

The European Regulation defines a trade mark in Article 4 as follows

" .. any signs capable of being represented graphically, particularly words including personal names, designs, letters,

numerals, the shape of goods or their packaging, provided that
such signs are capable of distinguishing the goods or services of
one undertaking from those of other undertakings "

It follows the trade mark must be a sign, be represented graphically, and
give some distinction to the goods or services with which it is going to
be used. Traditional trade marks such as names, logos, and some slogans
will not pose any particular problem for registration as a trade mark.
However the extent to which in any particular country more elaborate
trade marks can be registered is still developing. The shape of goods and
packaging will in fact be accepted under the trade mark rules operating
now in Europe if the shape is considered to be distinctive.

What is a Community trade mark with legal rights?

If the proposed trade mark is a "sign" as defined for trade mark
purposes, then the trade mark can be registered if it satisfies the
requirements for registration. Once registered, it becomes a
Community trade mark with associated legal rights. Some of these are
procedural such as completing the correct form with all the necessary
information. However, the main requirements are that the trade mark
is distinctive and not descriptive. These concepts are important ones
in trade mark law generally.

Distinctiveness and Descriptiveness

The European Regulation requires distinctiveness to be addressed by
reference to two categories of grounds for refusing an application to
register a trade mark. These are absolute grounds and relative grounds.
Some are based on public policy or to protect the rights of others. Some
grounds are to prevent descriptive trade marks being registered.

Registration procedure

The registration procedure in most countries will follow a general
pattern. There are bound to be national idiosyncrasies. The
application for a Community Trade Mark can be made at a central
office or at the equivalent in a country in Europe. The central office
is the Office for Harmonisation in the Internal Market (Trade Marks
and Designs) usually referred to by the awkward acronym "OHIM"
and which was instituted by the Regulation. This office is located in
Alicante, Spain. The equivalent office in the UK is the Patent Office
which despite its name deals with applications to registered patents,

trade marks and designs. The registration procedure is similar to that discussed in relation to patents although simpler.

Goods and services are divided into 45 classes. Trade marks are registered by reference to these classes. The classification system is international. The application is begun by completing a form and filing it with a national trade mark registry accompanied by a fee. The application must show a graphical representation of the trade mark, state the class of goods or services for which registration is sought and the specification of the goods or services within the class for which registration is sought. The specification of goods is used to assess the infringement rights of the owner and to assess the extent of use during the course of the application process and if there is a revocation or validity challenge. Once filed, the national trade mark registry will in due course scrutinise the application. In some countries, a detailed scrutiny is made together with a search for similar registered trade marks. In others countries, this does not happen. On the basis of the result of the search and scrutiny, the mark will be accepted or rejected. If rejected, usually a dialogue ensues between the examiner at the trade mark registry and the applicant or the applicant's professional agent. The purpose of the dialogue is to see if there are reasons why the trade mark should be registered perhaps with amendments. It is not the purpose of the trade mark registry to prevent registration but rather to ensure that trade marks are registered which are valid.

Once the trade mark has been accepted, perhaps after amendment, the application is published by OHIM for a given period. This is three months. This period is one in which opposition by any person who has trade marks rights which might be adversely affected by the acceptance of the application in question can be lodged to the registration of the trade mark. If an opposition is lodged, then an opposition procedure commences with the exchange of evidence and ultimately a hearing to decide whether the trade mark should be registered or not. If there is no opposition or after an unsuccessful opposition challenge, the trade mark proceeds to be registered on the national register of trade marks.

Once registered, the rights of the trade mark owner date back to the original date of filing and the initial duration of the trade mark is ten years. The trade mark must be renewed every 10 years. But no rights to enforce the trade mark come into effect until the trade mark is actually registered. Other countries may have different provisions. Once granted, the trade mark proprietor receives a trade mark certificate.

The renewal is to be paid during the period six months before the end of any such ten period. It can be paid in the six months afterwards as well provided that an additional late renewal fee is also paid.

Ownership

The person – individual or organisation – making the application is taken to be entitled to the registration of the Community Trade Mark unless it appears from the application that the person is not or may not be so entitled. Processes exist including an opposition procedure by which a persons entitlement to the registration can be challenged later.

Scope of protection and infringement

Infringement means the right to prevent another person using the registered trade mark without the consent of the owner. The national laws of each country where the trade mark is registered will determine the extent of protection given to a trade mark in that country. This will be a combination of the laws of that country and the interpretation of them by the local courts. The legal rights given by the Community trade mark can be enforced in any country in Europe by using the national courts of the country in which the Community trade mark is to be enforced.

Limitation on Community Trade Mark rights

Certain activities cannot be prevented by the legal rights given by a Community Trade mark. These are set out below and can be taken as a good guide to the sort of commercial activity which Community trade mark rights can not stop. Article 12 of the Regulation provides

Limitation of the effects of a Community trade mark

A Community trade mark shall not entitle the proprietor to prohibit a third party from using in the course of trade:

(a) his own name or address;

(b) indications concerning the kind, quality, quantity, intended purpose, value, geographical origin, the time of production of

the goods or of rendering of the service, or other characteristics
of the goods or service;

(c) the trade mark where it is necessary to indicate the intended
purpose of a product or service, in particular as accessories or
spare parts,

provided he uses them in accordance with honest practices in
industrial or commercial matters.

Validity and Revocation

The registration of a trade mark is only a good indication that the
registration is correctly registered. As with patents, the fact of a trade
mark being registered is not a guarantee that the trade mark will
continue to be registered. There are two grounds on which the
registration of a trade mark can be attacked.

First, that the registration is invalid. Secondly, that the registration is
liable to be revoked. The difference between these two is broadly as
follows. A finding of invalidity means that the registration should
never have been granted. A finding of revocation means that because
the trade mark has not been used or because of some activity during
the life of the registration, the registration should be cancelled.

Dealing with the Community Design

The rights in the Community Trade Mark may be transferred and
otherwise dealt with as a property right and as if a national registered
trade mark of the country in which the holder is based. The details
are a more complex but this is sufficient to understand that
ownership of the rights can be transferred.

Rights in Trade Marks in the UK

Registered Trade Marks in the UK

There is a separate national registered trade mark law and procedure
for the United Kingdom as in most other countries. The law was, in
1994, changed to implement the European Directive (EC Directive
89/104) in respect of designs. The law is now effectively the same as
for the registered Community Trade Marks in the European

Regulation (Council Regulation No. 40/94) although the rights obtained are only for the United Kingdom.

The application process is again similar in its concept and basic procedural steps to that of OHIM. Differences of detail exist which it is not necessary to explain in this book.

Non-registered rights in trade marks or Passing Off

Many countries give rights to businesses which have used the trade mark in trading activities whether for goods or in respect of services. These laws are often referred to as laws preventing unfair trade practices or rights in passing off. Many European countries have unfair trade practice laws. In the UK there are no unfair trade practice elaws as such but instead rights in passing off. Passing off is sometimes referred to as protection of the goodwill in a business or concept. Many countries which have been influenced by the UK system have passing off laws, for example, Australia, Canada, New Zealand, Hong Kong, and Singapore.

Rights in passing off arise out of trading or activities akin to trading. For example, charity organisations have been found to have passing off rights although they don't really trade as such.

The three elements required constitute a classical statement of the law. They are that there must be:

- a reputation or goodwill required by a business for its goods or services or which relate to a logo, a character or style;

- there must be a false statement not necessarily deliberate in relation to that reputation or goodwill leading to confusion amongst the public or a section of the public;

- there must be damage suffered by the person who has the reputation or goodwill.

There is a mass of case law about passing off and what constitutes a protectable reputation, what constitutes a misrepresentation, whether deliberate or false, and what sort of damage can be recovered. The vast majority of these cases are all unique in the sense that the outcome is dependent upon the facts of the case not on principles of law.

Consequently, the only statement of the law which can be used as a guide is that involving the three elements mentioned above. Everything else depends on the facts of a particular case.

The type of damages which can be claimed is pretty straight forward. This will range from the more certain type of loss such as lost sales to the more speculative such as compensation for loss of the opportunity of expanding into a related market sector.

Rights in Designs

Introduction

This subject has much in common with copyright but the subject has sufficient differences to merit a section on its own. The rights in designs in many countries including in Europe arise out of registered designs and from deign rights which do not require registration. Registration gives stronger and longer rights. In some countries other registered rights exist for product designs called utility models or petty patents. The extent to which these give protection depends on the law of the country in respect of which they have been registered. In the United States, designs can be the subject of a design patent to which we referred in the "Overview of the US patent system" on page 402.

In Europe the rights in designs are based on two regimes providing the rights. This is similar to the rights in trade marks where the rights can be acquired for the whole of Europe by a European trade mark registration or nationally by a national trade mark registration in a particular country. The legal rights in designs is yet more complicated than this. First, laws and procedures exist for Europe wide rights in designs through registered designs and design rights not requiring any registration. Then national laws and procedures exist giving registered rights and rights which do not require registration. In the UK, the national rights in designs are from registered designs and designs not requiring registration.

European Design Rights

In recent years, two legislative changes have been instigated at the for the whole of the European Union. One change is effected by a European Directive (EC Directive 98/71) in respect of designs with the intention of harmonising across Europe some aspects of the rights in designs. The other change is brought about by a European Regulation (Council Regulation No. 6/2002) providing laws and procedures for rights in designs applicable to the whole of Europe rather than at the national level only. Remember that a European Regulation gives rights directly to people and to businesses and other orgainsations operating in Europe. A Directive does not. A directive requires countries in Europe to implement laws at the national level to give rights as required by the Directive.

Community Design

The definitions and qualifying criteria for the Community Design are the same whether the design is registered as a Community Design or not. The rights given by the Community Design are longer – 25 years – if the design is registered than if not – 3 years only.

The rights in designs given by the European Directive (EC Directive 98/71) and European Regulation (Council Regulation No. 6/2002) are recent statements of the law about designs in European context. Court decisions about them are not yet available based on which a commentary could be given to help understand the way in which the new concepts work in practice. Until such time as these laws have been interpreted by courts and some accepted meanings established, they must be read and understood in the particular context based on experience and judgement which comes with that experience.

Meaning of a design

The definition of a design from the Regulation gives a reliable guide to the types of designs for which registration can be obtained in Europe. The definitions are from Article 3 f the Regulation.

Article 3

Definitions

For the purposes of this Regulation:

(a) "design" means the appearance of the whole or a part of a product resulting from the features of, in particular, the lines, contours, colours, shape, texture and/or materials of the product itself and/or its ornamentation;

(b) "product" means any industrial or handicraft item, including inter alia parts intended to be assembled into a complex product, packaging, get-up, graphic symbols and typographic typefaces, but excluding computer programs;

(c) "complex product" means a product which is composed of multiple components which can be replaced permitting disassembly and re-assembly of the product.

Definition of a Community Design with legal rights

The design to qualify for the legal rights given by the Community Design right must satisfy several criteria set out in the Regulation. Again these are a reliable guide as to the requirements to register designs in Europe. The requirements are complex and detailed.

Is the design new?

This is alternatively stated – does the design have novelty? It is one of the two main requirements for a design to be registered. The concept of "novelty" is one which appears in several guises intellectual property law and procedure. As originality in copyright law, as distinctiveness in trade mark law, and as a requirement for a patent to be novel. This is a further instance of it.

Does the design have individual character?

The requirement for individual character is the other of the two main requirements for a design qualify for legal protection as a Community Design. This is in Article 6 of the Regulation.

Some excluded designs

This is again a complex part of design law with many details. However, three important aspects of design are excluded which are important to understand in the context of protection for innovative designs in Europe. These exclusions are in Articles 8 and 9.

Article 8

Designs dictated by their technical function and designs of interconnections

1. A Community design shall not subsist in features of appearance of a product which are solely dictated by its technical function.

2. A Community design shall not subsist in features of appearance of a product which must necessarily be reproduced in their exact form and dimensions in order to permit the product in which the design is incorporated or to which it is applied to be mechanically connected to or placed in, around or against another product so that either product may perform its function.

3. Notwithstanding paragraph 2, a Community design shall under the conditions set out in Articles 5 and 6 subsist in a design serving the purpose of allowing the multiple assembly or connection of mutually interchangeable products within a modular system.

Article 9

Designs contrary to public policy or morality

A Community design shall not subsist in a design which is contrary to public policy or to accepted principles of morality

These exclusion are part of a balancing act performed by the European Commission between the desire for a free and open market within Europe and the need to protect the rights of individuals and businesses. These exclusions are part of the free trade side of the balance.

Scope of protection and infringement

The main legal rights given by a Community are the right of the owner the exclusive right to use the design and to prevent anyone else using the design without the consent of the owner. Use according to the Regulation ".. shall cover, in particular, the making, offering, putting on the market, importing, exporting or using of a product in which the design is incorporated or to which it is applied, or stocking such a product for those purposes."

The scope of the Community Design, again according to the Regulation ".. shall include any design which does not produce on the informed user a different overall impression." This is one of those expressions capable of being interpreted many different ways. Advising on whether a particular design which is not identical or very closely similar to the Community design actually comes within the scope of the a Community Design based on this expression will be difficult to do with any certainty. Once this expression has been interpreted by the courts, this task will be easier but not easy.

Length of protection

The rights in the unregistered Community Design last for three years form the date that the design was first made available to the public within the European Community.

The rights in a registered Community Design last for 25 years provided that renewals are paid at five yearly intervals. If a renewal is not paid the rights are lost from that time. The renewal can be paid late within a period of six months after the due date provided an extra fee is paid.

Ownership

The rights in the design are owned by the designer unless designs created by an employee "… in the execution of his duties or following the instructions given by his employer, the right to the Community design shall vest in the employer, unless otherwise agreed or specified under national law." A design will be jointly owned if two or more persons have jointly developed the design.

Registration procedure

The application for a Community Registered Design can be made at a central office or at the equivalent in a country in Europe. The central office is the Office for Harmonisation in the Internal Market (Trade Marks and Designs) usually referred to by the awkward acronym "OHIM" and which was instituted by European Regulation (EC) No

40/94 of 20 December 1993 on the Community trade mark. This office is located in Alicante, Spain. The equivalent office in the UK is the Patent Office which despite its name deals with applications to registered patents, trade marks and designs.

The registration procedure is similar to that discussed in relation to patents and trade marks although simpler. The procedure is to make an application including representations of the design. The application is examined to ensure that it meets the relevant criteria. It may be necessary to overcome objections raised in the examination process either by successfully arguing the objection is not a correct one or by making amendments. This process normally takes several months. Once any objections are overcome the registration will be granted as a registered Community Design.

Invalidity

A registered Community Design may be declared invalid either by OHIM or a by national court as a counter claim in court proceedings about infringement of the design. So to invalidate a registered Community Design, an application must be made to OHIM which is in Alicante, Spain unless infringement proceedings are current in a national court when the national court may decide whether the design is invalid as a counter claim to the infringement claim.

In contrast, an unregistered Community Design can be declared invalid by a national court either by an application for that purpose or as part of a counterclaim in infringement proceedings in respect of that design.

The grounds for invalidating a Community Design are detailed. The most important grounds mirror the qualification requirements for the subsistence of the design and the obtaining of a registration for it where registered. If these did not or do not exist, then the rights in the design whether registered or not should cease to exist.

A registered Community Design which has been declared invalid on certain grounds maybe maintained in force if amendments are made which correct or overcome the objections which lead to the registration being found to be invalid in its original form.

Dealing with the Community Design

The rights in the Community Design whether registered or unregistered may be transferred and otherwise dealt with as a property right and as if a national design right of the country in which the holder is based. The details are a more complex but this is sufficient to understand that ownership of the rights can be transferred.

Rights in Designs in the UK

Registered Designs in the UK

There is a separate national registered design law and procedure for the United Kingdom as in most other countries. The law has been recently changed to implement the European Directive (EC Directive 98/71) in respect of designs. The law is now effectively the same as for the registered Community Design in the European Regulation (Council Regulation No. 6/2002) although the rights obtained are only for the United Kingdom.

The application process is again similar in its concept and basic procedural steps to that of OHIM. Differences of detail exist which it is not necessary to explain in this book.

Design Right in the UK

This right is similar to copyright. It was introduced in the United Kingdom to give product designs protection against copying. It replaces copyright protection for these designs which was perceived in the late 1980s to give too much protection and to stifle competition. The right applies to designs created after 1st August 1989. The design must be original and fall within the relevant definition of a design.

Definition of a Design Right design

The definition of design covers " any aspect of the shape or configuration (whether internal or external) of the whole or part of an article." This definition will cover most manufactured products. There is no artistic criteria so that purely functional designs will have protection against copying. Some designs are specifically excluded. First, methods or principles of construction and surface decoration are excluded. So in one case the shape of a garment was protected by the unregistered Design Right and the design on the fabric of contrasting colours was copyright protected. Secondly, the so called "must fit" and "must match" exclusions. The "must fit" exemption only excludes those particular features which enable the article to "fit" to other features of the design whereas the "must match" would exclude all those features which enable the article to match the appearance of other parts of an overall design to make the whole complete.

These two exemptions are to prevent owners of the Design Right from using the rights in the design to stop competitors making products to be used with the Design Right owner's products. This again is part of the balancing of free trade with the rights of individuals and businesses. The competitors may be producing accessories or spare parts. For example, a replacement body panel, bumper, or instrument panel "must match" the rest of the design of the car to be of any use. But car seats, steering wheels and road wheels generally do mot have to "match" any aspect of the design of the car. Wing mirrors are useful to illustrate the boundaries of this exceptions. The design of the wing mirrors of a car may well be an integral part of an aerodynamic shape and so the design would match the overall car design. But in other cases the shape of the wing mirrors have no direct relation to the overall shape of the car.

The shape of a sophisticated alloy car wheel will have features design to enable the wheel to fit on a car. These features will be covered by the "must fit" exclusion but the remainder of the attractive design of the wheel will have Design Right protection.

Original and not common place

There are two qualifying criteria in relation to the design if Design Right is to subsist in it. First, the design must be original. Secondly, it must not be "commonplace in the design field in question at the time of its creation". The circumstances of each case will be used by a court to determine if a design is original and not commonplace.

Subsistence of Unregistered Design Right

For the Design Right to subsist there must be a record of the design. The Design Right will subsist in the record. The design can be recorded in two ways. By making an article to the design or in a design document. In most cases a design document will exist. If not, the fact of making a product to the design will be sufficient to record the design for Design Right to subsist in it.

Ownership of a Design Right

The position on ownership is similar to that for copyright with one important difference. The difference is that the unregistered Design Rights in a design which has been commissioned will belong to the person who commissioned the design not the designer. This is not the case with copyright. Nor with the Community Design. UK law states that "the designer is the first owner of any Design Right in a design which is not created in pursuance of a commission or in the course of employment." If there is a commission, the first owner is the person who commissioned the design. If the design was created by an employee during the course of employment, the employer is the first owner of the unregistered Design Right There is a fourth type of person who might be the owner. One of the ways that a design may qualify is by publication. If the design qualifies for unregistered Design Right protection through publication, then the person who made the qualifying publication will be the owner of the right.

Qualifying for Design Right

The provisions of UK law relating to the Design Right are similar to those for copyright but not identical.

Duration

The rights given by the Design Right continue for either 15 years from the date when the design was recorded or an article was made to the design or 10 years from the date when articles made to the design were first put on the market if that date was within 5 years of the first recording or making to the design. However, any person is entitled during the last 5 years of the Design Right to a licence to do anything which would otherwise be an infringement of the Design Right. If the terms of the licence cannot be agreed a mechanism is provided to settle the terms. The availability of such licences will have a big impact on the value and commercial assessment of designs which are only protected against copying by an Design Right. The exclusivity will have been lost and competition can be expected. The level of royalty for the kind of design only given this protection is likely to be low, in the 1–5% bracket.

Infringement rights

Any person infringes the Design Right who does or authorises another to do anything which is the exclusive right of the Design Right owner. The exclusive rights cover almost every commercial activity. So any person who reproduces the design either exactly or substantially by making an article will infringe. So will a person who imports, sells, or has possession of such an article. It is these exclusive rights that may have substantial value in that other businesses can be prevented from making products to the design.

Know How

Introduction

Know how is the riskiest type of intellectual property in which to invest, whether that be to take a licence and gear up for manufacture or to acquire a business whose commercial success is at least partially based on know how. But in many instances, other intellectual property rights will be combined with know how giving more certain protection often making any investment decision less risky. Know how is the riskiest intellectual property because of its nature. There is no registration to evaluate. It is not like copyright or designs where a particular "thing" is protected which can be seen. Rather know how is information that has value because it is confidential. Confidential means not in the public domain. Not known to everyone. The extent of the know how is often difficult to establish with any certainty. It is common to see know how described as "..financial information about..." or "... the technical specification for ...".

UK Common Law of Confidential Information

In the UK it is the law of confidential information which underpins know how as intellectual property protected by rights. The law of confidential information is a common law legal doctrine based on fairness between persons – individuals or organisations. The legal doctrine is a set of principles developed over hundreds of years in the UK by its courts. It is the application of those principles in particular circumstances which determines whether information is to be regarded as confidential or not. To achieve fairness the principles allow considerable flexibility. As a necessary consequence, there are no hard and fast rules but instead broad principles. These principles are interpreted and applied by the courts in each set of circumstances.

The fundamental principle on which the UK law of confidence is based is that a person who has received information in confidence from another will not take unfair advantage of it or profit from the wrongful use or publication of it. On this fundamental principle has been built a complex law of confidential information in the UK.

The requirements to be met under UK law for information to be protected as confidential are that a confidential relationship must exist between the owner of the confidential information and the person to whom it has been disclosed, the information must actually be confidential in the sense of not being in the public domain, and is the type of information recognised as protectable. The right in confidential information is broadly the right to prevent the unauthorised disclosure and use of the information.

Type of information

Any information can be protected as confidential if and to the extent that it is not in the public domain. There is no requirement that the information should be inventive as in patent law or original as in copyright law in the sense of having been the result of skill and effort. But information which is of a general or trivial nature is unlikely to be regarded as confidential by a court unless the circumstances are exceptional.

The know how must be sufficiently detailed and not simply a general concept. The more general the concept, the less likely a court is to find that it has been used in breach of confidence. It is much more likely that several persons could have thought of the general concept.

Public Interest Disclosure

In UK law, an obligation to keep information confidential will not extend to prevent disclosure of the information where a serious risk of public harm exists. But the permitted disclosure will only be to the extent necessary to prevent such harm. The harm might be, for example, the commission of crimes, the perpetration of a fraud, or some physical harm to the public. A disclosure in the public interest will only avoid being a breach of the obligation of confidence if the disclosure is limited to those who need to know to prevent the harm.

Disclosure, for example, to a national newspaper will not usually be justified. Disclosure to the police or a regulatory body is more likely to be meet the requirements of a public interest disclosure. So it would not be in the public interest to prevent the disclosure of confidential information about a product which would reveal that the product would be harmful to the public.

This UK law common law about public interest disclosure based on the court decisions over the years has know been made a statutory law in the Public Interest Disclosure Act 1998. The application and interpretation by the courts of the rights given in this statute will indicate to what extent, if any, the previous common law position on public interest disclosure has changed.

Confidentiality and employees

The extent to which a former employee can and cannot use information gained whilst working for an employer has been the subject of regular legal disputes in the UK for most of this century. The legal position in the UK law of an employer to prevent that employee, whilst still employed, disclosing or using information about the employer's business is strong. The employer's rights are based on the obligations of confidence and good faith owed by an employee to the employer.

The legal position of the employer, however, changes after the employment of an individual ceases. The employer cannot prevent a former employee from disclosing and using general skill and knowledge acquired whilst employed by the employer. The type of information which an employer can prevent a former employee from using is limited to information learnt whilst employed that is of a sufficiently high degree of confidentiality as to amount to a trade secret.

The position of the employer can be improved by having a contract of employment with an express term dealing with the use of confidential information and terms preventing an ex-employee soliciting customers and working in a competing business. Terms of an employment contract to ensure that information is kept confidential are usually not difficult to evaluate. However, evaluating the rights given by express terms to protect know how by seeking to prevent an ex-employee soliciting customers and working for a rival business for a period time after the of that employee's employment requires considerable knowledge and experience.

European Convention for the Protection of Human Rights and Fundamental Freedoms

The UK ratified the Convention many years ago but no UK government brought it into effect as the law of the UK. The UK labour government elected in 1997 decided that it would do so. The Convention became part of UK law on the 2nd October 2000 when the Human Rights Act 1998 comes into effect. The Convention has two relevant Articles which are Article 8 giving a right to privacy and Article 10 giving a right to freedom of expression. The Convention was an influence on the law of the UK before the Human Rights Act came into force. The UK appellate courts in various cases involving newspapers have stated that the rights in the Convention should be taken into account as having a persuasive influence on the decisions that the UK courts make.

It remains to be seen how the direct effect of the Convention and the Human Rights Act will affect the law of confidential know how in a business context.

In the public domain

Information to qualify for protection as confidential information must not be in the public domain. This means that the information must be not generally accessible by any person who wants to look for it. The qualification that the information must not be generally available is important because information can still be confidential in law yet be known and available to a limited number of individuals. For example, to a research group at a research institute or to certain employees in a company R & D department. So even though one organisation has information, the same information in the hands of a second company could still be regarded as the confidential information of that second company. Information which has been disclosed only in the course of a confidential relationship is clearly not in the public domain. Information which has been widely disclosed publicly is equally clearly in the public domain. But some cases will be in the grey between these two. The disclosure of an invention to a professional advisor in order that a patent application might be filed is clearly a confidential disclosure. Once the patent application has been published by the relevant patent office, the information in the application is available to the general public and the information in it is clearly no longer confidential.

Information which is publicly available can still form the basis of confidential know how. If a person researches publicly available sources of information to produce useful new information or know how, the results of that work will be protected as confidential information. It is the intellectual effort required to produce this information or know how from publicly available sources that gives rise to the protection against another person taking the know how and avoiding the effort to find the information by the same effort.

Confidential relationship

By agreement

Reaching an agreement to keep information confidential is a familiar event in business life. Employees are usually required to keep their employer's business information confidential by a term of the contact of employment. Non-disclosure agreements are sought before sensitive business information is disclosed in any negotiation or if an inventor is seeking backing from a potential business partner or provider of finance. The use of such non disclosure agreements is discussed later. Confidential information is exploited commercially often by a license from one person or organisation to another using know how agreements which require the information to be kept confidential and that a payment for use is made. Typically, a lump sum and a royalty.

The requirement to keep information confidential is a specific obligation in these contracts. But an obligation to keep information confidential can be implied into any contract if justified by the circumstances. It is not possible to give a check list of factors which if all or most were present would indicate that such an obligation would be implied. The best guide would be to imagine what one party to an agreement being a reasonable person would think if receiving the confidential information. Did an obligation arise to keep the information confidential?

By circumstances

An obligation to keep information confidential arises in many relationships without any doubt and this has been recognised by the law. For example, in the relationships between doctor and patient, solicitor and client, and banker and customer. But other relationships can give rise to an obligation to keep information confidential. For example, in a business negotiation where valuable business information is disclosed in trying to reach a deal. The obligation is more likely to arise if the information communicated is either detailed or highly valuable or both. But where the information is communicated in a social setting rather than a business one, the obligation is less likely to arise.

This ambiguity makes assessing whether or not a confidential obligation arises (if there is no confidentiality agreement in place) in particular circumstances difficult, at least with any precision. There are no hard and fast rules except in those few types of relationships mentioned above where the law is clear. The best guide that can be given is similar to that in relation to obligations of confidence being implied into a contract. Imagine what one person being a reasonable person would think if receiving the confidential information. Did an obligation arise to keep the information confidential?

The Non Disclosure Agreement

Disclosing secret information involves a risk that the information escapes the control of the person who owns it and becomes generally available. The chance to exploit commercially that secret information is lost. Yet often if the information is not disclosed, it is not possible to maximise that commercial potential. The aim must be to manage this risk and the non-disclosure agreement is an important part that risk management.

CHAPTER 4
VALUING INTELLECTUAL PROPERTY AND INTANGIBLE ASSETS

Contents

CHAPTER 4
VALUING INTELLECTUAL PROPERTY
AND INTANGIBLE ASSETS

Introduction

From previous chapters, the reader knows that the key assets that create wealth are now non-physical. They are capable of separate identification and valuation and, as one of the most important advances in wealth creation for centuries, this magnifies risk and liability assessment. In most acquisitions intellectual property and intangible assets ("Intellectual Capital") are likely to account for a large proportion of consideration. Every public and private business has these rights, even if they are only in the name under which it trades. Just as importantly, every business uses other people's intellectual property. More often than not, the questions to be answered are:

•   What is goodwill and what are the intellectual property rights used in the business or project?

•   How do you protect them in non-contentious (registration etc) and contentious (litigation etc) situations?

•   What is their value?

•   How do we increase intangible value?

•   How can it be transferred and exploited?

There are many situations when proprietors, directors and professionals will require an expert opinion of the valuation and creation of value in respect of these unique assets. They may be considering insurance, lending, credit risk and recovery, a sale or purchase of the company or asset, assessing damages following infringement or for a variety of other reasons. These assets can be transferred to low tax jurisdictions and valuation for tax purposes will often be required. Licensing is a key tool for exploitation.

A company's published accounts are prepared for many good reasons but not for representing worth and value. A Balance Sheet sets out a series of facts: a statement of the assets and liabilities of the company at a given moment in time; but it does not purport to represent a valuation of the company as a going concern. To suggest that it should do so would make the already over-burdened accountant's life completely impossible. It is common practice to see regular re-valuations of real estate and plant and machinery. Management and institutions have long since acknowledged that the most valuable assets of successful companies are not bricks and mortar but of an intangible nature. Management and institutions obviously need to know the value of what might be the single most valuable asset in a company and business managers need to know, or should know, the value of all assets under their stewardship and control.

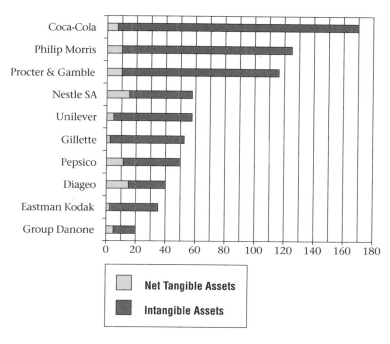

Source: *Citibank*, April 1999

Intellectual Capital: A Distinction

There is a distinction between legally protectable assets and those that cannot be directly legally protected. This distinction is important in valuation.

Intellectual Property

The essential characteristics of Intellectual Property are derived from the *legal system* for example:

- Patents (Patent Act 1977)
- Copyrights (Copyright Designs and Patents Act 1988)
- Trade Marks (Trade Mark Act 1994)
- Registered Designs (Registered Designs Act 1949)
- Design Rights (CDPA 1988)
- Data Protection Act (1998).

These issues are explained in Chapter 3 and the Appendix: More on Intellectual Property Rights.

Intangibles

Intangible assets also may account for a significant proportion of the total value of a business:

- Brands
- Subscription Lists
- Know-how and Show-how
- Negative Knowledge
- Research and Development
- Trade Secrets
- Proprietary Technology
- Agreements
- Information

Put another way, intangibles cover the spectrum of creative thought – this short list is therefore far from exhaustive. Together, intellectual property and intangibles are referred to in this chapter as "intellectual capital".

The Importance of Intellectual Property

When Pope John Paul II wrote in his encyclical of a new important form of ownership, "the possession of know-how, technology and skill", he was acknowledging that what has been christened intellectual capital is increasingly being recognised as the most important asset of many of the world's largest and most powerful companies. Intellectual capital is the foundation for the market dominance and continuing profitability of many leading corporations and is often the key objective in mergers and acquisition.

We have seen in the Introduction how intellectual capital is coming into its own. It is increasingly being recognised as an asset, the possession of which confers major economic benefits. Companies are licensing, selling and trading intellectual property around the world, and it provides one of the foundations of the global economy.

As further illustrations of this trend, the number of designs registered in the UK increased in 1999 by 13% and trademark applications by 11%. March 2000 broke Patent Office records and was responsible for more trademark applications than they had ever received in one month of their history.

The correlation between industrial and economic performance, and innovation seems to be a fact of life.

The Inefficient Market and Competitive Advantage

The efficient exploitation of their intellectual property assets must be a key objective for business enterprises. Those that are able to manage these assets properly are poised to take commanding positions of economic power. It is no longer an exaggeration to say that the business world is dividing between those companies and corporations that possess intellectual capital and effectively exploit it and those who do not. The have-nots will tend to diminish in status and importance, unless they can gain access to items of intellectual capital such as patents or well regarded trademarks and manage them.

Industrial muscle is no longer enough to ensure a future of growth and profitability. At the extreme a manufacturing company lacking intellectual capital has two choices, manufacturing for other corporations in a sub-contract relationship, or the mass production of a commodity. In either case the likely result is poorer growth and profits than the owner of intellectual capital. This, coupled with the increasingly global nature of the marketplace, is leading to a new form of international commercial activity: transaction based, and involving the transfer of intellectual property rather than the goods or services that the property supports. This commercial activity has changed the face of international business: whether taking the form of outright sale, joint ventures or licensing.

There is inherently a window of opportunity to obtain intellectual property at bargain prices or low royalty rates, due to the current inefficient market in which intellectual property rights are bought, sold and licensed, and the fact that accurate economic values are not being attributed to these valuable assets.

Making the Most of the Opportunities

Those companies that have developed clear strategies, based on accurate appraisals of the strength and value of intellectual property rights are out in the market place enhancing their earning power, productivity and market-share, harnessing home developed as well as acquired intellectual capital in their expansion.

"The process is very simple but extremely powerful. It allows the analysis of where Dow and key competitors are in the market place and in the innovation race, and allows decisions on research direction and intangible asset protection to be made in a reasoned and structured manner"

Gordon McConnachie,
Intellectual Asset Manager, Dow Chemical Company.

Investors look for the returns they hope to get either by way of income or by way of a future capital gain on realisation, or a combination of both. In arriving at the expected return an investor or investing company will have to consider a number of factors which will vary in their relative importance depending on the facts of the particular situation. Bearing in mind that no two say patents or trademarks are exactly alike, and that the circumstances in the industry at the date of valuation may vary from case to case it is essential to examine many factors.

Industries may show by their past history that trade is cyclical or even completely unpredictable. Political situations may have a vital bearing upon some sectors and this includes, the (in)stability, of the governing legal regime intellectual property in another part of the world.

The quality of management is an important factor, particularly in the small private limited company whose prosperity often depends upon one or more individuals who may be difficult to replace. The larger the company the greater the opportunity for training future executives and managing knowledge.

Valuation Overview – Arriving at an Expected Return

To set in context the sections that follow, we set out the key issues in valuation and outline the basic techniques and language. Throughout these sections we summarise the purpose of each, so that readers may find their level or read discrete sections understanding the context within our argument.

In order to make an appraisal of intellectual capital, it is necessary to examine the past. However history often only provides a simplistic guide to what may happen in the future and it is the net present value of a future return that is the most rigorous basis of valuation methodology.

A usual process in valuation has been to use average turnover, profits etc over the last three to five years. Where there is no discernible pattern, it may be necessary to examine figures over a much longer period, before arriving at forecasts. *Weighted* averaging techniques are also applied. For example where profits are steadily increasing you may weight to the final year when your figure will be more representative of future trends:

Date	Straight Average	Weighted Average Profits		
1999	10	10×1	=	10
2000	8	8×2	=	16
2001	12	12×3	=	36
2002	15	15×4	=	60
	$45/4 = 11.25$			$122/10 = 12.20$

However there are several reasons why earnings and their averaging fail to measure changes in the economic value. The most important of these are:

- different accounting techniques;

- the nature and level of risk, particularly when debt is a fixture of a businesses capital structure;

- investment requirements and capital expenditure are excluded;

- future dividend policy is not a feature; and

- such earnings calculations ignore the time value of money.

The Time Value of Money

The time value of money is calculated by adjusting expected future returns to today's monetary values using a *discount rate*. The discount rate is used in mathematical modelling to estimate economic value and includes compensation for risk and for expected rates of inflation. This will be dealt with in detail later, but is illustrated below.

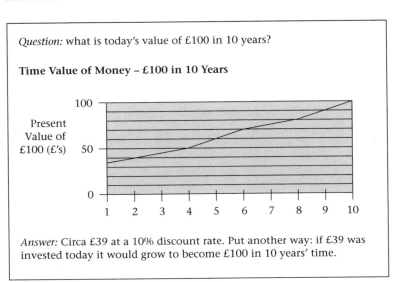

Question: what is today's value of £100 in 10 years?

Time Value of Money – £100 in 10 Years

Answer: Circa £39 at a 10% discount rate. Put another way: if £39 was invested today it would grow to become £100 in 10 years' time.

Predicting Returns

Consideration of the estimated future profits and net present value of those profits leads naturally to the next, and in many cases, the most important factor. Assuming that there are no immediate foreseeable prospects of liquidation, sale of the intellectual capital or take-over of the business, a shareholder's or investors' main interest will be centred on the yearly return he expects to receive by way of dividend distribution or salary. If there is no ready market comparator available among quoted companies, such as is the case with many SMEs, there is no industry "standard" yield (or yearly percentage return) to be applied. There are no "normal" SMEs. *In this case, the yield will be a function of management's ability to manage the intellectual capital – both legally protected intellectual property and other intangible assets.*

Many valuers when faced with this problem prefer to arrive at *required returns* on a comparative basis, by averaging the yield from companies and using comparable licensing in the same line of business and making an allowance for the unmarketability of intellectual property and intangible assets. This involves two further problems – the choice of comparable companies and the size of the allowance for unmarketability. Rarely is it possible to find an individual quoted company and/or intellectual capital similar to the one being valued. If this is the process chosen, and it is certainly not appropriate in a number of situations, it is better to take a group of similar *assets* and average the yields, or to look at the yield shown for the particular *sector* in the financial press. Often the yields required by investors in intellectual capital- and intellectual capital-owning companies are endowed with special requirements and special purchaser situations when compared to a sector. The process has dangers. It would, for example, be absurd to use an aerospace and defence index if you are valuing a small parts supplier in the same sector. The inclusion of large companies with extensive property and interests in intellectual capital will be reflected in a low yield and it would be more logical to take a representative selection of financial ratios of small parts suppliers generally.

Valuation Overview – Applying the Expected Return

Having decided on the expected return we come up against the next problem – to what financial information do we apply it. The purchaser is concerned with the future and the past is merely a guide. Hence he is not concerned simply with last year's return or the average return for the past ten years; he is concerned with next year's return and those for many years in the future. We must make an estimate of the prospective returns. Calculation of the prospective future returns will depend on the prospective cashflows and the task of forecasting these is not always easy.

For example:

• You would not adopt the same prospective future return for a company or asset with steadily rising profits as that for a similar company or asset where returns have dropped steadily and, say, where there is major capital expenditure in prospect.

- You may also be led to use the same estimated future profit where cashflows in the two companies or an asset had followed the same pattern.

In both cases averaging over a three or five year period could be identical and that is a nonsense.

Profit through cashflow is still what people want. Assets of whatever description, unless surplus to requirements, represent an investment which has to be made in order to generate earnings.

Generally the following need to be established as regards earnings:

- What has their trend been over recent years and how should these be adjusted for extraordinary events?

- What were the profits and cashflow in the last completed year?

- Is current financial information likely to be in line with historic trends – if not why?

- Are margins adequate and being maintained?

- What strategic (semi-capital) expenditure has been incurred? If little, has this weakened the future of the intellectual capital? If substantial, what adjustments should be made?

Problems with Forecasting

Forward projections will need to be used to establish the profit-earning potential of the intellectual capital. There is no alternative. Where substantial profit increases are expected, few people would rely upon that as a reasonable base upon which the present value of the intellectual capital could be established without question.

Reasons include:

- Inability to forecast crisis, recessions and other events delaying profitability.

- Difficulties in accurately estimating total cash outgoings. Often at a later date more cash is required than expected while major problems can remain unresolved.

- Frequently with intellectual capital, new management has to be recruited and proved. Many appointments fail. Recruiting is costly in time and money.

- Lack of knowledge of competitive activity and technological changes within the sector.

However where is it sensible to produce a prudent forecast this must be an ingredient to the earnings based valuation. Critical path and scenario analysis with assumptions should be stated in each case. Most businesses require a minimum cashflow to maintain their size, competitive ability and profitability. Replacement cost accounting procedures help with such assessments.

Using cashflow

Cashflow remaining after supplying debt and other fixed outgoings is free either to invest in growth, reduce gearing and improved liquidity (so giving the company or a particular piece of intellectual capital a stronger financial base) and to pay returns. The free cashflow should be ascertained, if possible. The reason why some sectors fall out of favour is that they have not been very popular with the stock market because their "free cashflow" has been so low as to threaten dividends and investment plans.

There is no standard method of valuing intellectual capital on the basis of its earnings and cashflow and every situation has to be treated on its merits. Discounted cashflow techniques will inevitably be utilised in this form of valuation appraisal. It is sensible to be very cautious when considering companies whose intellectual capital has a poor cashflow at the moment and which demand considerable injections of capital. Discounted cashflow analysis is one of the most comprehensive of the appraisal techniques and will reflect forecasts of revenue and operating expenses as far into the future as prudent.

The appropriate rate of return for use in discounting these cashflows is dependent upon risk and rates of return perceived at the valuation date. It will be necessary to look at comparable companies worldwide and compare market returns. The exercise will need to contrast returns where companies have either rate of return or price control regulation. Adjustments may be necessary to researched rates of return for issues such as different inflation rates in different countries and different accounting standards, for example historical cost and current cost. Inflation has played havoc with accounting principles and the interpretation of accounts. Adjustments for inflation must be handled with particular care.

The final year of the projected cash flow usually does not mean that all cashflows will cease. To be complete, the discount factor in the final year should represent a capitalisation that discounts perpetual cash flows into present value without having to show specific cash flows into infinity.

The Capital Asset Pricing Model which specifies the relationship between risk and the rate of return is one of the easier models that may be considered and this will be covered in detail later.

The following sections track the sequence and process of the valuation exercise. Each section represents a step in the appraisal. If taken out of turn or omitted, the valuation conclusion will be fundamentally flawed.

Section 1:

Understand the Reasons for Valuing Intellectual Capital

> The greatest resource any organisation has is the knowledge of its products or services, its marketplaces, its processes and all the ancillary issues which affect its business. This is held in the brains of its people and, to a lesser extent, within its form of databanks.
>
> Leif Edvinsson, Skandia AVS

Needless to say the reason the valuer has been instructed to make a valuation is crucial to understand. Reasons are not mutually exclusive and are here presented in no particular order.

1: Portfolio review

2: Knowledge Management

3: Selling or Purchasing Control

4: Arranging a loan

5: Tax

6: Mergers, Strategic Alliances and Fair Value

7: Valuing for balance sheet purposes

8: Public sector assignments

9: Transactions and Flotations

10: Allocation of Purchase Cost

11: Fairness Opinions and Comfort Letters

12: Fixed assets and occupational premises

13: Insolvency and Administration

> **Each of the above may introduce various concepts of value (see Section 2 at page 132 below), some governed by statute and case law.**
>
> **The two key questions we must first answer are why are we valuing? and what rules shall we adopt?**

1: Portfolio Review and the Audit of Intellectual Capital

The author had a health check recently and recalled a lawyer's comment some time ago that in the same way a wise man would attend his doctor for a general check-up from time to time, the wise IP manager or executive should regularly conduct an audit of his company's intellectual property and intangible assets: its "intellectual capital". If managers do not know the 'true' returns that are being generated on the investment in the business somebody else may be better informed. Often high percentages of sales are spent on gaining market share and developing, launching, protecting and nurturing this intellectual capital. Inevitably the next question is: are you maximising value or is an alternative strategy preferable? A portfolio review simply describes a process of understanding of where, in your portfolio of assets, value and hence risk lies.

As a first step the concept of an intellectual property audit is growing in importance, and is being offered by a growing number of professional firms. During the process, typically a lawyer will establish what intellectual property and intangible assets are owned and used, locally and abroad, and if your rights are effective outside of the United Kingdom. Schedules of patents, trade marks and registered designs will be examined, as well as applications pending. The nature and rights given by licences will be reviewed. The review will include existing products and supporting intellectual property and intangible assets, to compare this information with a list of registrations to check optimal legal protection is available (see further Chapter 3 and the Appendix).

At every stage of the process the security of rights is an essential question. Whilst the identification and protection of key intellectual property assets is clearly of crucial importance, the quantification of the returns earned from those assets is still not commonly undertaken. The intellectual properly audit, in conjunction with a detailed appraisal of the assets identified by the audit, will provide a company with significant competitive advantage.

Obviously the formal protection of intellectual capital needs to be placed in the wider context of the management of intellectual capital for the purposes of the business.

Where there is an unquoted business, particularly one with significant IPR, consideration must be given to the subsequent imbalance and possible lack of liquidity in the portfolio and associated risk. Perhaps the future role of a family as owner/managers must be considered. Where there is no continuing owner management prospect the owners might well consider selling control.

2: Selling or Purchasing Control

An essential first step when considering either selling or purchasing a business is to understand the likely value from which will follow a preferred deal structure. This should be calculated by either party from the perspective of *both* vendor and purchaser. An example of the questions to be answered when taking a vendor position might be:

- what is your business worth to you?

- what do you think it is worth to a purchaser (often there is a specific purchaser(s) in mind)?

- how do you think the purchaser will calculate your value? and

- what do you think that he thinks you think you are worth to him?

Needless to say an overlap position needs to be incorporated otherwise no deal can take place. Thus we begin to think of synergistic benefits and how the intellectual capital is used in one party's hands or how it will be used in the other's.

If the maximum that can be achieved on a going concern basis is probably the sum of the revalued assets less tax, logic demands that the most significant asset owned by the most trading companies is that commonly described by the accountancy profession as "goodwill". Goodwill in its true sense includes of trademarks, patents, design, copyright, knowledge, know-how, proprietary technology, customer relationships, workforce. These assets need to be valued and the calculation will be different from each of the vendor and purchaser perspective.

A trade buyer is normally buying a great deal more than the accounts show which influences the premium to be paid over the "desk" benchmark valuations in the accounts. Considerations revolving around acquired intellectual capital will include:

• market share;

• how much the acquired assets will cost;

• how profitable will the use of the assets be once acquired?

• what risks would be incurred exploiting the assets (e.g. infringement)?

• how will the market develop?

• will this acquisition pre-empt a competitor?

• will the existing product range and sales distribution actually benefit from the purchase?

• will the patents, know-how and development projects etc being acquired produce the required rate of return?

• are the vendor's skills required to maintain and provide upkeep for the assets? and

• how, generally, will the acquired assets help, tactically and strategically?

These thoughts and others never produce a single valuation, which introduces many complex techniques used by valuation professionals including scenario analysis modelling, option pricing and Monte Carlo simulations.

In practice, vendors often hold out for prices which are only obtainable from the right buyer at the right time or one who will only buy when conditions are favourable. This market and psychological background will make the value and deal structure unpredictable. Knowledge of trade practice or the needs of a specialist buyer may be unique and make more conventional approaches to valuation irrelevant.

Many sectors have their own practice on valuations. Where this is so it should be discovered and understood. It may not be valid. Value in these instances is often linked to turnover or other rule of thumb techniques and it can be of use as a negotiating tool. It can be useful to discover the reasoning behind such practices, if evident.

It is not uncommon to find proprietors with a subjective view of the value of their business, beneath which they will not sell. This is fundamentally an owner-value and bears no correlation to economic modelling. However the facts need to be ascertained and built into the value ranges.

The key is to calculate synergistic benefits to a purchaser or licensee and to capitalise those returns alongside the benchmark valuation process, acknowledging that a vendor can only hope for a proportion of the "synergistic benefit" element of the valuation.

3:   Arranging a Loan (see Chapter 6)

The value of intellectual capital, including both legally-protected intellectual property and intangible assets, is one of the factors to be taken into account when a bank offers a loan to a company, together with key people being able to efficiently and effectively run the company and manage the intellectual capital. The difference between High Street banks and venture capitalists is that the former work on much lower investment returns, avoiding risky investments. By contrast, venture capitalists would not expect all investments to succeed but expect much higher rates of return. The US is generally more tolerant of failure so that lenders in that jurisdiction have been less cautious.

Historically, despite their value, intellectual capital has rarely been used in isolation; however the following are examples of debt finance supported by intellectual capital:

Examples Of Debt Finance Supported By IPR

Borrower	Intellectual Property	Transaction	Date
Borden	Trademarks	$480m	1991
Disney	Copyright	$400m	1992
Liggett	Trademarks	$150m	1992
Chemical Company	Patents	$100m	1994
Calvin Klein	Trademarks	$58m	1995
GE Capital	Trademarks	N/A	1995
Fashion Company	Trademarks	$100m	1996
News Corporation	Copyright	$260m	1996
Nestle	Trademarks	N/A	1996
David Bowie	Copyright	$55m	1997
Dream Works	Copyright	$325m	1997
Universal	Copyright	$1.1b	1997
Rod Stewart	Copyright	$15.4m	1998
Polygram	Copyright	$650m	1998
Cecchi Gori	Copyright	It. Lire 525b	1998
New Line Cinema	Copyright	$350m	1998
Holland-Dozier-Holland	Copyright	$30m	1998

Source: les Nouvelles June 1999

Typically lenders have looked for more tangible security such as land and buildings, but it is often the case that these assets are only nominal in the overall scheme of a business's value. Small innovative concerns will not have tangible assets and may only show an R&D spend.

In English law, security may be taken over property in one of three ways: namely by mortgage, charge or pledge. For intellectual property the borrower is restricted to the former two. If it is a single item of intellectual capital or an entire portfolio then a mortgage is more common. If the intellectual capital portfolio is of mixed economic significance, a floating charge either instead of or in addition to a mortgage is typical. Using intellectual capital, particular intellectual property rights, as security for a loan is dealt with in Chapter 5.

The volatile nature of intellectual capital does not sit squarely with a banker's natural instinct to base investment decisions on highly predictable income streams. To meet these goals the securitisation of intellectual capital has become big business. Securitising assets can be very tax efficient, very cost effective, carries high credit ratings and can attract a wider investor pool. It separates ownership from management and satisfies a world wide demand for quality securities. Securitisation is dealt with in greater depth in Chapter 5.

Experts have estimated that the increased multiple attributable to securitisation to be about 1.7 on average (John C Edmonds, "Securities; the New World Wealth Machine" *Foreign Policy*, September 1996). For example if future cash flow from a portfolio is valued at £500 million, securitisation would value the portfolio at £850 million.

The valuation process in securitisations is no different from any other. In the Cecchi Gori securitisation the fair market value of the film library was appraised using a Monte Carlo simulation (this method is beyond the scope of this book). This model was used to assist in estimating the discounted cashflow rate so as to arrive at the net present value using the discounted cashflow method. Net realisable value (see page 138 below) was determined for the benchmark for the loan to value ratio.

Over time the market will understand better the accepted methodologies described in this book and this will result in more regular and larger securitisation of intellectual capital generally, hopefully for much smaller concerns.

4: Tax

Valuation of intellectual capital and potential tax liabilities associated with efficient exploitation are important areas for tax planning and tax mitigation. There are a number of aspects to this including:

- valuation of R & D for tax relief

- valuation to ensure tax efficiency

- valuation for probate, stamp duty and gains taxes

- transfer pricing

As an example of tax treatments, in the UK following various consultative documents, the April 2002 Budget provided from 1 April 2002 that companies will be eligible for tax relief for expenditure on the creation, acquisition and enhancement of intangible assets (including goodwill, patents and know-how and other such assets). In the past intellectual capital has been subject to a variety of different treatments, depending on the precise nature of the rights involved. There have been capital allowances for the purchase of some types and no relief at all for the purchase of others. The new rules allow companies to obtain tax relief on the costs associated with IPR in accordance with the accounting policy of the company. Relief will also be given for expenditure on the preservation or maintenance of intangible assets. For longer life intellectual capital there will be a tax allowance at a fixed rate of 4% per annum. There will be a conflict with the substantial shareholding exemption for the sale of shares in that a purchaser will want this new relief for the assets themselves. Clearly a number of issues remain unresolved and subject to negotiation in each case but equally certain is that it is likely that there will be an increase of the arguments as to the value of the intellectual capital.

Since April 2000 SMEs have been able to claim a deduction in computing their taxable profits equal to 150% of qualifying research and development expenditure. Since the cost to create or recreate intellectual capital is one of the determinants in the valuation of intellectual capital, well informed advisors and those involved tax have always advanced interesting argument about valuation.

For some time UK tax law has contained special rules for intellectual property and other intangibles and provisions against avoidance such as withholding taxes and withholding tax on royalties in the UK double tax treaties. Tax and transfer pricing issues arise where intellectual capital is featured in floatation planning, inter-group transfers, international franchising and cross border transactions. Planning valuations and lowest defendable values are essential when transferring shares and intellectual capital offshore. Large multinational companies earning from substantial intellectual capital rationally centralise the ownership of these assets in a low tax jurisdiction and licence their use to subsidiaries. The transfer of assets offshore is particularly attractive when the current value of these assets is seen as low compared to their potential value. While ultimate ownership can remain with a UK parent an offshore location can shelter brand earnings, allowing better management of the asset and optimal use of cashflows. In certain other jurisdictions investment in IPRs can be depreciated for tax purposes and tax rates on income receipts are often more favourable. Why repatriate earnings into a high tax area before it is absolutely necessary?

The Inland Revenue internal manual recognises a name as an asset in respect of which it is appropriate to make some payment. It is implied that a name can be separated from a business in considering a payment of a royalty. Super royalty provisions were incorporated into the Internal Revenue Code in the US as part of the Tax Reform Act as long ago as 1986. Super royalty provisions generally have the goal of requiring that payments by the affiliated licensee to the licensor must be at an amount that is commensurate with the income that arises from use of the IPR (an appropriate rate of return on their value).

For tax purposes the paramount principle in the case of transfer pricing and other issues between associated enterprises is that proposed intellectual capital transactions are deemed to have been calculated on an arm's length basis. Arms length pricing for intellectual capital must take into account the perspective of both the transferor and the transferee.

From the prospective of the licensee a comparable independent enterprise may or may not be prepared to pay this price depending on the value and usefulness of the intellectual capital to the transferee in its businesses.

For wealth tax and in the UK Inheritance Tax the value of intellectual capital could be the single most important asset, for example copyright, in the estates of JR Tolkein and J Lennon.

5: Knowledge – Managing a Key Asset (See Chapter 2)

Knowledge management has become a key tool for most influential businesses because they have realised that their intellectual capital (their intellectual property and other intangible *knowledge* assets) must be identified, protected, measured and leveraged.

"...the experience of CIBC, Skandia, Dow Chemical, Hughes Aircraft and others makes it clear that the knowledge asset of a company can be identified, that management processes can enhance them, that it is possible to describe and measure how such knowledge adds value, and that managing intellectual capital improves financial performance".

Fortune, October 1994

Like any other key resource, knowledge needs to be properly managed for the future prosperity of any business which owns it. Any knowledge management programme should be a continuous process and allow organisations of all sizes to meet the challenges of the immediate and long term strategic future. Key ingredients are:

- The audit of intellectual capital;

- Assessment of needs and opportunities;

- Evaluation of market environment;

- Knowledge mapping;

- The unlocking of corporate creativity;

- Strategies enabling innovation and the management of know-how;

- Development of knowledge and learning procedures.

Having identified the measurable knowledge assets it is for the valuer to provide the measures of value to management as a regular appraisal. See, further, Chapter 1.

6:   Merger, Joint Ventures, Strategic Alliances and Fair Value

For intellectual capital of any description benchmark valuations and valuation formulae are required for entry and exit. For a joint venture or alliance, it is important to set a fair value to ensure that the appropriate incentivisation exists and thus the success of the venture is as assured as it may be. The potential problem with intellectual capital developed as a result of collaboration will be ownership and the valuation processes to be triggered at termination. There may be additional intellectual capital outside the core of the activity in question that requires licensing to the venture. Valuations can build in the aspirations of all parties and can cover relevant areas of initial input, ongoing contribution, and exit routes. Valuations create the opportunity to set down the terms on which parties will enter into a business with another and provide a degree of commercial certainty. Each party is likely to make their own valuation of costs, rights generated and returns due in any event. Formal valuation, using methods agreed by the parties, helps to cements the relationship.

Usually a notion of fair value drives such appraisals with the aim of being equitable between the parties. Arms length valuations also create the perception of fairness and that alone can be the building block that determines success.

7: Balance Sheets and Accounts

It is important generally for company boards, institutions and shareholders to be informed in public accounting statements about the value, and hence returns generated on probably their most valuable assets. Thus there are many reasons why companies report the value of IPR in Notes to Accounts in addition to the requirements following the two reporting standards referred to below.

UK Financial Reporting Standard 10 – "Goodwill and Intangible Assets"

This standard is effective for accounting periods ending on or after 23rd December 1998.

A problem with earlier standards was that management was not held accountable for the amount that it had invested in goodwill; it was not taken into account when measuring the assets on which a return must be earned: and there was no requirement to disclose a loss if the value of the goodwill was not maintained. Standard 10 is to ensure that purchased goodwill and intangible assets, which may include protected rights and other assets such as brands, are charged to the profit and loss account over the period in which they are depleted. An intangible may be classed as an asset if access to the future economic benefits that it represents is controlled by the reporting entity.

Purchased goodwill and intangible assets can now be capitalised as assets and this removes the option to write-off goodwill straight to shareholders' reserves which existed under the previous Statement of Standard Accounting Practice 22.

Unfortunately, the standard does not allow internally generated goodwill to be capitalised unless the asset is separately identifiable and has a readily ascertainable market value with the key requirement that there is "an active market, evidenced by frequent transactions".

Where goodwill and the intangible assets (including intellectual property rights) are incapable of ongoing measurement, or where they have only a limited useful economic life, they must be written-off in the profit and loss account on a systematic basis over a prudent period.

The useful economic life of purchased goodwill is the useful economic life (i.e. period of time) over which the entity expects to derive economic benefit. The useful economic life of an intangible asset (here both protectable intellectual property or other intangible) is defined as the period over which the entity expects to derive economic benefit from that asset. Put another way the period over which the value of the underlying acquired business is expected to exceed the value of its identifiable tangible and intangible assets (where goodwill is an unidentifiable factor).

Durability depends upon a number of factors, such as the nature of the business, its stability and that of the sector, life-spans of products and market competition. There is a "rebuttable presumption" that the useful economic life of purchased goodwill and of individual intangible assets cannot exceed 20 years from the date of acquisition. The 20 year presumption can be rebutted where the useful economic life of an intangible asset can be demonstrated to be greater than 20 years and where the asset is capable of continued measurement. Intangible assets with finite useful economic lives should be amortized over the appropriate period and intangible assets with indefinite lives should not be amortized.

Impairment reviews must be performed to ensure that goodwill and intangible assets are not carried at above their recoverable amounts. If necessary the amount impaired will be charged to the profit and loss account in the year of impairment. The recoverable amount of an intangible asset is defined as the higher of net realisable value (the amount at which an asset could be sold) and its value in use (the present value of the future cash-flows obtainable as a result of an asset's continued use plus any residual value on its ultimate disposal).

A full independent impairment review should be conducted one year after acquisition for all intangible assets and annually thereafter for all assets which are deemed to have an indefinite life. Intangible assets with a finite life will be subject to a more limited review.

For accounts purposes the basis of valuation of the assets, the grounds for believing that a useful life exceeds 20 years or is indefinite and the treatment adopted for any "negative goodwill" (arising where the value of identifiable purchased assets exceeds the price paid in an acquisition) must be disclosed in the Notes to the Accounts.

UK Financial Reporting Standard 11 – Impairment of Fixed Assets and Goodwill

Effective for accounting periods ending on or after 23rd December 1998

The standard is to ensure that fixed assets and goodwill are recorded in financial statements at no more than their recoverable amounts, any resulting impairment loss is measured and recognised on a consistent basis, and sufficient information is disclosed in the financial statements to enable users to understand the impact of the impairment on the financial position and performance of the reporting entity.

Fixed assets including intangible assets and goodwill should be reviewed for impairment if events or changes in circumstances indicate that the amount carried forward in financial statements for the intangible asset or goodwill may not be recoverable. Individual assets should be tested for impairment. However, if cash flows are not generated by a single asset this may not be possible. In such cases the smallest possible group of assets, or "income generating unit" ("IGU") should be tested, subject to practicality. The income generating unit is defined as "a group of assets, liabilities and associated goodwill" that generates income that is largely independent of the reporting entity's other income streams, (in many cases IGUs will be defined by reference to brands although this will be up to the judgement of management).

Impairment should be measured by comparing the value of the goodwill or fixed asset (either tangible or intangible) being carried forward with its recoverable amount. The recoverable amount is the higher of the amount that can be obtained from selling the fixed asset or income-generating unit (net realisable value) or from using the fixed asset or income-generating unit (value in use).

Value in use is calculated by discounting future cash flows of the income generating unit at a rate of return which the market would expect from an equally risky investment. Impairment losses must be recognised immediately in the profit and loss account. Past impairment losses can be written back in certain circumstances. If an external event caused the impairment, the amount can be written back if subsequent external events clearly and demonstrably reverse the effects of the initial event in a way not foreseen in the original impairment calculations.

8: Public Sector

Valuations in the public sector are typically in privatisations and in the tendering out of central and local government and public sector services. For example, in the UK, work on behalf of the National Audit Office in respect of value for money studies of the benchmark valuation procedures in privatisations – all concerned intellectual capital.

An example is the qualification of the UK's 1999–2000 accounts of the UK's Ordinance Survey. In his report to Parliament, Sir John Bourn said that the decision not to value the National Topographic Database had resulted in a significant understatement of the Agency's tangible fixed assets. It may also have distorted the view given by measures of reported financial performance e.g. the return on capital employed. The Comptroller and Auditor General instructed the author's organisation to value the database and our conclusion was that it was unlikely to be less than £50 million.

9: Transactions and Flotations

In the UK, independent expert valuations of intellectual capital, acceptable to Sponsors, Nomads and the Stock Exchange for Yellow Book instructions are used in the prospectus and Offer Document Reports, for example, pursuant to the requirements of Chapter 20 (Scientific Research Based Companies) of the Stock Exchange Listing Rules. Offer Document Reports are normally published in the Offer Document and would address issues such as:

• the merits of the company's products;

• the company's business plan including the critical path and timescale to commercial exploitation; and

- any projections of the market potential for the company's products and intellectual capital.

10: Allocation of Purchase Cost

Companies typically merge or acquire at greater assessments of value than the fair value of net tangible assets. The residual is broadly goodwill. This may need experts to allocate the purchase cost more precisely.

Valuations in connection with the mergers to form listed companies are typical examples of this. In the diagrams below, a company has reported in its Consolidated Financial Statements that based upon an independent valuation, its allocation of the purchase price in excess of the fair value of the net tangible assets acquired to intangible assets totalled $65m. The USA Securities and Exchange Commission required the company to report on purchase cost allocations. Instructions to valuers arose due to conflict of interest rules which dictate that independent experts and not the auditors, must undertake the valuations. The appraisal apportioned the purchase price of the assets acquired for accounts purposes. Many of these assets were intangibles such as brand names, patents, workforce and copyright with a residual goodwill element. In this instance:

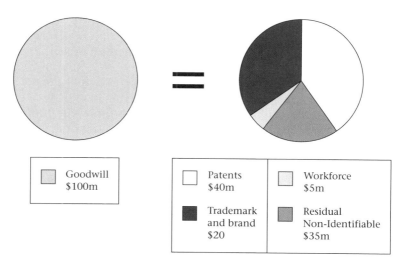

11: Fairness Opinions and Comfort Letters

These documents support financial diligence in sale and leaseback transactions.

For example, a corporation may issue a large currency note under an indenture for which a substantial trust company will be the Trustee. The independent valuer delivers a letter setting out the result of the transaction procedures to the corporation on behalf of the noteholders under the indenture, typically described as Bondholders, in connection with the sale agreement.

The scope of the engagement would include verifying the original cost of the assets, performing limited-scope research into the market for similar assets and investigation into transactions involving assets with characteristics similar to the asset and finally, given a stated set of assumptions and limiting conditions, give an opinion of on the fairness of the agreement to the Bondholders. Additionally, it may be required to perform limited-scope statistical analysis related to the expected useful life of the IPR and investigate the range of interest rates commonly applied in similar lease transactions.

12: Fixed Assets and Occupational Premises

Valuers of intellectual capital are instructed by international surveying practices in connection with occupational premises such as hotels, nursing homes, schools, retail premises and theatres.

Many in the surveying world recognise in principle (but not always in practice), the need for a combination of valuation skills, notably fixed asset skills *and* intangible asset skills. This process acknowledges that the basic challenge is valuing not only real estate and a business, but a combination of business and real estate. Clearly premises and businesses such as hotels, nursing homes, retail outlets and schools include elements that represent a going concern, as opposed to simply being realty, personalty (furniture and equipment etc) and improvements.

For example, generally occupational premises, particularly first tier hotels, are unique forms of real estate. In addition to land and improvements, they are labour intensive retail businesses that are extremely dependent upon the management skills and brand of the hotel operator. Typically chain affiliated hotels will outperform independent concerns and affiliation to a group produces premium value which is again indicative of intangible "brand" value.

13: Insolvency, Administrative Receiverships and Liquidations

Although there have been some changes in the law, phoenix companies can still be a problem for creditors and professionals involved. Businesses and assets sold at derisory prices sometimes to new companies with the same proprietors have long illustrated the problems with Section 216 of the Insolvency Act 1986, which was clearly inadequate. Professionals that work in this area require comfort from valuers in order to achieve maximum returns for creditors, particularly following the important decision in the *Western Intelligence* case. In this UK case, Robin Jacob J pronounced upon Phoenix companies and generally about businesses and assets sold at derisory prices, sometimes to new companies with the same proprietors.

Section 2:

Valuation: A Summary of the Rules and Guidelines

At this juncture the reason for valuation has been established. The direction may introduce one or more of these concepts of value:

- Tax Valuations
- Fair Value
- Fair Market Value
- Open Market Price
- Investment Value
- Owner Value
- Net Realisable Value

Depending upon the 'rules' of that concept, the valuation conclusion in respect of the same asset may, and probably will, be different.

For example, preparing valuations of intellectual property and intangible assets for a strategic alliance could involve consideration of each of fair value, tax value, investment value and owner value.

The reader should consider which concepts of value apply to their situation or to their client's situation. The "other side" will also have a concept of value: for example, the tax authorities being very different from a merger partner.

Valuation for Tax Purposes

For the purposes of a hypothetical sale to assess value for tax purposes, the valuer must envisage a number of scenarios:

- An imaginary willing seller
- Not anxious to sell
- Not reluctant to sell
- Happy to remain a shareholder
- Prepared to sell if offered a reasonable price

In practice this means, from case law in England, the *best price obtainable*.

Legal Basis

Fiscal applications of valuation in different tax structures can be very different. However, the legal basis of valuation in the UK is broadly the same for stamp duty, capital gains tax, inheritance tax and Schedule E. The statutory "open market" first appeared in the Finance Act 1894 where section 7(5) provided that "the principal value of any property shall be the price which in the opinion of the Commissioners such property would fetch if sold in the open market at the time of the death of the deceased".

Open Market Value

The valuer in fiscal situations is confronted with an open market rule far removed from reality. There is rich ground for argument and dispute, principles have been tested by the courts and it is essential for the valuer to be acquainted with the major decisions. In summary:

- an imaginary sale is hypothesised and the practical impossibility of an actual sale is to be ignored (*Attorney-General* (1) v *Jameson* (1905) 1 IR 218, *Duke of Buccleuch* v *Commissioners of Inland Revenue* [1967] 1 AC 506).

- the fact that legally a sale would be impossible is to be ignored (*Ashcroft, Clifton* v *Strauss* (1927) 1 CR 313).

- any and all forms of open market may be considered and all possible purchases must be included in the open market (*Commissioners of Inland Revenue* v *Clay* (1914) 3 KB 466).

- the best price obtainable must be assumed and that may involve division into saleable lots (*Ellesmere* v *Commissioners of Inland Revenue* (1918) 2 KB 735) or

- getting the best price may involve combining holdings (*Attorney-General of Ceylon* v *Mackie* (1952) 2 All ER 775 PC).

- the sale is assumed only on the relevant date for the purposes of assessment (*Buccleuch* v *Commissioners of Inland Revenue* and *Re Lynall*), and

- events after the relevant date must be ignored (*Holt* v *Commissioners of Inland Revenue* (1953) 1 WLR 1488).

- the hypothetical purchaser is a prudent man who makes appropriate enquiries about the subject matter (*Findlay's Trustees* v *Commissioners of Inland Revenue* (1938) 22 ATC 437, *Salvesen's Trustees* v *Commissioners of Inland Revenue* (1930) SLT, 387 9 ATC 43)

Information

The open market does not operate in a vacuum. Information which may have a bearing on valuation includes information about the industry and the general economic background on the date of valuation. It also means information relating to the intellectual capital, such as published material, and any other information a purchaser could find out himself.

Case law also dictates in the UK that there shall also be available to any prospective purchaser all the information which a prudent prospective purchaser might reasonably require if he were proposing to purchase the intellectual capital from a willing vendor by private treaty and at arm's length. This implies that provided the information required is reasonable it will be forthcoming, and it seems to follow that one should envisage a purchaser acceptable to the owner.

The valuer will look to the specialist knowledge of the asset's owners, the financial press, trade journals, stockbrokers and Government reports and information services such as that provided by the Financial Times and Extel.

Profit: Upper and Lower Limits

A range of values should become apparent within which the price may be expected to fall. There is nothing precise in valuation. The Shares Valuation Examiner at the UK's Capital Taxes Office will also prepare a range of values within which a price can be agreed. That range will be moulded by the strength of the initial presentation to him. In negotiation, the examiner should also illustrate flexibility by asking himself whether continuing the correspondence is cost effective in terms of tax or duty at stake. Very rarely do cases proceed to the UK's adjudication authorities, the Tax Commissioners and many have experienced a 'without prejudice' letter which may indicate agreement outside of the range of value considered appropriate.

Fair Valuation

"Fair valuation" is the amount that will fairly compensate an owner who is deprived of the economic enjoyment of the intellectual capital where there is neither a willing buyer nor a willing seller. Fair value is primarily a legal concept and it is important to study the relevant 'local' jurisdictional law and precedent (see, further, page 55). Fair value is intended to estimate a fair or reasonable or equitable amount. It is not necessarily intended to reflect a likely open market price for the IPR. Fair value can relate to involuntary transactions and those in Agreements.

The essence of fair value is the desire to be equitable to all parties. The constraints of fair value dictate a limited marketplace where vendor and purchaser are not free to market for the highest or lowest price. To be fair, therefore, the value determined must recognise what the seller gives up in value and what the buyer acquires in value, through the transaction. In some ways it is closer to owner value (see below) than any other of the main concepts of value.

Fair Market Value

There is no single definition of fair market value because it is largely a theoretical exercise. Numerous definitions have come from various statutory authorities, judicial precedent, and administrative rulings worldwide. Generally both the buyer and the seller are seeking their maximum economic self-interest. Unspecified hypothetical vendors and purchasers are assumed to have equal knowledge, negotiating abilities, and financial strength. Transactions are assumed to be consummated at the highest available price, but not at an unrealistically high, non-economic price. Thus there can be a difference between fair market value and open market price (see below) that does not concern itself with fairness.

Factors disregarded in a fair market valuation are:

• Legal and contractual restrictions that prevent an unfettered sale

• The possibility of imprudent actions is not considered.

• Forced or compulsive acts such as a forced sale are not considered.

Factors considered when formulating the value conclusion are:

• Existing restrictions.

• The hypothetical vendor and purchaser are aware of all information, circumstances and facts relevant to the valuation at the valuation date.

• An assumption of arm's length dealing is made.

• The transaction is assumed to be consummated for cash.

While fair market value is often referred to in a regulatory or litigation context, and is practical because a transaction is not immediately contemplated, it can have little relevance in the real world of intellectual property and intangible asset ("intellectual capital") transactions. This is because, in actual transactions, the participants do not care what Mr. Hypothetical Seller will accept or what Mr. Hypothetical Buyer will pay. In the real world, a specific buyer consummates a transaction with a particular seller, given their own unique set of interests and criteria. Special transactional circumstances inevitably dictate that there will be a departure from fair market value.

Open Market Price

This is largely a practical exercise. In the open market special purchasers are common; prices are negotiated between parties with different knowledge, negotiating skills and financial strength. Sales of intellectual capital may be at unrealistically high (for example to gain a new geographical market) or unreasonably low prices (for example intellectual property with pending litigation). Rarely will all potential purchasers have been solicited, and some purchasers may be unable or unwilling to transact. Unlike open market value in taxation and fair market value, the legal and contractual restrictions that prevent an unfettered sale cannot be ignored. Either the vendor, the purchaser, or both may not be appraised of relevant information concerning the intellectual capital that might influence price. The vendor and purchaser may not be dealing at arm's length and a price may have been agreed as a result of compulsive acts by the vendor, the purchaser or both. And often consideration may not be all cash, but may all or in part be comprised of non-cash consideration, such as shares.

Investment Value

Investment Value is the value of an intangible asset given a defined set of individual investment criteria (e.g. given a definite investment criterion such as a specific internal or external rate of return or payback period). This standard of value may be relevant to answering questions such as: what is the value of the subject intellectual capital if it is only in commercial use for the next five years? What is the value of the asset if its owner requires a 20 percent after tax, cash-on-cash internal rate of return on the investment in that class of IPR? And so on. Internal rate of return is defined as that discount rate which reduces to equality the present value of expected cash outflows to the present value of expected cash in-flows. Simply a Net Present Value of zero.

Owner Value or Existing Use Value

Often adopted for financial reporting purposes, owner value is the value of the intellectual capital to its current owner, given that its owner's current use of the intellectual capital and current resources and capabilities for commercially exploiting the asset. The value of the assets corresponds to the loss in value if the owner were deprived of the property. Thus it is the value of the assets, given the owner's circumstances, including resources, management, strategy and business plans etc. Owner value is not tax value, fair market value or the price that would be fetched in the open market where a purchaser would necessarily manage and exploit the intellectual capital differently.

Net Realisable Value

Financiers, particularly major clearing banks, in the same breath as asking for fair market value, will seek a view about the net proceeds obtainable upon the sale of the intellectual capital after providing for all costs of disposal, including taxes and professional fees. It is not uncommon for the valuer to 'negotiate' within this instruction a 'reasonable time' clause in respect of the sale, that is to avoid the absurdity of a hypothetical forced sale situation. Although the latter is important when considering the hybrid, liquidation value.

Section 3:

Valuation in Practice: Interdisciplinary Study and Fundamental Must-Do Research

This section presents a series of checklists for consideration as part of the valuation process.

The valuer cannot contemplate mathematical or financial ratio modelling until a thorough analysis of the following takes place:

- **Business activities and history**
- **Management structure and personnel**
- **State of Industry**
- **General economic outlook**
- **Political situation**

Business Activities

Typical Information requirements

1. Description and history of the assets:
   - registered
   - unregistered?

2. Information about intangibles supporting the 'core' assets, for example
   - know-how,
   - marketing know-how,
   - technical know-how,
   - research and development,
   - documentation,
   - design graphics,
   - manuals.

3. Precise activities for the company
   - its associate companies
   - subsidiaries where appropriate; or
   - of the proprietor of the intellectual capital assets.

4. Previous valuation reports.

5. The product(s) dealt in, supported by or extended by the assets.

6. Is anyone permitted to use the intellectual capital and knowledge?
   - are there plans to do so?

7. The company's market(s) and competition, ask for:
   - Business Plans and
   - Due Diligence if undertaken.

8. Details of:
   - licensing,
   - strategic alliances,
   - joint ventures.

9. What is the intellectual capital dependant upon? For example is there:
    - one source of raw materials or
    - a few large customers?

10. Does the company:
    - wholesale or retail the product(s),
    - install (if so by own employees or sub-contractors),
    - manufacture from raw materials,
    - assemble bought in components,
    - import goods or materials (if so where from, what are the countries of origin, are they economically and politically stable? Are supplies likely to be interrupted?),
    - export goods (if so where to and is the market stable?)

11. Who are the company's suppliers?
    - are the suppliers sound or are they likely to go out of business?
    - might they change their style of business?
    - have they been taken over recently?
    - are they few or many?
    - are they likely to be affected by economic or political changes either in the home jurisdiction or worldwide?

12. Can contractual arrangements relating to the intellectual capital be assigned or transferred or any royalty agreements?

13. Any major customers?

14. Objectives/developments or trends expected in the industry?

15. How are these likely to affect the company?

16. How does the company perceive its own strengths and weaknesses?

17. Are there any key factors, e.g. monopoly?

18. Is any major capital expenditure in prospect?

19. Who are the competitors? or

20. What is the standard industry clarification?

21. What is the market share by the company for its products?

22. Who uses the products? Why?

23. Seasonable or cyclical trends?

24. Technological changes?

25. Is there a trade association? If so, are there:
    • any directories available or
    • any annual reports?

26. How vulnerable are profits?

27. How vulnerable is the source of raw materials?

28. Have there been any recent acquisition/mergers in this sector around the valuation date?

29. Anything significant since the latest accounts?

30. Is the intellectual capital contributing to corporate strategy?

31. How is R&D managed, (non-disclosure agreements, subcontractors, training and incentives)?

The emphasis in all valuations concerning intellectual capital and companies owning such assets is on the future and the need to establish the level of maintainable earnings and cash flow with prudent assumptions.

The valuer assesses future expectations and risks *by reference* to past records shaping those expectations for the future, based on the published accounts (for the three to five year period up to the date of valuation), with such supplementary information as can be reasonably required, including the latest details available of the trading position at the valuation date and forecasts for future profits and cash flow.

Needless to say, such broad-based information gathering is a requirement in each and every case. The care taken in preparing this information will have a direct bearing on the "accuracy" of the resulting valuation.

The role of "financials"

Financials are the basis for understanding the business activities and past financial performance which together with the other information obtained can provide an insight into the prospects for the future as well as the risks inherent in the investment. In particular, request the detailed trading account and other plans which do not form part of accounts.

The principal source of internal information will be the annual report and accounts, business plans and other such strategic documents, trading account, profit and loss accounts, the directors' and auditors report and the Chairman's statement. Any reports from executives managing the intellectual capital should also be used.

Because you are concerned with the future, it is unnecessary to go too far back in time although if the activities of the company and IPR are cyclical in nature then it may be appropriate to obtain five years' accounts or even longer.

Understanding financial statements

There is no such thing as standard analysis which can be adapted, where necessary, to suit the particular circumstances of each case. Information should be noted which is relevant to the assessment of information obtained including the following:

- assumptions and possibly real options analysis underpinning forecasts

- exceptional or extraordinary items of revenue or expenditure in the cash flows

- a break-down of profits between exploitation activities, including that with licensees and other partners.

Because valuation is relative not absolute, an art not an exact science, to be of any use at all the context and meaning of the figures inserted into the analysis must be understood. Ratio analysis is a means by which this case-specific information can be presented in a series of key points. Ratio analysis includes financial ratios, performance (or activity) ratios and cash profitability ratios. The ratios by themselves will be of little use to the valuation but are useful for making comparisons with previous years (to establish trends) and as a comparison with other companies operating in the same industry. As comparisons they are a means of judging the present and future risks and return prospects for any particular company exploiting similar intellectual capital.

Management Systems, Management and Workforce

Assessing the quality of management and workforce in the valuation process is vital, even with substantial companies who own intellectual capital. Assessing management ability is fraught with difficulties, especially since for the most part the information will be sensitive. Questions that lead on the path of discovery include (in no order):

Management systems

1. Is there a management plan for intellectual property and other intangibles?

2. Is there an asset schedule setting out the extent of ownership of such intellectual capital, and the interests of third parties (if any)?

3. What audit systems are operated to track the creation and management of intellectual capital?

4. Is other intellectual capital separately identified?

5. What security systems are there to protect commercial sensitive know-how?

6. What policing systems are there to detect infringement of IPR?

7. What enforcement procedures are there?

8. Is valuation for intellectual capital model included within the management information systems?

9. Is any of the intellectual capital licensed? If so, how are royalty rates calculated?

10. Has management identified opportunities for exploiting the intellectual capital in other markets?

11. As a percentage of turnover, what proportion of revenue is derived from licensing income? Is this projected to change over the next three years?

Customer and Supplier management

1. When disclosing proprietary information, are appropriate markings placed on the documentation to signify that it is confidential and proprietary?

2. Are design or manufacture out-sourced or sub-contracted?

3. Has a competitor used or threatened to use the technology?

4. Are you involved in any joint ventures with other organisations involving research and development?

People management

1. Do your staff know what the management polices are for the intellectual capital business?

2. Are there appropriate confidentiality, intellectual property ownership and non-compete clauses in staff contracts and consultancy contracts?

3. Where work is out-sourced, is ownership of intellectual property clearly documented?

4. How is knowledge managed, retained and shared in the organisation?

In most cases it may be desirable to ascertain the names, ages, length of service and positions of whoever is involved in managing intellectual capital.

Age is particularly relevant. Many of the purchasers in the value concepts described in Section 2 above need to have a long-term view concerning investment in intellectual capital which means that the valuer must consider (amongst other things) when key managers could be expected to retire and what provisions have been made for their replacement. Another factor is associated with age – older managements may be more conservative in outlook which could be reflected in not fully exploiting the intellectual capital, for example in extending the 'core' assets for exploitation in other areas and sectors. A younger management is more likely to be an alert management (but may equally be an inexperienced one!).

As regards corporate structures, if the directors are also the principal shareholders, this could indicate that they have a continuing interest in the company's prosperity. Generally attributes of good management must not be ignored and include:

• firm financial control through management accounting,
• good labour relations,
• the ability to discover and open up new markets,
• being alive to new developments and techniques and
• making adequate provisions for management succession.

Key Personnel

Sole traders, inventors and small private companies are more likely to rely on the talents of key individuals and are unlikely to have management succession in place. The central importance of the role of key personnel applies particularly to a business with intellectual capital at its heart. If a change in ownership, management etc of the business will affect the value of the assets, it is vital to establish details of any service agreements and the period each still has to run. It is rare to find that anyone is irreplaceable, albeit often at a higher cost, though sometimes it may be found to be lower than the remuneration package currently enjoyed.

The Sectors in which the Intellectual Capital is Exploited

The general conditions in a sector (and any sectors to where the intellectual capital may be extended) affect all business, although not all in a particular sector will necessarily be affected in the same way. It is essential to understand the industry in which the intellectual capital is exploited and the competitive position in relation to that industry.

A valuer must have access to, and understand, sector or industry reports prepared by (for example) Investment Banks' analyst teams, industry reports by experts in their field. In addition to ascertaining the general background to the industry, the following questions are pertinent:

- is the sector "fashionable" – different sectors are popular with investors and acquisitive companies at different times. For instance some in the electronics sector are recovering after being out of favour with investors following the dramatic collapse of a small number of companies, whereas only a few years earlier this sector had been the choice of the market.

- Are smaller companies being taken over by large companies?

- Is the sector dominated by one or two giants?

- As a whole is the sector expanding or contracting?

- Is the intellectual capital dependant upon any single large customer or has its owner a particularly large share of the market through its exploitation?

General Economics and Politics

Economic considerations such as inflation will affect all industries in all sectors and there may be special economic factors affecting particular industries or companies worldwide. This is of particular consequence with the exploitation of intellectual capital because typically its efficient exploitation crosses geographical boundaries with ease. Political factors and Governments clearly affect future earnings (wars, protectionism, exchange control) though valuers, like others, cannot be expected to predict these with accuracy!

Section 4:

Introducing the Valuation Methodologies

At this stage valuation fundamentals already established are:

- Identification of the intellectual capital in question

- Determination of whether it is transferable

- Is its earning power enduring

- Does its existence in the market give rise to some barrier to entry by competitor?

- What is the market?

- Who are the managers and how is it managed?

- Why you are being instructed?

- The valuation rules you are going to adopt.

Next steps

- **Determine the most appropriate valuation methodology**

- **Quantify the likely value**

This section outlines the main arguments.

We have described the fundamental principle of valuation theory that the value of any asset is the present value of the future economic benefits that can be anticipated to accrue to the owner of that asset. However whilst this principle is generally accepted by valuation professionals, there is no universally accepted valuation methodology.

The reader needs to be familiar with each, to know the implications of each. There are examples where the authors would use one approach or another. But also the authors regularly encounter others using one methodology rather than our preferred method for that circumstance – with very different results.

Assessing value isn't easy

Whoever said valuing brand names was a joke? Elastoplast giant Smith & Nephew has sold the rights to the Nivea brand name for a soothing £46.5m. The price is remarkable because S&N only made £2m from its £20m sales of Nivea. The buyer is Beiersdorf AG of Germany, which sells Nivea everywhere outside the UK and what was the British Empire. The deal means the Germans regain mastery of Nivea's £400m plus world sales. The British rights were confiscated from them during the war.

Source *Daily Mail*

Valuation Methodologies – Overview

Valuation theory, in very broad terms, recognises three distinct approaches to the appraisal or valuation of any asset, including intellectual capital. These are usually described as the cost, market and income approaches: each is examined further in the next section.

The Cost Approach

The cost approach is utilised to arrive at the value of an asset by ascertaining its replacement cost. The assumption underlying this approach is that the price of the new asset is commensurate with the economic value of the service that the new asset can provide during its life. The principle disadvantage of this method lies in its correlation of cost with value. This is a particular problem in high technology areas. A commonly cited example is the US Government's attempt to build a nuclear-powered aircraft in the 1950's. The costs of this ultimately abortive project will have amounted to many millions of dollars, yet the value of the aircraft, which would not fly, was zero.

Even in cases where the cost of replacement might reasonably be expected to provide a reasonable representation of value there is an additional complication. The appraiser or valuer has to quantify the necessary reduction from the brand new state of the replacement asset to the actual state of the asset under consideration, taking into account the physical, functional, economic and legal life of the asset.

The Market Approach

The market approach arrives at the value of an asset by obtaining a consensus of what others in the market place have judged it to be. Problems here include the requirement for an active and public market, with a record of exchange of comparable properties. Not surprisingly, perhaps, this is not a common state of affairs for intellectual capital.

The Income Approach

The income approach looks at the income-producing capability of the asset to be valued. The future economic benefits are equated to the present value of the net cash flows anticipated to be derived from ownership of the property. The quantification of the future cash flows takes into account incremental fixed asset and working capital investments.

The calculation of the present value of the cash flows is arrived at by utilising an appropriate discount value of the factor. The factor itself can be derived from a number of different rate of returns models, about which considerably more in the next section (see page 154).

What and how: factors in operation of any valuation method

Bundle of Rights

The ownership of intellectual capital confers a number of separate privileges. The owner can sell the property, or give it away. He can license it, and there are many separate rights that can be licensed; the right to make, the right to use, to disclose, to lease, to sell etc. Valuation therefore is often concerned with a composite of a series of rights.

Highest and Best Use

The concept of "highest and best use" is an import from real estate valuation, where the valuer usually is able to assume that knowledgeable parties will know the potential uses of the land under consideration, and the particular use that will provide the highest economic return.

This concept is crucial to the valuation of intellectual capital. The various potential uses of any item of intellectual capital should be considered in any appraisal or valuation of that asset. Typically the highest and best use of intellectual capital will be within a business: the ability to maximise the potential of the asset is a key ingredient in value.

Valuation in Practice

As we have seen, any methodology developed for the valuation of intellectual property and other intangibles should consider the marketing, financial and legal aspects of intellectual property and should follow the fundamental accounting concepts of prudence and consistency. It should also allow for revaluation on a regular basis, if required, and be suitable for both 'home grown' and acquired intellectual capital.

The starting point for the adoption of any methodology is a recognition that the intellectual capital provides some barrier to competition or a competitive advantage.

Current valuation practice and theory also requires that the intellectual capital is separable, protected (or protectable) transferable, and relatively long-lived. The National Companies and Securities Commission in Australia as long ago as the early 1990's,

deliberated succinctly upon such criteria and the following
paragraphs of this section summarises our joint views:

Separability

The value of all intangible assets is determined by the benefit of
future earnings or cashflows that can be obtained from the use or
ownership of that asset. Intellectual capital rarely changes hands and
detailed information difficult to obtain unless the valuer was a party
to the negotiations: more usually a deal is between special purchasers
from which historical data can rarely be derived. If an asset is to be
valued in the absence of an established market in comparable assets,
the future economic benefits from the employment of that asset must
be calculated and it can be difficult to segregate the future economic
benefits deriving from the individual asset being valued from those
other assets that comprise the business. It is important as well to
'isolate' assets that may 'travel' with the subject asset, for example a
brand does not travel in a vacuum and assets supporting it, for
example a patent, may be exploited additionally, elsewhere.

The valuer must therefore exercise judgement in allocating a
composite intangible value, typically described by the accountancy
world as simply goodwill, comprising the unidentifiable and the
separate identifiable intangibles.

Protected (or Capable of Protection)

While trade secrets, know-how, and other intangible assets can be
hugely valuable, in order for an asset to retain or increase its value,
authorities and regulators typically look for some form of obvious
protection. For example with brand names there is generally protection
by virtue of the trademark and registered design legislation, in addition
to protection under common law. The strength, duration and extent of
this protection have to be carefully considered in placing a value on
any piece of intellectual capital.

Transferable

In order to be consistent with the standard definition of fair market
value, the asset must be capable of being exchanged. In some
instances, the asset itself may not be capable of direct sale, but may
effectively be transferred by some other means, such as a licensing or
franchise agreement.

Long Lived or Enduring

The characteristics of the asset should be such that it can properly be regarded as a capital asset rather than the carry-over effects of some recent expenditure. The greatest difficulty with respect to this criterion is the segregation of the benefits, for example when valuing brands, of current advertising expenditure from the value of a trademark or brand name.

An indication of relative longevity is the continued success or dominance of a product in the absence of high levels of supporting expenditure. An assessment of the future economic benefits of the intellectual capital should be net of the ongoing costs associated with the maintenance of the assets.

Section 5:

Valuation Methodologies – Three Basic Approaches

> **More detail on the methodologies. Strengths and weaknesses compared – with various versions of each explained.**
>
> **This section and the next examines the methodology and merits of each of the approaches below. Each is used in practice and the valuer must understand the effects of the chosen approach on the end value.**
>
> Market Approach
>
> - Comparable market transactions
>
> Cost Approach
>
> - Historical or replacement cost
>
> Income Approach
>
> - Capitalisation of historical profits
> - Gross profit differential method
> - Excess profits method
> - Relief from royalty method
> - Future economic benefit modelling

The Market (or Comparability) Approach

"How can such shares in such a company with such articles have their value estimated at the price which, in the opinion of the Commissioners, such property would fetch if sold in the open market? An actual sale in the open market is out of the question. A feat of imagination has to be performed."

Thus, according to Lord Ashborne in one of the leading UK share valuation cases (*Jameson* CA (1905) p 226), we are required to use our imagination to see the tax "open market". In a perfect world, one would always prefer to determine fair market value, the most common direction for the valuer, by reference to comparable market transactions. Revenue Rulings in the US provide similar directions.

In practice, this is difficult enough when valuing assets such as companies and property because it is rarely possible to find a transaction that is exactly comparable. However, in valuing a patent or brand, for example, finding a sale that segregates a transaction sufficiently is extremely rare. There is no active market for the sale of intellectual capital (intellectual property and other intangible assets).

This is not only due to lack of comparability, but also because IPR is generally not developed to be sold, and any sales are usually only a small part of a larger transaction of which the details are kept confidential. In any event by its nature intellectual capital is unique.

Additional caveats that were identified by the aforementioned Australian Commission and endorsed by the authors are:

• Observed transactions will seldom represent values to the existing business, but often reflect transactions where identifiable intangible assets are (or are deemed to be) much more valuable to the new owner, and such "special values" may not be reflective of market values;

• The implicit value placed upon identifiable intangible assets in the acquisition of a company may be based upon a limited level of knowledge of the underlying business, or the allocation between tangible and intangible assets is often wrong or driven by taxation or stamp duty considerations;

- Values placed on business or identifiable assets may vary as markets rise and fall in cycles. It is essential to eliminate the distorting effects of these peaks and troughs; and

- The particular characteristics of identifiable assets may differ both within and across industries. A direct comparison therefore may often not be possible.

In summary, whilst theoretically this method may be acceptable, it has practical difficulties. Accordingly, its utilisation by any valuer should be conducted only after the valuer is satisfied that appropriate adjustments have been made in the valuation process to overcome these practical limitations, particularly the limitation of inadequate, specific and detailed information relating to the comparable transaction(s) chosen.

Market Approach Example

- The VLI Corporation was a one patented product company; a contraceptive device with sales soaring to $17 million in 1986 from zero in 1983.

- In 1987 a key supporting patent expired because the company failed to pay the renewal fee.

- In 1987 a predator offered $7 for each of VLI's circa 12 million shares, contingent upon the key patent's renewal, valuing the company at circa $83 million.

- Prior to the October 1987 stock market crash the shares were trading at $4.

- Is the $3 difference, multiplied by the circa 12 million shares the value of full patent protection, that is some $36 million?

- Is it an underestimate? The $4 market price was trading at this level at the time of indications that there was a likelihood that the Patent Office may relent.

- Balanced against this the company has a market lead over generic competitors.

Comparability Example

- Coca-Cola negotiates to buy 30 Cadbury brands for $1.75 billion.

- Total sales of the brands were estimated at $262 million.

- Annual operating profits attributed to the brands – $94 million

- Are the turnover and profit multiples indicative enough to use for the valuation of similar brands? Possibly.

Historic or Replacement Cost Approach

> An Army spy plane is in danger of being scrapped because, after ten years and £227million, it still does not work. Defence sources said yesterday that six years after it was due to go into service, the Phoenix unmanned aircraft project was 'under review' and could be cancelled. The Army may now buy a cheap and reliable Israeli alternative that has already been sold around the world. The project's possible failure leaves a new question mark over the reputation of GEC Marconi, Britain's biggest defence contractor, which was also behind the £1billion fiasco of the Nimrod early warning aircraft, scrapped eight years ago. The Phoenix UAV unmanned air vehicle was supposed to replace the Army's obsolete airborne artillery drones, which contain film that has to be recovered and processed.
>
> *Daily Mail* January 1995

Cost-based methodologies assume that the value of the intellectual capital is related to the costs incurred in developing it. The cost to create must be distinguished from the cost to re-create. The formula might be best described as:

Fair Market Value = New Replacement Cost minus Functional Obsolescence minus Economic Obsolescence minus Physical Obsolescence

Costs typically included are:

- Raw Materials
- Salaries
- Overhead Costs
- Consulting Expenses
- Advertising and Promotion
- Extension Costs

Building Example: An Investor's Intellectual Capital from Costs

	200X	200X	200X	200X
Actual Gross Expenditure to Date	10,000	5,000	6,000	5,000
Tax Relief	3,000	1,500	2,000	1,500
Net Expenditure	7,000	3,500	4,000	3,500
Inflation Based on RPI	2%	3%	3%	2%
Expenditure Adjusted (in this case with negligible inflation figures unchanged)	7,000	3,500	4,000	3,500
Rate of Return	10%	10%	10%	10%
Rate Return factor	1.33	1.21	1.10	1
Cost (rounded)	9,300	4,200	4,400	3,500
Total Cost £21,400				

Problems with Cost-based Methods

Other than for the obvious application and assistance with regard to the valuation of a workforce, distribution networks or software, this approach has very little to recommend it. There have been numerous examples of expensive re-branding exercises or new product launches which have been a failure, and hugely successful intellectual property created with extremely low costs. Cost rarely correlates to value. The spy plane in the quote above shows the dangers – unless the technology has a secondary market, the value of the Phoenix UAV may be 0 rather than £227 million in cost.

Practical problems that arise in using this valuation method are:

- Lack of information.

- Future economic benefits are excluded.

- Historical costs do not equate to current costs. Capitalised costs that have built up ignore the time value of money over the period chosen, the effect of investment rates of return and alternative uses of that money including compound interest.

- Most intellectual capital requires support and further R&D to maintain its value and increase its earning power. Capitalising past costs may require a judgement on the extent to which expenditure relates to the R&D, or alternatively to support the asset.

- Costs do not correlate with technological, legal or physical life.

- Obsolescence is difficult to quantify.

- Maintenance is often ignored.

There are, however, examples of where the cost approach is optimal – in part because of weaknesses in the application of other methodologies. As stated above, this may include valuation of a workforce.

Workforce Valuation: Applying the Cost Approach

A trained and assembled workforce is a highly valuable intangible asset for many companies. In addition, several court cases (principally in the US) confirm that an assembled workforce can be properly identified as having a separate measurable value. The various valuation methodology's strengths and weaknesses in relation to workforces are as follows:

Workforce: the Cost Approach

Estimating the fair market value of a human capital intangible asset using the cost approach typically involves estimating either the reproduction cost or replacement cost of the asset. The reproduction cost equals the cost to construct an exact replica of the subject intangible asset, while the replacement cost is identified as the cost to recreate a property with an equivalent utility of the subject intangible asset.

The replacement cost method is frequently used to estimate the value of an assembled workforce. Costs to replace an assembled workforce include the cost to recruit, hire, and to train a replacement workforce.

Typically the estimated costs to recruit hire and train are expressed as percentages of total compensation for employees. In some instances, if employees are separated by grades, it may be appropriate to separate the estimated cost to recruit hire and train by employee grade. Another refinement would be to include a differentiation between the various groups of employees on the basis of the number of years employed.

The estimated cost to recruit, hire, and to train are then multiplied by the historical annual total compensation to result in a value for the assembled workforce.

Workforce: Income Approach

The income approach is based on the premise that the company will receive specified rewards or returns from human capital in future periods.

The income approach is less commonly used than the cost approach because it is difficult to estimate the economic income that will be generated by each specific employee.

Workforce: Market Approach

In the market approach, transactions involving similar intangible assets are used as reference points to estimate the value of the workforce.

Again the market approach is less commonly used in the valuation of assembled workforces, because transactions involving the sale or transfer of company workforces are not common, or not within the public domain, or the information is not complete.

An example using the Cost Approach

As stated above cost approach is the best methodology to use.

XYZ Ltd has a work force of some 100 employees that can be categorised into the following broad salary bands:

- Up to £9,999   3 employees
- £10,000 – £19,999   63 employees
- £20,000 to £29,999   22 employees
- £30,000 to £39,999   8 employees
- £40,000 +   3 employees
- The Board   3 members

The table below represents a spreadsheet showing an analysis of the XYZ Ltd staffing list showing salary split, number of employees per band, average remuneration per band, and total average remuneration per band.

Total Salary	Number	Av. Rem.(£)[1]	Actual Costs(£)	Hire Cost[2]	Training Cost[3]	Total Cost[4] (Hire & Training)	Value(£) (Actual x % total cost)
to £9,999	3	6,900	20,600	5%	10%	15%	3,090
£10k–£19,999	63	17,700	1,113,920	15%	20%	35%	389,872
£20k–£29,999	22	24,300	534,500	20%	25%	45%	240,525
£30k–£39,999	8	32,900	263,500	25%	35%	60%	158,100
£40k+	3	47,300	141,800	30%	45%	75%	106,350
Board	3	83,000	250,000	35%	50%	85%	212,500
TOTALS	**102**		**2,324,320**				**1,110,437**

Notes

1. Details in this column only shown to enable the 'banding' in the first column.

2. Hire Costs

   A percentage of remuneration has been allocated to each of the grades in the XYZ Ltd staff list. This percentage is to take account of the totality of hire costs and will include some or all of the following:

   • salaries of the employees involved in the recruitment of employees

   • overhead costs

   • head-hunter fees

   • direct recruit and hiring expenditure such as advertising, travel etc.

The percentages that we have used have been crosschecked against a sample of actual costs in each of the categories, and the following percentages have been adopted for hiring staff:

- Up to £9,999   5%
- £10,000 to £19,999   15%
- £20,000 to £29,999   20%
- £30,000 to £39,999   25%
- £40,000 +   30%
- Board   35%

3. Training Costs

We have further added a percentage to reflect the cost of the training with regard to each of the employees in each band. Whilst this is to some extent a subjective exercise, the figures that we have used are internationally accepted as being typical for the band involved, in the industry.

The basic premise is that the more senior the staff the more expensive will be the training, and therefore the more valuable they are.

The percentages that we have used are as follows:

- Up to £9,999   10%
- £10,000 to £19,999   20%
- £20,000 to £29,999   25%
- £30,000 to £39,999   35%
- £40,000 +   45%
- Board   50%

4. Total Cost

The total cost therefore for each of the bands is the sum of the hire cost and the training cost percentages outlined above and are summarised as follows:

- Up to £9,999   15%
- £10,000 to £19,999   35%
- £20,000 to £29,999   45%
- £30,000 to £39,999   60%
- £40,000 +   75%
- Board   85%

Total Value

As per the Table above, we show the percentages for each band of employee and the application of the total cost percentage to the total salary cost for each band to arrive at a value in respect of each band. The total value is £1,110,437, **say £1.1m**.

Income Approaches

Super Profit Methods

It is a fundamental principle of valuation theory that the value of any asset is the present value of the future economic benefits that can be anticipated to accrue to the owner of that asset, by virtue of his ownership of it. However whilst this principle is generally accepted by valuation professionals, there is no universally accepted valuation methodology.

Capitalisation of Historic Profits, Gross Profit Differential, and Excess Profits are methods that attempt to measure the so-called "super profit" being produced by the intellectual capital over and above the profit that is generated by the tangible assets.

Capitalisation of Historic Profits

This method arrives at the value of intellectual capital by multiplying the maintainable historic profitability of the asset by a multiple that has been assessed after scoring the relative strength of the intellectual capital. This multiple is arrived at after assessing the intellectual capital in the light of factors such as leadership, stability, market share, internationality, trend of profitability, required support and protection.

The intellectual capital is then marked for each of these factors according to the strength attributed to them. Historically associated with brand and trademarks the resultant total is described as the brand strength score from which a resultant price/earning ratio or multiple may be derived.

While this method recognises some of the factors that should be considered, it has major shortcomings. Being based upon the historic profitability this method does not take account of future profit growth or decline attributable to the intellectual capital, nor the likely future effects of other key variables or alternative future uses to which it might be put.

The Example of a Music Library

£m's	1999	2000	2001	2002
Net Profit Before Tax	20	15	25	30
Average	90/4 = 22.5			
Weighted Average	$(20 \times 1) + (15 \times 2) + (25 \times 3) + (30 \times 4)$ $= 245/10 = 24.5$			

Notes: The latter is the better method to adopt because of the increasing profits and there is no reason in the valuation to question the trend. An analysis of the market place and the sale of like assets suggests a pre-tax multiple of 5. Capitalisation of historic profits thus produces thus a valuation of £122m using a weighted average.

There are numerous examples of significant brand names which have been consigned to the history books.

Further problems and caveats are:

• Tangible assets responsible for profits must be taken out of the equation, together with their returns.

• In cases where this method is used the selection of the price earnings multiple has typically been made without reference to analysts' reports in sectors and the stock exchanges generally. It is therefore inevitable that the method will not reconcile the total value for the business and the values of the intellectual capital.

• When used for brand names little regard and account seems to be paid to supporting patents, design and copyright, most of which will have separate economic values outwith of the brand. Brands do not travel in a vacuum.

• Scoring is akin to customer surveys, where questions and their interpretation are wholly subjective. Subjective based judgements should be minimised in good valuation practice, not as in this methodology, maximised.

Gross Profit Differential?[1]

While gross profit has no universal definition this is another method which is often used for single patents, trademarks and brand names. The methodology adopts the difference in sales prices, adjusted for differences in marketing costs. The difference between the margin of a branded and/or patented product and an unbranded or generic product is used to 'drive out' cashflows and calculate value. In calculating the margin, both prices and volumes need to be considered and an allowance is made for the cost of support to the intellectual capital.

---

1.   Some caveats and descriptions on this methodology, the excess profit method and relief from royalty are summarised from a paper by Kenny & Loel and C&L, Brisbane, September 1991.

Gross Profit Differential Method: An Example

Stage 1

Branded/Patented product's price	50
Generic equivalent	30
Gross premium	20
Allowance for Brand/Patent costs (e.g. legal protection, marketing spend, design and packaging, R&D, etc)	(10)
	10
Tax @ 30%	(3)
Profit differential or premium	**7**

Stage 2

Annual Profit differential or premium	7
Estimate of the shortest of economic, legal, technological lives, say	10 years
Discount for risk and inflation (per annum)	10%
Value circa	**43**

Care in the use of this method is important because:

- The gross profit calculation does not directly value the net tangible assets and either take into account the internal rate of returns or the required rate of return on those assets. Accordingly it is possible to compare branded and generic products without comparing the real costs of brand maintenance to the respective producers.

- The calculations may reflect the distortion of a one-off huge advertising or unusual R&D spends, cost efficiencies in production and/or distribution attributable to economies of scale.

- Comparability exercises are fraught with difficulty unless you have 'inside' knowledge of all costs, volumes and marketing budgets.

- It may be difficult to find a suitable non-branded or generic product available for comparison and even if there is a similar generic product, it may not be strictly comparable due to differences in quantity, quality and/or availability.

- It is rare, in practice, for there to be much (if any) empirical evidence on the price elasticity of the branded and/or patented versus generic product.

- No allowance is made for trends in relative market shares over time (e.g. a generic competitor may have only recently entered the market).

Excess Profits or Gross Contribution of the Subject Intellectual Capital

In this method, the current market value of the net tangible assets employed is calculated as the benchmark and then an estimated rate of return is utilised in order to calculate the profits that are required in order to induce investors to invest into those net tangible assets. Any return over and above those profits required in order to induce investment is considered to be the excess return attributable to the intellectual capital and as with the capitalisation of historic profit, this return is then capitalised.

This methodology is a variation of the methodology of valuing a business as a whole and subtracting from that value the current market value of net tangible assets employed. In either case, one method should be reconciled to the other (i.e. the sum of the parts cannot exceed the total of the whole). Although this method theoretically relies on the pure economic benefits obtained from the use of the assets, both tangible and intangible, it has the following major limitations:

- Identification of the gross contribution of the subject asset from the tangibles and other intellectual capital is tricky.

- The required rate of return may reflect risk and other factors which cannot be separately assessed with precision.

- Determination of the net profit contribution is difficult.

- The method itself does not allocate between any constituent components (e.g. such as different patents).

- The valuation of some of the tangible assets employed may also incorporate some of the intangible value (i.e. plant and machinery may be valued on a going concern basis).

- Information about technological developments in potentially competitive products is generally not available and/or its impact is difficult to assess.

- The assets being valued may not be employed in the best possible manner (highest and best use).

- Asset values and reported profits may be calculated on different bases.

- Theoretically, any company earning an excess profit margin will generally have that margin eroded over time by competitive pressures.

- Branded products, if successful, generally have the benefit of lower depreciation charges (because of fully depreciated assets or assets acquired at a lower historic cost base) and the benefit of the learning curve at all levels of operation.

- The required rate of return may be taken into account in setting the sales price of the product.

- This method ignores the potential earnings to be derived from alternative uses of the intellectual capital.

An American appraiser, Michael Paschall (*Business Valuation Review* 2001) recently succinctly also set out his views on the main problems with this approach, as follows:

- The returns on tangible and intangible assets cannot be realistically separated.

- There is no way to reasonably estimate what "normal" tangible equity should be.

- There is no way to reasonably estimate what a "normal" rate of return on "normal" tangible equity should be.

- There is no way to reasonably estimate what the capitalisation rate for intangibles should be and there is no empirical support for such a rate.

- The method has been roundly and loudly denounced by its creator, the Inland Revenue Service in the U.S.A..

- The method has been widely criticised by the business valuation profession.

- Sophisticated buyers and sellers in the real world do not use this method.

Relief from Royalty

Royalty relief valuations are based on the theoretical assumption that if the intellectual capital had to be licensed from a third party there would be a royalty charge based on turnover, which would be levied for the privilege of using that intellectual capital. By owning the asset(s), royalties are avoided, hence the term 'royalty relief'. Hypothetical post-tax royalties less costs of a licence are capitalised.

There are many examples of royalties being applied for the licensing of intellectual capital between companies. The valuer must be able to source like information to be able to use this method. Information is not widely available nor are the terms on which the royalties were based, so the exercise is time consuming. Rates often incorporate payments for the use of patents, copyright or shared marketing costs. They vary depending upon tax considerations and market circumstances from time to time. It is difficult, therefore, to identify an appropriate rate for a particular valuation. However, notional royalties assessed with the help of the previous methods are acceptable.

Thus the relief from royalty approach is similar to a sale and leaseback of real property. It assumes that the intellectual capital is sold and then licensed back by its previous owner. The method calculates the maximum royalty the business could afford to pay for the licence, whilst still achieving an acceptable return on the assets remaining in the business, being its investment in such things as plant, working capital and goodwill. Hence, the royalty is equivalent to the super profit mentioned earlier.

The royalty stream is then capitalised at an appropriate rate of return to produce the value of the rights to use the intellectual capital. The rate of return will need to reflect the risk/return relationship implicit in the investment in the intellectual capital.

Relief From Royalty DCF Approach (No Residual Or Terminal Value): an example

Years ended 31 March (£m's)	1994	1995	1996	1997
Sales Attributable to IPR	5	10	15	10
Royalty Rate	20%	20%	20%	20%
Royalty Savings	1	2	3	2
Taxes at 40%	0.4	0.8	1.2	0.8
After Tax Savings	0.6	1.2	1.8	1.2
Discount Factor at 15% (mid year)	0.9325	0.8109	0.7051	0.6131
NP Value of Post Tax Cash Flows	0.56	0.97	1.27	0.74
Total Present Value (NPV)	3.54			

Note: The NPV of tax savings resulting from the amortisation over useful life, if applicable, should be calculated and added to the royalty savings of £3.54m.

The advantage that this method has over those three mentioned in the Super Profit section above, is that the notional royalty rate used in the valuation can be compared to the royalty rates actually being paid in the market for "similar" intellectual capital. Also, the approach specifically considers the profitability of the intellectual capital and takes into account factors such as the number of times the royalty is covered by profit.

Some of the problems associated with the relief from royalty approach are:

•   Without adjustment it does not reflect the owner's complete control of the intellectual capital.

•   There may be no separation of the other intangible components that may be implicitly included in the determination of a prevailing royalty rate. Therefore, the licensee will, in addition to the brand name, pay for the geographic goodwill or monopoly that may be a component of the business.

- The selection of a comparable royalty rate has practical difficulties:

  - The reference rates may be out of date and may not properly reflect current economic conditions;

  - The normalised rates are established with respect to an average of a number of transactions about which detailed information may not be available; and

  - The licensing arrangement may preclude the alternatives uses to which the intangible asset may be put.

The relief from royalty approach does have some conceptual problems but it is probably the best of the super profit capitalisation approaches, and provides the conceptually soundest starting point as long as the valuer makes the appropriate premium calculations to account for the fact that an owner, has complete control over the asset and the ability to exploit it beyond a single licensing strategy.

Relief from Royalty is an extremely useful method for 'driving out' the cash flows that will be subject to the discounted cash flow calculations. This is explained in greater detail in the next section.

Royalties Foregone/Relief From Royalty – Summary

Method

- Capitalise royalty stream by rate of return

- More prestige = higher royalty rate

Features

- Estimate future royalty stream

- Basic premise: sale & lease back

- Usually calculated as a maximum possible with the acceptable rate of return in the market as a check

- Alternatively looked upon as a payment for use: a rent

- Royalty equivalent to excess profit component

- Greater availability of independent economic & trade association forecasts

- Facilitates comparisons with royalty rates of similar intellectual property in marketplace

Special factors to consider when calculating the royalty rate

- Relative dominance of the brand, patent etc

- Geographical area covered

- Rate of return acceptable to all parties

- Probable level of continuing sales

- Commercial obligations of licensor(ee)

- 'Market rates' or 'industry norms' are not always correct

- Royalties often represent mark-ups and reflect complex warranty and indemnity terms in agreements

Problems

- Separation of intangible components

- Other factors often an ingredient in determining current royalty rate e.g. geographical goodwill or monopoly.

- Comparables may be out of date, detailed information not available and arrangements may preclude for example extensions to the intellectual capital, that is the premium for total control.

Section 6:

Income Approaches: Economic Use

> This section aims to establish how valuation needs to reflect a rate of return for its owner. One owner's cost of capital will be different from another owner's. The risk of the market in which the asset is deployed will differ from another market. This chapter builds a basic example of how to reach a rate of return for a particular valuation.

Income Approach and Pure Economic Use Valuation

"Valuation models for IP companies typically employ discounted cash flow analyses based on assumptions of market sizes and penetrations. One critique of most DCF models is that they will provide almost any conclusion an analyst chooses, but with well defined and conservative underlining assumptions, the DCF can be a useful tool. Indeed CSFB has based its valuation and share-priced targets on this methodology. In the current market, we believe that investors have largely abandoned or are treating with skepticism the DCF based valuation method, preferring instead more simple methods such as P/E or market capitalization/sales. We believe while easy to understand, these metrics do not capture the growth that technology companies can achieve in the medium term."

Source: *CSFB* 12 August 2002

While simple capitalisations, such as those in the previous section, use a multiple or a combination of a multiple and discount rate, 'economic use' valuations, based on discounted cashflows (DCF), are the most widely recognised approach to valuations where intellectual capital is involved. Such valuations consider the economic value of the use of the intellectual capital to the current owner and to others. Any of the previous methodologies applied initially can help in driving out cash flows and to determine income. The valuer can subsequently either capitalise maintainable earnings or cashflow using a multiple or adopt discounted cashflow.

The reader will recall it is a fundamental principle of valuation theory that the value of any asset is the present value of the future economic benefits that can be anticipated to accrue to the owner of that asset, by virtue of his ownership of it. However whilst this principle is generally accepted by valuation professionals, there is no universally accepted valuation methodology.

Income approaches look at the income-producing capability of the asset to be valued. The cashflow model used in economic use valuations comprises future income streams less costs represented on an annual, six monthly or quarterly basis. The future economic benefits, i.e. income, are equated to the present value of the net cash flows anticipated to be derived from ownership of the asset. The quantification of the future cash flows should take into account incremental fixed asset and working capital investments. For an example of calculation from cashflows, see pp 204–211.

Present Value

The calculation of the present value of the cash flows is the quantification of the fact that £1 in your pocket today is of more value than £1 sometime in the future. The value of money to be received in future stated at today's value, factoring in risk, is calculated by utilising an appropriate discount factor. This factor can be derived from a number of different rate of returns models which are referred to later in this section.

£1 in your pocket today is worth more than £1 next year or the year after and the discount rate copes with this by making a judgement about risk free rates of return and also the riskiness of the investment opportunity. Different discount rates or required rates of return can have a huge effect on the valuation outcome.

For example £100 invested today and projected forward at a return rate of say 10%, 20% and 30% would be worth, in 10 years time, approximately £250, £600 and £1,400 respectively. Similarly £100 in 10 years time is worth £39, £16 and £7 respectively in today's terms using the same discount rates.

Most financial analysts value companies on the basis of free cashflows discounted back to a net present value. Free cashflows are:

• net profit before interest and tax

- less tax
- plus non-cash items such as depreciation
- less capital expenditure
- plus or minus working capital requirements

Similarly the calculation of future cashflows rendered back to a Net Present Value for IPR avoids the distortions of accounting adjustments which bear no relationship to the underlying economic facts. Thus just as modern business valuations now focus on the sustainable cashflows from the business, and put a value on that cash stream, so IPR led valuation and licensing appraisals consider sustainable cashflows from the IPR exploitation and puts a value on them.

Thus Economic Use Valuation Analysis is effectively DCF applied to the Business Enterprise or the subject intellectual capital under consideration.

The Net Present Value (NPV) of a strategy or business or intellectual capital is thus the sum of its expected free cash flows to a horizon (H) *discounted* by its cost of capital (r):

$$\text{NPV} = \frac{\text{Year 1 Cash Flow}}{(1 + r)} + \frac{\text{Year 2 Cash Flow}}{(1 + r)^2} \text{ ...}$$

$$\text{... to say } \frac{\text{Year 5 Cash Flow}}{(1 + r)^5}$$

PLUS

A terminal value (see also page 210) i.e. the value of the business or intellectual capital at a horizon (HV):

$$\text{HV} = \frac{\text{Cash Flow at Year 5}}{(r - \text{growth})} \quad \text{also discounted back to present value.}$$

Growth (%) is a variable affected by the strategy of the business, but often projected as anticipated inflation. This factor in effect projects the last cash flow in a series forward into the future by reducing the discount rate applied by r.

How far is the Horizon?

Before getting down to the detailed cash flow spreadsheets, quantification of the remaining useful life and decay rate associated with the use of the intellectual capital is required. This remaining useful life analysis will quantify the *shortest* of the following:

- **Physical life**
- **Functional life**
- **Technological life**
- **Economic life**
- **Legal life**

Forecasting – how long for? Examples of Risk in Intellectual Capital

Patents ruling wipes £9bn off GSK's value

Almost £9 billion was ... instead of this wiped from the market value of GlaxoSmithKline (GSK), Europe's biggest drugs group, after a US court ruled that patents protecting its second biggest selling drug, the antibiotic Augmentin, are invalid. The ruling means that three generic drug companies are free to launch a cheap copy of the drug, which had sales in the US of almost £1 billion last year. GSK shares plunged 9 per cent amid heavy selling as analysts downgraded profit forecasts for the company, which has suffered a wave of patent challenges against its best-selling products. JP Garnier, GSK's chief executive, said his company would appeal against the Augmentin ruling but gave warning that earnings growth in 2002 would fall about a third to just 10 percent if generic Augmentin was launched on July 1.

He said: "We are clearly disappointed with the court's decision. We have provided this additional EPS (earnings per share) guidance in order to be clear on the impact should a generic Augmentin be launched before the appeal, although I should emphasise that there is still no certainty whether this will ultimately occur." Generic companies usually wait until after an appeal before launching drug copies, because of the threat of punishing damages if the appeal reverses the initial decision. Mr Barnes, pharmaceuticals analyst at Merrill Lynch, forecasts that Augmentin sales in the US, which were £912 million last year, will fall to £706 million this year before collapsing to £176 million next year. ... instead of this Augmentin is covered by other patents due to expire in 2017 and 2018 but they were also recently ruled invalid. The patent challenges were brought by three generic companies: Geneva Pharmaceuticals, the generics division of Novartis, the Swiss drugs group, Teva Pharmaceuticals, an Israeli company, and Ranbaxy, an Indian drugs group.

Geneva already has regulatory approval from the Food and Drug Administration for its generic Augmentin, so could launch immediately. Teva's mode highlights the increasing aggression of the generics industry, whose cutprice drugs are attractive to cost-conscious healthcare providers. GSK has suffered a series of assaults from the generics industry. Patents for Paxil, its blockbuster antidepressant, have been challenged. A generic version of Wellbutrin, another antidepressant, which had US sales last year of £628 million, is about to be launched. Merrill Lynch downgraded the stock from "buy" to "neutral" and cut its earnings-per-share forecast for the current year by 5 per cent to 80p.

Source: *The Times*, May 2002

Prozac rivals send Lilly's profits tumbling by 22%

Eli Lilly, the US pharmaceuticals group ... revealed the huge impact of patent expiry in the drugs industry when it unveiled a 22 per cent fall in first-quarter profits following generic competition to its ubiquitous antidepressant, Prozac.

The company reported a 9 per cent fall in the first quarter sales to just $2.56 billion (£1.78 billion), compared with $2.81 billion in the same period last year.

Prozac, which was once one of the world's biggest selling drugs, fell victim to generic competition last summer. The rapid speed with which sales have collapsed underlines drug companies' vulnerability when their patents expire.

Sales of Prozac, an anti-depressant in a class of drugs called selective serotonin re-uptake inhibitors (SSRIs), fell 70 per cent in the first three months of this year to about $186 million. In 2000 Prozac boasted sales of $2.6 billion. Lilly shares added $2.43 to $75.85 in early trading in New York, showing that the market had anticipated depressed first-quarter trading. But analysts at Deutsche Bank said Lilly's pipeline of new drugs "is the richest in the industry and should drive robust, high-quality growth over the next few years".

Lilly's biggest-selling drug is Zyprexa, for schizophrenia, which had sales of $819 million in the first quarter, compared with $637 million at the same time last year. However, two deaths in Japan of diabetics using the drug mean additional warnings might be necessary when the drug is prescribed. Lilly's other big-selling products include Gemzar, the cancer treatment and Evista, the osteoporosis drug.

Lilly said its anti-impotence drug Cialis is on track for launch in the second half of this year, even though its manufacturing plant in Indiana is the subject of a rigorous regulatory inspection.

The company reported a 22 per cent fall in first-quarter earnings per share at $0.58 and a similar fall in net income at $629.2 million. Analysts expect the company to report flat profits this year, returning to growth in 2003.

The Times

Summary of Economic Use Valuation

C A S H F L O W	1. A Financial Forecast
	This involves a review of data and if they exist a review of historic data relationships and trends. The objective is to identify a reliable set of assumptions and a range of business earnings flowing from use of the intellectual capital.
	2. Identifying Specific Intellectual Capital Earnings
	A review to apportion total business earnings between the products and IPR. This income allocation is essentially a judgmental process based on all available research.

and a third element now due to be discussed

COST OF C A P I T A L	3. Discount Rate Determination and Risk
	This involves modelling sometimes individual risks, and forecasting realistic outcomes and probabilities for the risks and then identifying an appropriate discount rate(s). The discount rate transforms the future cashflows into net present value reflecting risk and the time value of money. The discount rate must be greater than the return on risk free investment opportunities and a usual starting point is the risk free cost of long term debt.

Risk

To calculate discount rates, the relative risks of an investment must be understood.

Harry Markowitz identified two types of classic risk:

1. *Unsystematic risk* (also called specific risk, stock-specific risk or unique risk). In effect this is individual stock risk that can be diversified away by holding stocks in portfolios.

   Specific risk factors can be positive (e.g. the discovery of a new patentable product) and negative (e.g. a fire in a warehouse).

2. *Systematic risk* is inherent in stock markets and unavoidable. It consists of business and financial risks which are caused by macroeconomic factors. No matter how many stocks an investor

holds, the overall portfolio will still be subject to changes in the economy.

A business's Systematic Risk depends on many factors including the contracts it makes with suppliers and customers, for example:

- If a company locks in supply prices with a long-term contract, it is passing on inflation risk to its suppliers

- Similarly, if it locks in prices to its customers, it is bearing more inflation risk.

It would be all but impossible to measure the risks of each of a company's contracts (even if the information were available).

While you can *increase* systematic risk by investing in a high risk portfolio of shares, say in an emerging market or unfashionable sector, this type of risk is caused by factors which affect *all* investments. An investor's required return amounts to a risk free rate of return (see risk free section below) plus a market risk premium.

Specific risk can be made less risky because it is largely in the owner's control although like the fire in a warehouse not one that you may have wished. Contrast systematic risk above which on the other hand consists of business and financial risks which are caused by macroeconomic factors which effect all investment situations.

Interest rate risk is a hybrid and is sometimes used to explain a situation where markets go down when the cost of money goes up, particularly because in these economic conditions companies find sales at good margins more difficult.

The strength of intellectual capital also determines the applicable discount rate. Strong intellectual capital would attract a lower rate reflecting lower risk to associated earnings. Weak intellectual capital would attract a commensurably higher rate, other modelling being equal. To develop decision trees, probability distributions and other representations of the risks, the research referred to in Section 3 above is invaluable. Once complete, the valuer will notice that the shape and volatility of risk will alter, determined by the probability assumptions.

Rarely does a situation demand consideration of every possible variable, for example by an expensive Monte Carlo model which considers the implausible and downgrades the plausible by default. To echo the sentiment of Dick Brealey – *Principles of Corporate Finance, (McGraw-Hill)* – *"The model that was intended to open up black boxes ends up creating another one."* It does have its uses – occasionally – but such uses are beyond the scope of this work.

Discount Rate Determination and its Basic Application

> This requires two steps:
>
> 1. Identifying and applying the cost of capital to known cash flows.
>
> 2. Calculating a terminal value and discounting appropriately.

1. Apply a Weighted Average Cost of Capital (WACC) as a discount rate to the unlevered "free" cashflow in each year (see pages 187 below). That is, pre-interest cashflows, with calculation of a tax charge on pre-tax, pre-interest profits. The Weighted Average Cost of Capital process reflects the blend of required debt and equity returns, dependent on the likely gearing of the company or investor in intellectual capital, adding or subtracting the current year cash or debt from the valuation. These are explained further below.

plus

2. Calculate in addition a terminal value ("TV"), as a multiple of earnings before interest, tax and depreciation or EBITDA (earnings before interest, tax, depreciation and amortisation) in the first year that forecasting becomes futile (steady state year) to reflect the perpetuity value of the subsequent cashflows – if indeed they do not fall off a cliff such as at the end of a patent or a technology shift. At this point revenue and market penetration can still be enjoying good growth. This can be done by using EBITDA merger multiples of similar companies in the sector and discounting by around 15%–25% to obtain public market multiples.

or

Calculate and apply as indicated on page 192 an Equity Rate of Return to the terminal value in the steady state year. This uses the reciprocal of the discount rate less the long-term growth rate of the business, all multiplied by the final operating cashflow in the last year say 2015.

$$TV \quad = \quad \frac{\text{Year 2015 Operating Cashflow}}{(r - g)}$$

where

TV = Terminal Value

r = The cost of equity

g = The long-term growth rate of the business.

Regarding the two terminal value calculations above the authors prefer the last methodology and it is often regarded as the most relevant for equity investors.

On the basis of these analyses, the value of the exploitation of the IPR can be calculated.

We have now:

- **made a financial forecast**

- **identified earnings**

- **shown what needs to be done to reduce those earnings and projected earnings to current values to an investor.**

We must now move on to look further at the cost of capital.

The Weighted Average Cost of Capital ("WACC")

WACC or the weighted average cost of capital as referred to in the introduction to this section is the least understood and requires further explanation. To recap:

Value = $\dfrac{\text{Expected Cash Flows}}{\text{Cost of Capital}}$

- If the valuer doesn't know the cost of capital, then whether value is being increased or reduced is not known

- The cost of capital must match the risk of the associated cash flows

However, Corporate and Business Value has two major components namely equity and debt:

	Equity Value	(value that belongs to the owners)
+	Market Value of Debt	(the borrowing of the owner, at "market" rates – as if they were refinanced)
=	Corporate Value	

- Debt holders have a prior claim on a business's assets
- Equity holders have a residual claim

	Corporate Value
–	Market Value of Debt
=	Equity Value

Precisely how the proposed capital structure of the business would have resolved itself depends on individual circumstances but it is not unusual to assume a typical target structure consisting of either 70% equity capital and 30% debt, or debt free.

Estimating the Cost of Equity

- From the investor's perspective it is simply the return that would entice an investor to invest in the equity of a business:

  | Investor's required return (%) | = | Risk-free rate of return (%) | + | Premium for the investment's level of risk (%) |

- From a shareholder's perspective the cost of equity is sometimes calculated using the Dividend Discount model (%)

  | Investor's Required return (%) | = | Dividend Yield (%) | + | Capital Appreciation (%) |

Dividend discount caveats

- Fails to link returns to the risk of the investment

- Dividend policy varies widely and is under the whim of management

- Cannot be used when growth is greater than the expected return

---

The two basic ingredients of the cost of capital are therefore the cost of debt and the cost of equity. WACC is a weighted average of these two aspects. This is derived from the fact as illustrated above that all corporate and business value has two major components namely equity and debt. Value in intellectual capital is no different.

Determination of the appropriate discount rate or capitalisation rate to be used for the purpose of capitalising the incremental economic benefits associated with the intangible asset should consider the following *cumulative* factors:

– current yield on short term, risk free, money market instruments

– inflation risk premium

– a term to maturity premium, based upon the current term structure of interest rates

– an illiquidity risk premium

– a lack of marketability risk premium

– a premium for the systematic risk factors associated with a comparable investment

– a premium for the non-systematic risk factors associated with the specific technology or intangible asset and

– a business's cost of capital (see WACC above)

Building a Discount Rate – A Basic Example

A basic model to understand the nature of a required rate of return or discount rate could be built up in the following way. Figures are rounded (often up) because, of course, predicting the future is not an exact science.

1. *Purchasing Power Risk*   %

E.g. consumer price inflation, say Eurozone

Forecast 2002 – 2.2 % y/y
         2003 – 1.9% y/y

& UK

Forecast 2002 – 2.3% y/y
         2003 – 2.4% y/y   say   + 2

2. *Interest Rate Risk*

E.g. US bond yields in 2002 were well past a trough. At that time, with weakness in global demand, the low inflationary environment when yields should not rise dramatically, and given the fact that European bond yields will track US yields, these investments are comparatively safe opportunities to measure against the intellectual capital appraisal. Bonds can be anticipated to have a yield of (say) 4% – or 2% more than purchasing power risk.   say   + 2

3. *Business Risk*

The daily cut and thrust of business – consumer loyalty, customer loyalty, competitors, capital expenditure, business cycle, trends etc. No exact percentage can be put forward for this. Lenders would usually require at least 3%, however.   say   +3

4. *Market Risk*

E.g. concerns for recovery, a consumer sector
overstretched, high debt levels in any sector,
persistent under performance in sectors such
as manufacturing, and telecoms. Is there
some light at the end of the tunnel or will
a combination of these and other elements
relative to the sector, the general economy
and politics likely to impact on the sector
and intellectual capital being appraised?   say   + 3

5. *Risk Free Rate of Return*

See page 194 below   say   + 5

Therefore required rate of return or discount rate   15%

Conclusion

Thus an albeit crude but logical first step to understand the mechanics
of arriving at a discount rate to bring back future earnings to today's
value. We are beginning to think about a *required rate of return*, to value
intellectual capital income streams, of something in excess of 15%.
However IPR attracts the above risks and usually a *lot more.*

It is timely to introduce Capital Asset Pricing Model ("CAPM") in
detail to perhaps better illustrate and better calculate the risks you
cannot control and throw up a discount rate below which percentage
figure you should not consider.

The only adjustment to the CAPM rate is upwards: it provides a
benchmark. With its relative rigour it is widely used by financial
institutions as providing the starting point for pricing capital assets:
including intellectual capital.

The Discount Rate to Adopt

Our recommended tool in most valuations uses CAPM to estimate the discount rate to apply to the cash flows you have calculated. This section shows how, using an example in which a cumulative approach builds a rate used at the end of this section.

First a *debt-free* CAPM is calculated as a benchmark. Then, say, an investor or lender's risk is reflected in an uplift – largely based on valuation experience.

Cost of Equity and the Capital Asset Pricing Model ("CAPM") in Detail

To assist in the calculation of the appropriate rate of return and discount rate the valuer can utilise a number of different methodologies including the Capital Asset Pricing Model, Arbitrage Pricing Theory and Venture Capital models depending on the particular circumstances, as well as the preference and judgement of the valuer. If carried out thoroughly and conscientiously each of these models should produce acceptable results. CAPM is probably the easiest model to use to arrive at the cost of equity capital, because the assumptions introduced are containable, is the CAPM and this is the focus of this section. The cost of equity capital is, as stated above, crucial to determining a discount rate to use to achieve a present value appropriate to the risk of an investment.

CAPM is the relationship between individual stocks, their rate of return and risk, and the market as a whole. CAPM uses a Market Risk Premium (MRP) plus a Beta to calculate the premium for Systematic Risk.

Remember systematic risk is caused by factors which affect all investments. The required return of the whole market can therefore be expressed as:

Investors' required return $=$ Risk free rate of return $+$ a Market Risk Premium

CAPM provides a means to apply this formula to a particular asset or share. CAPM's main strengths are that:

– Historical inputs are accepted and the calculations are observable in larger financial markets

– CAPM has been widely used and accepted when data is available (which it invariably is) currently and historically.

To recall: the Cost of Capital (K) is used to discount the expected cash flows to calculate value:

- The cost of capital is also referred to as "the discount rate" or the "required rate of return"

- It represents the weighted average return that debt and equity holders demand in return for investing in a project or an asset

- K is a function of risk: the higher the risk the higher the required rate of return.

The Capital Asset Pricing Model (CAPM) formula

$$K_e = R_f + (ß) (R_m - R_f)$$

where

K_e = Cost of Equity Capital

R_f = Risk Free Rate

R_m = Return on a diversified market portfolio

$(ß)$ = Beta – the market volatility of an equity security

$R_m - R_f$ is commonly referred to as R_e

K_e – the Cost of Equity Capital

Statistical measures can be used to measure systematic risk and estimate the cost of equity:

- The additional risk a stock adds to a diversified portfolio can be found by measuring the extent to which it relates to efficient and well-diversified portfolios

- The standard deviation of the 'expected' rate of return is the measure of a share's total risk

- Beta (ß) measures the sensitivity of a stock's 'expected' risk premium to movements in the market's 'expected' risk premium

- The Capital Asset Pricing Model (CAPM) and Arbitrage Pricing Theory (APT) are simply two ways of measuring this risk and translating it into the require return for a given stock

Each of the K_e components is discussed below. The conclusions are specific only to this text and will be utilised in an example to illustrate the methodology.

1. R_f – The Risk Free Rate – the first component of K_e

The valuer needs to begin to arrive at the discount rate which is appropriate to the risk inherent in the given valuation appraisal. A common benchmark is the risk free rate which is usually determined by safe investments such as Government bonds. For example the best available approximation to this in the UK is the yield on 5 to 15 year Government bonds and that currently stands around 5% (a rate simply sourced from the London *Financial Times*).

Needless to say there is a problem in emerging economies and those subject to scrutiny by the IMF. Generally the valuer should only use yields where there is no risk of default. Research by Ibbotson Associates, probably the leader in its field in providing this kind of data, has detailed calculated rates of return for portfolios of long – term Government bonds.

For the example that follows: conclusion 1

Thus we have calculated the first constituent part of our CAPM formula, **R_f** is **5%**

2. R_m minus R_f (sometimes referred to as R_e) – the second component of K_e.

R_m is the return on a diversified market portfolio or the expected return from the market and a market portfolio of shares.

R_m minus R_f is the expected *market risk premium*. It is commonly measured as the historical difference between the return to the market as a whole and the risk – free return (R_f). This equity premium is calculated post tax.

In the UK, historically ($R_m - R_f$) is in the range of 6 – 8%. However research by the Boston Consulting Group has shown that this has dropped to between 3% and 4% in the recent past.

To take forward to the example: conclusion 2

Thus in our model example let us follow suit and adopt **4%** for **$R_m - R_f$, or R_e**.

3. Beta (ß) – the third component

Beta is the commonly used description for the degree to which a business is more or less risky than the market represented by a fully diversified portfolio of investment. Thus a beta of 1 implies that when the market went up or down 10%, on average the stock also went up or down 10%. In other words it has systematic risk *the same* as the market portfolio. A beta of 1.5 implies that when the market went up or down 10%. In other words the stock went up or down 15% i.e. the stock is *more* risky than the market portfolio. Thus, to the safe starting point of risk free debt, are added beta factors for the market as a whole and sometimes for the intellectual capital in particular. These beta factors are generally determined by reference to standard industry risk analysis, supplemented by specific intellectual capital risk analysis.

Total risk is reduced when stocks are combined in a portfolio:

- For example, a portfolio consisting of 50% Tesco and 50% Shell has lower risk than the stocks individually

- Overall risk is reduced as one firm's random misfortune is offset by other companies' random good fortune

- Larger portfolios spread over different sectors reduce the risks even further.

Beta is a relative market measure of a business or stocks' volatility or sensitivity to movements of the market as a whole. Intellectual capital and companies holding intellectual capital are particularly risky and Beta is a measure of a risky assets' level of risk relative to the market.

Key features of Beta (ß)

- (ß) is a measure of variance – the degree to which a stock moves relative to a well diversified portfolio (the market).

- (ß) shows whether a firm is more or less risky than the market as a fully diversified portfolio.

- A (ß) of 1 implies that when the market went up (down) 10%, on average the stock also went up (down) 10% (It has the same systematic risk as the market portfolio).

- A (ß) of 1.5 implies that when the market went up (down) 10%, on average the stock also went up (down) 15% (The stock is more risky than the market portfolio).

- (ß) is commonly calculated by regressing 5 years of monthly stock return data against returns for a designated "market portfolio".

Thus the Beta is a measure of a stock's sensitivity to market movements. The best method of obtaining the Beta in our example is to use the Beta of companies in a similar field as our subject intellectual capital – in our example the most appropriate Beta is 1.20 (Source: London Business School Risk Measurement Survey) being the figure currently showing for this sector of the FTSE – Actuaries Index.

For the example: conclusion 3

The Beta is 1.2

4. CAPM in a situation that is debt free, i.e. where no debt is being introduced.

In the first instance the Capital Pricing Model is used to arrive at an appropriate discount rate on the assumption that the intellectual capital will be funded solely by equity (not unusual with many intellectual capital investment scenarios) and no debt. An illustration of the potential effect of debt in our example is shown on pages 212–215.

Given the assumptions and conclusions as to the figures for the three components above, the cost of equity (K_e) can be calculated thus:

$$K_e = R_f + B(R_e)$$
$$K_e = 5\% + 1.20(4.0\%)$$
$$K_e = 9.8\%$$

You sometimes see this expressed as follows:

$$K_e = 5\% + (1.2 \times 4\%)$$
$$K_e = 5\% + (120\% \times 4\%)$$
$$K_e = 5\% + 4.8\%$$
$$K_e = 9.8\%$$

 Adjusting the Benchmark

We can therefore *benchmark* an equity discount rate of 9.8% in considering the valuation in our example. Often substantial uplifts are required to this benchmark and are considered next.

Uplifting the CAPM Benchmark

> The reader will realise, by now, there is no "right answer" here. Experience and the market behaviour of lenders is the guide: here we present typical target returns and where they originate.

The valuer of unquoted businesses and shares applies adjustments to ratios and yields derived from the quoted sector in comparability exercises for:

- lack of size,
- liquidity,
- a lack of market in the shares, and
- diversity of business.

The valuer undertakes a similar exercise, putting the benchmark in the context of financial realities such as the rates required by venture capitalists. They look at risk evaluation and discount rates in start-up seed capital situations by requiring a rate of return after tax of between 60 and 70 plus percent (after tax). This is compared with early start-up rates of returns of between 50 and 70 percent after tax. (Dauten suggests a post-tax rate of return of 70+% whilst Guil Rhaus suggests 100+% – Dauten, KP *Venture Capital Risk/Reward Primer and Glossary of Terms*, NASBIC VC Institute, Chicago 1986 and Guil Rhaus, FW in *Accounting Forum*, June 1985). Rates of return decline markedly as the business and intellectual capital matures.

These rates of return are based on *uncertain* projected cashflows. That is, they represent a risk-adjusted discount rate applied to risky cashflows. In our example, the cashflows have been prepared in a rigorously prudent manner with stated assumptions in which case the cashflows are largely risk-adjusted. Accordingly the discount rate applicable should acknowledge that fact, particularly to avoid a double discount.

The Securities Institute of Australia Diploma Course notes (Advanced Security Analysis, 1989), for example, state that after-tax rates of return on equity capital are 'in the range of 30% to 40% for risky industries' and are 'higher for new projects than established areas of activity'.

If, as in our example, it is accepted that the enterprise has passed the 'seed' capital stage and is in a start-up phase, an after-tax rate of return of approximately 50% to 70% may be applicable to unadjusted cashflows. This range of discount rates equates to approximately 30% to 45% on an adjusted basis (employing efficacy and certainty factors to 'risky' revenues.)

However, it is our view in the example that the intellectual capital, although in theory in a start-up phase, is technology acknowledged to be of immediate application by the envisaged parties in a mature industry.

Target returns: some examples

Valuation theory advanced by James H Schilt ("A Rational Approach to Capitalization Rates for Discounting the Future Income Stream of Closely Held Companies", *The Financial Planner*, January 1982), and supported by Shannon P Pratt (*Valuing a Business*, 2nd Edition, Business One Irwin, 1989) endorse risk premiums added to a risk-free rate to determine a usable capitalization rate as follows:

- Established businesses: good trade position; good management; stable past earnings; predictable future – 6 to 10 percent.

- Same as above except in more competitive industries – 11 to 15 percent.

- Companies in highly competitive industries, with little capital investment and no management depth, although with a good historical earnings record – 16 to 20 percent.

- Small businesses that depend on the skill of one or two people, or large companies in highly cyclical industries with very low predictability – 21 to 25 percent.

- Small personal service businesses with a single owner/manager – 26 to 30 percent.

It is also wise to be aware of typical target returns expected by Venture Capitalists (Source ACT October 2001) as follows:

Stage	Expected Return %
Seed	80
Start-up	60
First Stage	50
Second Stage	40
Third Stage/Mezzanine	30
Bridge/Debt	25

These returns should be placed in context and ACT helpfully also set out an example of a view of a Venture Capitalist's risk evaluation process:

	Probability %
Product Development	85
Production and Material Supply	85
Competitor Behaviour	80
Pricing/Margin	75
Management Capability	70
Sufficient Capital	70

This is cumulative percentage reduction to 'score' a probability of success percentage of some 20% in the example given.

In our experience VC's will often demand a 100% plus return at the seed stage.

Therefore a discount rate of 9.8% (see CAPM conclusion on page 198) is not considered appropriate for the valuation of the subject intellectual capital in the example that follows. And further to academic studies, the following points of difference are among those that need to be considered in arriving at an appropriate discount rate to apply to the intellectual capital:

- While our subject intellectual capital is proven technology, ... it does not have a history of profitability.

- CAPM utilises data derived from transactions in quoted stock ("CAPM stock") that has historically paid dividends and can be expected to do so in the future.

- CAPM stock usually has considerable tangible asset backing.

- CAPM stock usually has full access to the capital markets.

- CAPM stock usually comprises of very substantial businesses with mass and diversity.

A substantial uplift to the CAPM result is obviously required to reflect the increased risk of an intellectual capital investment compared to the market as a whole.

Valuation experience suggests an uplift for intellectual capital by some 2.5 times.

However, this level may not always be correct – well protected patents may be lower, speculative e-commerce ventures higher. The uplift is not scientific – it draws upon the knowledge about what those involved expect when lending to businesses at their various stages and about what mature businesses would be expecting to negotiate.

Because the logic of the CAPM is so intuitive and compelling, it has become the standard model taught in virtually every MBA and finance program. The assumptions used to develop the model do not require that a firm be publicly traded; therefore, it can be used as a starting point to estimate the cost of equity even for a privately held firm. However, the only data available for estimating the parameters come from publicly traded companies. As a result, adjustments will need to be made to any available data. This is conceptually similar to the problem with debt in that adjustments must be made to the returns offered by liquid securities to reflect the actual return required by investors in small companies... ... .

... ...Because of extraordinary difficulty in estimating the cost of equity capital for small illiquid businesses, venture capital companies, which specialise in buying and selling small illiquid businesses, will often use a discount rate in the range of 20%–50% for the cost of equity capital. The cost of equity for a small business with several years of history would likely be in the lower end of this range since it would have a much longer history and an established market for its product. However, a history of highly erratic and unpredictable profitability would likely still place the cost of equity for many small businesses at a minimum of 20%. Failure to adjust for a liquidity premium would represent a major flaw in an appraisal report on a company without equity and that is actively traded in the market. This adjustment is obvious, recognized by both academics and professional investors, and widely known.

Hal B Heaton – Professor of Finance,
Brigham Young University, Provo, Utah – January 1998.

For the example: Conclusion 4

We will use 9.8% × 2.5 to reach a **discount rate of 25%.**

Introducing a Valuation Example

Table A – Our Subject Intellectual Capital – Estimate of Potential Total Revenue

YEAR	YEAR	LOCAL SALES £'000	LOCAL REVENUE £'000	EXPORT SALES IN £'000	EXPORT REVENUE £'000	TOTAL SALES IN £'000	TOTAL REVENUE £'000
2002–03	1	2,500	5,000	1,000	27,600	3,500	32,600
2003–04	2	4,000	8,000	2,500	69,000	6,500	77,000
2004–05	3	5,000	10,000	7,000	193,200	12,000	203,200
2005–06	4	7,000	14,000	15,000	414,000	22,000	428,000
2006–07	5	11,000	22,000	23,000	634,800	34,000	656,800
2007–08	6	15,000	30,000	33,000	910,800	48,000	940,800
2008–09	7	18,000	36,000	44,000	1,214,400	62,000	1,250,400
2009–10	8	22,000	44,000	58,000	1,600,800	80,000	1,644,800
2010–11	9	26,000	52,000	73,000	2,014,800	99,000	2,066,800
2011–12	10	32,000	64,000	90,000	2,484,000	122,000	2,548,000
2012–13	11	35,000	70,000	98,000	2,704,800	133,000	2,774,800
2013–14	12	37,000	74,000	105,000	2,898,000	142,000	2,972,000
2014–15	13	40,000	80,000	110,000	3,036,000	150,000	3,116,000
		254,500	509,000	659,500	18,202,200	914,000	18,711,200

Our subject intellectual capital will generate cash flows both in a local market and overseas. It is important that explicit assumptions are quantifiable, stated and permutations are left for scenario analyis, that is by different cash flow models.

For the purposes of the example it is here assumed that the most appropriate method of valuation is the income approach and in these circumstances the best methodology for assessing the value of the intellectual capital is via Discounted Cashflow ("DCF") methodology.

We have conducted our scenario analysis of the likely length of the life of the intellectual capital as a cash-generator as indicated in the previous sections. As such, the value of the forecast cashflows to a given horizon should be discounted back to a value today taking account of the time value of money and risk.

Cashflows – How Much

After estimating potential total revenues, it is necessary to establish the net cashflows to be used and for this we will adopt the Relief from Royalties method. As described on page 170 this method looks at the royalties one would have received if the intellectual capital were to be licensed out to a third party in exchange for an income stream.

The valuer here conducts research into comparable royalty rates in the market place. Although usually unable to find any direct comparables from our database searches, the following licensing agreements exist relating to broadly similar technology in the sector of our subject intellectual capital – in practice one would complete the list in detail.

Licensor	Licensee	Business & Sector	Royalty Fee
Poppy	Wisteria	Describe	5% of Gross Revenues
Penstemon	Narcissus	Describe	6 to 7.25% of Gross Revenues
Lilac	Hydrangea	Describe	8% of New Contract Volume
Clematis	Hosta	Describe	3% of Gross Revenues
Fuchsia	Tulip	Describe	6% of Gross Revenues
Lobelia	Camellia	Describe	2.5% of Gross Revenues
Primula	Lupin	Describe	3% of Gross Revenues
Magnolia	Rose	Describe	6% of Gross Revenues
Iris	Orchid	Describe	4% of Gross Revenues
Canna	Proteas	Describe	5 to 15% of Gross Revenues

Although the above will not be directly comparable with the subject intellectual capital they at least provide a reasonable starting point on which to base our calculations.

For the purposes of this exercise here are excluded from the calculations transactions involving special situations and terms, say for example, the fourth licence between Clematis and Hosta above involved a large up-front payment. An average is then taken of the other deals (taking an average of the range of the two deals involving ranges), which gives a royalty rate of 5.7%, say 6%.

Therefore using cashflows in table B (page 96) and a royalty rate of 6% of the forecast revenue for the period up to 31 March 2015 (Table A above at page 204 illustrates overall forecasts of sales and revenue).

And to arrive at our post-tax cashflows we will adopt the Tax Rate of 30% that is (in this instance) that of the proposed purchaser of our subject intellectual capital.

How the royalty rate, tax rate and discount rate are applied to the total revenue will also be shown in Table B on page 208.

We will apply the discount rate to the cash flow in each year. The discount rate reflects the risk that the cashflows will not be achieved and also the time value of the money.

Valuation of our Example IPR

As table B opposite, a discount rate of 25% applied to the forecast cashflows for the period through to 31 March 2015 implies a value today for those cashflows of £105,836,000, say £105m.

The spreadsheet at Table B below shows the application of the 6% royalty rate, the 30% tax charge and the discount rate together.

This valuation conclusion assumes that when patent protection ends in 2015 all of the income streams fall over a cliff in 2015. That may not be the case because of market share and if, say, the valuation is of a substantial brand, the income streams would endure beyond 2015.

The theoretical answer to this problem was introduced as the second basic step, in addition to the key parameter of overall discount rate determination earlier.

After a discussion about terminal values, the spreadsheet Table C at page 98 illustrates what happens to the valuation if a terminal or horizon calculation is appropriate, that is, to allow for the fact that the subject intellectual capital is long and enduring and acknowledging that one cannot forecast with any sense or certainty after 2015.

Table B

	Year Ended 31–Mar 2003 £'000	Year Ended 31–Mar 2004 £'000	Year Ended 31–Mar 2005 £'000	Year Ended 31–Mar 2006 £'000	Year Ended 31–Mar 2007 £'000	Year Ended 31–Mar 2008 £'000	Year Ended 31–Mar 2009 £'000	Year Ended 31–Mar 2010 £'000	Year Ended 31–Mar 2011 £'000	Year Ended 31–Mar 2012 £'000	Year Ended 31–Mar 2013 £'000	Year Ended 31–Mar 2014 £'000	Year Ended 31–Mar 2015 £'000
Total Revenue as shown in Table A	32,600	77,000	203,200	428,000	656,800	940,800	1,250,400	1,644,800	2,066,800	2,548,000	2,744,800	2,972,000	3,116,000
6% Royalty	1,956	4,620	12,192	25,680	39,408	56,448	75,024	98,688	124,008	152,880	166,688	178,320	186,960
Corporation Tax at 30%	587	1,386	3,658	7,704	11,822	16,934	22,507	29,606	37,202	45,864	50,006	53,496	56,088
Net Post – Tax Income[1]	1,369	3,234	8,534	17,976	27,586	39,514	52,517	69,082	86,806	107,016	116,682	124,824	130,872
Discount period (months)	12	24	36	48	60	72	84	96	108	120	132	144	156
Discount period (years)	1.00	2.00	3.00	4.00	5.00	6.00	7.00	8.00	9.00	10.00	11.00	12.00	13.00
Present value factor[2]	0.8000	0.6400	0.5120	0.4096	0.3277	0.2621	0.2097	0.1678	0.1342	0.1074	0.0859	0.0687	0.0550
Present value of cash flows[3]	1,095	2,070	4,370	7,363	9,039	10,358	11,014	11,590	11,651	11,491	10,023	8,578	7,195
Year	105,836												

Table B

Discount Rate 25.0%

Notes

1. These represent the notional cash flows of the royalty rate less tax.

2. Present value factors $= \dfrac{1}{(1 + r)}$ in the first year

$$= \dfrac{1}{(1 + 0.25)} = 0.8000.$$

3. Calculated by $\dfrac{\text{Cashflow}}{(1 + r)}$ or $\dfrac{1{,}369}{(1 + 0.25)} = \dfrac{1369}{1.25} = £1095.$

The Terminal Value Calculation and Table C

In considering a terminal value after the year ended 31 March 2015, we have used the reciprocal of the discount rate less the long-term growth rate for the intellectual capital, all multiplied by the final operating cashflow in year 5. However, there is some difficulty estimating the long-term growth rate of any business this far into the future. We have used the UK Government long-term inflation forecast of 2.5% as being a conservative estimate. The formula can be stated as follows:

TV = Terminal Value
r   = The cost of equity
g   = The long-term growth rate of the business

A discount rate of 25% applied to the forecast cashflows to year 2015 implies a rounded down value for those cashflows today of some £105m, as Table B page 208.

The same discount rate applied to the year 2015 cashflows into perpetuity and assuming growth of 2.5% implies a rounded down terminal value of some £32m, see Table C opposite.

The total value of the subject IPR based on all projected income streams including an horizon value is therefore £105m (as Table B) + £32m = £137m.

Table C

Discount Rate	25.0%
Growth	2.50%

Perpetuity calculation

Cash flow terminal year	130,872
+ growth (1 + g)	134,144
Cap rate (r – g)	0.225
Terminal year value	596,195
Discount period (months)	156
Discount period (years)	13.00
Present value factor	0.054

Present value of terminal **Year cash flow (b)**	**32,776** (rounded down 32m)
Total value (a) + (b)	**137m**

Table C

	Year Ended 31–Mar 2003 £'000	Year Ended 31–Mar 2004 £'000	Year Ended 31–Mar 2005 £'000	Year Ended 31–Mar 2006 £'000	Year Ended 31–Mar 2007 £'000	Year Ended 31–Mar 2008 £'000	Year Ended 31–Mar 2009 £'000	Year Ended 31–Mar 2010 £'000	Year Ended 31–Mar 2011 £'000	Year Ended 31–Mar 2012 £'000	Year Ended 31–Mar 2013 £'000	Year Ended 31–Mar 2014 £'000	Year Ended 31–Mar 2015 £'000
Total Revenue as shown in Table A	32,600	77,000	203,200	428,000	656,800	940,800	1,250,400	1,644,800	2,066,800	2,548,000	2,744,800	2,972,000	3,116,000
6% Royalty	1,956	4,620	12,192	25,680	39,408	56,448	75,024	98,688	124,008	152,880	166,688	178,320	186,960
Corporation Tax at 30%	587	1,386	3,658	7,704	11,822	16,934	22,507	29,606	37,202	45,864	50,006	53,496	56,088
Net Post – Tax Income	1,369	3,234	8,534	17,976	27,586	39,514	52,517	69,082	86,806	107,016	116,682	124,824	130,872
Discount period (months)	12	24	36	48	60	72	84	96	108	120	132	144	156
Discount period (years)	1.00	2.00	3.00	4.00	5.00	6.00	7.00	8.00	9.00	10.00	11.00	12.00	13.00
Present value factor	0.8000	0.6400	0.5120	0.4096	0.3277	0.2621	0.2097	0.1678	0.1342	0.1074	0.0859	0.0687	0.0550
Present value of cash flows	1,095	2,070	4,370	7,363	9,039	10,358	11,014	11,590	11,651	11,491	10,023	8,578	7,195

Total (a) 105,836 (Rounded down 105m)

Introducing Debt

Estimating k_d – the Cost of Debt

In many situations the valuer cannot ignore the element of debt, in addition to equity, in the business structure. As has been seen in the previous pages, the cost of equity was adjusted upwards significantly to take account of the risk of the venture in the discount rate. The cost of debt must also be calculated in order to ensure there is not *additional* risk to be factored in – in other words to check that the cost of debt does not raise the weighted average cost of capital.

The Cost of Debt is the return that debt holders require for bearing the debt's risk.

*   The cost of debt generally increases with financial leverage (i.e. as the proportion of debt: equity increases).

*   Therefore, a change in the target capital structure will change the cost of debt.

*   Where interest on debt is tax-deductible, the rate of return that a business must earn on debt-financed instruments is the after-tax cost of debt.

Thus, where t = the tax rate and I is the interest rate:

$$K_d - (K_d \times t) = K_d \times (I–t)$$

There are several other ways to Estimate K_d

1. Find similar debt instruments that have known yields.

2. Find similar businesses and use their bond rating to estimate K_d.

3. A good peer group should have similar operations and debt structures (short term v long term, duration etc).

4. Create a synthetic bond rating for the firm, identify yields on bonds of similar rating and duration and use that yield as the cost of debt.

5. If similar instruments are not available, divide interest expense by the book value of debt to estimate the cost of debt.

Additional Information Needed

Calculating the yield to maturity of private debt requires additional information:

* Individual debt securities are valued on the basis of cash flows and risk.

* Cash flows consist of periodic coupon payments and the repayment of the principal (face value) at maturity.

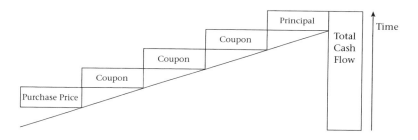

* Risk is reflected in the interest rate used to discount these cash flows

* The greater the risk, the higher the investors' required rate of return

* For debt instruments this discount rate is used to calculate the Yield to Maturity (YTM)

Thus the way to calculate the cost of debt depends on the available information.

If the firm's capital structure is not expected to change and you know the yields and market values of the relevant debt instruments, use the average Yield to Maturity of those instruments as the cost of debt. This is particularly appropriate for large companies as the bond market may play a role in finding them. This can be done in two steps:

1. Find or calculate the current Yield to Maturity for each instrument.

2. Use the market value of each instrument to weight each instrument's yield and produce an average.

A simple example of calculating the cost of debt

*   Say the business structure you are appraising as a potential purchaser of the intellectual capital, has three debt instruments

*   The cost of debt is the weighted average yield to maturity of those three instruments

Instruments	% of Total Debt	Yield to Maturity	% x Yield
Instrument 1	25	12.0	3.00
Instrument 2	40	8.5	3.40
Instrument 3	35	7.3	2.55
	100		8.95

The cost of debt in this example is therefore 8.95%

Information

For public debt instruments for use in valuations for large corporations or organisations the Yield to Maturity (YTM) can be found from market data

*   Bond prices are quoted in the financial press.

*   The YTM can be calculated as the interest rate that equates to the present value of a bond's cash flows to its current market value.

*   Whenever a bond's market value is less than its face value (i.e. the YTM is greater than the coupon rate) the bond is said to be issued at a discount.

- Whenever a bond's market value is greater than its face value (i.e. the YTM is less than the coupon rate) the bond is said to be issued at a premium.

Caveats

- Information about instruments may not be available

- The target capital structure may change rendering information about past or current debt instruments irrelevant

- For smaller companies or projects, using bank base rates may be more appropriate

The YTM is affected by several risks which may need to be taken into account for businesses with higher debt:

- *Interest rate risk:* The risk that interest rates will increase, decreasing the present value of a bond's future cash flows.

- *Inflation risk:* The risk that inflation will increase, decreasing the present value of a bond's further cash flows.

- *Default risk:* The risk that the bond issuer will default on payments of coupons or principal.

- *Liquidity risk:* The risk that debt holders will not be able to liquidate their investment in a timely manner.

Returning to the Example

Returning to our working example, having ascertained the cost of equity, we consider the cost of debt. In the light of the fact that UK Bank Base Rate is of the order of 4% at the valuation date we suggest that the appropriate uplift to this figure would be one of 3%, giving an overall cost of borrowing in the order of 7%.

However, payment of interest can be set off against tax. Therefore, after Corporation Tax at 30%, the effective rate is reduced to 7% × 0.70 = 4.9%.

Accepting a target structure of 70% equity and 30% debt, and the already calculated CAPM cost of equity capital of 9.8%, we arrive at a weighted average cost of capital with debt of 8.33% as follows:

$(0.7 \times 9.8) + (0.3 \times 4.9\%) = 8.33\%$, say 9%

As referred to in the debt free calculation in respect of the cost of equity (the 9.8%), in the light of the difference between this business and those that comprise the quoted sector and in view of the relative immaturity of our subject IPR, we must adjust this cost of capital significantly upwards.

In the light of the small difference between the non-debt result and this debt introduced result, we would therefore again adopt a cost of capital of 25% for this intellectual capital as at page 203.

Needless to say, calculations are rarely this convenient and straightforward and it might be that a debt-laden company has a markedly different WACC to which to apply the risk multiplier.

Exploitation of Intellectual Capital and Licensing

In this section, we examine the implications of the high cost of capital for a major tool of exploitation of intellectual capital, namely – the licence.

For both licensor and licencee, we ask:

"Is the licensing model still attractive?"

before moving onto calculating royalty rates and structuring deals.

"Is the licensing model still attractive to investors? We answer in the affirmative – just because the market is no longer as bullish as it was two or three years ago, it does not mean the benefits we have articulated previously cease to apply. These include:

- recurring (often multiple) long term revenue streams;
- high gross margins;
- high scalability of the business;
- low sales and marketing costs typically;
- low capital intensity/manufacturing overheads;
- rapid growth as the licensee ramps up production volumes;
- high cash generation; and
- high barriers to entry due to patent position.

We believe that the recent market has exposed some of the downsides of the model, namely;

- lack of control over the licensees' strategy;
- lack of revenue predictability; and
- vulnerability to product launch delays.

Despite this, we continue to support the IP model and believe the benefits of licensing will resurface when corporate buying-power returns. Ultimately, the model allows technology acquirers to bring new technologies into their product development programmes without the need to invest heavily in R&D themselves – often a risky process. Through licensing, these companies can control their exposure to technology risk to a greater degree while still having access to innovations that can drive their next product cycle.

The licensing companies have responded to the new market environment by adapting their model. Some have restructured their licensing agreements, for example by reducing the up-front commitment in return for a higher back-end royalty rate. Some licensing deals may involve an element of the licensee's equity instead of cash, or there may be cross-licensing to mutual benefit.

In addition, the IP companies have understood the need to become much closer to key licensees."

Source: CSFB August 2002

The key to successful intellectual capital exploitation is often licensing, joint ventures or strategic alliances. The adoption of a "no license" strategy is often done by default. While a conscious no license decision affirms control, it is sometimes a strategic decision to shelve the intellectual capital to hide it from the marketplace.

Reasons for "licensing in" technology

- Speedy market penetration

- Reducing reliance on in-house R&D

- Access another's synergistic intellectual capital

- Specialist R&D companies are often more innovative and efficient than larger manufacturing/distribution companies

- Reduces product development time and costs

- Cost of acquiring technology my not have to be incurred until revenues commence

- To acquire intellectual capital useful to competitors

Reasons for "licensing out" technology

- Reducing the licensors' risks

- Specialist R&D companies can concentrate on what they do best and use others for manufacturing and distribution

- The technology may not be of strategic importance for licensor but may be for licensee or can be licensed for use in a sector which does not compete with "core" activities

- Freeing up existing production, marketing and distribution facilities can reduce costs

- Market extension: Licensing is an effective method of entering foreign markets

- Licensing can accelerate cash flow and/or profits.

The successful exploitation of intellectual capital requires the employment of additional, often substantial, resources. In broad terms, the exploitation of intellectual property can be either direct or indirect.

Direct exploitation

Direct exploitation involves the intellectual property employed by its inventor or developer, with the business or individual retaining all the various rights. This option is adopted for one of a number of reasons. These would typically include:

- the view that the intellectual capital was in the mainstream of the enterprise's activities;

- the availability of the necessary resources to exploit it successfully; or

- the fact that the potential royalties might not be economically worthwhile.

A typical example of direct exploitation would be a pharmaceutical company developing a drug in-house and then exploiting it and reaping the benefits from the marketing and sale of that drug.

Indirect exploitation

Indirect exploitation, by contrast, involves the owner transferring all or part of the bundle of rights, in return for some share of the returns. Indirect exploitation typically involves one or other of the following: outright sale, licensing, joint ventures or franchising.

Outright sale is the simplest method of indirect exploitation, where the owner, in exchange for some form of consideration, transfers all interest in, or at least control of, the intellectual capital. The consideration can be structured in a number of ways, including a one-off payment, or deferred or contingent payments.

Licensing involves a licensor, the owner of the intellectual capital, or intellectual property right, availing another, the licensee, of some form of permission to utilise one or more associated rights with the asset which the licensee would not otherwise have access to, in exchange for some form of consideration.

Key issues in this area include:

• the amount of the potential income (for both licensor and licensee) to be derived from the arrangement;

• the duration of that income;

• the risk of the anticipated benefits not being achieved;

• together with the costs of achieving the potential payments.

Valuation of Intellectual Capital in Licensing

Value may vary according to whether the form of license granted is exclusive, or non-exclusive. Many licensing deals can involve a myriad of rights in different countries or territories. This leads to a situation where a single royalty rate can be agreed for the whole package, without regard to the individual economics of particular aspects of the deal. This is a relatively delicate area in view of the continuing tension between the concepts of protection for intellectual property and the advantages of free competition. Competition law in general is suspicious of such blanket arrangements, although this is changing.

A trend can be identified whereby the courts and enforcement authorities are coming to recognise that even from the licensee's perspective it can be beneficial to have an easily understood and relatively straightforward method of calculation royalty payments.

Notwithstanding this trend it is desirable to analyse and appraise each facet of an intellectual property licensing package. For example, if a license comprises rights to utilise patented technology, know-how and trade marks, a diminishing royalty for the IPR could be argued to be appropriate, say as a patent's life terminates.

Often, although the intellectual capital such as patents or trademarks may be the basis of the exploited technology, the key elements in ensuring the commercial economic returns may in fact be derived from know-how and show-how.

As licensors or licensees, executives and fiscal authorities have become more aware of the nuances of licensing economics and the importance of royalty rates, thorough evaluation of each aspect of a licensing package becomes more and more necessary.

The Importance of Quantifying Royalties

Royalty payments generally represent consideration or compensation for allowing the use of an asset, or collection of assets by another party. In theoretical terms the amount of the royalty paid for using any aspect of intellectual capital should be equal to a fair rate of return on the value of the intellectual capital that is being used.

A royalty rate that represents a rate of return below a fair rate of return is poor intellectual capital management of what might be an important corporate asset. Conversely, it can also be argued that a required royalty rate providing for a higher rate of return than a fair return will tend to discourage potential licensees and again reflects poor management.

Intellectual capital is usually utilised as part of a business enterprise, where the intellectual capital, tangible assets, such as plant and machinery and working capital are together utilised to achieve a return on the sum total of those assets. Intellectual property and intangible asset valuation theory suggests that the global return can be allocated or apportioned between the various assets that constitute the business. This then provides a basis for calculating the element of the return that can be attributed to the intangible assets or intellectual property.

This in turn then provides the starting point for the quantification of the appropriate royalty rate.

The process of allocating economic returns to specific items of intellectual capital has to address both the degree of importance of the particular asset to the achievement of the overall returns, and the required rate of return. This latter factor has to allow for a range of considerations including economic life, risk and return and the particular details of the intellectual property or capital asset under consideration – including an assessment of the strength and weaknesses of that asset, from both a legal and an economic point of view.

The recognition of the importance of accurate quantification of royalty rates and the like is a relatively recent phenomenon. The old pricing methods of, for instance, the 25% rule, industry norms, return on R&D costs, or return on sales are at best inadequate, and at worst, dangerous.

This is not least the case where tax authorities become involved. Structuring licences for tax optimisation is big business: low tax versus high tax jurisdiction, location of R&D deductions, tax savings from intellectual capital profits, treatment of disposals for gains taxes, withholding taxes, controlled foreign company legislation and inter-group licensing etc.

> ### *Transfer pricing*
>
> Transfer pricing as an issue is growing in importance and the following sets out by way of a general illustration, the basic steps that should be followed in a transfer pricing valuation:
>
> - Identification, including a strategic and technological assessment, of the intellectual capital transferred.
>
> - Projection of an incremental stream of revenue, cost savings, net income or net cashflow associated with the use, ownership or license of the intellectual capital, based upon (among other things) a technology valuation and micro economic analysis.
>
> - Quantification of the remaining useful life and decay rate associated with the use of the intellectual capital, and
>
> - Quantification of the amount of value of the appropriate inter-company transfer price (or royalty rate) as the product of the fair market value of the intellectual capital multiplied by the fair return on investment for such an asset.

Royalty Rate Calculations

Much of what has been said in the intellectual capital valuation section of this book is relevant in the calculation of the appropriate rate of return in royalty rate calculations and again we can utilise a number of the same methodologies including the Capital Asset Pricing Model (see page 192), Factor Build-up, Arbitrage Pricing Theory, or Venture Capital models depending on the particular circumstances as well as the preference and judgement of the valuer. If carried out thoroughly and conscientiously each of these models should produce acceptable and defendable results.

In practice a rate is estimated by reference to some or all of the following:

- existing licences for the intellectual capital (the *comparables approach*),

- industry norms for licenses for similar inventions (the *market approach*),

- allocation of economic benefits derived from the use of say the patented invention (sometimes referred to as the *available profits* or *analytical approach*) and

- licensing practice (*rule of thumb approach* or the 25% rule).

A licensor's established practice: the Comparables Approach

In litigation on intellectual capital the courts will examine carefully royalty rates established by the licensor in previous licence agreements. The licences previously negotiated have to be similar to the licences suggested for the subject intellectual capital.

This approach (see also Deal Structure below) examines specifics such as:

- How other licences were negotiated
- The intellectual capital and support required to maintain it
- The length of the agreement
- Exclusivity
- Special terms for special deals
- Geography
- The sector in which the intellectual capital is licensed
- Special relationships

Even if previous licensing practice is comparable, it can only provide a benchmark. Intellectual capital by its nature is unique and it is often a thankless task making numerous and required adjustments to allow a fair comparison.

Industry Norms and Rules of Thumb

Many industries have built up a folklore of average royalty rates. This information is accessed by valuers from sector analysis, experience and essentially from the valuer's own proprietary database. That database of information needs to summarise main terms and conditions, lump sums and rates in order that valid comparative data can be withdrawn. This information is an essential tool for relief from royalty calculations see page 170 above. It is usual to search for:

- Obvious comparables in the same or very closely related sectors.

- In the US, the establishment of a Delaware Holding company (a company set up for tax effective exploitation of intellectual capital) and inter-company rates disclosed and other public domain knowledge.

- Close comparables from transactions in respect of closely related intellectual capital.

- Transactions of different intellectual capital (typically a brand), but licensing in the same sector eg. clothing or food.

Market practice may not be representative of the circumstances of your appraisal because:

- Royalty information regarding similar intellectual capital is very rare. Seldom can a reasonable comparison be found and still more seldom is third party royalty rate information available.

- The licensor would not have granted a licence to just anybody the licence may not be typical.

- Special licensees and related party transactions may have an effect.

- The adjustments required to compare a substantial running royalty rate for an exclusive licence will be worthless in evaluating a non-exclusive license on different, but related technology (for example, 2% running royalty on technology that can be effectively designed around is equally misleading in setting a value on, say, leading edge intellectual capital *critical* to the competitor).

- The IPR may be important for only part of a product (a royalty based on the sales price of a product may demand a very low royalty rate and a royalty rate based on the sales price of the fraction of the product needs to be much higher).

- Information about rates that are available may reflect specific licensing clauses that affect the royalty rate that was negotiated. The effect of licence agreement clauses on the negotiated royalty may be appropriate for the conditions under which the rights are being licensed, but may correlate poorly with the conditions associated with outright ownership.

- Many rates have been negotiated by legal experts without consideration for business risk and investment rates return.

- Industry rates were often established years ago and reflected economic conditions, business risks, and investment rates of return that are no longer appropriate. Any mistakes made by the initial setting of an industry royalty are passed along.

With successive licences, the first to licence often has the advantage of a lower royalty rate. As more competitors sign up, a licensor's negotiation often and naturally gets tougher. Accordingly past licences of the same intellectual capital must be read in the context of the circumstances under which former licences were entered. As the number of licences at the same rate rises, the true value of the intellectual capital involved becomes more evident. A single prior licence or even two can be of little use. If prior rates seem to be too high one would look for evidence that prior licences were negotiated with an element of coercion, collusion or additional consideration in the form of trade secrets, technical assistance or licensees help if the prior rates are too low one would look for evidence of a less mature market, more risk or untested intellectual capital.

The role of industry averages

Even though industry averages are suspect as a royalty rate it is an essential exercise in any determination: Martin S Landis in his article 'Pricing and Presentation Licensed Technology' *Journal of Proprietary Rights,* August 1991, put forward a range of 8–15%. Figures typically are based on a *net sales price royalty base* and a *non-exclusive licence.*

A 20%–50% premium has been discussed as a reasonable average for *exclusivity of licence* (Finnegan and Mintz 'The Determination of Reasonable Royalty', *The law of IPR and 'Know How Licensing,* 1975) and as much as 300% premium for exclusivity has been reported in the pharmaceutical field Edward McKie Jr 'Pricing and Packaging Technology', in *Domestic and Foreign Technology Licensing* 1984.

For tax purposes the paramount principle in the case of transfer pricing and other issues between associated enterprises is that proposed intellectual capital transactions are deemed to have been calculated on an arm's length basis. Arm's length pricing for intellectual capital must take into account the perspective of both the transferring organisation of the rights and the receiving organisation. From the perspective of the licensee, a comparable independent enterprise may or may not have been prepared to pay this price depending on the value and usefulness of the intellectual capital to the receiving organisation in its business.

Thus a licensor and potential licensee sitting down to negotiate a licence of intellectual property right, if well advised, would normally complete two tasks:

1. They must identify the range of exclusivity defined by the intellectual capital; and

2. They must assign to that exclusivity an economic value limit. A licensor views his economic limit as the least amount he would be willing to accept for sharing with a licensee the exclusivity or degree of exclusivity, afforded by the intellectual capital. A licensee meanwhile would view her economic limit as the most

she would be willing to pay for access to the intellectual capital led technology, brand etc.

Assuming the owner and the licensee both calculate into their respective values an overlap area for negotiation a deal is possible. In the real world there can only be agreement if the calculated value overlaps with the licensee's calculated value, or a licensee is not well advised himself, and/or he does not undertake the analysis (horrifyingly common).

In summary: mostly because transactions of interest are confidential, this market approach rarely provides an effective substitute for analytical methods of evaluation described below.

Available Profits Approach (referred to as the analytical approach in the US)

A method particularly described by Henderson Garret & Dunner – J M Romary and also in *Application of Business Economics to the Licensing Decision* Stephen Willis 1987:

The Licensor Perspective

For the licensor there are many ways to determine the minimum he or she is prepared to accept. However a simple profit analysis method often works best remembering that this is an area with no mathematical certainty and nothing is precise. Simple examples of this approach follow:

*   In a growing market where the licensor has established a market share which would not be at risk by the entry of a competitor, his £X value will be determined by estimating the expected future incremental profit increase for the licensor both with and without exclusivity. That differential, discounted to present day value, represents the available incremental profit should exclusivity be lost. The licensor's analysis will also include the investment value of capital required to achieve the expected incremental profit increase. The investment value is the return-on-capital income that could be derived from the investment capital required from other business activities, say for expansion.

    If the investment value is greater than the expected incremental profit there is no objective profit motive to justify further expansion by the licensor. In the absence of subjective motivation, the licensor would seem better off to accept the income for the investment value of the required capital and forego expansion into the market. Objectively the value of his £X would fall to zero.

If the expected incremental profit is greater than the investment value, the difference is the £X value. The licensor must obtain at least this differential, the £X value, to justify abandonment of the market that requires the intellectual capital exclusively.

- In a mature market where there is little opportunity for increased market share or volume, the £X value should reflect any loss of established market share in the event that exclusivity is abandoned by the licensor. The simplest way to value this loss is to multiply estimated lost sales by profit per sale for each year covered by the intellectual capital and then discount those results to net present value. This number is then used as the licensor's £X value. Again if the licensor cannot secure at least £X value for a license, there is no objective reason to abandon market exclusivity.

When analysing either a growing or maturing market, the licensor should estimate the total incremental revenue expected to be affected by the loss of exclusivity. This analysis is akin to the analysis undertaken to determine whether to enter a market segment in the first place. The cost of entry is compared with the expected benefit. Also when analysing the marketplace the licensor would also factor in the effect of derivative sales. In the US there is also the expression "convoyed sales"; in Europe we often call these "extensions", which may be a significant factor, for example say, a sale of an item of haute couture can be expected to convoy or extend the sales of other luxury items (watches, leather goods etc) which could multiply any original profit calculations.

Calculations should be undertaken in respect of any additional production facilities needed in the absence of competition from a licensee, the cost of the increased marketing and sales force required to handle increased volume and the risk involved in any market expansion of the type contemplated in the absence of competition. In a mature market the licensor needs to consider the reduction in cost of production facilities, the reduced cost of marketing and sales force and the risk involved in anticipating market dilution.

Ideally these initial calculations set a ballpark of the value of exclusivity to the licensor. Ranges of value are produced in global terms not pretending to be scientifically accurate. Once a "ballpark" number for the net present value of market exclusivity is arrived at by the lost-profit analysis, secondary factors might be considered such as any dilution of goodwill should a competitor be allowed to enter an exclusive marketplace and the increase of supply anticipated by additional competition from the licensee which borders on a price erosion effect on the sales maintained by the licensor.

A final consideration could be that the product is not firmly established in the marketplace and there are risks of introducing a second source for that product. These costs can be significantly reduced if licensing takes place early in the development of a product as the licensees seek to maximise their investment by early participation. Other benefits to the licensor include the economic feasibility of entry into foreign markets, access to better technology through cross licensing and the ability to satisfy market demand without undesired costly expansion.

This process suggests a best guess of present market value for exclusivity. A guess which normally forms the cornerstone of the licensing process for it represents a first justification for the setting of the minimum value the licensor could accept for granting a licence.

The Licensee Perspective

If the licensee's analysis mirrors that of the licensor, the value to a competitor of entering the market covered by the intellectual capital should be exactly the same as the value for the licensor to expand the market itself. In this case no agreement to licence would be reached. In the real world factors affecting licensor and licensee differ because of factors such as manufacturing facilities with lower production costs, more efficient or better developed marketing and sales structure, access to a larger or different client base, better name recognition or lower profit expectations. In practice both parties seek to arrive at a value which is the maximum present market value to the licensee for the access to the licensor's exclusivity.

This value determination would include consideration of the licensee's incremental capital investment value, so too should this value take into account his alternatives. The first to consider is the investment value return on capital for the licensee.

The licensee will consider factors for non-infringing and potentially infringing substitutes include additional research and development, additional capital and plant, lost profits from any delay in the transaction, lost or gained profits as the result of marketing an alternative product, and higher manufacturing costs. The differential between the value of the licensee's net return and the value of his access to the licensor's exclusive market niches yields the value to the licensee.

These value positions will usually have been researched over many years often before negotiations take place. If the licensee's value exceeds the licensor's value you have room to negotiate.

The clauses in the final agreement need to be in place to relate to infringement, to balance protection issues for the licensor and the licensee. For example, joint action on infringement or the right of action for a licensee if a licensor refuses to act. Who pays for the actions will often be covered, and whether there is adjustment to royalties for enforcement cost. See further, page 232.

In franchise agreements a variety of intellectual capital is licensed under very strict controls, supervision sources and supplies are dictated, and geographical boundaries are rigorously defined.

A licensee may encounter important additional factors. If already in the market he may face the risk that the licensor may prevent all further activity of the licensee in the event of non-agreement for example because of infringement of intellectual property rights, with a corresponding loss of investment to the licensee. Needless to say there is also the risk of court imposed damages for any infringement. These factors may significantly increase the value to the licensee and greatly enhance the negotiating position of a licensor.

At this point in the calculations there are four different values:

- two minimum values the licensor would accept – one calculated by the licensor and the other by the licensee; and

- two maximum values the licensee would accept – one calculated by the licensee and the other by the licensor.

Assuming both parties calculate into their respective values an overlap negotiating position and any relevant factor such as the enforceability of the intellectual capital in court (and a likelihood of successful enforcement) an agreement can be contemplated.

Cost calculations that need to be taken into account include legal fees and disruption of business opportunity in the marketplace etc. The cost of enforcement may widen the overlap position or create one that obviously did not exist. However there can be agreement only if the licensor's calculated values overlap with the licensee's calculated values.

Royalty Rate Rules of Thumb and the 5% and 25% Folklore

Over the years a fiction has developed that, in general, a competitor should be willing to pay between 23% and 33% of the gross profit margin before taxes expected to be returned under licence. This is a rule of thumb method to allocate incremental profits between parties in those situations where the licensor has no presence in the market to be licensed. However, overall it is often not really even useful as a general guide upon which to begin calculations. Too many important factors cannot be reconciled. It may be used as a benchmark to compare a royalty rate arrived at from economic mathematical modelling.

This rule of thumb method allocates incremental profits between parties. The rough allocation of profits reflects the relative risks borne by the parties. The licensor has taken the R & D risk to develop the intellectual capital, the licensee takes on the risk of marketing the intellectual capital. The profit figure on which this rule is based should include identified savings to the competitor. Therefore this process resembles the methodology employed to determine the maximum present market value to a competitor for access to the licensor's niche of exclusivity (the same value position as in the licensor in the Available Profits Approach, above). However the licensee's value is based on the incremental difference between expected profit and alternatives and should take into account derivative sales. This rule is applied to the expected gross profit, regardless of alternatives.

In practice the parties must either agree that each year say 25% of the gross profit is turned over to the licensee or they agree on a value of the expected gross profit over the life of the intellectual capital and convert that amount into a running royalty. Neither is feasible in the real world. Few with prudence and disposition would allow a licensor sufficient access to its books and records on an annual basis to calculate gross profit even assuming agreement could be reached as to how gross profit is to be calculated. In addition, as projections are made into the future, expected gross profits can be totally illusory. It is one thing to project one's own business into the future and quite another to reach agreement in arm's length negotiations. The rule almost always fails to take into account the final profitability that is ultimately realised with the licensed rights.

Moreover this range is not necessarily a fair division of profit. In the well known US case concerning Bausch & Lomb the IRS (the US tax authority) held that 50–50 was a fair split in a super royalty analysis under Section 482 of the Internal Revenue Code. Further, it could be argued that the range should be on the one hand moved higher to benefit a licensee for new untested intellectual capital where there is real risk or alternatively lower the benefit to a licensee if the product has been fully developed and the market mature.

Gross profit can never be accurately defined. Based upon generally accepted accounting principles the definition includes the direct costs of production (labour, raw materials). Absent are selling, administration and general overhead expenses. Two products may cost the same amount to produce and yield the same amount of gross profit. Yet one of the products may require extensive and continuing sales support while the other does not. The added cost of this extensive and continuing sales effort make the first product less profitable to licence. While the two products may have the same gross profit it is very unlikely that they will command the same royalty.

There is an even cruder rule of thumb: a standard 5% of sales which has several primary weaknesses. The first is the proper allocation of the profits between a licensor and licensee. A precise and quantifiable method for dividing the net profits is rarely specified when this royalty rate methodology is described. Another area of weakness is the lack of consideration for the value of the intellectual capital that is invested in the enterprise as well as a lack of consideration for the value of the complimentary monetary and tangible assets that are invested. The method also fails to consider the relative investment risk associate with the intellectual capital.

Clues from Case Law as to a Reasonable Royalty

It is clear from US case law for example *General Tire* v *Firestone*, 1976; *Allen & Hanbury (Salbutomol)* 1987 and *Gerber Garment Technologies* v

Lectra Systems Limited 1995, that in assessing a reasonable royalty, the specific characteristics of the intellectual capital, the parties and the nature and impact of infringement require careful scrutiny.

Generally there is no definitive list of the factors to consider and the US contrasts with the UK where case law provides little if any guidance. Key factors to consider include:

- Exclusivity.

- The proportion of the marketable product attributable to the intellectual capital.

- The relative risks borne by licensor and licensee. (Bear in mind restrictions on certain types of licensed payments. It can be an abuse of a dominant position in the EU, achieved through ownership of intellectual capital, to charge excessive royalties on the intellectual capital i.e. competition law restrictions. This is a topic beyond the scope of this book.)

- The impact on the licensor's business.

- The rate of technological change within the industry and the state of development of the market.

- The cost of inventing or developing the intellectual capital (bear in mind that the *amount spent* for example in R&D is rarely equal to the *value* of a property and development *costs* rarely reflect future economic benefits and a *fair return*).

- Investment rates of return available from alternative forms of investment assessing comparable elements of risk.

- The commercial relationship between the parties and the time frame of the agreement.

- How the parties may structure a 'deal'.

- The effect on the licensee's sales of related products and services.

- Legislative changes.

The Cost Approach and Royalty Rates

It is perhaps worthwhile to mention the cost approach (meaning that the aim is to at least recoup the cost to create the IPR through a royalty stream) because it is one of the methodologies constantly referred to, although again invariably totally misleading. As laboured earlier in the valuation section, there is no basis to believe that the cost for the research and development of intellectual capital bears any correlation to future profit and value of the technology to a licensee. For example the *Gilbert Hyatt* example where his undisclosed licensing fees for the microchip invention, following negotiations with Motorola, no doubt far outweighed his costs. Equally the opposite may be true: recall the development of a nuclear powered aircraft in the US supported by a multi-million dollar R&D expense (see page XX). The plane never got into the air and was effectively worthless. The cost approach also ignores the skill of the inventor and assumes that the same technology, not the next best alternative, could have been recreated by the licensee.

There are numerous objections to the cost approach, and an ultimately successful technology should probably reflect the cost of past failures (particularly true in sectors where R&D costs for intellectual capital failures may run at more than 5 times the cost for R&D successes). Nevertheless time and time again one finds cost analysis in negotiations in setting a proposed licence royalty rate.

General Business Profile Approach

Closely associated with the standard cost approach above, is another, particularly described as the "general business profile approach" by Joseph Andonian (New Method to Determine Royalty Rates, *Les Nouveles* (1991) and Finnegan, Henderson, Faraborow, Garrett & Dunner (1995)) as follows.

The idea is to rely on the general knowledge of those in business and to cover the lost R&D spent to produce the intellectual capital that would otherwise have been available for other projects.

Costs are established as a percentage of sales for the total business. Following Andonian's example, production costs for a whole business may equal 30% of total sales revenue, marketing costs 20%, administrative costs 13% and distribution costs 7%, and ongoing R&D effort for the overall business is budgeted at 15% of expected sales, in total 85% leaving 15% of expected sales for earnings before taxes. The important figure is the 15% ongoing R&D costs. For the licensor to maintain this level of R&D in the face of sales lost to the competitor any licence would need to cover the licensor's R&D figure. Given this example the royalty rate would need to be 15% of the licensee's sales. It has been argued that this approach takes too much account of the costs associated with failures. If intellectual capital being licensed is only partially developed then a percentage of R&D costs can be allocated i.e. if only one-third developed any R&D factor would be reduced by one-third to a figure equalling 5% of sales.

Andonian concluded that the general business profile approach is probably the most appropriate in those circumstances where:

- The ultimate commercial outcome of the technology cannot be predicted accurately enough to justify using an income approach.

- There are insufficient examples of royalties as a proportion of selling prices for comparable technology in an efficient marketplace.

- Specific cost figures for replacement or reproduction are not accurately ascertainable.

The approach can be used in conjunction with the other approaches to provide greater support for any position a party wants to take in negotiations for a royalty rate.

In many ways the fundamental flaws are the same as for the cost approach. It is virtually impossible for an outsider to ascertain what intellectual capital has cost to produce. It is all too often possible to overpay for something and even if it were possible to determine underlying costs it would be impractical to use that information in any decision making process because, for the most part, it is irrelevant.

An Example of the General Business Profile Approach

Focuses on an overall general cost – success or failure – of discovering and developing the general type of technology under consideration:

Sales	100%
Costs:	
Production Costs	30%
Marketing Costs	20%
Administration & Misc	13%
Distribution	7%
R&D	15%
Total Costs	85%
Earnings Before Tax	15%

Notes:

(i)   Not the same as the cost approach which focuses on specific costs.

(ii) This basic calculation is to determine what royalty % will permit a company to maintain earnings expectations. The answer is given in the paragraphs above.

(iii) Not the same as the market approach which relies on the royalties being paid in other licence agreements.

Deal Structures

It is vital that lawyers and those negotiating keep the valuer appraised so that advice can be given on the highest or lowest defendable rate at any given time, particularly during the course of discussions. They will introduce and discuss many combinations and obligations, all of which will have a bearing on the calculation of economic value to each position and hence royalty rate. There may be fixed sums, maximum and minimum sums and percentages (in advance or in arrears). A licensor may provide maintenance for the intellectual capital, standards of quality and manuals. Specific licensee activity, minimum sales and advertising spend terms are not unusual.

Structuring the deal will thus have an important impact on the royalty rate agreed upon and there are various possible forms of agreement:

- *Lump sums* or running royalties may be agreed as a percentage of a licensee's gross income from the intellectual capital.

- A *gross sales* and *turnover base* (i.e. actual money received for sales) introduces less room for argument.

- Many licences and licensing agreements use a *royalty base* of net sales. It should be an easy measurement to verify and it adjusts automatically for inflation. Its disadvantages include the difficulty in isolating the amount of net sales specifically relating to the intellectual capital.

- A *running royalty* could be agreed, for example at 5% royalty on a product whose sale price is £1,000 and represents a £50 royalty payment for each license sale.

- Royalty rates may vary according to *volume*.

- Instead of net sales another frequently used base is *units of production* and a *unit royalty* for each item sold. These are again easy to compute and easily verifiable. However the method does not adjust for inflation.

- A licensor may agree to a less desirable royalty rate in return for guarantee minimum annual royalties or a higher royalty rate with a maximum value of royalty to be paid each year (particularly effective when a licensee insists that a lower royalty is justifiable because of a high expectation of sales).

- Use of up-front payments in combination with a running royalty rate is not uncommon and the upfront payment can, say, equal the cost of the intellectual capital being licensed or a recoupment of administrative costs of negotiating and executing any licence.

- Variable rates may be adopted that will lower rates as sales increase, thus incentivising a licensee, or a low rate may be set for an initial period to assist in a new or difficult market

In any chosen route, there is VAT and other taxes, transport, insurance, returns, commission and possibly sub-licensees' fees to consider and define.

When all is done the royalty rate is multiplied by the selected base over the estimated life to calculate the total royalty savings. This amount represents the benefit that would accrue to the licensee as a deductible business expense and for this reason the calculation should be made on an after-tax basis. The calculated amount is discounted to its present value using an appropriate discount rate. To determine this discount rate, the time value of money, the inherent business risk and the fact that these payments have been calculated on an after-tax basis should all be considered.

When considering deal structures one must consider the tax treatment of lump sums, immediate and deferred, as against ongoing royalties and if necessary remember currency risks in an international deal.

Licensees and licensors will be subject to provisions for breach of the licence terms. That risk should be factored into any scenario analysis over the agreement term, and may affect economic returns. In an extreme case, a licensee may cease paying royalties or a licensor may have rights to outstanding royalties.

The valuer must cost a deal out over the life of the agreement. Do not use simplistic industry norms, previous licensing practice or someone else's practice as to what is acceptable as a royalty level. Calculate the ratio of sales to profit over the life of licence. It is important to remember that although a flat rate may be satisfactory because of its simplicity it will ignore the time value of money. If a percentage royalty basis is adopted for calculations this to some extent takes account of inflation. Capital sum payments include lump sum paid up royalties, lump sum advances on royalties, minimum payment obligations, increasing royalty levels with turnover and lump sum options on improvements on later add-on's/extensions.

Structuring Deals to maximise profits

Note: this illustration shows how different deal structures affect *reported* profits. The value to each party will require calculation of the present value of the cash flows at their own cost of capital/discount rate. See, further, the Case Study as page 129–131.

Year	Sales	Licence 1		Licence 2		Licence 3	
		Cash	Profits	Cash	Profits	Cash	Profits
1	5m	100	100	75	225	75	300
2	10m	200	200	150	100	75	–
3	8m	160	160	120	70	75	–
4	5m	100	100	75	25	75	–
		560	560	420	420	300	300

Licence 1
The royalty here is 2% of licensee's sales every year.

Licence 2

The royalty here is 1.5% of licensee sales with minimum of 50,000p.a. for the first 4 years. Should the licensor wish to represent it as such this is a profit calculation as follows:

Yr(1) $4 \times 50 + (75 - 50) = 225$

Yr(2) $150 \ (1.5\% \times 10m) - 50 \ k \ (\text{taken in Yr 1}) = 100$

Yr(3) $120 - 50 = 70$

Yr(4) $75 - 50 = 25$

Case 3

300,000 payable in 4 equal annual instalments

Summary

To summarise intellectual capital rarely generates economic benefits alone. Complimentary assets, in the form of working capital and intangible assets, are typically combined into a business enterprise. This 'portfolio' of assets generates an overall economic return. Allocation of the overall return among the asset categories comprised in the 'portfolio' can isolate the amount of return that is attributable to the intellectual capital component. Simply, this stream of economic benefits from the intellectual capital, coupled with the appropriate rate of return associated with the asset is key.

Essentially this a debt-free calculation excluding interest expenses associated with such a debt. This debt-free net income includes all of the variable, fixed, selling, administrative, and overhead expenses that are required to exploit the intellectual capital. Omission of any of these expenses overstates the amount of economic benefits that will ultimately be allocated to the IPR as a first step to examine appropriate royalty rates.

Intangible assets and intellectual property are often considered to be at the risky end of business enterprise. For example intellectual capital -led technology can date as new research advances. A higher rate of return on these intellectual capital assets is therefore required. Since the overall return on the business is established as the weighted average cost of capital (see page 187 above) and since a reasonable return for the monetary and tangible assets can be estimated, the valuer is in a position to derive an appropriate rate of return to be earned by the intellectual capital. Without reflecting investment rates of return in royalty rate calculations leads to mismanagement, inefficient exploitation and the wrong rate.

Licensing economics dictate consideration of resources, secrecy, transferability, risk and reward scenarios, licensee capability, intellectual capital assistance, standards, exclusivity and territory.

A discounted cashflow model can be used to establish well defined royalty rate ranges. It clearly shows the overall affect on the value of a corporation and allows royalty negotiators to focus precisely on the income that is generated by the licensed intellectual capital.

The alternative to licensing between the values of £X to a licensor and £Y to a licensee is to seek to protect your intellectual capital and possibly enforce your intellectual capital in the general marketplace. See Chapter 3 for the legal aspects of protecting intellectual capital. Enforcement is therefore a key issue for licensing. The cost of enforcement is normally factored into any negotiation for licensing. For example, both the potential licensor and the potential licensee will incur legal fees. The licensor may be reimbursed for these fees if the licensee is found to have infringed the IPR. In this case, the potential for legal fees moves the anticipated negotiated value of the IPR somewhat higher. In any event both licensor and licensee would normally calculate a budget for this event and factor into their calculations.

Miscellaneous Question: Assessing the value of assigning rights

Question: I receive £2,000 per annum from the ownership of copyright in a book I wrote in 1975. The copyright income is relatively stable and grows by the rate of inflation each year (assumed to be a constant 4.5%). A required rate of return from an investment of this sort could be assumed to be around 13%.

I am offered £22,000 for assignment of the rights. Is this a fair deal?

Notes:

a   Using the formula (see page 178) $\dfrac{\text{Income} \times (1 + \text{Growth})}{\text{Discount Rate} - \text{Growth}}$

b   This formula is, in effect, for income in perpetuity, but in view of the fact that copyright owner is alive, and income will flow for 70 years after death, the difference from any other approach is negligible.

c   Answer on page 249.

Royalty Rate Determination: A Case Study

X Ltd has an electrical goods division. They have been offered the chance to manufacture and sell a new product which, while not unique, is protected by patent and copyright, and it would not be practical for the division to develop its own rival product.

The valuer has been given the following information and asked to suggest the maximum royalty rate that the division should pay. Alternatively, what is the maximum cash sum that the division should pay?

Part I – Estimating the NPV of the Division

(i) The division currently has sales of £100,000 per annum with expected increases of 6% per annum.

(ii) The divisions cost of sales are 65%.

(iii) Depreciation is currently £3,000 per annum and is relievable for tax purposes. Depreciation is also expected to increase at 6% per annum.

(iv) The division pays tax at 25%.

(v) Additional working capital of £800 is needed during 1992 and will increase at 6% per annum.

(vi) Capital Expenditure of £3,000 per annum is anticipated in 1992 and will increase at 6% per annum.

(vii)The cost of capital of the division has been separately estimated at 15%.

Part II – Estimating the NPV of the Division and the New Product

(i) The new product has projected sales of

2002	£1,000
2003	£5,000
2004	£10,000
2005	£25,000
2006	£50,000

with growth of 6% expected thereafter.

(ii) The cost of sales of the new product is only 40%

(iii) No additional depreciation will be allowable

(iv) Additional working capital has been quantified as follows:

(N.B. this **replaces** the assumptions in Part I)

2002	£1,000
2003	£1,750
2004	£2,500
2005	£4,750
2006	£3,000

(v) Additional Capital Expenditure has been quantified as follows:

(N.B. this **replaces** the assumptions in Part I)

2002	£3,000
2003	£4,000
2004	£4,750
2005	£5,000
2006	£5,250

(vi) New Working Capital and Capital Expenditure is expected to increase by 6% after these years

Part III – What is the maximum royalty rate that should be paid?

No additional information is needed: the valuer simply needs to calculate the rate at which the n.p.v. of future cash flows from the new product has zero net effect on X Ltd's overall position. That is, the rate at which all additional profits (at present value) are paid as a royalty to the licensor. At any rate better than this maximum it is worth licencing.

Royalty Rate Calculation Table 1

	Existing Sales Only				
	2002	2003	2004	2005	2006
Sales	100,000	106,000	112,360	119,102	126,248
Sales Increase %		6%	6%	6%	6%
Cost of Sales	65,000	68,900	73,034	77,416	82,061
Cost of Sales %	65%	65%	65%	65%	65%
Gross Profit	35,000	37,100	39,326	41,686	44,187
Gross Profit %	35%	35%	35%	35%	35%
Depreciation Expense	3,000	3,180	3,371	3,573	3,787
Depreciation Increase %		6%	6%	6%	6%
Admin, Overheads etc.	25,000	26,500	28,090	29,775	31,562
% of Sales	25%	25%	25%	25%	25%
Operating Income	7,000	7,420	7,865	8,337	8,837
Taxation at 25%	1,750	1,855	1,966	2,084	2,209
Net Income	5,250	5,565	5,899	6,253	6,628
Add back depreciation	3,000	3,180	3,371	3,573	3,787
Total Cash Flow	8,250	8,745	9,270	9,826	10,415
Less Additional Working Capital	800	848	899	953	1,010
Increase in Working Capital %		6%	6%	6%	6%
Less Capital Expenditure	3,000	3,180	3,371	3,573	3,787
Increase Capital Expenditure %		6%	6%	6%	6%
Net Cash Flow	4,450	4,717	5,000	5,300	5,618
PV Factor (15% Discount)	0.869565	0.756144	0.657516	0.571753	0.497177
Present Value	3,870	3,567	3,288	3,030	2,793
Total Present Values		16,547			
Residual Value*		32,897			
Total Value		49,444			

$$* \quad \frac{\text{Maintainable earnings} \times (1 + \text{growth})}{\text{Discount Rate} - \text{Growth}}$$

$$\frac{5,618 \times (1 \times (0.06))}{0.15 - 0.06} = \frac{66.168}{0.497177} = 32,897$$

Royalty Rate Calculation Table 2

	With New Product Sales				
	2002	2003	2004	2005	2006
Sales	100,000	106,000	112,360	119,102	126,248
Sales Increase %		6%	6%	6%	6%
New Product Sales	1,000	5,000	10,000	25,000	50,000
New Sales Increase		400%	100%	150%	100%
Cost of Sales	65,000	68,900	73,034	77,416	82,061
Cost of Sales %	65%	65%	65%	65%	65%
Cost of New Sales	400	2,000	4,000	10,000	20,000
Cost of New Sales %	40%	40%	40%	40%	40%
Gross Profit	35,600	40,100	45,326	56,686	74,187
Depreciation Expense	3,000	3,180	3,371	3,573	3,787
Depreciation Increase %		6%	6%	6%	6%
Admin, Overheads etc	25,250	27,750	30,590	36,025	44,062
Operating Income	7,350	9,170	11,365	17,087	26,337
Taxation at 25%	1,838	2,293	2,841	4,272	6,584
Net Income	5,513	6,878	8,524	12,815	19,753
Add back depreciation	3,000	3,180	3,371	3,573	3,787
Total Cash Flow	8,513	10,058	11,895	16,388	23,540
Less Additional Working Capital	1,000	1,750	2,500	4,750	3,000
Less Capital Expenditure	3,000	4,000	4,750	5,000	5,250
Net Cash Flow	4,513	4,308	4,645	6,638	15,290
PV Factor (15% Discount)	0.869565	0.756144	0.657516	0.571753	0.497177
Present Value	3,924	3,257	3,054	3,796	7,602
Total Present Values		21,633			
Residual Value		89,535			
Total Value		111,168			

Royalty Rate Calculation Table 3

	With New Product Sales and Royalty Payment				
	2002	2003	2004	2005	2006
Sales	100,000	106,000	112,360	119,102	126,248
Sales Increase %		6%	6%	6%	6%
New Product Sales	1,000	5,000	10,000	25,000	50,000
New Sales Increase		400%	100%	150%	100%
Cost of Sales	65,000	68,900	73,034	77,416	82,061
Cost of Sales %	65%	65%	65%	65%	65%
Cost of New Sales	400	2,000	4,000	10,000	20,000
Cost of New Sales	40%	40%	40%	40%	40%
Gross Profit	35,600	40,100	45,326	56,686	74,187
Depreciation Expense	3,000	3,180	3,371	3,573	3,787
Depreciation Increase %		6%	6%	6%	6%
Admin, Overheads etc.	25,250	27,750	30,590	36,025	44,062
Royalty Payment	240	1,199	2,398	5,996	11,991
Royalty Rate % New Sales	23.98%	23.98%	23.98%	23.98%	23.98%
Operating Income	7,110	7,971	8,967	11,091	14,346
Taxation at 25%	1,778	1,993	2,242	2,773	3,587
Net Income	5,333	5,978	6,725	8,319	10,760
Add back depreciation	3,000	3,180	3,371	3,573	3,787
Total Cash Flow	8,333	9,158	10,096	11,892	14,457
Less Additional Working Capital	1,000	1,750	2,500	4,750	3,000
Less Capital Expenditure	3,000	4,000	4,750	5,000	5,250
Net Cash Flow	4,333	3,408	2,846	2,142	6,297
PV Factor (15% Discount)	0.869565	0.756144	0.657516	0.571753	0.497177
Present Value	3,768	2,577	1,871	1,225	3,131
Total Present Values		12,571			
Residual Value		36,873			
Total Value^2		49,444			

---

2. The maximum royalty rate is therefore 23.98% of new sales, the total value figure is the same as the existing sales value in Table 1.

Example answer – establishing an appropriate royalty rate

This simple example models the process of establishing an economic royalty rate in a situation whereby intellectual property is used to enhance a business operation.

Table 1 introduces a discounted cash flow analysis of the value of the business based on forecasted sales, expenses, working capital and hence cashflow for five years.

The £100,000 worth of sales forecasted for the first year are expected to grow at a steady but unexciting 6% per year. Imagine that this company is in a sector with slim profit margins, strong competition and a mature market. Production costs of the company's sole product are running at 65% of sales and this is expected to continue for the foreseeable future.

Administration costs and overheads, etc. have historically amounted to 25% of sales and this will continue to be the case. Depreciation, which is a non-cash expense, is based upon the estimated market value and a 15 year life for the production equipment presently used in the business. The additional working capital and fixed asset expenditure reflect the continuing, necessary re-investment in the business.

Table 1 shows the results of utilising a 15% discount rate reflecting the hypothetical firms weighted average cost of capital. The residual value is calculated by projecting the final years sales, together with the projected 6% growth rate. The business is therefore valued at £49,444.

Table 2 shows the effect of expanding the business by the introduction of a new product line, with production costs of only 40%. The administration overhead costs are assumed to continue to run at 25%.

The value of the business increases as a result of the new product, to £111,168. However the improved cash flow only results from an independent company making available technology associated with the new product through a licensing deal. The owner of the technology anticipates earning a fair return for the licensing of technology to the company.

It therefore becomes necessary to include a royalty payable to the licensor, in the cash flow calculations, and the question, is at what level should the royalty rates be calculated?

In **Table 3** a flat royalty rate is shown as an expense item, while still leaving enough cash flow from operations to maintain the present value of the company at £49,444, identical to that shown in Table 1.

In the above example the company has not contributed to the intellectual property value, and therefore a licensor would, arguably, not permit the retention of any of the cash flow generated by that property. More realistically however, one would anticipate some sort of attribution of the intellectual property income between the licensor and licensee. Therefore the 23.98% royalty rate effectively represents the upper limit, and provides the starting point for the subsequent negotiations.

These calculations go to the core of what has been said in the text earlier about the need to appraise the respective licensor and licensee value positions, before negotiations, remembering to build in an 'over lapping' position where a 'deal' can be done.

Answer (from page 242)

$$\frac{2000 \times (1 + 0.045)}{0.13 - 0.045} \quad = \quad £24,588$$

Though in numerical terms this deal might not look attractive, it should not be forgotten that the purchaser needs a margin too. This is a good offer – the value of that £22,000 over the period is less than the total of the cash flows but more certain for the vendor of the licence *and* better business for the purchaser.

Tools of Analysis

 This section provides a short "glossary" of techniques for future reference.

The Derivation of DCF

Modern valuation analysis is effectively DCF applied to the business enterprise under consideration.

The formula for discounting cash flow is derived from classic compound interest as follows:-

Compound Interest

If FV = Future Value, the $FV = PV(1 + r)^n$ where:–

PV = present value
r = periodic rate of interest expressed as a decimal and representing risk
n = number of periods

Present Value of a Future Payment

It follows from the above that $NPV = \dfrac{FV}{(1 + r)^n}$

Present Value of a Stream of Cash Flows

If C is taken to denote future periodic cash flows, it then also follows that:–

$$PV = \frac{C^1}{1 + r} + \frac{C^2}{(1 + r)^2} + \frac{C^3}{(1 + r)^3} + \dots\dots\dots + \frac{C^n}{(1 + r)^n}$$

Net Present Value of an Investment

The Net Present Value (NPV) of a strategy or business is the sum of its expected free cash flows to a horizon H discounted by its cost of capital.

If then NPV equals net present value (i.e. present value of stream of n cash flows net of the initial investment required to generate them.)

$$NPV = C' + \frac{C^1}{1 + r} + \frac{C^2}{(1 + r)^2} + \frac{C^3}{(1 + r)^3} + \dots\dots\dots + \frac{C^n}{(1 + r)h}$$

where C represents the initial investment and is negative and r the cost of capital.

The terminal value is the value of the business at a horizon *(h)*

$$H \text{ Value} = \frac{\text{Cash Flow}}{(r - \text{growth})}$$

Also discounted back to present value.

Assuming proper selection of r in accordance with the Capital Asset Pricing Model see page 192, any project giving a positive NPV will increase the total net present value of an enterprise and should be undertaken. NPVs may be used to rank mutually exclusive projects in order of attractiveness and may be summed to determine the total value to a business of combinations of non-exclusive projects.

The Capital Asset Pricing Model (CAPM)

CAPM uses a market risk premium and a Beta to calculate the premium for Systematic risk. Systematic risk is caused by factors which affect all investments.

The variable r in the DCF formula is the rate of return required from the project under analysis to compensate the investor for the use of the money (i.e. to replace the return which could be earned by placing the funds in a risk-free investment), for non-diversifiable market risk (i.e. risk relating, for instance, to macroeconomic factors and general economic conditions which affect all investments) and for diversifiable specific risk (i.e. risks specific to the nature of the project), also called unsystematic or unique risk, that can be diversified away by holding stocks in portfolios.

KE, which represents the cost of equity capital (KE) total return (i.e. the return accruing both from income and from movements in capital value), can be estimated using the CAPM, which postulates that

An investor's required return = risk free rate of return × (Beta × market risk premium) or $KE = rf + \beta(rm - rf)$

where:–

rf = rate of return on risk-free investments such as Treasury bonds

rm = rate of return on equities ie a diversified market portfolio

$rm - rf$ = premium available for accepting market or non-diversifiable risk

and

β = *Beta*, a constant reflecting the degree to which the specific or diversifiable risk of the project varies from non-diversifiable or market risk. The degree to which a stock moves with a well diversified portfolio (the market).

$\beta(rm - rf)$ therefore represents the premium over the risk-free rate of return available in respect of both specific and market risk. That is to say, the total risk premium element in *KE*, being $r - rf$, can be expressed as

$KE - rf = \beta(rm - rf)$

which is simply a rearrangement of first equation.

Specific risk, as quantified by β, can itself be decomposed into a number of elements, being the risks associated with the business of the industry, entity or project, the risks associated with its operating leverage and the risks associated with its financial leverage.

CHAPTER 5
INTELLECTUAL PROPERTY DUE DILIGENCE

Contents

CHAPTER 5
INTELLECTUAL PROPERTY DUE DILIGENCE

Introduction

The due diligence process assesses the three essential attributes in relation to any intellectual capital. First, that legal rights exist in the intellectual property. This chapter is predominantly about these legally-protectable rights: the intellectual property element of intellectual capital. For example, that there is a patent or a trade mark registered. Secondly, that a good title can be established. If you were going to buy or rent a house, you would always check out who owned if first. It is the same process but in a very different context. Thirdly, that rights can be enforced to prevent others using the rights without permission to generate revenues. This latter attribute refers to the strength of the intellectual property rights and is the most difficult aspect of due diligence in relation to intellectual property. Using the house analogy again, this aspect of due diligence seeks to assess the boundaries of the plot of land you call yours.

These attributes directly relate to the effect any intellectual capital may have in a business context. The effect can be regarded as either positive or defensive. Due diligence in the *positive* sense seeks to evaluate the intellectual capital as a commercial asset seeking to identify intellectual property rights which can be exploited to enhance the earnings of the business. These intellectual property rights might be owned by the business but under-exploited. Alternatively, the identified intellectual property rights might be owned by another business requiring a license to use the identified intellectual property rights. The *defensive* sense is where a business is concerned that the existence of any intellectual capital might prevent a business activity continuing or being started because the intellectual property rights will be infringed or that a serious risk of infringing those intellectual property rights exists. In either case with the potential of a substantial damages claim, unless a license to use the particular rights can be agreed.

Defensive due diligence seeks to establish whether any intellectual property rights exist which may give rise to the risk of infringement and substantial damages being paid in respect of a business activity the subject perhaps of an investment proposal. Then if any intellectual property rights that may be relevant are found to exist, the strength of these rights must then be evaluated and a judgement made as to the extent of the risk in the particular circumstances. Back to the house analogy, this is knowing the boundaries of the plot of land and assessing whether your activity might be a trespass. A decision can then be made as to whether the investment in the business activity should be made or continued.

The due diligence process – whether positive or defensive – will cover many of the same points such as assessing the existence of rights and their strength. The due diligence requires judgements to be made about such things as sort of searches should be carried out, about the strength of the rights which the searching has revealed, and about the infringement risk posed in particular circumstances.

A simplified version of a report following an actual due diligence investigation is set out in Addendum 1 to this chapter at page 329. Many of the complex details have been omitted. An intellectual property due diligence aide memoire is in Addendum 3 at page 339.

Positive Due Diligence

Know your own and any licensed intellectual property

Objective

The objective of this type of due diligence is to carry out sufficient investigation into the intellectual property identified as being used or which is to be used in a business. The investigation is principally to check and assess that the claimed legal rights actually exist and also on ownership. Checks and assessments may also be made about the strength of the rights and their validity. "Sufficient investigation" means all those checks it is prudent to carry out in the circumstances. These circumstances will determine by how much money and time is spent on the checks.

Intellectual property rights are business assets. They give competitive advantage. Patents can prevent competing products being developed. Brands can enable high margins to be maintained. Alternatively, these rights can be licensed to earn revenue which mostly goes straight to the bottom line. This is the power and value of owning intellectual property rights. It is now a vital skill for any successful chief executive, for accountants and those involved in business investment, particularly in equity funding to understand the positive and defensive sides of intellectual property due diligence. So is the ability to successfully negotiate a licence for the use of any required or desirable intellectual property rights or the acquisition of those rights. Many business plans for a new business or for a new project in an existing business are now based on the use in some way of intellectual property rights.

The positive side is the process of identifying and assessing the intellectual property rights in a business and the extent to which those rights protect the intellectual property form being used by others without permission, and the intellectual property rights of other businesses the use of which might add value. The defensive side requires the same skills. The positive and defensive may overlap. Defensive due diligence aims to identify intellectual property rights which might be infringed unless a licence is negotiated or the particular rights acquired.

Any business seeking to invest in its own intellectual property rights or to licence them out or which is seeking to acquire the right to use intellectual property rights must be satisfied that the intellectual property rights exist and be certain of the identity of the person who owns them. This process involves many of the same basic principles as when acquiring any other property such as checking that the asset exits and that the person claiming to own it does have legal ownership not just apparent ownership through possession or because the rights are being used.

Reducing doubt

The holy grail of the positive due diligence process is to eliminate any doubts about the existence and ownership of the particular intellectual property rights, and to know precisely the extent of protection given by them if enforced against others. In practice, doubts about the existence of the rights should be few, if any.

But in relation to ownership and the protection given by the rights eliminating doubt is more difficult and often impossible. Intellectual property rights are still national rights except in a few cases such as the Europe wide trade mark and design laws referred to in chapter two. All these rights are subject to the laws of different countries. The decision about the ownership of intellectual property rights or infringement of those rights in one country might be binding in other countries but doubts will remain. The amount of doubt depends on the countries involved. A decision in a French court is very likely to be recognised and enforced in other European counties. But more doubt would remain about that decision being recognised and enforced in some developing countries or where the political regime is volatile. Recently, in a case involving Yahoo, a French court banned the advertising for sale of Nazi memorabilia on websites of Yahoo. US courts refused to enforce the decision in the United States. A decision about ownership, say from a court in a European country, might not be recognised and enforced in the United States. Doubt remains. Eliminating the doubt might well involve taking court action in the United States. The decision then would be about justifying the cost involved and balancing these against the need to eliminate rather than reduce the doubt.

Doubts can also arise out of circumstances. Ownership might depend on whether a patentable innovation was made by an employee in circumstances such that the employer owns it. In most cases this will be straightforward but in others not so. In a collaboration, if ownership of intellectual property rights is not made clear in an agreement, serious doubts about ownership are likely to arise. Or if a new product design is commissioned, the person commissioning will own the design rights but often the arrangements by which the design was created are more like a supplier and customer relationship where the supplier takes the risk that the cost of creating the design will be recovered in sales. This may not be a commission.

Similarly in relation to the scope of protection given by intellectual property rights, much depends on the circumstances. A person using an identical trade mark for the same products or services is infringing the trade mark. This will be the same in most countries. Doubts arise if the trade mark is not identical but similar or the products and services are similar but not the same. The less similarity, the more doubt about whether the trade mark rights are infringed. The same point could be made about patents and designs. The *Improver* case study on page 407 illustrates this point particularly well.

So doubt can arise as a result of the effect of national laws and enforcement of decisions across national boundaries as well as from the circumstances of a transaction or dispute. Eliminating doubt may not be possible or only possible at a cost which may not be justified. In such circumstances, the positive due diligence process then is all about reducing doubt, not eliminating it. Information should be obtained and professional advice taken. Then an assessment should be made about the level of doubt and its effect. This will involve very careful judgement by a person with knowledge and experience.

Registered rights – existence and ownership

The first place to check for the existence and about ownership of a registered intellectual property right is at the registry where these rights should be registered. Searching is covered in more detail in relation to defensive due diligence at page 277 below. Since intellectual property rights are essentially national rights, a search will be necessary in the registry of each country or region where the intellectual property rights are being considered for exploitation.

The results of the search should confirm the existence of any registered rights such as patents, trade marks, or designs and who owns them. But the search results are often not the whole story. Ownership of intellectual property can be transferred like any other asset. Frequently, the change of ownership is not registered as it should be. In practice, usually one business is clearly using the intellectual property rights in question and claiming ownership. The discrepancy between claimed ownership and the register entry will be apparent. Appropriate enquiries can be made. Prudently, proof of the ownership of the person claiming to be the owner (though not registered as such) will be needed and the true owner to be properly registered. If the intellectual property rights are to be sold or licensed, the assignment or licence document may have a warranty requested by the new owner or licensee together with a suitable indemnity that during the time that the true owner was not properly registered as such, no other conflicting rights have been granted or exist. This is a contractual safeguard against an unfair result which can occur if the person, still registered as owner but who had in fact already transferred ownership to A which had not been registered, purported to sell or licence the rights again to a second person, B.

The value of such a warranty and indemnity, of course, depends on the financial strength of the business or person giving it. To have any real value these must ultimately be capable of leading to compensation being paid in the event of a breach of the warranty causing loss. In the UK, there is a legal safeguard about this unfair result for most rights. Put simply, it is that a person (B above) acquiring rights in intellectual property such as by a transfer of ownership or a licence from the "owner" named on the register will take effect in preference to the rights of the new but unregistered owner (A above) or anybody who has obtained rights from that new but unregistered owner. This is one reason why transactions involving registered intellectual property should be recorded at the relevant registry. The legal rule does not apply if the person (B above) acquiring from the "owner" as shown on the register had knowledge or reasonable suspicion that some other person (A above) may in fact own the intellectual property rights.

Case Study

The following illustrates some of these points. It is about the acquisition of a business, the assets including a valuable patent. It is based on a real transaction although simplified. The patent position was not satisfactory. The patent had been owned by a company which had gone into receivership. This company had been owned by the management of a second company – lets call it Sellout. The management had bought the assets out of the company in receivership into the new company Sellout or at least thought they had. That new company was given effectively the same name as the old company. The search of the register of patents showed the patent remained in the name of the old company but that all the renewal costs had been paid by the new company Sellout. There were three possible routes from this position. First, that Sellout now seeking to sell the assets had agreed to acquire the patent rights from the receiver of the old company but no assignment document had been registered at the relevant patent office to record the change. To correct this, it would be necessary to record the details of any existing agreement which showed the assignment. The second possibility was that Sellout had agreed to acquire the patent but no document to complete the transfer of the legal title had been concluded. Therefore, only an imperfect title and not the full legal title had been transferred to Sellout. A document would need to be prepared and signed by or on behalf of the old company to transfer the legal title. The third possibility was that Sellout had never purchased the patent from the old company. The first possibility could be eliminated. The second possibility would have required reinstating the old company that had gone into receivership and which at the time had been struck off the companies register in the UK. This company could then sign an assignment to transfer legal title. Sellout could then pass good legal title. Alternatively, the assignment could be direct from the old company. The rules about the restoration of companies in the UK are detailed and it is by no means certain that the company could in fact be restored. If the old company in receivership never agreed to assign the patent rights to Sellout, the patent would have passed to the ownership of the UK State since the old company had been struck off. It would be necessary to persuade the relevant state official to assign the rights either to the Sellout or direct to the acquiring company. This would undoubtedly involve payment of some consideration for doing so. This case study is taken from case study A on page 447.

The circumstances in this example illustrate the difficulties that can arise. The legal and practical problems here in confirming title lead to considerable expense. The money being paid for the business and the intellectual property rights (including the patent) were substantial. The person undertaking the due diligence must have both the legal knowledge and the experience to be able to do two things. First, spot the problems. Secondly, find solutions to overcome the identified problems and advise on the likely effectiveness of these solutions. Some solutions are likely to retain an element of risk which needs to be assessed and a judgment made as to whether to proceed or not.

An incomplete or uncertain title to the intellectual property rights in question will directly effect the value of those rights. Licensing the rights will be difficult if not impossible. Investing in technology developed by the business will be a more difficult. Raising venture capital or other funding will be difficult for a technology based business if the existence and ownership of the intellectual property rights is in doubt. A sale or stock market floatation of the business would need the title to the intellectual property rights to be audited. Any holes in the rights to fundamental intellectual property, which could not be plugged, may well lead at least to a reduction in the value of the business.

This next case study should act as a wake up call to all investors in technology based businesses. A substantial investment was made in a business set up to exploit a patented innovation to be used in a machine for industrial cleaning. It had the potential to be as successful as the Dyson innovations in the domestic cleaning market. A world wide patent was being obtained for the sophisticated material made of fibres. The density and dimensions of the fibres were the clever bit. The patent rights were claimed by reference to the density and dimensions. The patented product was successful and had huge potential. Hence, the investment. Ownership of the patent rights was clear and had been transferred to the company into which the investment had been made. Inevitably, the success lead to copying and apparent infringement of the patent rights. Investigation and due diligence was carried out before court action was taken. An analysis of the product alleged to infringe and the product being made by the business owning the patent rights revealed that they had the same fibre density and dimension. Unfortunately, neither the alleged infringing product nor the product of the patent owner had the density and the dimensions of the fibres as specified in the patents rights! Yet each product was just as effective as a product made as specified by the patent rights. So no infringement. The alleged infringer was a large business operating globally who could not be stopped. Other competitors began to use the technology. The patent was perfectly valid but useless. The new business could not attract further funding and was squeezed out of the market. It was liquidated shortly afterwards with the loss of a substantial investment.

The original positive due diligence before the substantial investment was ineffective. The due diligence in relation to both the technology and the patent protection being sought was also ineffective. The patent rights had not been written in broad enough terms. The full extent of the innovation had not been protected. This could not be rectified since the invention had been made public. As a result, any business could make material which would be just as effective as material made as described in the patent rights and without infringing those patent rights. In many jurisdictions the patent would be worthless. The courts in some jurisdictions might possibly take a wider view that the inventive concept had been infringed even if the precise density and dimensions of the fibres are not replicated. Germany might be one such jurisdiction. Even in these jurisdictions, the outcome would not be certain depending in each case on the circumstances of the alleged infringement.

Unregistered designs – existence and ownership

The requirements for these rights to exist and who might own them have already been covered earlier in this book. The problems which can arise in connection with work done by employees and sub-contractors follows were identified. The due diligence here when checking that the rights exist and who owns them requires the background facts to ascertained. This is the equivalent to searching when checking the existence of registered rights. To do this effectively, again needs both legal knowledge and experience. Take a copyright work such as a computer game, the following questions need to be considered and answered:

- Are copyright works involved such as computer programs and images?

- Are these works original?

- Do they qualify for copyright protection in the countries in which rights are to be acquired or licensed?

- Who is the author of them? Is there more than one? Are these persons employees? If so, of whom?

- Do any agreements exist dealing with ownership?

- Were any of the works commissioned? If so, does this affect ownership in any relevant country?

- What will be the value of any warranties and indemnities given about such things as originality and ownership?

Two case studies are illustrative. In the first, the designs of an international fashion business were being copied in Singapore. The copyright and designs law in Singapore at the time gave the designs no protection in Singapore unless those designs had been registered. The particular designs were not registered. It made no commercial sense to spend substantial sums registering everyone of the many designs created each year since a design typically would be in fashion for only about 18 months. So in Singapore, no copyright existed. This meant that the designs could be copied in Singapore and products made to those designs sold there. However, selling of those products in other countries with different laws protecting designs would infringe the intellectual property rights in the designs. In this particular case the brand name of each design had been used as well as the name of the international fashion business which enabled court proceedings to be taken in Singapore to stop this activity using rights of passing off in Singapore.

The second case study involves a due diligence investigation in respect of a manufactured product which had an innovative design closely allied to its function. The product was commercially successful. A rival began to manufacture and sell an identical copy of the product. Two intellectual property rights might exist to make the coping an infringement, namely copyright and design right. The relevant works for copyright purposes were several complex drawings. The business was a Swedish company. The author of the drawings and creator of the design was a Swedish national and employee of the company. The design was first published in Sweden. The copy of the product was being sold in the UK. This is the type of information which was to be verified as part of the due diligence.

The drawings were artistic works in which copyright in the UK could exist. But did they qualify for copyright in the UK? Yes. Sweden is a qualifying country so that works created by its nationals qualify for copyright protection in the UK. Once the relevant information had been confirmed, it was clear that copyright existed. But copyright in the UK does not protect many types of manufactured products against copying. This was covered in the section on designs in chapter two. Design Right was the only intellectual property right which could be used to stop the copy being sold in the UK. The design of the manufactured product was not registered as a design. Did Design Right exist? The knowledge that the design was created outside the UK should put the person doing the investigation on notice to check that the design qualifies for Design Right protection in the UK. The qualifying provisions for the Design Right are not as comprehensive as for copyright. First, was the design likely to be found sufficiently original? Here, yes. Was it commonplace? No. The next questions to answer was whether the design qualified for Design Right in the UK. Qualification is judged by reference either to the creator of the design or to the employer of the creator owning the rights in the design. The design would qualify for protection if the Swedish creator or Swedish employer was a qualifying person as defined. This depended on whether Sweden was a qualifying country. A qualifying country includes a member state of the European Union. Sweden did not join the European Union until 1995. The design was created before 1995. So at the time that the design was created it would not qualify for design right protection in the UK.

The amount of effort put into this kind of investigation should depend on the relative cost of doing the investigation weighed against the cost of the rights either not existing or not being owned by the person from who they were acquired. The cost might reflect the loss of opportunity in having exclusive use of the rights if the intellectual property rights do not exist or the wasted time and money invested in a project based on these rights. The cost might be the royalties that will have been paid which would not have been if an investigation had been carried out showing that the rights did not exist. Another cost could be the cost of infringement if the rights are actually owned by somebody other that the person who was thought to be the owner.

Doubts about the existence and ownership of the intellectual property rights may still remain even after the investigation and assessment are complete. A judgement will need to be made about whether the risk that this doubt introduces is worth taking in all the circumstances. This is where a person with broad and detailed knowledge and experience carrying out the due diligence can make a real difference.

Confirming and securing ownership

Introduction

It is easy to assume that a business which has developed technology will be the owner of it and all the intellectual property rights that might relate to it. This should not be taken for granted. Often as part of a due diligence investigation, business managers or executives claim with complete confidence that the intellectual property rights are owned by the company for a new technology. On probing into the detail of the development of the technology, the strict legal position is often different. The confident claim to ownership on probing is often followed by a statements such as "ah well we employed a design house to develop that part" or "well, the software to control the machine was developed by XYZ Software House".

The commom assumption is that intellectual property is owned by the business that paid for it to be developed. This is not necessarily so. The payment is either for its own employees to undertake the development work or for a another business or person to do it.. This is a dangerous assumption to make. In many cases, the assumption will be correct but it might not be. Life being what it is, the assumption may be wrong when the intellectual property is important or valuable or both. If the intellectual property is or is likely to be important, prudence suggests checking and making sure.

Often the terms and conditions of the business creating the design or doing other work will provide that the intellectual property rights will belong to them. Terms and conditions printed on the back of quotations for work are, in a busy corporate life, often overlooked. They should not be. Businesses developing technologies using outside contractors should take special care to ensure that the intellectual property rights belong to the company.

Checking means understanding the law which applies to the particular relationship. Relationships are typically employer and employer, and contractor and sub contractor. Each of which are discussed in more detail below. However, the relationship might equally be joint venture or collaboration relationship.

Being sure of ownership for an employee means having a detailed contract of employment and obtaining a confirmatory statement or assignment from an employee. For a business which has created the development that is the subject of the intellectual property, being certain means obtaining a confirmatory assignment. However, this needs care because in some cases the relevant law will dictate how and to what extent this is possible.

Commissioning developments and products

The ownership of intellectual property needs to be considered carefully and ownership agreed at the beginning and before any work is started or any payments made. The agreement must, of course, be in writing. It must be as sufficiently comprehensive as the circumstances require. This is again about risk reduction. A comprehensive agreement should leave less room for doubt. But the time and cost involved might not be justified.

The legal considerations about ownership when commissioning a development can be illustrated well using copyright and Design Right in the United Kingdom where ownership is often in issue and neglected at the start.. The due diligence point will be about ownership of intellectual property rights in designs.

In UK law, if any aspect of the design has been commissioned and is protected by a Design Right, the Design Right is owned by the person who commissioned the design. But if any aspect of the design is commissioned and protected by copyright, the copyright will be owned by the person who created the work or that person's employer not the person who commissioned it. This is the position in the absence of any agreement about who would own the design. It is possible for the copyright to be owned by one person and the design right by another. Any person undertaking a due diligence investigation must be aware of this possibility and check for the existence of both copyright and Design Right and the ownership of both rights.

A case about the copying of a fashion garment shows that this is not just a legal technicality. The garment became popular with younger people. Sales were huge. Counterfeit garments began to be sold. The garment had a unique cut as well as a distinctive pattern in the fabric. The cut was protected by Design Right and the pattern by copyright. A confirmatory assignment was required to ensure that the copyright as well as the Design Rights were owned by the fashion business and could be enforced by it against the counterfeiters. In this case, the agreement was obtained with out dispute or extra cost. In other cases, awkward disputes and substantial costs have been involved in regularising the ownership of the rights.

Much better to be aware of these potential problems and deal with them at the time the design was commissioned or created.

Employees and sub-contractors

Development work undertaken by an employee is likely to result in any intellectual property right belonging to the employer. The ownership of intellectual property rights created by employees will depend on the law that is applicable. In any due diligence process the legal position under the correct applicable law will need to be considered, the facts investigated and collected and then a judgement made about whether the employer is the owner of the relevant intellectual property rights. In the vast majority of cases under UK law, the employer will be the owner. Nevertheless, the relevant background should be ascertained from the employer so that in a due diligence process an assessment can be made as to whether there is any serious likelihood of the employee owning the rights rather than the employer.

To eliminate any risk, a simple assignment could be taken from the relevant employee or employees to ensure that all the intellectual property rights are owned by the employer and available in the transaction whether it is a licence deal or an acquisition of the intellectual property rights. Alternatively, the employee should be asked to confirm that the relevant intellectual property rights are owned by the employer. An assignment would be better. Care should be taken with patents since as between an employer and employee, ownership is determined according to the provisions of the UK Patents Act and cannot be overridden by an agreement. Typically an agreement will be a contract of employment. But with copyright, for example, the relevant law allows ownership to be determined by the contract of employment as well as providing a regime to determine ownership if not contract exists. Also the employee could be asked to sign a confirmatory form. An example is shown in addendum 2, page 337.

Transfering ownership

The ownership of intellectual property rights is often transferred from one person or business to another. If so, the person who has the legal title to the intellectual property rights will depend on the agreements effecting the transfers. One defective agreement in the chain of agreements passing ownership will be enough to prevent a good title being shown. This is no different really to when business premises are being acquired either outright or by lease. Good legal title needs to be shown. An early decision as part of the due diligence will be about how much time and money should be spent checking the chain of agreements transferring ownership to the intellectual property rights. This takes us back to assessing the cost of the checking against the risk that cost later will arise from not having good title.

If, at the end of the due diligence investigation and assessment, doubt about the ownership of the intellectual property rights in question remains, agreements can often be put in place between all relevant parties involved. The purpose of the agreements being to remove or substantially reduce the doubt that existed. If agreements cannot cure the defects or remove the doubts sufficiently, the final decision will be to go ahead with the defects and doubts identified or to pull out.

In this case study, an engineering business operating globally sold part of its worldwide business in one sector to a rival. The intellectual property rights used in the business being sold were owned by several companies in the group and not all of these were the operating companies of the part of the businesses being sold. Stage one was to transfer all the intellectual property rights into effectively a intellectual property holding company. This was achieved successfully. The intellectual property rights being both registered rights (patents, designs and trade marks) and unregistered rights (mostly product designs and important know how). The tax position was carefully checked before doing so. Stage two was to agree the sale and enter into a binding contract for the sale. This sale agreement provided that the the intellectual property rights would be grouped by reference to two broad business sectors and each of these groups of rights transferred to a separate company on completion. The deal was completed.

Subsequently, one of the products the subject of the transferred intellectual property was copied and court action proposed. A due diligence investigation into the ownership of the relevant intellectual property revealed two problems with the title to the intellectual property. First, the sale agreement did not include the unregistered intellectual property rights only the registered ones. So the new operating companies owned by the purchaser were using intellectual property rights they did not own and could not enforce to stop copying. Secondly, the groups of intellectual property rights had on completion been assigned to the wrong operating companies. So that each operating company was using intellectual property rights which it did not own. The latter problem was really a matter of internal reorganization although some accounting reporting changes had to be explained. Suitable confirmatory agreements were put in place. The former was more serious. However, since all the intellectual property was clearly meant to be transferred, agreement was eventually reached and again a confirmatory agreement was agreed transferring the intellectual property rights missed out first time.

Defensive Due Diligence

Be aware of competing intellectual property

Objective and introduction

The objective is to know of any intellectual property rights which might be , or worse are likely to be, infringed by any activity planned by a business. These rights can then be assessed and a careful judgement made by a person with knowledge and experience about the risk of any infringement. It may be possible to make changes to the original plans so as to reduce any risk of infringement identified by the assessment. A decision whether to proceed can then be made taking the infringement risk into account with the planned activities or to abandon the plans.

Clearly it is prudent that this assessment is done as early in the planning of the particular activities as possible, just in case the plans have to be changed or abandoned. By doing the assessment early, any costs wasted as a result can be kept to a minimum.

Due diligence to ascertain whether any intellectual property rights exist which might prevent some business activity is about risk management, not risk elimination. The latter may not be possible, but management of risk is essential. The risk is that some intellectual property right will, or might be, infringed. Due diligence here has two aspects. The first is about searching and investigating to find information about the existence of such rights. The second is making an assessment as to the risk of infringement based on the information available as a result of the searching and investigating.

Risk management

The more information about any intellectual property rights which might be relevant the better. But the cost of an extensive search for such information can be substantial. There are two elements to the costs which will be incurred. These are the cost of searching and the cost of evaluating the results of the searching. Recent examples indicate the range of costs. One case involving trade marks and copyright required a relatively simple investigation and analysis. This involved costs of about £5,000. This due diligence process did not require extensive searching and evaluation. But in another case involving a patent in the telecommunications sector, extensive patent searching was done to reveal prior art information. This information was analysed, further searching carried out, and a dossier produced showing that each aspect of the target patent looked invalid. This due diligence work incurred costs of about £100,000. The dossier was used as a basis for negotiating a licence of the target patent. The cost incurred enabled the risk and costs of a patent infringement law suit to be avoided.

The detailed information from a comprehensive search and investigation will allow the risk of infringement to be assessed accurately. In practice it is often difficult to determine with confidence that all relevant intellectual property rights have been identified and detailed information about them obtained. In each case, a decision must be taken as to how much due diligence is carried out. The cost of carrying out a detailed search and investigation needs to balanced against the risk that costs will be incurred if the business venture did or might infringe an intellectual property rights. Generally, two considerations drive this decision, namely the amount of time and money being invested, and the likely level of liability for infringement damages. If a substantial investment is to be made, then an extensive carefully conducted due diligence investigation and assessment should be undertaken. There are two risk areas. First, the risk that the investment is wasted as a result of a concern over intellectual property rights infringement. Secondly and possibly worse, a liability to pay substantial amounts of compensation for infringing the intellectual property rights may have arisen. Both could have a serious impact on the financial position of the business which is making or has made the investment.

In Chapter Two, an example used was the *Kodak* v *Polaroid* patent infringement battle. We used this in relation to intellectual property management Principle Nine – Be ready to protect your rights. It bears repeating here. The Polaroid patent related to the number and order of layers of chemical in a photographic film. A court in the United States in the 1990s held the patent to be valid and infringed by Kodak. Kodak paid Polaroid damages said to be over $900 million which had the effect of almost putting Kodak out of business. Kodak could have avoided infringement by using earlier public domain techniques!

Usually, the larger the investment, the greater the cost of pulling out of the project. If the investment is not substantial, typically much less or no due diligence is undertaken. Similarly, if the liability for infringement damages is likely to be substantial, then more due diligence would be prudent than if such liability were to be assessed as likely to be small. In some cases even these decisions cannot be taken until after some basic due diligence work has been carried out.

The type of business under consideration will have an impact on whether any due diligence work is carried out and, if so, the extent of that work. For example, businesses that developed original characters for merchandising or for use in software can control the development and should be less worried about infringing copyright and any design rights. The risk of a rogue employee copying other works perhaps from a previous employer would remain but the risk can be controlled with proper management. The extent of due diligence might limit searching for registered trade marks and designs and being aware about the work these employees have previously done which might lead to allegations of copying. But in the development of a film or game where new and existing images and sounds are to be included, the amount of due diligence would be extensive – the objective being to secure the permission to use existing works from all those who have rights in such work. This process is often referred to as "clearing rights" and is covered in more detail later in this Chapter. Also the process checks for existing trade marks and designs the same as, or similar to, the new trade marks and designs being created. The objective is to assess if rights in any such trade marks and designs would be infringed.

The case for extended due diligence

- A business wishing to launch a new confectionery product with a new brand would incur huge wasted costs by launching a brand which had to be changed subsequently because another person has rights already in the chosen brand.

- Before building a substantial chemical plant to manufacture a product, it would be wise to check that no patents exist to prevent the product being processed and sold.

- If a film or video game is being made, the main issues will be securing the right to use all the content such as graphics, music, film or vides clips and text. All contributors to the project who may have rights must be asked to transfer or waive their rights to the fullest extent possible before work begins. If this is not done, some person might well have the right to block the commercial exploitation of the film or video unless additional payment is made.

The case for appropriate due diligence

- A business has developed a new grain hopper. Arranging for the product to be manufactured is not expensive. Margins are low. Patents are unlikely to be involved. No copying has occurred. A substantial due diligence investigation is not justified.

- An individual has written software. It has been independently created and not based on any other software. The software becomes the foundation of a design business allowing the creation of websites cheaply and easily using the internet. A brand is adopted. The business is launched. The main risk comes from the use of the brand. So some simple searching can be done to check for existing registered trade marks the same or similar to the proposed brand. In the early years, the brand could be changed, if prudent to do so because another person claims that using it is an infringement of another trade mark. Again after some initial checking for any registered trade marks, an expensive detailed due diligence investigation is probably not justified before the business is launched.

The possibility of patenting software and now some business methods will mean that businesses which had not needed to consider carrying out any extensive due diligence in relation to new activities will now have to do so or at least considered doing so. For example, this will affect industries such as software development and fulfillment businesses. This is particularly important if these businesses are providing products or services into the e-business sector.

Intellectual property gives rights that are specific to a country or possibly a region. Businesses now often operate globally. The business revolution taking place as a result of the internet and in mobile communications together with the possibilities for e-business may turn even quite small businesses into global ones. A due diligence investigation about intellectual property rights globally, or at least in several countries, may involve professional advisors from many countries. This will not just be expensive and need to be carefully coordinated, but will also take time as information is gathered and the professional advice is sought. Their respective opinions will need to be considered and assessed. That time also has a commercial cost.

A due diligence assessment as to whether rights exist which will or might be infringed can lead to a conclusion that in some countries such rights exist but not in others. The commercial assessment will then be – is the business venture viable if limited to those countries where the rights do not exist?

Patents

Patent rights can be infringed irrespective of any intent to do so. A good example of this is a recent case involving a chemical patent in the health care sector. The patent was for a combination of several chemical products which gave a surprisingly good and beneficial effect. One of the chemicals was only required to be present in very small quantities. A rival found that a similar effect could be achieved by leaving out one of the chemicals required by the patent and adding another. But the added chemical had, as an impurity, sufficient of the chemical intended to be omitted to bring the whole of the rival product unintentionally within the scope of the patent rights. This was an infringement even though the rival had no intention to infringe the patent rights.

Patent rights are potentially dangerous to anybody considering launching a new product or starting a new business. Developing a new product or starting a new business without copying is no guarantee of avoiding patent infringement. Motive is not relevant to patent infringement. Realising this is particularly important for businesses based on new technologies in chemicals, pharmaceuticals, electronics and in telecoms, and for software businesses and those businesses developing around the use of the internet for doing business.

Software is now regarded as patentable in many countries and has been confirmed as patentable in Europe following a recent decision to allow a software patent to IBM. Business methods are now being patented in the United States since a court decision there in 1998. About several hundred business method patents have been granted and many thousands are pending. Two developments indicate the value these types of patent will have. First, in October 1999, Amazon.com Inc. sued its arch rival Barnesnoble.com Inc. for infringement of its patent for the Amazon "1-Click" process to allow customers to enter credit card and address details only once. Secondly, in September 2000, Apple Computer Inc announced that it had taken a licence to use the Amozon patented "1-Click" technology. The details of the licence agreement were not disclosed.

Damages for patent infringement are not always payable. The usual reason is that the patent rights were not known to the person accused of infringing. But often the risk of having to pay damages is only half the story. The other half is the business venture being stopped voluntarily or as the result of a court order. Once the existence of patent rights are known, actual infringement or the risk of infringement leads on to a liability for damages. This may mean that the only option is to voluntarily stop the particular activity. In one case an injunction was enforced in a patent infringement dispute against a business making nappies. The order required the managing director to shut the production line down. He left his office followed shortly afterwards by the noise of the production line being stopping. Followed by silence. At that point, the managing director was not thinking about damages but rather of the investment made, the bank loan to repay secured on his house, and the workforce soon to be laid off. The due diligence investigation seeks to reduce the risk of this happening. If possible, the objective is to be able to say with certainty that the proposed business will not infringe any patent rights.

Not all new products or business ventures are likely to involve a patent infringement. It is possible to identify business sectors where innovations occurs frequently. Often in these sectors innovating is the key to being competitive and profitable. Patents are common in electronics, chemicals, telecommunications, biotechnology and recently for software and (in the United States at least) for business methods for use in internet applications. Anybody launching a new product or business in any of these sectors needs to have a strategy about obtaining their own patents and where appropriate undertaking a negative intellectual property rights due diligence investigation. This does not mean that in other sectors it is safe to proceed without undertaking such a negative due diligence. Rather that patents are not so prevalent. If a substantial investment is being made, due diligence should still be done.

Searching for patents

The purpose of the search needs to be agreed. The search may be to identify any patents which might be infringed or which might be prior art relevant to a new invention. The purpose might be to find prior art about a known patent to see if the patent can be attacked.

The first step is to identify the technical field. Patents can be thought of as registered for broad technical subjects and then by reference to more specialist categories within that subject. Once the technical field has been identified, searches for patents and patent applications can be undertaken.

Patent searching is a complex process. First, patents are granted for regions or countries. So before commencing a patent search as part of the due diligence, a decision has to be taken about this. Will the search be a worldwide one or limited to certain regions or countries? The answer is directly related to the purpose or business opportunity being considered, whether it has actual or potential worldwide application or just local to some territory. If the latter, a search can be made for patents and applications for the countries in that territory.

Secondly, searches are usually undertaken in the technical field in question *and* related fields if those involved in the due diligence investigation think that patents or applications could exist in related technical fields which may affect the product or business being considered. So, electronics, telecommunications and software might be regarded as related fields in a complex internet development. Or biotechnology and chemicals in a pharmaceutical innovation.

Thirdly, the searching may be carried out in a number of phases. The results of one search being considered and then perhaps further searches carried out. This process can be repeated many times until a comprehensive search has been carried out and all the patents or applications which might cause a problem have been identified. Copies of the specifications of the patents will be obtained.

In technical fields where many patents are filed such as electronics, the searching will be extensive and expensive. But not as expensive as infringing a patent owned by Sony or IBM! In other technical fields only a small number of patents or applications are likely to be relevant so that the searching will usually not be as expensive.

The benefits of searching

In a recent example involving industrial doors, the search process revealed two patents which the new door design appeared to infringe. But the search also turned up six other patents. Two of these six patents were for closely similar inventions and pre-dated the two patents causing concern about infringement. The assessment made was that probably no infringement would occur. The outcome was not certain. Concern remained. The six other patents for innovations in the same sector had been found by searching. These gave information which eventually lead to two door manufacturers being found. Both had made and sold doors before the date on which the two patents causing concern were filed. These doors came within the scope of the two patents but were made and sold before the priority date of those patents. Consequently, the two patents were invalid and unenforceable. This was one of times when advice could be given with certainty. There would be no infringement. A subsequent court case proved the advice correct.

Once the searching has been completed and copies of relevant patents and applications obtained, a specialist often together with a person having experience in the technical fields in question will analyse them. The purpose of this is to identify any patents or applications which might be infringed by the new product or business, assess the strength of such patent rights and whether any infringement is likely and determine if any of the patent rights which might be infringed are invalid. This is a difficult task especially if a large number of patents have to be considered. Except in the simplest of patents, the patent specification is a complex document. Each one must be read, understood, and the scope of the rights given by the patent in question assessed. A patent specification in some technical fields such as electronics and biotechnology can run to hundreds of pages. These are not the norm.

Once the scope of the patents or applications has been assessed, a judgement can be made about the two important questions in the negative due diligence process in relation to patents. Do any patent rights exist which might be infringed? If so, are these patent rights valid?

One area of uncertainty will remain. The patent search, however comprehensive, will not reveal pending but unpublished patent applications. The patent application process requires that an application be published after 18 months from the priority date. Publication typically occurs at that time or shortly afterwards. Also the file relating to the application at the relevant patent office can be inspected and copies of most documents on the file can be obtained. The exception is the United States where publication of the patent contents including the application does not occur until the patent is *granted*, although recent changes may result in some applications for US patents being published if the application was first made in a country other than the US. A patent usually takes several years to be granted, typically three to four years.

Since the content of these unpublished applications is not known, they cannot be evaluated to decide whether or not the new product or venture will infringe any patent rights which may be eventually granted. It is usually possible to find out that a patent application has been filed in a particular technical area and the application number. The progress of the application can be tracked at least. But the practical implications of this remain worrying. In the UK, if a business activity or preparations for it had begun in good faith before the priority date of a patent, this activity would not be stopped by the granting of the patent rights. In many other countries the situation is the same. But for the period between filing the application and publication, the uncertainty and risk remain. However, to be a serious problem the patent application would need to remain undisclosed until published by the relevant patent office and no information about the innovation the subject of the patent made public. This is unlikely, though it does happen. Normally, once the patent application has been filed, the invention is commercialised and information about it will be known in the relevant business sector.

Case Study

The writer was involved in a case about a dispute as to the ownership of an innovation arising out of a joint venture. One partner to the joint venture filed for a US patent unknown to the other and in breach of the joint venture agreement. This party did not reveal what it had done and evaluation of the product being jointly developed continued. The US application was not published, and in fact was held up in the patent process, so that the other partner could not find out anything about the patent application filed even if it had become aware of the application. In order to obtain worldwide protection another application was filed by the first partner. This was based on the US application, was later published, and eventually came to the attention of the other partner to the joint venture. The contents of the US application were still not available but an educated guess about the contents could be made from the later application which was published in Europe. The subsequent dispute about who owned these patent rights was settled based on a joint ownership.

This last example illustrates that most often, in practice things are not as bad as they theoretically could be. First, even if the US application is not published for many years, an equivalent application in another region will be published within about 18 months of the date the US application was filed. If not, patent protection outside the United States is probably not being sought. Secondly, in many businesses more than 18 months will pass from preparation to substantial investment. Pending applications which might cause trouble can be monitored. Here the due diligence will involve monitoring the position and making a judgement on all the available information as to whether or not a patent application is likely to be lurking unpublished which could torpedo the project.

In other businesses, the period from preparation to investment will be much less than 18 months. If a search reveals the possibility of an unpublished patent, the judgement about whether a torpedo is lurking in the form of an unpublished patent will be a lot more difficult and the resulting risk greater. The patent search will reveal if the technical field relevant to the business is one in which innovations are being regularly made and, consequently, in which many patent applications are being filed and patents granted. At the moment, particularly in the US, many applications for software and business method patents are being filed relating to doing business on the internet. The due diligence in a technical field with this kind of profile would need much greater care. The possibility of unpublished patents with torpedo capabilities will be higher. Hunting them down if they exist will be a priority in the due diligence.

If the risk of patent infringement exists, is the venture sunk?

Possibly, but not necessarily. If the result of the due diligence is that the proposed activity may infringe some patent rights, then consideration must be given to abandoning the activity proposed or changing to something which will definitely not infringe. This may involve substantial investment of time and money being thrown away. Alternatively, there is the option of seeking permission to use the patent rights by negotiation. The answer may be "no deal". But often a licence can be negotiated. If the proposed business activity itself is based on a patented invention, sometimes these patent rights are licensed in exchange for a licence in respect of the patent rights found in the due diligence investigation. Alternatively, if a convincing argument can be made that the patent rights might be invalid, the owner may prefer to grant a licence than have the patent rights revoked or at least the weaknesses in the rights publicly exposed. This approach worked in relation to a patent for an innovation in the electronics sector. A French company thought that one if its innovations might infringe the patent owned by a large company based in the Asia Pacific region. A full due diligence investigation was undertaken into the validity of the patent in question. A detailed dossier was prepared running to many pages and summarised in an opening section. This dossier was then the subject of a formal presentation. This was done in a commercial context not as an overt threat to undermine the patent. The effect after a time was to convince the owner of the patent rights that the rights were vulnerable to being revoked worldwide and that giving a licence was beneficial to both businesses.

In many countries, the patent laws allow activities to be continued which would otherwise infringe the patent rights if these activities have commenced in good faith before the patent was published. The right to continue typically relates strictly to the activities already

---

1.   [1990] F.S.R. 181.

commenced. It does not allow other activities commenced later which would still infringe if covered by the scope of the patent.

A further possibility is to spend more time and money carrying out a really thorough due diligence into the patent rights and then judge whether an infringement really will occur. This is the most high risk strategy. This may lead back to a decision to abandon or alter the proposed activity which has already been mentioned. If not, the cost of defending patent infringement suits in several jurisdictions should prudently be built into the financial model on which the investment decision is to be taken. The example mentioned on page 278 on industrial doors is a good example of this approach. The due diligence showed that the patents were invalid. But the owner sued anyway. About a year later, when the case was all but lost by the patent owner, a satisfactory settlement was achieved with all legal costs recovered.

The 1989 UK of *Improver Corporation* v *Remmington* illustrates the care that needs to be taken when assessing patent rights in different countries. This case has been explained at page XX of this book as a case study. The legal battle in the European arena was conducted in Germany and UK. In the UK the "Smooth & Silky" product did not infringe the Improver patent because the patent specified a helical spring which was not in the "Smooth & Silky" product. The German Court found that there was an infringement of the Improver patent in Germany by the "Smooth & Silky" product essentially because the inventive concept had been taken even though the specified helical spring was not used.

The Remmington product with the rod and slits was not the same as the helical spring specifically mentioned in the Improver patent. However, it did use the innovative idea of the patent. A due diligence assessment before the court case had begun would have concluded with confidence that in the England the patent rights would not be infringed. But in Germany at the same time the conclusion about no infringement could not have been reached with any confidence. In this case, a settlement was eventually reached. The terms are not known but the Remmington product continued to be made and sold, becoming the market leading product.

Finally, remember that other rights may exist such as design rights and copyright. Care will need to be taken that these are not infringed by copying the designs to which those rights relate.

Summary of due diligence and patents

- Patent due diligence is about risk management not risk elimination;

- Specialist advice should be sought from someone with both expertise and experience. Experience is important because due diligence is often about making a judgement in given circumstances;

- Searching will reveal the existence of relevant patents and published patent applications. The rights given or likely to be given by these patents or applications will need to be evaluated;

- The evaluation of those rights will be crucial to deciding if any substantial risk of infringment of any patent rights exists;

- Seeking permission to use patent rights revealed by the due diligence may be necessary if an infringement risk is identified. The alternative being a costly infringement case even one where no infringement is likely to be the outcome;

- A patent strategy should be adopted including procedures to decide when to carry out a due diligence investigation and equally importantly to identify those innovations which might be patentable. Considering patenting innovations is important, particularly as patents for software and business methods in relation to the internet. Patent rights will give a business a better chance to negotiate the use of other patent rights if it has identified rights which might be infringed.

Film, music, broadcasting and similar rights

Copyright exists in most types of creative works produced in the media and entertainment industry. For example in music, lyrics, recordings and films. Any person who wishes to use such a creative work or part of it for commercial exploitation will almost certainly need permission from the owner of the relevant rights to do so. Copying the work without that permission would amount to an infringement of any copyright in that work or any of the related rights. Those related rights are discussed in chapter two and

Appendix 1 under the headings author's rights (page 68), performer's rights (page 68) and recording rights (page 69). The expression used in the entertainment industry for this process is the *clearing* of the rights to use a copyright work. The process of clearing rights is an everyday activity in the entertainment industry and is most relevant to recordings of literary works, typically plays, music and in relation to films and broadcasts. However, copyright does protect works created in other business sectors and the need to check for infringement applies to these equally. For example, the use of a graph as an illustration in a book, or the copying of a fabric design or the copying of a computer program are all likely to constitute copyright infringement if permission is not sought.

The purpose of the defensive due diligence when clearing rights is to know who owns the rights and to seek the permission from the owner to use the rights in the work created. Clearing rights is mainly required to be done in the media and entertainment industry because existing works are re-used to create or be included in new works. For example, the re-recording of a classic pop song will need the permission of the writer of the lyrics and of the music, as well as possibly the owner of the rights in the original recording since the new version may be regarded as an adaptation of the old. Clearing rights is of much less relevance to businesses in other sectors. But the importance of the internet as a channel for doing business and for providing information has brought the possibility of having to clear rights into other business sectors. So major websites about sports, news, and all kinds of information which may contain sounds and moving images to make the websites interesting and easy to use will require rights to be cleared.

The concept of "clearing rights"

Clearing rights means making sure that all the required permissions have been obtained to enable the product being produced to be used and sold as envisaged by the producers and financers of the production. The production could be a television programme, a film or video, a computer game, a music CD, or the creation of a portal website on the internet. The clearing of rights effectively is about careful planning and management. In a properly managed production process, the following should be considered with the producer:

- What is the origin of the production? Have all the rights from the originators of the project been obtained? For example, to use a screen play or to adapt a play or book into a film.

- What existing works are to be used? Can the permission of the rights owners be secured to use these works?

- How is the production to be commercialised? This is an important part of rights clearance given the way that rights are "sliced" by the rights owners. All likely ways of exploitation must be considered and appropriate permissions secured. A balance must be struck usually between obtaining permission for all likely uses ("slices") and the cost of doing so. Some less likely uses may have to be omitted on cost grounds. If these uses are important later, permission can be sought then and the payment for such permissions negotiated.

- How will author's rights and other related rights be dealt with if waivers cannot be obtained or the rights overcome? Will the existence of these rights adversely affect the viability of the project?

- Do rights have to be cleared for worldwide distribution or just for certain regions or countries? This is important. Clearing rights worldwide can be difficult, time-consuming, and expensive.

The person who has the task of clearing all the rights that may be necessary must know the answers or at least the likely answers to these questions and must do so preferably before the production starts. The cost of obtaining the necessary permissions should form part of the budget for the production. The necessary permissions to use rights can be obtained early if the production is planned properly and the person clearing the rights involved in the project at an early stage.

Identifying rights in an existing work to be used?

The point here is to find out if any rights actually exist which would prevent the product such as the television programme, a film or video, or a computer game or part of it being used. These rights could be any of the rights mentioned namely copyright, design rights, author's rights, performer's rights or recording rights. If there are no such rights the work can be used without further investigation. It would be unusual for any work worth exploiting to have no intellectual property rights protecting it.

Is a substantial part of the work to be used?

If only an insubstantial part of the work is to be used, in many cases this would not amount to an infringement of any copyright or rights in designs in the work. The product being produced can use that part without permission of any rights holders. This is an easy statement to make. It is far from easy to make the judgement confidently and correctly as to whether a substantial or an insubstantial amount of the work is being used. Getting this decision wrong will be very costly. At worst the product – television programme, a film or video, or a computer game – which has been made will not be usable. At best, some extra payment will be required to use the product which will not have been in the production budget. Guidelines on what constitutes a substantial part in this context can not be given since each time the decision would depend on circumstances. Some organisations have tried to give guidance on this by indicating that so many lines out of particular work will constitute an insubstantial amount. The idea is laudable but the practice is dangerous. For example in the case of *M S Associates* v *Power*,[2] at a preliminary hearing, the judge concluded that in the circumstances of that case, copying 90 lines of code of a software program out of a total of 7000 lines was the copying of a substantial amount sufficient to be a copyright infringement.

Can reliance be placed on any uses permitted by the relevant law?

These are often referred to as being "fair dealing" exceptions to copyright and cover such things as use for research in private study, use for criticism, review and reporting of current events, and educational use. There are others. It is not necessary in this book to go through them all. Most of them are aimed at non-commercial activities anyway. It is worth mentioning two recent cases about the attempt to rely in the UK on the concepts of fair dealing in copyright work. In the 1998 UK Court of Appeal case of *Pro Sieben Media AG* v *Carlton UK Television Limited*[3] shows these fair dealing provisions being applied by the courts. Pro Sieben made and broadcast a nine minute report about a women who became pregnant through infertility treatment and was carrying eight embryos. The use of a thirty second clip from this report in a programme about cheque

---

2.   [1988] FSR 242.
3.   [1998] FSR 43.

book journalism was not a copyright infringement since it was covered by the fair dealing exceptions. The court decided that the clip which was copied from the Pro Sieben programme had been used for the purposes of reporting current events and for criticism.

Another recent UK case about this arose out of media interest in the circumstances surrounding the death of Diana, Princess of Wales. She died in a car accident in August 1997. Mr. Al Fayed publicised his version of events leading up to fateful day. He suggested that his son Dodi and Diana were soon to be married and had spent two hours viewing one of his villas in Paris effectively as the matrimonial home. *The Sun* newspaper paid for some still photographs taken from a security camera which showed the two of them entering and Diana leaving the villa in about 30 minutes not two hours. *The Sun* published the photograph in typical lurid fashion as part of an exposé of Mr. Al Fayed's story as untrue. *The Sun* was sued for copyright infringement amongst other things. It relied on "fair dealing" in reporting current events. Even though a year after the death, the court was prepared to accept for the purpose of a preliminary ruling that the media interest in the circumstances about the death and Mr Al Fayed's account were current. It rejected *The Sun's* claim that they had acted fairly. The information about the times of the visit could have been used without the need to publish the photographs which had previously been unpublished. A defence that the publication was in the public interest also failed. There is a difference between in the public interest and of interest to the public. This case was the latter.

The process of clearing rights

The process has two phases. First, ascertaining the owner of the rights in the existing work to be used. Secondly, obtaining the permission of the owner to use the existing work in the project in question. Ascertaining ownership of registered designs and registered trade markes requires a similar process to that for patents.

Clearing rights in relation to well known media and entertainment works is usually not so much about checking legal rights. It is more about planning the rights which might be needed in producing and commercialising a new work and obtaining any permissions necessary. This task can be simple or complicated depending on the circumstances. Obtaining the rights to record music and lyrics written by an individual should be straightforward. But clearing all the rights in connection with a film will not be so straightforward. The rights of many individuals could be involved. For example, the person who wrote the original story, the person who wrote the screen play, writers of music and lyrics being included, and those who had recorded the music and lyrics. Many of these individuals will either have signed contracts with publishing and recording companies or will have appointed professional organisations to handle their rights. These organisations are generally referred to as collecting societies or similar.

Ownership of copyright or rights in designs in less well known work is about finding out who was the author of the work and if the rights have been transferred or are still owned by the author. For example, rights in a song may have been transferred to a music publishing company or to a record company. Any related rights such as author's rights should then also be identifiable or at least the need to check and clear any such rights should be identified. The identity of the author is a question of fact. In most cases making the identification is easy because the identity of the person who created the work is known and soon confirmed. Otherwise a detailed investigation may be necessary to ascertain the author's identity. In other circumstances there might be a dispute as to authorship. If so an investigation and a determination of the identity of the author will be necessary based on the facts revealed during the investigation. If the outcome of either investigation is inconclusive, uncertainty about who owns the rights may make the use of the work being considered too risky. Any decision to invest in any venture based on such copyrights would need to reflect that uncertainty.

A large part of the money made in the media and entertainment business derives from payments for the use of created works in which copyright, rights in designs, and related rights subsist. Many individual artists and performers make their living out of exploiting these rights either directly or through collecting societies. The revenues of many of the large and profitable businesses in this sector are made by exploiting copyrights and other rights which subsist in various works. Disney is a high profile example. The consequence of this is that these individuals and organisations are good at exploiting the rights in created works. Permissions to use them will be given for one project in return for one payment. Another use of the same work for another project will be require another payment. Even the use of the product of the project in a different context will require another payment. So the use of a recording in a film to be shown in a cinema may not include the right to use that recording to broadcast the film on television or to distribute it on video. If the bundle of copyrights and other rights which subsist in these works is considered as a loaf of bread, the rights owners will seek to slice the loaf as thinly as possible and then rent out the slices for payment. As new media come along such as DVD and the internet, more slices become available for which payment can be required.

The clearance process should start early in the production. If the necessary permissions cannot be obtained or only at costs which would make the production not profitable or sufficiently so, changes can be made before substantial production costs have been incurred. Leaving the clearing of rights to the last minute risks failing to secure the permission required so that the production cannot be exploited or parts must be left out or remade. The cost of this remaking could put the production over budget. This in turn may lead to difficulties with others involved in the production and financing of the project if the outcome will, as a result of a failed rights clearance, be quite different from that originally planned. Leaving parts out may affect the success of the production.

It may take some time to clear use of the rights in question. Rights clearance will require the procedures of any organisation which holds rights to be followed. Securing permission usually takes time as these procedures are followed. Alternatively, the rights are held by individuals who are often not inclined to be rushed into granting permission assuming they can be located in the first place. So another risk of leaving the rights clearance until late in the project is that if the person clearing the rights is then on a tight time scale, the rights holder may have to be told of the urgency. In these circumstances, the rights holder may see the producer needing the permission as being over a barrel. The price of the permission is likely to reflect this. Again budgets might be over-run with all the consequences previously mentioned.

Copyrights and other rights are national rights. Rights in designs are usually national but European design rights are now available. The extent of the rights given vary in each country. Care needs to be taken that the right to use the particular work in all countries where the work is to be exploited have been obtained. If not, another "slice" of the rights will be required which may require another payment depending on the rights owner. Equally important are the rights of authors and performing artists in the countries where the work is to be exploited. The extent of these rights also varies from country to country. The rights of authors and performing artists in the different countries are complex. Clearing these rights either worldwide or across many countries is a difficult task. It is also time consuming and a minefield. So, for example, in one country like England an author agrees to waive any author's rights in a particular work. Tick in the box. Relevant rights cleared. However, in some countries like Germany and France, authors cannot legally waive their rights so that in these countries the same author could object to some forms of exploitation of the particular work, for example, an adaptation of the work or to the way that the work was promoted or sold. This could either mean another "slice" of rights had to be purchased or that the author's views had to be taken into account in exploiting the work in that country or both.

Clearing copyright use (but take care in case other intellectual property rights exist)	
Is the work protected by copyright?	
Yes go to next question	No the work can be used without permission or infringement
Is a substantial part to be used?	
Yes go to next question	No the work can be used without permission or infringement
Do any fair dealing exceptions to infringement apply?	
No go to next question	Yes the work can be used without permission or infringement provided the terms of the relevant exception are strictly complied with
Who owns the copyright? (1) Was the work created by an employee?	
No author will be the owner unless an agreement provides otherwise	Yes employer will be the owner unless an agreement provides otherwise
(2) Does an agreement exist about ownership?	
	Yes Assess who is the owner of the copyright.
Finally, seek from the identified owner the necessary permissions	
• for each copyright work; • for all types of exploitation; • for all countries where work to be exploited.	

Summary of points about clearing rights

Clearing rights in works in which copyright rights in designs and related rights subsist is really all about identifying the rights involved and the ownership of them, knowing the uses for which permission will be needed, and making the required payments. The result should be that the exploitation of the new work will be free of the risk of infringement of copyright and other rights. Imagine planning to create a computer game or a complex website. The right to use the following will need to be obtained:

- the images which form part of the game;

- the software which drives the functionality of the game or the website;

- any screen play or story outline for the game or website;

- any animation;

- the music;

- the lyrics;

- the recording of the music and the lyrics;

- the synchronisation of the recording with the animation;

- any text;

- author's rights;

- any performer's rights.

These are the rights in respect of which permission is needed. It is likely that features such as the images and software will be specifically commissioned so that identifying the individuals is easy. In fact, the individuals are likely to have agreed that the business commissioning these will own all rights in them. Identifying the rights owners to well known music and lyrics and any recordings of them is not difficult nor should obtaining permission be difficult. The cost can be high. The rights owners to less well known works can be more difficult to trace. If they can be found, the cost should not be as high as for works by well known artists. Sometimes it is less trouble to commission new works and new recordings if, for an existing work, the rights owner cannot be identified or found or the cost of obtaining the rights is high or permission cannot be obtained to use the work in all the ways and all the countries where exploitation of the work is anticipated.

Any agreement in respect of a new work or new recording must ensure that either the commissioning organisation owns all the rights or has all the required permissions to use the work.

Trade Marks

Can I use my new brand, trading style, or packaging design?

The intellectual property rights which may exist in relation to a trade mark were described in the section on trade marks in chapter two (see page XX). These are registered trade marks, rights arising out of the use of the particular trade mark, and design rights as a result of recent changes in the law about designs. In the UK, the rights arising out of use are referred to as rights in passing off. Similar laws exist in countries such as Canada, Australia, and Singapore. Some other European countries have developed laws to protect trade marks against misuse known as unfair trade practices. In the United States, the concept of trade dress gives similar rights to protect unregistered trade marks.

It is worth recalling here that a trade mark can be any distinctive sign. The meaning of a sign includes brand and business names, packaging styles, logos, colours and smells. See page 410 for more detail.

These intellectual property rights for trade marks exist side by side. Knowing this is important for a defensive due diligence assessment in connection with a new trade mark. A search for any registered trade marks or applications may not turn up any existing registered trade mark rights which would prevent the proposed trade mark being used. But such a search will not necessarily indicate the full extent of the trade mark rights of others. A business may have been using the trade mark or one similar to it already. This business may have decided not to register a trade mark but would still, in the UK for example, have passing off rights. Both a registered trade mark search should be carried out and enquiries made in the trade to find out if anybody is using the same or a similar name. These enquiries can seem like looking for a needle in a haystack. At least any business which has been using the name prominently and extensively should be found through these enquiries. Once again, the due diligence is about risk reduction not risk elimination. It is inevitable even after these enquiries that some doubt will remain. The more extensive the enquiries the more the doubt about infringing someone's rights can be reduced. But some risk is likely to remain. Trade marks rights just like other intellectual property rights are really national rights enforced locally. So any trade mark searches and other enquiries will need to be made in all those countries where the proposed trade mark is to be used. That means all those countries where goods or services bearing the trade mark are likely to promoted and sold.

Once the results of the searches and enquiries are available, these will need to be analysed. The process should be easier and not as expensive as a search for patent rights. As with patents, the assessment of the results may lead to more searching and enquiries. This in turn will lead to more assessment and so on. There are several factors which influence how long this process of searching and assessment continues, some of them are:

- the importance of the chosen trade mark;

- the cost of the searching as against the cost of later changing the trade mark including the wasted investment in the promotion of the trade mark in the market or of paying damages for infringement;

- whether further searching is likely to increase certainty that either the trade mark can or cannot be used without infringing any intellectual property rights;

- whether in any of the major markets the trade mark cannot be used.

Recently a business devised a new concept in the entertainment sector. The concept needed the co-operation of famous personalities. The idea was to have involved visitor centres, themed bars, and merchandising of products. Two trade marks – a name and logo – were chosen. A due diligence investigation was carried out. The name trade mark was free to be used. But the logo trade mark would have clashed with an existing registered trade mark in England but not elsewhere. Further investigations showed that the existing trade mark was owned by a business based in California and that it had not been used much in England if at all in recent years.

The existing trade mark had probably not been used enough and so an application could be made to revoke the registration. This would open the way for the use of the logo trade mark as part of the new concept and also enable that logo trade mark to be registered. The difficult decision here was whether to launch the business using both the name and logo trade marks and if an infringement law suit was made, defend the claim by seeking to revoke the trade mark registration. Since the chance of doing that was good, the chance of some agreement being reached, if necessary, about the use of the trade mark would also be good. The alternatives were first to challenge the validity of the trade mark registration before launch. This would have taken over a year, maybe longer, and delayed the launch. Secondly, to seek such an agreement about using the trade mark before the business was launched. The threat to revoke the registration would also be mentioned. If no agreement could be reached, the threat could be carried out and a further attempt to agree use could be made.

In fact the business concept was launched with plenty of funding behind it. The infringement claim was raised and the counterclaim for cancellation made in return. The outcome was that the trade mark was acquired by the business promoting the new concept at a value which gave the owner a good return for an under performing trade mark. However, the price was probably less that the likely unrecoverable legal costs, avoided management time being involved in a dispute at a critical time of the launch of the new venture, and gave certainty.

In any trade mark due diligence, once the searching and assessment has been completed, a judgement must be made based on the results of the assessment. This again is risk management. If the assessment is that no trade mark rights exist which prevent the chosen trade mark being used, the decision is easy. Similarly if trade mark rights exist such that the use of the chosen brand or name in a particular country would be an infringement or there is a reasonable risk of infringement, then the decision here too should be easy and involve a change to a different brand or name. This may involve further searching and enquiries.

The difficult decisions are where the existing trade mark rights probably will not be infringed but might be. Circumstances will probably determine the best course to take.

If a major launch is planned for the new trade mark or a business based on using it, the decision will probably be to avoid any possibility of being required to withdraw the trade mark and relaunch under a new trade mark. This might be achieved by seeking agreement before launch of the owner of the existing trade mark rights if the trade mark is a particularly good one. The agreement could be to acquire the trade mark or licence its use. Much will depend on who owns the trade mark. A major rival is unlikely to agree or the price is likely to be too high. If certainty cannot be achieved by agreement and the trade mark is important, the decision may be to go ahead anyway. As with patents, the cost of defending a trade mark infringement case must then be built in to business plan for the launch of the new business in which the trade mark is to be used. More than one such case might be involved if the launch is in several countries. If the trade mark is not so important, the prudent course would be to proceed with a different one. The money which might have been spent defending trade mark infringement law suits being used to promote the business or taken as profit.

Domain names

These are not really intellectual property rights. However, when considering the adoption of a trade mark, the availability of the domain name must be considered. At the time of writing, the rights of a trade mark owner to obtain the use of a domain name containing the owner's trade mark, registered by someone who is not the owner of the trade mark, have become clearer. There have been some high profile cases of individuals registering domain names equivalent to well known trade marks with a view to demanding large sums to transfer them. Such individuals had some early success. One individual is known to received several thousand US Dollars for a high profile sports related domain name just before a major championship.

Recent cases have shown that such profiteering may be over. For example, the World Wrestling Federation took an individual to the World Intellectual Property Organisation's domain name dispute resolution forum. The individual had registered the domain name "worldwrestlingfederation.com" and four days later offered to sell it to the Federation for a $1000. The individual was quickly ordered to hand the domain name over.

The legal position in relation to trade marks and domain names is still developing. There are two routes to resolving disputes between domain name owners and the owners of rights in a trade mark used in the domain name. First, the procedural dispute resolution processes of the organisations such ICANN and NOMINET who registered domain names. The World Intellectual Property Organisation (WIPO) also has a dispute resolution process for domain name ownership disputes. These broadly require certain published criteria to be met and require written representations which are considered by an adjudicator who then makes a decision. The other route to resolving such disputes is to take action in the courts. The outcome will depend on the attitude of the courts in the jurisdiction where the action has been or is required to be taken. The dispute resolution processes involve less cost than court action and tend to be relatively quicker. Owners of strong rights in trade marks have generally found them effective.

The current position in general is as follows. Any organisation with strong trade mark rights – that is a well known trade mark probably used for many years – preferably registered as a trade mark, will be able to stop the use of a domain name which includes the trade mark in question or one similar to it. This will be so whether action is taken in the courts or one of the domain name dispute resolution processes is used. A decision adverse to the trade mark owner, through such a process, is not binding on the courts and the trade mark owner can have a second bite at the cherry through the courts.

Owners of new or less well known trade marks face a more uncertain outcome, especially if their trade marks are not registered. The owner of the domain name may have a plausible argument explaining why the domain name containing the trade mark or one similar to it was registered as a domain name. This argument will be likely to make the point that the owner of the domain name was unaware of the new or not so well known trade mark. Stopping the use of the domain name in these circumstances is unpredictable. The courts probably being the better route than the domain name dispute resolution processes. The costs will be higher in the courts.

In many cases, if the trade mark owner is successful in preventing the continued use of the domain name which incorporates a trade mark or something similar to it, then an order will be obtained to transfer the domain name into the ownership of the trade mark owner.

So one important practical point must be made. If a trade mark is to be adopted, check the equivalent domain name. Not just for who owns it but to find out what information can be accessed using the trade mark as a domain name.

Recently investors sought to build up a British brand which has considerable potential. Unfortunately, the top level domain name "brandname.com" is owned by a United States based individual and when accessed brings up a large number of hard core pornography sites. The domain name has been registered for over five years. The brand owners in allowing the brand to languish had not been alive to the possibility of registering the domain name themselves or of checking if someone else had done so. The former is understandable since five years ago the potential of the internet and the need to register domain names was not widely known. Less forgivable is failing to check in the last two to three years and take appropriate action. Action is currently being contemplated probably in the United States which will seek to stop the use of this domain name and to have it transferred to the brand owners and the new investors. The outcome is uncertain. The trade mark is not widely known although is prestigious. The use of it to access pornography is likely to help influence a court in favour of the owner of the brand.

Designs

These can go under several different names depending on the country involved and were explained in chapter two (see page XX). In the UK and many other countries, a design which is registered becomes a registered design. But other names are used in some countries for protection given to designs by registration such as utility model or design patent. A rather older expression for a utility model still used is petty patent. A further complication is that the scope of protection given by these legal rights depends on the interpretation of them by national courts in given circumstances.

A due diligence investigation for design registrations is done in a similar way as for patents. Searches are carried out in respect of those countries which are the major markets for a product. The search and analysis stages will be similar as for patents. The results of the searches are then analysed and a judgement made about whether or not the product is likely to infringe any design registrations. The aim as with patents is risk management. In many cases, elimination of the risk will not be possible.

The analysis of the rights in designs found by these searches should take less time and be less complicated than for patents. The registrations for designs usually do not take as long to understand as a patent specification running to many pages. The judgement as to whether the rights are infringed or not is likely to be just as difficult.

Licensing Intellectual Property Rights

Introduction

Licensing is the most usual way to acquire the right to exploit intellectual property. Most owners are reluctant to transfer ownership of their rights outright except through an up-front payment reflecting the value of the rights. If the intellectual property rights are mature in the sense of generating substantial royalty revenue, valuing the intellectual property rights with reasonable certainty is possible. The selling price is likely to be high. The following examples from the financial press over the last few years of intellectual property rights being sold are interesting and illustrative. The Enid Blyton copyrights were sold for £13 million. EMI bought a half interest in a catalogue of Motown classic songs and recordings for $132 million. SC Johnson &

Co sold four household brands – Spray 'n Wash, Glass Plus, Vivid, and Yes – for $160 million. The film rights to a best selling book Cold Mountain were bought for $1.25 million. The UK health service paid £1.25m for the copyrights and other rights in a computer coding system for use in a computerised clinical information system.

If the rights are not mature in the sense of having a track record of generating substantial royalty payments, the price at which the rights might be acquired would have to be based on some assumed revenue stream generated using the intellectual property rights. In these circumstances, putting a value on the intellectual property rights is much more subjective. Agreeing a price might be difficult. The risk would exist that the owner would sell for too little and that the buyer would pay too much. This risk for both parties can be largely removed by a royalty based licence, perhaps linked to an option to buy these rights later where the revenue being earned is more certain.

The licence and related agreements should be properly prepared in writing although with many intellectual property rights a written licence agreement is not a technical legal requirement. It is, nevertheless, prudent in most cases to have a written agreement. Much depends on the local law and the particular rights involved. The agreement should contain all the basic agreed terms. It should also make provision for ending the relationship in an orderly fashion.

Keep an open mind!

Technology licensing is conceptually simple. One person has intellectual property rights for use by others in return for payment. Another person needs or wants to use the rights and is willing to pay. Each licensing deal depends on the prevailing circumstances. Some will be simple, others very complicated. But all too often the first move is to begin considering straight away the standard licensing structure such as the rights to be licensed, the territory, any lump sum, and royalties. Then perhaps exclusivity and minimum performance standards.

But to do this misses out an important strategic step. A careful commercial analysis is essential about the use to which the intellectual property rights will be put and the likely revenue generated as well as covering other strategic aspects such as the way the business and the market is likely to develop, attitude of competitors, technology obsolescence, the possibility of modifications and improvements. Then the detailed consideration about the licensing terms, particularly the commercial terms, should begin as if with a blank sheet of paper. It is too easy to be railroaded into standard terms and not to use imagination to structure the terms of the licensing deal. It is likely that some of the standard type of terms will end up in the agreement but these should be included because in the circumstances they are needed not because they are standard.

Structuring the licensing deal – the important areas

Even starting conceptually with a blank piece of paper, some terms of a licencing deal need to be covered and will be a feature of any licensing deal. They are the parts of any licensing arrangement where negotiation is at its most intense unless one side can effectively impose terms on the other. These terms are about:

- the commercial activities licensed;

- payment for the use of the intellectual property right;

- whether the deal will be exclusive or non-exclusive;

- who will tackle others who may infringe the licensed intellectual property rights;

- to what extent warranties and indemnities will be given that use of the rights will not infringe the intellectual property rights of someone else;

- and about modifications and improvements.

Rights licensed and territory

It is important to think carefully about the commercial activities in respect of which the licence to use the intellectual property rights is required. This is particularly so with the use of copyright works and similar rights in the media sector and in software. Careful consideration also needs to be given to the countries where the commercial activities or some of them are to be carried out. Then in the negotiations the required rights can be requested and any limitations considered in the context of the earlier assessment of the extent of the rights needed to make the use of the licence successful. So the question needs to be: is a licence to manufacture and sell to be, for example, a licence to do this anywhere or in given countries? Or is manufacturing going to be carried out in only some specified countries with selling and supply being over a wider area? If some processes need to be subcontracted, rights to do this under the licence need to be obtained and safeguards put in place for the owner of the intellectual property rights. For example, is it important who can be awarded a sub-licence? Does the owner of the rights have a veto? Will the licensee guarantee the obligations and payments of the sub-licensee or be directly liable?

Payment

The payment arrangements in any licensing deal depend on the terms negotiated by the parties to the deal. There are no hard and fast rules. Many licensing deals are complex involving highly structured payment terms. However, lump sums at the start, royalties on sales, and minimum royalty payments are common in licence deals. A lump sum is often paid at the start of the licence. Many arguments can be made to justify the request for the payment of a lump sum. For example, the lump sum pays the administration of the licensor or is the price of acquiring the licence with its royalty payment obligations. But really the lump sum is just part of the cost of licensing the use of the intellectual property rights. Recognising this reality, the lump sum is sometimes described as a payment on account of future royalties to be set off against royalties generated in the future.

Royalty payments are usually linked to sales. A calculation of the amount payable is best pegged to net sales value although, for example, many franchises require franchise fees (otherwise known as royalties) to be calculated on gross sales. The obvious danger in using gross sales is that too much of the profit is taken up in royalty payments to make the deal sustainable. In one instance a US franchise was brought over to the United Kingdom. It became clear that the franchise fees based on turnover were too high. The costs of property to locate franchise outlets, in particular rent and local government taxes, as well as the ever increasing cost associated with the regulation of employment, and the minimum wage, were much higher than in the United States. To make the franchise sufficiently profitable, lower franchise fees needed to be charged to keep the margin equivalent to the average net margin being achieved by a typical franchisee in the Untied States.

Minimum royalties to be paid each year are an incentive to the licensee to make good use of the intellectual property rights and generate royalties for the licensor. If the intellectual property rights have a track record of generating royalties paid by licensees, then setting a minimum accurately is possible. Take for example a licence to use Disney characters for merchandising products. The payment terms including minimums will be virtually standard because of the experience of Disney at licensing and merchandising and their ability to effectively dictate terms in many cases. But with a new technology or brand, setting minimums is difficult. In theses circumstances, it is common to start with a low level and build up over several years.

Terms will need to be included to provide for what will happen if the minimums are not met. Will the owner be able to terminate the agreement? Alternatively if the licence has some exclusivity built into it, will the owner be able to end the exclusivity but keep the agreement going? What about the person who has acquired the licence? Does this person have the chance to make up the difference between the royalties actually generated and the minimum amount or have the right to terminate the agreement on the basis that enough business cannot be generated to earn sufficient royalties?

But with no track record, the minimum figures are forecasts only. Any business investing in the licence will be reluctant to do so if the agreement can be terminated in the event that the forecasts figures are not achieved. None of the parties to the agreement can say with any certainty that the forecast figures will or will not be achieved. It requires a proactive and imaginative approach to find an acceptable middle way in particular circumstances. The owner needs some reasonable certainty that the rights will earn royalties through effective exploitation. The licensee needs the assurance that the rights cannot be taken away if, in good faith, the rights have been exploited but the sales or other uses achieved have not matched up to expectations.

Remember no matter what the agreement says, it is always possible to seek to renegotiate. If both parties can see the market requires something different, new terms might be possible.

Exclusive or non-exclusive

Exclusivity is usually given for a territory – a region or a country. Less often worldwide exclusivity is agreed. The first important point to appreciate about an owner of any intellectual property rights giving an exclusive licence of them to one person is that the owner cannot then use the intellectual property rights. An alternative for the owner is to grant a sole licence which means that the owner and the person licensed only can use the intellectual property rights. An exclusive licence is more valuable than a sole or non-exclusive one. A sole license could be more valuable than a non-exclusive one but much will depend on the relative market power exercised by the owner and the licensee. The payment terms should reflect this. Minimum performance targets are important especially with exclusivity over a large territory. A worldwide exclusive deal would be imprudent without some measurable performance targets. Without such targets, the worldwide exclusivity could result in the products or services to which the intellectual property rights relate not being exploited. The failure to exploit the rights could be deliberate or because the licensee is incapable of exploiting the rights for whatever reason. In these circumstances, the owner of the rights – the licensor – would have little or no royalty revenue and may not have any clear sanctions to encourage performance or which would enable the agreement to be terminated.

Once a non-exclusive licence has been given for a territory, an exclusive one cannot be agreed for that same territory unless the first non-exclusive agreement can be ended. Before a decision about exclusivity is taken, a strategic assessment should be made of the likely best way to maxmise the licensing revenue from the market in the territory. Then a decision can be made about giving exclusivity or not taking everything into account.

Two cases studies based on recent deals illustrate this point well. The first involved technology developed in the United States. It was patented worldwide. An exclusive licence was given to a European based business for most of the European Union countries and also countries such as Poland and Romania. A few years later the US owner of the patents had the chance to licence on a non-exclusive basis a multi-national United States business. This would have been lucrative. But a major market for this multi-national was Europe where an exclusive licence was already in place blocking the deal. The only real options for the US owner were either to buy out the exclusive rights for Europe or to make the exclusive licensee part of the agreement and share some of the benefits.

In the other case, software was licensed to a business in one country on an exclusive basis. This was done before the software was successful. About a year later, in the home market of the owner of the copyright in the software, the sales of the software increased rapidly. The value of the business grew hugely. The exclusive deal in the neighbouring territory enabled the exclusive licensee to ride on the back of the success in the home market and to achieve a similar business valuation. This business with the exclusive rights was disproportionately successful from the neighbouring territory where the exclusive rights had been granted compared to the owner of the rights.

Competition law/anti-trust compliance

The effect of licensing territories exclusively can be to divide a region up. Limiting the rights by country or groups of countries can lead to breaches or potential breaches of the regulations about competition or so called anti-trust laws. The licensing transaction and the agreement need to be structured so as to be compliant with these laws taking advantage of published exemptions and guidance. These laws are complex and are both national and regional. The consequences of failing to comply can be the agreement or parts of it are ineffective and heavy fines can be imposed by the competition authorities. These authorities have extensive powers of investigation and to search premises for information.

The concern is that an exclusive licensee in one part cannot promote or sell the licensed product or service in the territory of another exclusive licensee. If this type of scheme is put in place, it can have the effect of reducing competition in each territory. This, in turn, can inflate prices and have other adverse effects for business purchasers and consumers. Consequently, the authorities charged with enforcing the laws against anti-competitive activities may investigate such schemes where the owner of the intellectual property rights has substantial market power. In Europe, it is possible to structure the licensing scheme to meet various exemptions or to obtain clearance of the particular scheme. Obtaining clearance can be a laborious process and is now discouraged. The regulatory authorities now effectively requiring businesses to "self certify" that they are compliant. One serious disadvantage in seeking clearance is that it usually involves disclosing a great deal of sensitive business information. If an exclusive licence scheme is to be set up for parts of Europe which may reduce competition in the market, the terms of the licences should be made to fit into one of the exemptions wherever the business strategy allows.

Dealing with infringers

This is another area of often hot discussion in a negotiation over a licence. The ability of a licensee to take court action to prevent infringements of the licensed intellectual property rights depends on both the law applicable to the agreement and of the country where the alleged infringement is happening. Some laws allow licensees to sue, others do not. Others again only allow exclusive licensees and the owner of the particular rights to sue.

If a licensee has the legal capacity to sue, it is possible to adopt one of several negotiating positions. The position adopted by a party to a negotiation is not always one of principle but rather because it suits the interest of that person or business in the negotiations. The most common positions to take are as follows:

- *"You own the rights, you sue"*. This approach means the licensee argues that the owner of the rights should take any required action against an infringer because that person is being paid for the use of the rights. If the rights are being infringed without penalty, the person paying royalties is paying for nothing.

- *"You're using the rights, you sue"*. Here the licensor argues that the person licensed should tackle infringers because that person is making most money out of the exploitation of the intellectual property rights in that territory. This is often argued forcefully if an exclusive licence is being granted. The licensee will argue equally forcefully that all the business risk is being taken by the licensee and the added risk of taking on infringers should be borne by the owner of the rights.

- *"We can both sue"*. Here either the licensee or owner of the licensed rights can take on infringers. The extent of the profits being earned, or the potential to earn them, by the licensee will determine if the licensee will attempt to stop an infringement so as to protect the profits being earned.

The licensee will typically argue that royalties should not payable whilst infringements are continuing unchecked. If the licensee tackles infringers, terms will be demanded in relation to the legal and other costs of doing so. Sharing them or deducting them from royalties payable are common. The licensor will argue that infringement is a fact of life and the licensor will take all appropriate action. In the meantime the licensee should keep paying. The negotiations can move on to what happens if the licensor takes no action or is ineffective in preventing infringements. The deal must them reach some compromise position or the negotiations will fail.

An infringement may not be clear-cut. Terms are, therefore, often included which provided a mechanism for determining whether an infringement is taking place or not. Some link this to taking independent advice from legal counsel in the territory where the infringement is said to be occurring. The conclusion that infringement is happening can be important since it will be the trigger for all the other terms about infringement to operate, notably who will sue the infringer, how the costs will be borne, and what happens to the payment of royalties in the meantime.

In one deal a large international business was negotiating to take an exclusive worldwide patent licence from a much smaller, though successful, business. One of the major markets was the Asia-Pacific region. The large business produced a draft agreement which stated that if an infringement occurred in any territory and the infringement went unchecked, royalty payments would be suspended. The product in question would be relatively easy to counterfeit. The smaller business was rightly worried that either all its royalty income would be spent chasing shadowy counterfeiters or if it did not, royalties would be suspended. Poor deal either way.

The larger business clearly had the money and the legal advisors in place to attack counterfeiters. It was better placed to do so. The compromise terms involved a complicated formula but basically the larger company would sue all infringers, royalties would not be suspended if counterfeiting was the type of infringement taking place. But if the patent rights were challenged in any major jurisdiction such as in an infringement action against a rival legitimate business, the cost would be off set against royalties payable in respect of sales in any part of the world. The agreement needed to be more specific about precisely what would constitute a challenge in a major jurisdiction. The overall financial value of the licensing deal to the owner of the patent rights was reduced to reflect the risk of having to tackle infringers and counterfeiters.

Infringement indemnity

The licensee will be concerned to be sure or to be as sure as possible that no infringement of the intellectual property rights of any other person occurs when using the intellectual property rights licensed. This is the same concern addressed by a defensive due diligence investigation. The licensee will seek a warranty that by exploiting the intellectual property rights no infringement of other rights will occur and an indemnity in respect of any loss caused if the warranty is breached and other rights are infringed. The attitude taken to such a warranty indemnity by lawyers and business people varies enormously and often reflects a personal approach to licensing. The spectrum of these approaches ranges from the formal legal to the practical deal making.

The licensee, if properly informed or advised, will usually ask for an indemnity from the owner of the rights to cover any liability arising from such an infringement. The aim is to reduce the risk associated with building a business, or part of one, around someone else's intellectual property rights. But the owner of the intellectual property will not know for certain whether or not use of the rights will infringe the intellectual property rights of another person. Any searching for rights in connection with the registration of its own rights and the prosecution of the registration of its own rights will have revealed some relevant intellectual property rights of others. However, the owner, if properly informed or advised, will resist a request for such an indemnity. The section on defensive due diligence in this chapter clearly established that being certain as to whether or not using the intellectual property rights licensed will result in the infringement of other intellectual property rights in the vast majority of cases will not be possible.

The important point, therefore, is that giving or not giving such an indemnity is all about who bears the risk of infringement of other intellectual property rights. This is an aspect of defensive due diligence. The argument is often put forward that an indemnity must be given because the owner of the rights is charging for their use and should in effect certify that the rights can be used risk free.

If a proper due diligence investigation has been carried out, the risk of infringement of other intellectual property rights can be assessed. Inevitably, some uncertainty and, therefore, risk remains. But the cost of such an investigation to the licensor could be substantial and may not be justified if the likely payments under licence are not anticipated to be substantial. The cost, even if substantial, could be justified to the licensee if a major investment of time and money is to be made or if the infringement damages could be high. All these factors will form part of the negotiation about the terms of the licence.

Some important practical points follow from this. If giving an infringement indemnity, the prudent owner of the rights to be licensed should undertake some due diligence investigation and reveal any worries about other relevant intellectual property rights. This is similar to giving a disclosure letter common in corporate transactions. If the owner of the rights is a small company or an individual inventor, the owner is unlikely to have the money or assets to back the likely liability which would arise if other intellectual property rights were infringed. So the licensee may decide to undertake a defensive due diligence investigation anyway. The owner of the rights being licensed should consider capping the amount of the liability, possibly as a way to break any deadlock in negotiations over this point. It is likely that insuring against this type of liability will be difficult and, if such insurance is available, the premium will be expensive.

The risk is more difficult to assess as to whether or not infringement of the copyright and unregistered designs belonging to some else will be infringed by using the licensed intellectual property rights. This is because copyrights and some design rights are not registered and cannot be searched. But to infringe any copyright or designs often requires copying to be proven. The rights owner should be able to state with certainty at least that the licensed copyright or designs are original works and not copied. This is a significant statement if made as a warranty and backed up with an indemnity. It reflects the risks that the licensor should be able to control. The rights owner as licensor will be reluctant to go further and give a warranty that no infringement of any other intellectual property rights, particularly copyright and design rights. The risk assessment here is much harder for the licensee but easier for the licensor who has access to relevant information. This is a good argument for the licensor to give some assurance and indemnity.

In the end the giving or not of this type of indemnity is all about who takes the risk or about risk sharing. The outcome of the negotiation on this point as with others depends on the usual factors – relative bargaining positions, the need or desire to do the deal, and whether, if necessary to do the deal, those involved can find a way to balance the risks acceptable to both sides of the agreement being negotiated.

Modifications, improvements, and adaptations of patented inventions

This is another difficult aspect of technology licensing particularly where patents are involved. These three words effectively cover similar but not necessarily the same things. They are often used either together or individually in licence agreements. Careful consideration needs to given to what these words mean in a particular agreement because it might be very important whether a subsequent innovation by either the licensee or licensor is covered by the agreement.

A further aspect of the case study referred to on page 323, about the exclusive patent licence for the European countries, shows just why careful consideration of improvements and modifications can be vitally important.

The exclusive licence was blocking another deal the US owner of the patent rights wanted to do. It had made an improvement in or possibly an adaptation of the original patented recycling process based on a chemical reaction. This modification was also patented. But the exclusive licence had clearly expressed terms that included in the licence all later modifications, improvements or adaptations of the original process. The exclusive licensee argued that the later innovation in the process was, as a result of these terms, covered by their exclusive licence. The US owner was still blocked. The US patent owner argued that the modification was sufficiently different so as not to infringe the first patents and so could not be regarded as a modification, an improvement or an adaptation. It was not covered by the exclusive licence and they were free to licence this later innovation to someone else.

The result was a practical commercial outcome. The large US patent owner went ahead and licensed the later innovation to another major US corporation. The exclusive licensee decided not to sue either of them for patent infringement or the patent owner for breaching the agreement.

The licensor and owner of the patent rights knows the technology and technical field well. Further innovations are likely. The licensee will normally want further innovations on the initial licensed technology to be included in the licence and disclosed as soon as possible. Since a licence agreement is in place, including these later innovations is relatively easy. The parties to the agreement will still have to negotiate the basis on which these later innovations will be included in the licence, if at all. For example, will additional payments be made or the costs of patenting them be shared?

Much more difficult is dealing with subsequent innovations by the licensee based on the licensed technology. If the owner and licensor of the original patents negotiates and obtains agreement that these innovations will be made available to it, a mechanism to make this part of a binding agreement is difficult certainly under English law. It is not possible to have an enforceable agreement as to how the licensee will licence back innovations it has made to the licensor, unless all the terms of that licence-back are set out at the time the first agreement is reached. Of course, the licensee may never make any innovations so the cost of setting up the agreement just in case would then have been wasted.

Instead, many different types of good faith mechanisms can be included. Some of these can have elements which are legally enforceable such as giving rights of first refusal, exclusive negotiating periods or rights to be offered a license on no less favourable terms than the best deal done with another business.

The competition authorities regard the pooling of patents for innovations made by linked orgainsations such as a licensor and several licensees of a particular technology as potentially anti-competitive. So when negotiating and agreeing the terms of a licence of patented technology, be aware that including modifications improvements and adaptations might be regarded as preventing competition. The circumstances will be all important in determining if competition is being prevented or is likely to be so.

Intellectual Property Agreements – Licences and Assignments

Validity of agreements

Agreements are an integral and essential part of transactions in intellectual property rights. A due diligence investigation may reveal weaknesses in the title or the rights to use intellectual property. These weaknesses can often be removed by a suitable agreement. When intellectual property rights have been transferred or are licensed, a due diligence process must assess the validity of the agreements in question. The agreements could constitute a weak link. The intellectual property rights may be strong but the title to them or the right to use them may be weak as a result of poor agreements.

The effect of an inadequate agreement

This case involved a dispute about a design of a security product. Allegations of copying were made. These were denied. Investigations by the defence lawyers lead to the conclusion that the design probably had been copied but that the ownership of the design by the business alleging copying looked vulnerable after requests for information and further investigations. The design had been originated by a company which had gone into liquidation and been dissolved. The rights had been transferred to the business making the allegations by an "agreement". The agreement was short, just about identified the design but not clearly, did not meet all the legal requirements to be enforced, and was signed by an individual stated to be the "general manger" who probably did not have authority to sign the agreement and who could no longer be found.

So the ownership of the design was seriously in doubt. The company which originated the design had been dissolved and could not be asked to sign a confirmatory assignment of the rights in the design. A court might conclude after all the evidence came out that the "agreement" was effective or at least in all the circumstances showed a sufficiently certain intention that transfer of ownership should be recognised. A very uncertain prospect. The case was withdraw later. The copiers got away with it. The costs of the investigation were easily justified.

The uncertainties over ownership had the effect of making the rights unenforceable throughout the world. The value of those rights was, therefore, reduced to nothing.

Every agreement will be governed by the law of a particular country usually referred to as the "applicable law". The courts of a particular country will have jurisdiction over disputes arising out of the agreement. The rules to determine applicable law and jurisdiction even when plainly stated in an agreement are complex and in many instances are governed by international treaties. The applicable law and the courts having jurisdiction will set the legal context which will determine whether an agreement is a valid one or not. For example, the extent to which oral evidence about the nature of the agreement, and what was intended, can be given in court could effect the resolution of any ambiguities in the agreement. For example in the UK, there are restrictions on the extent to which oral evidence can be given in such circumstances.

Check formalities

When considering an agreement in a due diligence exercise the obvious formalities will need to be checked. These will include the names of the parties, that the agreement was signed, that the agreement has relevant terms to cover the transaction in question. These may seem obvious but they are nonetheless important to check.

Case Study

This example illustrates the point. In a patent licensing deal, a subsidiary of an international manufacturing company agreed on its own behalf and on behalf of all its subsidiaries and its holding company to use for a number of years a patented product exclusively in all the major markets including the United States rather than a rival product. Leaving aside any anti-trust or regulatory objections that there might be to this deal, at the time the agreement with the subsidiary was signed, the holding company had signed, a few months previously, a deal to buy the rival product for use in the whole of the United States. The subsequent dispute about a breach of the agreement centered around whether the subsidiary had made an agreement which bound the holding company. If not, the only route left to the first company would be to sue the subsidiary for breach of contract. The weakness made the agreement possibly ineffective in a major market the United States. The value of the transaction was totally different to that which appeared at first sight on reading the agreement. The deal really should have been done with the holding company not the subsidiary. The subsidiary was later sued, found to have breached the agreement, and paid substantial damages.

Other legal technical requirements must be met for the agreement to be valid and enforceable. Again this would depend on the applicable law. For example, in the UK an agreement will not be enforced if its terms are not sufficiently certain or, in some circumstances, unless it has been executed as a deed. For other agreements, consideration must have been given at the time the agreement was signed.

Case Study

Another case study involved an attempt to enforce an agreement which arose out of a patent infringement dispute which was settled after difficult and lengthy negotiations. The settlement agreement contained an option for the company alleged to be infringing the patent to take a patent licence. Draft terms of the licence were attached to the settlement agreement. Both the settlement agreement and the draft licence had clauses making the laws in England and Wales the applicable law. Rather than recite all of the terms of a patent licence, the main terms that one would expect were included, duration, royalty rate, products covered, times for payment and the like. But not all the terms were included. A provision was made that if there was any dispute about the terms to be included the usual terms for a patent licence would be included and in the case of dispute those terms would be determined by a Queen's Counsel of at least 10 year standing practising in the UK "at the patent bar".

Shortly after the settlement was reached, the company accused of infringement sought to exercise the option to take up the patent licence. The company who owned the patent reneged on the deal and refused to grant the licence on the basis that the terms of the licence could not be determined with sufficient certainty. The company given the option sought to enforce the terms of the agreement and issued proceedings in the UK courts using a summary or fast track procedure rather than the normal court process which could have taken about two years to reach a conclusion if no appeal was made. It was not commercially worth a drawn out dispute. In the summary procedure, the court of first instance and the UK Court of Appeal both found the terms of the licence to be insufficiently certain to be enforceable.

A case of this sort – which is real – should be taken as a salutary lesson to both professional advisors and to those in business. The business person would often prefer a short agreement whereas a legal advisor will insist that only a weighty document will do the trick. Here, the attempt to have a short agreement came unstuck. The legal advisor's nightmare and commercially useless too!

To be binding, an agreement must be signed by a person in authority. If the agreement is to be signed by an individual, then the individual can sign and the agreement will be binding on him. Any person signing on behalf of a company must be duly authorised. If the applicable law of the agreement was UK law, then directors of companies will normally have actual authority or authority consistent with their status through the concept of ostensible authority. Nevertheless, if the agreement is important, it is prudent to obtain, in relation to a company operating under UK law, a resolution of the board of directors of the company authorising a named person to enter into the particular agreement on its behalf. Equivalent procedures will exist for businesses operating under the laws of other countries.

One case illustrative of this point involved a dispute about the ownership of a particular intellectual property right. One party was a UK company, the other was an international investment company with offices in many parts of the world including Switzerland. The parties had entered into a collaboration agreement to undertake research into a particular technical field. The agreement provided the usual things such as the keeping of confidential information, the sharing of technical results and the use to which they would be put. Agreements were also reached about joint ownership of any intellectual property rights that arose out of the collaboration. Suffice to say for our purposes that that collaboration agreement was not as clear as it might have been. A dispute arose as to the ownership of patents. The UK company relied on the agreement providing for joint ownership. The investment company put forward a different meaning of the agreement namely that it would own all intellectual property rights. As the case unfolded this position looked increasingly untenable. The international investment company then sought to rely on a technicality. The agreement was entered into by the company's subsidiary based in Switzerland. The company argued that under Swiss law only specific named persons in a public register had authority to sign agreements binding the company. Since the agreement had not been signed by such a person it was not binding even though both companies had operated under the terms of the agreement for several years. The outcome for the Swiss company would have been much better if the agreement was not enforceable. The dispute was settled so the point was never determined by a court.

Incomplete or incorrect agreements

A written agreement should be an expression of what the parties have agreed to do relative to one another – that is, express their mutual obligations. It should be complete and certain. However, no one can anticipate every eventuality that will arise and, therefore, the terms of an agreement are unlikely to cover every such eventuality. One might call these unforeseeable gaps. Occasionally, terms may simply have been omitted or incorrectly expressed by mistake. One might call these foreseeable mistakes. In either case, the express terms of the agreement will not be sufficient.

The law of the agreement and the likely attitude of the courts having jurisdiction will be critical to the outcome of any attempt to use the law to fill any gaps or resolve any mistakes in an agreement. An English court under English law, will, by suitable evidence, seek to establish the complete agreement where the parties have failed to state the full terms of their agreement. It will do so by interpreting the true meaning of the agreement, by implying terms where appropriate, and by rectifying mistakes in certain limited circumstances. Being aware of these approaches, and the possibility of similar legal doctrines in other jurisdictions, could in particular circumstances enable the person undertaking the due diligence investigation to suggest ways to resolve mistakes, and reduce uncertainties and risks, which may be sufficient to allow a particular transaction to proceed either on the original basis or a different one.

Registering intellectual property agreements

In the transfer of intellectual property rights there are some technical requirements to be met. In UK law an assignment of a patent for example must be in writing and, for damages to be recoverable in infringement proceedings, the transfer or the licence being granted must be registered within some time at the UK Patent Office. The recording of agreements affecting or relating to any registered intellectual property rights at the registry where the particular intellectual property right is registered is important but often overlooked.

Renewals

Registered intellectual property rights require to be renewed at defined intervals. The renewal periods vary depending on the intellectual property rights in question and the countries in which they are registered. Intellectual property rights being essentially a collection of national rights, local national laws will determine the regulations and procedures of renewal which will apply. The renewal attracts a fee which must be paid. If the renewal fees are not paid the registered intellectual property rights will eventually lapse. In many cases, if a payment is missed, it can be made late subject to a penalty being paid within a defined period: often six months. These are referred to as grace periods. If a renewal is not made and the grace period has expired, it is usually difficult if not impossible to reinstate the intellectual property rights which will have gone for good.

Clearly in any due diligence investigation, one of the first tasks in checking if any registered intellectual property rights exist will be to ascertain if any rights in question have been properly renewed. If not, can the renewal be effected late and the rights preserved, albeit at a cost?

Parallel Imports

Legal position

Parallel imports are products made available for sale by the owner in one country, bought by another person, often an intermediary, and made available for sale in different country. The motivation to do this is usually that the price is higher in the first country than in the second. These products are sometimes alternatively called "grey market products".

The existence of intellectual property rights can enable a higher price to be charged in a country where those rights exist. For example, in pharmaceuticals and for products sold under well known brands. If in some countries the product is available at a lower price, the possibility of a price differential may create a market for buying in one country and selling in another where a higher price can be charged. Recently, in the UK, Honda motorcycles and well known perfume brands have been imported and sold at cheaper prices than the brand owners would like. There are many reasons why these grey market products become available. For example, price differentials between regions or countries make it profitable to import products from one country to another. Or surplus stock from one business can be bought at a discount and sold on for a profit whilst still undercutting the retail price that the brand owner or their retailers charge.

The price differential may come about because in those countries where no intellectual property rights exists, rivals of the intellectual property rights owner will begin to make or sell the product if there is good business in it. To obtain a share of the market in these countries, the owner of the intellectual property rights existing in other countries, may need to compete at a price below that in markets where the intellectual property rights do exist. Higher quality and service may enable the higher price to be sustained. But if not, the problem for the intellectual property rights owner, and the opportunity for competitors, becomes clear. Competitors can buy the genuine products (put on the market in one country by the intellectual property rights owner) at the lower price and import them into other countries where intellectual property rights exist and where prices are likely to be higher but without infringing those intellectual property rights. In many cases,the intellectual property rights owner can do little about it.

The legal doctrine which makes this process legal is called exhaustion of rights and has been developed in the European Union. The effect of the exhaustion of rights legal doctrine is easy to describe. If an owner of a product protected by intellectual property rights, say a patent or a trade mark, puts that product on the market or it is put on the market with the owner's permission, say by a licensee, in a member states, that product can then be used, resold, and imported into any other member state. The intellectual property rights cannot be used to stop this occurring. The courts have laid down some requirements which must be met for the doctrine to apply. The effect of the doctrine does not mean that any person can, after a product has been put on the market, make products themselves and sell them because to do so would infringe the particular intellectual property rights.

The law relating to the grey market is complex within the European Economic Area and involves the understanding and application of laws of the European Union as applied by the European Court of Justice. The doctrine does not extend to products put on the market outside the European Economic Area. The case law in this area does lay down some safeguards for the intellectual property rights owners. These cover, for example, deterioration of the product, alterations to packaging and similar.

For a few years prior to 2001 there was uncertainty about two points. First, exactly when and in what circumstances trade mark proprietors could use their trade mark rights to object to their branded products being imported into the European Economic Area where the goods had originally been placed on the market outside the European Economic Area. Secondly, when they could object to their branded goods being re-packaged for import into another market.

In 2001 the European Court of Justice clarified these two important issues. In a case involving trade mark proprietors Davidoff and Levi

Strauss the question was whether the proprietors had consented to the goods being imported into the European Economic Area.

The goods in question had originally been put on the market in Singapore, the US, Canada and Mexico. The parallel importers argued that since no restrictions had been placed on the persons who were authorised to sell the goods in those countries, then the trade mark proprietors had impliedly consented to the further marketing of the goods anywhere else in the world.

The English court agreed with the parallel importers saying that if the trade mark proprietor did not place restraints then they could be said to have consented to the further commercialisation of the goods in question. But this question of consent was referred to the European Court of Justice which, in November 2001, held that consent must be expressed positively. Silence cannot amount to consent nor can a trade mark proprietor be said to have consented simply because the goods do not carry any warning that they are not to be placed on the market within the European Economic Area.

It is for the parallel importer to prove that consent has been given and although a trade mark owner can, in certain circumstances, be said to have impliedly consented the circumstances in question must unequivocally demonstrate that the trade mark owner has renounced the intention to enforce the trade mark rights.

The second issue, regarding repackaging of branded products, was decided by the European Court of Justice in April 2002. In that case, concerning pharmaceutical products, the court was asked to consider when a trade mark proprietor could object to the repackaging of branded products; whether the repackaging had to be necessary. What "necessary" meant, and whether the importer had to give notice to the trade mark proprietor.

The court held that a trade mark proprietor cannot oppose the repackaging of goods if the repackaging is necessary to enable the product to be imported. To object would be a disguised restriction on trade in the European Economic Area and would contribute to the artificial partitioning of the markets in the European Economic Area. The trade mark proprietor can, however, oppose repackaging which is dictated by consumer preference so long as the importing state allows the goods to be imported in their original packaging.

The court held that in some cases there may be such strong consumer resistance to the original packaging that repackaging is necessary to achieve market access. In those cases repackaging is acceptable but it is for the national courts to decide whether those circumstances exist.

In all cases the parallel importer must give reasonable notice of the repackaging (the court suggested 15 days) and the repackaging must not affect the condition of the product or damage the reputation of the trade mark.

Strategy implications

One strategic decision for the intellectual property rights owner is whether to sell products or allow products to be sold in countries where it 'does not have intellectual property rights protection. Competitors will be able to offer a rival product in these countries probably at a lower price which in another country would infringe intellectual property rights. If the products are sold by the intellectual property rights owner at an uncompetitively high price, little business will be attracted unless the product can be successfully sold on other qualities such as service or durability. If the price is reduced in order to be competitive, the products might well be exported into other countries as parallel imports. A strategic assessment will need to be made as to which course of action is the best.

Case Study

Two case studies illustrate exhaustion of rights in practice. The first involved a UK University which had undertaken research into controlling a pest which attacked the skin of certain animals. The research led to the invention of a preventative treatment based on natural materials. The product had market potential across the whole of the European Economic Area since it was a product for the agricultural sector. The invention was made the subject of a UK and then an international patent application. Further development was carried out necessary to demonstrate that scaling up production to commercial quantities would produce a stable and efficacious product. This took longer than anticipated. But no business partner would commit to the invention until this preliminary scale up work had been completed successfully. Not able to commit further money to the expensive stages of an international patent application, the University abandoned all but the UK patent application.

Later the product proved both stable and efficacious. Businesses took an interest in the product and its uses. The analysis of the investment opportunity in summary went like this. The product could be produced and sold without infringement of the patent everywhere except the UK. The published UK patent disclosed how to make the invention. Any business selling the product based on the patent rights could limit its activities to the UK where the price of the product could be kept high using the patent rights to stop infringers selling at lower prices. The price everywhere else would be comparatively low since no patent rights existed outside the UK and the product would be a commodity product with potentially several suppliers in the agriculture sector. If the product was sold by the owner or licensee of the patent rights in parts of the European Economic Area other than the UK, the price would need to be low to compete with the products of other manufacturers. If the price was higher in the UK, any person could buy the product from the rights owner or user and import it back into the UK and sell it at a price just below the higher UK price. Their defence would be based on the exhaustion of rights principle and likely to be successful.

The patent rights were only of any value if a high price or larger market share could be maintained using them. This could only happen, if at all, in the UK. The patent rights could only have any value if the business based on the patented product was limited to the UK. As soon as products were sold in other European Economic Area countries at competitive prices, imports of those products from these countries would force the price of the products in UK down to the level or nearly of the rest of the European Economic Area. The patent would then have no real value on this analysis. No business took up the patent rights for the UK. Most of the research had been put into the public domain when the patent application was published.

The second case relates to a similar problem. It involves a company making chemical products with patents throughout the European Union except for the Republic of Ireland. At the time the European Patent application was made, the Republic of Ireland was not part of the European Patent Convention and so a separate application would have been required there. For whatever reason, the separate patent application was not filed in the Republic of Ireland. For many years, this did not cause a problem. The belief in the existence of worldwide patent rights prevented a competitor challenging the patent or the product in the market. Product prices were high and margins good. However, later the level of business undertaken by the patent owner in the market in the Republic of Ireland became sufficiently large to attract a competitor. This company realised that no patent rights existed, began selling a rival product at a cheaper price, and immediately took a substantial part of the Irish market. In Ireland, the patent owner would have to compete on price. The new competitor took market share by cutting its prices as well as providing a reasonable level of service. The patent owner was left with two choices. To withdraw from the market in the Irish Republic or to compete on price to retain market share. If the price was dropped to compete, the product would without question be exported to other European countries where the patent was keeping the price was higher. A decision was made to withdraw from the market in the Republic of Ireland in which healthy profits had been made for several previous years.

Anyone seeking to put a valuation on those patent rights would need to have a thorough understanding of the exhaustion of rights principles in order to be alive to the fact some of the business could be lost. That loss could have an important impact on the valuation of the intellectual property rights, in this case patent rights.

ADDENDA

ADDENDUM 1
DUE DILIGENCE IN PRACTICE

1 Company Records

An inspection of the company's own records relating to the registered intellectual property rights revealed a number of trade mark registrations and patents and patent applications in the name of "ABC" companies and other companies, in particular XYZ Limited a wholly owned subsidiary prior to the receivership of ABC Plc in about 1991.

In Schedule 1 we have attached copies of relevant documents from the records of the company.

2 Searches

We have carried out **searches** in the relevant databases of registered rights held by ABC and XYZ named companies. These searches would reveal UK and international;

2.1 patents and patent applications;

2.2 registered trade marks;

2.3 design registration numbers.

There are no registrations in the name of XYZ Ltd. The only relevant "XYZ" company name mentioned is XYZ Products Limited as to which see below.

Further searches can be undertaken quickly if appropriate.

3 Patents

3.1 The European Patent 123 456

The only patent currently in force is European Patent Number 123 456. This patent also designated Germany, France, Spain and Italy. It is no longer in force in those countries because the *renewal* has not been paid. It is, therefore, effective only in the UK.

3.2 **Exhaustion of Rights**

The effect of intellectual property law in the European Union is likely to be interpreted such that a product sold lawfully in countries where there are no patent rights would allow that product to be resold in the UK despite the patent rights. Similar conditions apply in respect of designs and trade marks within the European Union. This is only relevant if there is a substantial price differential and only if the sales outside the UK are lawful, i.e. made or sanctioned by the intellectual property right owner.

3.3 **Entitlement Claim**

An ABC Group Plc subsidiary, XYZ Products Limited, applied for a patent which was given number GB 1 234 567. This application never became a granted patent as it was allowed to lapse.

It was the invention claimed in this application that was the subject of the failed attempt by Mr Smith to obtain an order that he was the owner of the invention and entitled to apply for a patent for it. His claim was rejected by The Patent Office by a decision dated 26th May 1995.

Warning

Mr Smith has six weeks from 26th May 1995 in which to appeal this decision. If he did appeal it, he is unlikely to succeed in maintaining his claim. If he did succeed, he would have the right to pursue a patent application in respect of the development of the drainage system and related products having a two piece snap fit arrangement. If this application went on to become a granted patent, it could affect the ability to sell the drainage product being developed by ABC Group Plc at the moment. It is not possible to give a more certain opinion on this point without much further investigation.

4   Designs – Registered Design Protection

There are a number of designs owned by ABC Group Plc as appear from Schedule 2 under the designation "D" in the left hand column. The UK designs numbered 2 000 000, 2 000 001, 2 000 002, and 2 000 003 are *in force*.

The UK designs numbered 2 000 004 and 2 000 005 both *ceased* to exist on 20 December 1994.

There was also a UK design numbered 1 000 000 in the name of ABC Products Limited but this *ceased* on 18 June 1991.

The German design is in force and the renewal fee for that according to the official records has been paid.

The Italian design number 0 101 000 is presently in force but the renewal fee is overdue.

Warning

It has not been possible to check if this fee has been paid in Italy. Enquiries of Apple & Pear, Patent Agents for ABC Group Plc led to an assurance that this renewal fee had *not* been paid but that ABC Group Plc had instructed Apple & Pear to pay it late within the allowed six month late payment period together with the appropriate penalty payment.

The Spanish design is still in force. The next renewal fee is due to be paid on 29 July 1995. The Spanish design is still registered in the name of RST Group, the name of the company on formation prior to the change of name to ABC Group Plc. A change of name will have to be filed in to the name of ABC Group Plc.

The French design is still in force and will remain so until 14 March 2006.

Warning

A letter from Apple & Pear to Mr Green dated 5 March 1996 states that the German and Italian designs have not been formally assigned from ABC Plc (which went into receivership). It will be necessary depending on the circumstances to either attempt to restore the company to complete the agreed transfer of these assets or if no such agreement existed, to obtain formal assignments from the appropriate official, probably the Treasury Solicitor. This will undoubtedly involve some payment and some professional fees being incurred.

Finally, amongst the records of ABC Group Plc was a letter from Upstart Polytechnic confirming that all intellectual property rights resulted from work undertaken by the Department of Three Dimensional Design at the Polytechnic will belong to ABC Plc. The letter refers to designs for drainage systems and products. There were no formal assignments amongst the records of ABC Group Plc in respect of those designs and any related intellectual property rights owned by ABC Group Plc.

Warning

In the absence of formal assignments from Upstart Polytechnic, the legal title to the registered designs cannot be assured. However, this is not likely to cause the registered design rights to be unenforceable by any person acquiring them from ABC Group Plc. There is a risk that a good title to these rights could not be given in any future sale. Further investigations could be undertaken and possibly an assignment obtained.

Designs – Copyright/Design Right Protection

The designs for the drainage products are also protected by non-registerable intellectual property rights. Any drawings for the clamps will attract copyright protection.

This copyright will remain with Upstart Polytechnic in the absence of a formal assignment. It appears from the Upstart Polytechnic letter that the copyrights belonged to ABC Plc and now to ABC Group Plc if transferred properly after the receivership. A written assignment is required to perfect the legal title prior to which only an imperfect legal title can be shown.

The actual design of product, as made and as depicted in the drawings, is protected by Design Right. This is distinct from copyright which protects only the drawing of the design or other recording such as on a CAD system. The protection given by a Design Right is similar to that given by a registered design but not as extensive.

If these designs were commissioned as seems likely by ABC Plc, the Design Rights would have belonged to ABC Plc and now ABC Group Plc if transferred after the receivership as mentioned above. An assignment would confirm that position beyond doubt. If the designs were not commissioned, ABC Plc would have acquired no title to these design rights unless either there existed an agreement to that effect or a written assignment was obtained from the Polytechnic.

To put this point in context, the registered designs, if the renewals are paid, last for 25 years. The Design Right lasts for a maximum of 15 years and more usually 10 years if the design is commercial. The copyright would last for the life of the person who made the drawings plus 50 years (soon to be plus 70 years). The copyright only protects copying of the drawing not the production of the design depicted in the drawing. The Design Right protects the design depicted against illegal copying. Therefore, provided the registered designs remain in force, the existence of Design Right and Copyright is less important in preventing others copying the design. However, if those rights needed to be passed on to other persons subsequently, it would not be possible to pass a confirmed good title to the copyright and probably the Design Right.

This may also be true for other designs created by sub-contracting organisations or in respect of designs other than the drainage products in relation to Upstart Polytechnic.

Schedule 3 contains a copy of the Upstart Polytechnic letter and draft assignment, letters from Orange & Co, Patent Agents, dated 21 March and two dated 22 March 1996 confirming much of the patent and design information referred to above.

5   Trade Marks

5.1 **Title**

In the letter dated 21 March 1996 from Orange & Co referred to in Schedule 3, there are listed various trade mark applications in the name of "ABC" named companies. Searches reveal the following trade marks as existing, the name of the registered proprietor, and the goods for which they are registered:

Mark	Registered Proprietor	Goods
ABC	ABC Plc	[Omitted]
BORER	ABC Group Plc	
DRAINER	ABC Plc	
CUTTER	ABC Plc	
RODDER	BC Group Plc	
ABC	ABC Plc	
ABC	ABC Group Plc	

At the moment we have not investigated further the status of these marks, for example, the renewal fees for them may be imminent, or may recently have been due for payment and not been paid. This should be raised with the patent agents, Apple & Pear for ABC Group Plc.

Warning

The trade mark registration for ABC number B 22222 (item 6 above) has not been formally assigned from ABC Plc to ABC Group Plc. Several of the other trademarks remain in the name of ABC Plc. These will require a formal assignment (see 3 above about the question of assignment under the heading Patent). This is likely to involve a payment and further professional fees being incurred.

5.2 **Non-Use**

Mr Green of ABC Group Plc stated that the trade mark [BORER] had not been used since 1991 when ABC Group Plc purchased the trade mark rights out of ABC Plc in receivership. He thought it may have been used by ABC Plc but could not confirm it. The registered trade mark [RODDER] had never been used.

Warning

These marks are vulnerable to being struck off the register of trade marks for non-use. Other trade marks owned by "ABC" companies or their subsidiaries which have not been used for more than five years would be similarly vulnerable to be struck off. No further information is available without further investigation into the background.

UK trade marks continue without limit in time provided the relevant renewal fees are paid when due.

6   Other Intellectual Property Rights

ABC Group Plc may own other intellectual property rights which are not registerable. These might be in respect of other designs for which registered design have not been sought but for which Design Right and copyright protection may exist. The company may also have confidential know-how which is important for the commercial exploitation of its products. It is not possible to report on rights such as these without a much wider investigation.

7   Receivership

The agreement by which ABC Group Plc acquired, amongst other property, the intellectual property rights from the receivers of ABC Plc was not available for inspection amongst the company records relating to the registered intellectual property rights. This must be carefully scrutinised to ensure that ABC Group Plc can give a good title to the intellectual property rights that it is purporting to sell or at least title not worse than that of ABC Plc prior to its receivership .

8   Assignments

It will be necessary to obtain individual formal assignments for registration in the various national states where rights exist. In respect of the intellectual property rights still remaining in ABC Plc it will be necessary to obtain a contractual entitlement for the assignment of those rights either through ABC Group Plc or with that company's consent direct to FGH Investments Plc.

9   Validity

The validity of the intellectual property rights can be challenged. The challenge typically occurs when the rights are to be enforced. On your instructions we have not carried out a detailed validity investigation in respect of any of the registered intellectual property rights of ABC Group Plc.

Apple & Pear state in their letter of 5 March 1996 that they have no information which would lead to a conclusion that the patent 123 456 is invalid.

We have mentioned the information given by Mr Green about the use of the trade marks. The lack of use can lead to the trade marks being invalid.

10   Summary

10.1   The only relevant patent is European Patent Number 123 456. If the renewal fees are paid, this expires on 29 January 2010;

10.2   The UK registered designs in force are numbers 2 000 000, 2 000 001, 2 000 002 and 2 000 003. If renewals are paid they will remain in force for 25 years from their filing date;

10.3 The German, Italian, Spanish and French equivalent design registrations last for the following periods:

Years from date filed or priority date if earlier

German	(Filed 14.12.90)	20 (5 year renewals)
Italian	(Filed 28.12.90)	15 (5 year renewals)
Spanish	(Filed 04.01.91)	20 (10 year renewals and tax every 5 years)
French	(Filed 14.03.91)	50 (25 year renewals)

Investigations indicated that these designs do not have earlier priority dates so their respective terms run from the indicated "filed date".

10.4 The registered trade marks continue in force for so long as the renewal fees are paid when due.

10.5 We have not been able to confirm good title to some of the registered intellectual property rights of ABC Group Plc. These are some of registered trade mark and the designs which are currently still registered in the name of ABC Plc. The cost of perfecting the title to these rights is difficult to estimate. FGH Investments Plc should budget to spend a substantial amount to resolve these problems. We can advise on a more precise amount in discussion with you.

10.6 Similarly, we have not been able to confirm good title to the designs which are not subject to the design registration. To do so would require confirmatory documents or statements from Upstart Polytechnic and anyone else to whom work was sub-contracted. In the circumstances, FGH Investments Plc may conclude that this is commercially unnecessary given the patent and registered design rights and if the payment for these unregistered rights does not form a major part of the purchase price.

ADDENDUM 2
DECLARATION OF COPYRIGHT OWNERSHIP

1 Name.	
2 Address.	
3 Place and date of birth.	
4 Nationality.	
5 Brief description of work in which copyright is claimed (the "Work").	
6 Period during which the Work was created.	
7 Employer during whose employment the Work was created.	
8 Was the Work created during the course of employment?	
9 Have you signed any agreement relating to the Work and/or the copyright in it?	
10 Was the Work derived wholly or partly from another work?	

I declare that the details written above are true and accurate to the best of my knowledge

Signature of declarant   Date

ADDENDUM 3
ESTABLISHING THE EXISTENCE
AND OWNERSHIP OF RIGHTS TO
INTELLECTUAL PROPERTY

Initial information gathering

Registered Rights – patents, trade marks, and design registrations/utility models.

- Check the register.

- Searching.

- National rights.

- Registered owner.

- Inter Group use.

- Look for registration of lenders and loan security documents.

- All good?

Unregistered Rights – copyright, some design rights, some brand rights/unfair competition rights, confidential Know How.

- No register to check.

- National rights.

- Information from owner crucial.

- Assess if have any rights.

- All good?

Risk Analysis

The Fundamentals

- Understand what is achievable.

- Risk management v risk elimination.

- Don't want a problem v enforceable rights to compensation and corrective action.

Validity of the registered intellectual property rights

- Registered rights might be invalid or revocable even though been granted by the registering authority:–

  - because did not meet the registration criteria when registered.

  - because some conduct of the owner.

Validity of the unregistered intellectual property rights

Unregistered rights might not exist because the qualifying requirements for protection under the relevant law

Validity of ownership rights

- Acquired form someone else.

  - within the Group.

    - still need due diligence.

    - should be easier to resolve any problems.

  - previous acquisition.

    - need very careful due diligence.

    - may be difficult or costly to resolve problems.

- links in the chain good?

- all agreements effective?

If not good chain/agreements – life savers

- Depends on law of the agreement or applying to the parties.

- Correcting mistakes.

- Incomplete agreements.

- Agreement interpretation.

- Confirmatory agreements.

Employees and their rights

- Which law applies

- Ask the right questions.

- Risk v cost again.

- Rely on warranties and indemnities again?

- Beware – sub-contractors.

- Beware – collaboration partners

Defensive due diligence – any third parties rights to stop me?

- Registered rights.
- Unregistered rights.
- The ambush risk.

CHAPTER 6
SECURITISATION AND LOAN SECURITY

Contents

CHAPTER 6
SECURITISATION AND LOAN SECURITY

Securitisation of intellectual property rights

Introduction

This section is intended to give a general outline to the subject of securitisation. It is now an established process in the United States, but still a relatively new topic in other countries like the United Kingdom where the development of securitisation has followed the lead given by the United States.

In the US securitisation was originally based on mortgages as assets to back securities issued to investors, but has now grown into a considerable business with the securities being backed by a wide range of other assets such as car loans and credit card receivables.

Whilst the majority of securitised assets are currently residential mortgages and other assets having a predictable revenue stream, the securitisation process has potential application to any number of assets with the potential to generate steady revenue streams. One of the most ambitious to date is the concept of securitisation of intellectual property rights, which was given prominence by the securitisation of parts of David Bowie's and Rod Stewart's back catalogues.

What is securitisation?

Securitisation is a complex financial technique that allows finance to be raised from cash flows received from a range of often illiquid assets. Suitable assets are pooled in a financial package, underwriting is obtained for the package and securities offered and issued to investors. These securities are supported by the securitised assets and the revenues generated by them. The key feature which differentiates securitisation from other asset backed offerings is the issue of securities to investors backed by the bundle of assets which have been securitised.

As previously mentioned the technique was originally used with mortgages which were pooled together and offered as security to investors, the use of such previously illiquid assets being highly innovative. Most types of receivables which generate a cash flow are capable of being securitised.

In a traditional security structure the borrower secures a loan with the relevant assets and if payment obligations are not met the assets can be seized for payment. In a securitisation the securities are not backed by the ability of the company to repay the loan, but by the expected cash flow the securitised assets will generate.

Companies that have numerous assets on their balance sheet can pool them, assess their creditworthiness and revenue generating ability and then, if suitable, use them to back securities issued in a securitisation transaction.

The basic process involves the owner of the relevant assets (usually referred to as the "originator") selling the relevant assets to a special purpose vehicle ("SPV") with the SPV raising the money to finance the purchase by issuing debt securities (such as bonds) to investors. Interest and principal payments due to investors on those securities are paid for out of the income generated by the acquired assets, with security for the payments usually being by way of charges created by the SPV over those assets in favour of a "security trustee" for the benefit of investors. The originator will usually manage the assets as agent for the SPV and deal with the day to day administration and payment collection from debtors in relation to those assets.

Why securitise?

There are a range of potential benefits to securitising intellectual property rights.

Value Realisation

Even though a company may be realising value from its intellectual property rights, it may not be able to realise their full value. It is usually difficult to raise debt finance over intellectual property and it may not be possible to reflect the true value of the portfolio on the balance sheet. It is possible that securitisation could unlock the unrealised value.

Cost Effective Cash Generation

By selling assets to the SPV the originator can realise cash which can, of course, be used to reduce existing borrowings or as new working or development capital. This can be a particularly valuable source of cash for growing technology companies where cash burn is high or where growth by acquisition may otherwise be difficult to finance.

Cash derived in this way can be cost effective compared with other alternative sources, even if those sources are available to the originator. The credit risk associated with the income from the securitised assets will usually be better than the credit rating of the originator since the pooling and packaging of a portfolio of assets by the originator in a securitisation transaction enables a security to be offered to investors with a known and fixed amount of risk. The effect is to increase the possibility of a more cost effective financing than the originator could itself obtain.

Wider Access to Funds

By its nature, securitisation will give the originator access to a much wider range of potential investors than may be available to it by way of more traditional methods of fund-raising.

Risk Management

The risks inherent in the securitised assets will typically be passed to the SPV and the investors, which may have significant advantages to the originator.

Control and Future Benefit Retention

As the originator will typically continue to manage the securitised assets, it will retain some degree of control over them and enable the originator to manage and preserve existing business relations. This control may be critical to the originator, particularly where the securitised assets are of extreme value and importance to the originator's business.

It is possible to structure the securitisation to ensure that future benefits derived from the securitised assets are retained by the originator. The residual value of the assets following completion of the financing and any surplus cash generated by the assets over and above that required to satisfy the continuing costs of the financing can be retained, with the additional advantage of improving the originator's return on capital. It is important, however, to consider how such future benefit retention will affect the ability of the originator to obtain potential balance sheet improvements as discussed below.

Balance Sheet Improvement

It may be possible for the originator to remove the securitised assets from its balance sheet with the proceeds of the sale to the SPV being shown as cash, but this will be dependant on the exact structuring of the securitisation. Originators will need to consider carefully with their auditors the application relevant financial reporting standards. In the UK, Financial Reporting Standard 5 (FRS 5) will determine how the securitisation is to be treated, particularly where future rewards relating to the securitised assets are retained by the originator. Even if complete off-balance sheet treatment is not available, it may still be possible for the balance sheet to be improved by obtaining a linked presentation for the assets.

Tax Advantages

It is possible that the securitisation may have tax advantages to the originator, but this will clearly depend upon the particular circumstances of the originator and of the exact structuring of the securitisation.

The securitisation process – legal and commercial aspects

It is important to remember that the detailed structure will be governed by the circumstances of the particular assets being the subject of securitisation and by the tax implications of a particular structure.

Suitability of the assets

It is clearly fundamental when considering any securitisation to determine whether the assets proposed to be securitised are suitable for securitisation. The assets need to be of a suitable type, both legally and commercially.

Most types of assets which generate predictable cash flows are capable of securitisation. The assets and cash flows they generate which are best suited to securitisation are those:

- where the legal rights of the originator to own the assets and to receive the cash flows are clear and which can easily be separated from other assets and cash flows of the originator;

- have performance information capable of being obtained and verified in relation to them; and

- are generating revenue from parties that themselves have high credit ratings (or are from a class of parties where credit risk can be determined in relation to them as a group).

The majority of intellectual property rights are capable, at least in principle, of satisfying these important requirements. Patents, copyright, product designs and brands could be considered for securitisation. The copyright in films, music, and sounds are all particularly suitable. The securitised bonds based on the copyrights in the back catalogue recordings of David Bowie and Rod Stewart are good examples. The revenues derived from a substantial portal on the internet involving the exploitation of the copyright in software, complex graphics and other media content would be another example. Several well known business corporations, including IBM, Xerox, and Dow Chemicals, have successfully developed business entities earning huge revenues from licensing their patents. The patent rights, clear ownership, and identifiable revenue streams would make these patent portfolios suitable for securitisation. In a similar way, the intellectual property rights in a successful range of products could be securitised if the intellectual property rights in the designs, their ownership, and relevant revenues are clearly identifiable.

Know how would, in most cases, be unsuitable for securitisation. The extent of confidential information comprising the know how, the ability to successfully transfer the legal rights to it, and the extent of those legal rights all point to their unsuitablility. The biggest risk is that the confidential information is disclosed. The exception could be a particularly valuable chemical formulae or recipe relating to a successful product but only if the formulation or recipe could not be obtained by analysing the end product available on the market.

In determining the suitability of an originator's assets, detailed legal and commercial due diligence should be undertaken in relation to them to determine whether there are, for example:

- any defects in the title to the assets;

- any flaws in the legal or commercial documentation that may make the relevant intellectual property rights unenforceable;

- any legal, regulatory or contractual restrictions on the ability of the originator to transfer the assets to the SPV or to assign the right to receive income from them; and

- any anticipated circumstances where the revenues generated from the assets may not be as high as the revenues historically generated from them.

It is unlikely that the legal due diligence investigation will produce a complete guaranteed bill of health in respect of the assets and it is likely that some element of doubt will remain. However, if the due diligence investigation is carried out by an experienced professional, these areas of doubt should be kept to a minimum, and it may be possible to find a way of eliminating or reducing the extent of any doubt revealed. If the end result is, however, that the doubt is sufficiently serious it may be that the assets are not suitable for a securitisation.

If the way in which the originator currently utilises its intellectual property portfolio makes the assets unsuitable for securitisation it may be possible for restructuring to make the assets more suitable. For example, intellectual property not currently licensed outside the group might be licensed or franchised to produce an appropriate revenue stream. Alternatively, it may be possible for certain intellectual property rights to be concentrated in a particular group company which grants licences in relation to it to other group companies in return for the payment of licence fees, with those licence fees forming the basis of a securitisation. Clearly the terms upon which any restructuring is carried out and the terms upon which any intellectual property is licensed outside or within the originator's group must themselves be prepared in such a way as to ensure suitability for securitisation, including in relation to transfer or assignability.

The Special Purpose Vehicle (SPV)

An SPV is a corporate entity that is formed specifically to acquire the assets to be securitised from the originator and which typically raises cash with which to acquire those assets by issuing debt securities (such as bonds) to investors by way of a public or private placing. The SPV will almost always be a public company and will have powers in its memorandum and articles of association to carry out the transaction.

Interest and principal payments due to investors on those debt securities are paid out of the income generated by the acquired assets, with security for the payments usually being by way of charges created by the SPV over the acquired assets in favour of a "security trustee" (typically a professional trust corporation). The security trustee will look after the interests of the investors during the life of the debt securities.

The debt securities may be of a fixed or floating interest rate type, but in the UK are typically of the floating rate type with the rate linked to LIBOR.

The documentation relating to the issue of the debt securities will be in substantially the same form as required for any debt securities issue. The documentation will set out and regulate the terms on which the securities are issued and on which they will be held by investors. In the event that the debt securities are to be listed on a stock exchange the documentation will need to comply with any relevant listing requirements relating to the market in question. In the case of a listing on the London Stock Exchange they will need to comply with the Listing Rules published by the Financial Services Authority (as the competent UK Listing Authority) and the SPV will need to comply with the continuing obligations contained in the Listing Rules and of the continuing requirements of the London Stock Exchange.

The SPV will have no assets or liabilities over and above those arising out of the securitisation transaction and will be structured in such a way that all relevant parties agree not to bring any insolvency or other proceedings against the SPV.

The most appropriate way in which to fund the SPV will depend upon the nature of the assets to be securitised, the amount proposed to be raised and the perceived marketability of the identity of the originator. If funds are raised on a public market there will be additional initial and continuing regulatory requirements that the SPV will need to comply with resulting in an increased cost and transparency going forwards.

A final consideration is the location of the SPV, as it may be possible, subject to the local tax authorities agreeing any intellectual capital valuation, to locate it in a tax efficient jurisdiction. However, careful consideration will need to be taken of the local legal and regulatory frameworks in the relevant jurisdiction, including any legal or regulatory rules relating to the issue of debt securities.

Transferring assets to the SPV

As we have seen, the basic structure of a securitisation transaction involves the transfer of the assets to be securitised from the originator to the SPV.

Typically the assets are sold to the SPV (for an amount slightly lower than their value) by means of a transfer of the full legal and beneficial title to them. Subject to the accounting issues discussed previously in relation to control and the retention of future benefits, the assets will be removed from the originator's balance sheet. An additional benefit of a transfer in this way is to protect against the sale being set aside as a sale at an undervalue or as a preference (for example in the UK under either section 238 or 239 Insolvency Act 1986 respectively). The asset transfer agreement will be between the originator and the SPV, but other parties (depending upon the particular structure of the transaction) may include a security trustee and any party providing credit enhancement. In the event of credit enhancement, there would also typically be a credit enhancement agreement between the SPV and the party providing the credit enhancement. The subject of credit enhancement is addressed in more detail in the section "Rating securities" later in this Chapter.

It is possible to structure the transfer so that any overperformance of the securitised assets will result in any excess revenues being payable to the originator. The transfer can also be structured so that assets (or the residual value of them) are transferred back to the originator on maturity of the securities issued by the SPV, typically in consideration of the originator agreeing to administer the assets on behalf of the SPV (as discussed in more detail in the section on "Administration" later in this Chapter). As indicated previously however, both of these actions will have an effect on the accounting treatment of the transaction in the balance sheet of the originator.

In the event that there are difficulties with structuring the securitisation in this way (because of legal, regulatory, or commercial difficulties with a complete transfer or assignment, for example) then an alternative "secured loan" structure may be appropriate. This involves the SPV granting a loan to the originator (or, alternatively, a subsidiary of the originator established to hold the relevant assets) secured on the assets to be securitised. The SPV in this situation grants fixed and floating charges over its entire undertaking to a "security trustee," and sells the cash flows generated by repayment of the loan, again typically by way of the issue of debt securities, using the proceeds of the issue to provide the loan to the originator.

The potential legal and commercial difficulties relating to transfers to the SPV can be particularly relevant to securitisations of intellectual property rights, and there can be particular advantages in structuring the securitisation so that the legal title to the assets remains with the originator, including the retention of enforcement rights by the originator. This is considered further in the section on "Potential problems and possible solutions" later in this Chapter.

Administration

It is not usual for the SPV to have any employees. This does, of course, have the advantage of avoiding any associated statutory and other legal obligations in this respect.

The securitised assets will however need to continue to be administered following their transfer to the SPV and this administration would typically be carried out by the originator on behalf of the SPV on the terms of an administration agreement between the originator and the SPV, and, in appropriate cases, the security trustee and credit enhancement provider.

The administration agreement will typically contain obligations on the originator to act as the agent of the SPV to exploit the securitised assets and to operate the portfolio to generate revenue for the SPV and is akin to facilities management arrangements now common in many sectors. This administration obligation would include the obligation to pay renewal fees and collect the revenues generated by the intellectual property rights and passing those through to the SPV.

As mentioned previously, leaving legal title with the originator has the advantage that powers of enforcement remain with the originator. As the originator is likely to have spent substantial time and money in developing and protecting the rights, transferring equitable title only would enable the originator to continue doing to do so (and, in fact, the administration agreement between the SPV and the originator would require them to do so).

It is normal to have a "fall back" administrator to cover the unlikely event of the originator or other administrator failing for some reason.

Any funding required in relation to the operation of the SPV will usually come from retained earnings derived from the securitised assets but may also be financed by way of loan to the SPV by third parties or by the originator. Any such loans would be subordinated to the rights of the investors.

Rating securitites

It is usually necessary to obtain a credit rating for any securities to be issued by the SPV. In this way access to public markets will be improved and investor confidence will be enhanced particularly where the underlying securitised assets are of a type with which the investor may not be familiar.

A number of factors are taken into account by rating agencies, but to receive a high rating for the securities issued by the SPV the assets to be securitised should be isolated from any other substantial risk of the originator's business and the quality of the assets to be securitised should be high.

Whilst separation of the securitised assets from the business of the originator is an essential element of the securitisation process, the extent to which the assets can be separated in any particular case will vary. The greater the isolation of the assets from other risks of the originator the easier it will be to obtain a high rating.

As indicated previously in relation to examining the suitability of assets for securitisation, the quality of those assets will depend upon a number of factors including the credit rating of the parties or class of parties providing the revenues in respect of the assets and the quality and predictability of those revenues.

There are various credit enhancement techniques that can be applied to mitigate any risks. One method is "overcollaterisation" whereby the value of the securitised assets and expected cash flow is higher than that required for the securitisation. Another method is to arrange for letters of credit to be issued by a substantial bank or financial institution to underwrite the revenue stream by guaranteeing a given percentage of the revenue against arrears or non payment. The bank or institution will, in these circumstances, itself need to be a highly rated institution.

Other techniques include obtaining financial guarantee insurance, implementing senior and subordinated debt structures and by the replacement of non-performing assets with better performing assets.

Potential problems and possible solutions

Isolation of the intellectual property rights

We have already noted that to receive a high rating for the securities issued by the SPV the assets to be securitised should be isolated from any other substantial risks of the originator's business. Whilst this may be possible in the context of legal isolation it may be difficult to isolate the assets commercially.

The cash flows generated from licences of brand names, for example, will be largely dependent upon the continuing value of the brand names. The uncertainty of such continuing value is clearly more difficult to assess in the case of relatively new brand names (and, of course, if the level of uncertainty is too high it may mean that the brand names are not suitable at all) which may be more dependant upon future marketing expenditure or new product development under the brand names than more established brands. A possible solution is to securitise only mature and strongly established intellectual property rights.

Whilst the transaction documentation will oblige the SPV to use its best endeavours to exploit the securitised assets, structuring the transaction so that originator administers the assets on behalf of the SPV (and delegating the exploitation duties to the originator) will help the originator ensure that this exploitation happens and that the continuing value of the assets is maintained by ensuring that they are properly and effectively promoted and protected.

Transferring intellectual property rights

Transferring legal title to intellectual property rights may cause adverse tax consequences in some jurisdictions. This used to be the case in the UK where stamp duty was payable on the transfer of legal title to intellectual property rights. Recent changes have abolished the payment of stamp duty on such transfers although the transfer of goodwill may still require stamp duty to be paid in some circumstances. Transferring legal title to intellectual property can however have other adverse consequences. For example, if the legal title to a registered intellectual property right like a patent or a trade mark is transferred the transfer will have to be registered in every country where the particular right is itself registered. This might be the transfer to the SPV. Registering such transfers is time consuming and costly. Another example, is the effect of such a transfer to the SPV would be to take away from the originator the power to enforce the intellectual property rights and move such powers to the SPV. All would depend on the law of each country where the rights might need to be enforced.

These problems can be overcome. Instead of transferring the legal ownership of the intellectual property rights to the SPV, a worldwide exclusive licence could be given to the SPV. The rights of the SPV would be effectively the same as if the legal title had been transferred without the possible tax consequences. Some important practical points should though be borne in mind. The rights of an exclusive licensee in some jurisdictions may not be the same as outright ownership and may be different for one type of intellectual property right compared to another. The granting in some countries of a worldwide exclusive licence may be regarded by the tax authorities as really a transfer of all the important legal rights and so treat the licence for tax purposes as if a transfer of the legal title had occurred. Also in many cases the exclusive licence will need to be registered, although this is usually easier and less costly that registering a transfer of ownership.

In some jurisdictions the exclusive licence will give both the SPV and the originator the right to bring legal action to prevent infringements of the intellectual property rights in question.

An alternative to transferring full legal ownership or an exclusive licence might be to transfer the right to own the intellectual property rights in question but not transfer the actual legal ownership. In UK law, this would be a transfer of the "equitable" ownership with the agreement being similar to granting an option to call for the ownership of the rights. The laws of countries other than the UK may allow a similar approach to be taken. The SPV can call for the transfer of legal ownership later when to do so becomes desirable or necessary. Not transferring legal title but granting a right to own the legal title would enable the originator to enforce the intellectual property rights yet still enable the SPV to control the ownership of the rights. This approach can, for example, avoid a tax burden being incurred if the trigger for the tax consequences is the transferring of legal ownership. A straight option arrangement would be another alternative.

Core and non-core business activities

The intellectual property portfolio generating the cash flows to be securitised may have a dual role in an organisation. The rights may relate to products or services which are core activities of the originator and the originator will want to retain ownership of assets which are vital to the continued success of its business. However many businesses gain substantial revenues from licensing the same rights for uses which do not compete with the core activities. These substantial revenues could be securitised to raise capital for the originator and not incur liabilities on the balance sheet.

Solutions to this dilemma could include option arrangements and the originator exclusively licensing the SPV to use the intellectual property rights for certain limited uses, i.e. the non core activities. Alternatively, it may be possible to transfer the ownership of intellectual property rights in relation to certain uses only. Care must be taken in doing this however since splitting ownership can cause other problems. An alternative but usually less attractive route would be to transfer the intellectual property rights to the SPV which would licence them back exclusively to the originator for certain agreed uses, namely the core activities of the originator.

Securitising revenues based on non-assignable agreements

The right to use the intellectual property being securitised may be based on agreements such as exclusive licences, music recording and distribution agreements, or manufacturing agreements. It is common for agreements to contain express terms that the agreement cannot be assigned to another organisation. Such express terms come in many different forms. Typically, one or both parties to the agreement are prevented from assigning the agreement. Sometimes the ban on assignments is limited to requiring consent to be obtained, often with the proviso that consent cannot be unreasonably refused. The justification for these terms is that to make the agreement and relationship successful, the contracting parties are both important in exploiting the assets. For example, it might well be that the licences by which large organisations allow other organisations to use their technology and patents have value because of the right to improvements made by one or both parties or that the licensed party has a good chance of exploiting the intellectual property to maximum advantage for the licensing party. Assigning the agreement to another organisation would potentially at least undermine these advantages, hence the ban on assignments. A valuable portal on the internet will involve the use of various intellectual property rights such a copyright in software but often agreements with other organisations bring substantial value to the portal. Such agreements might be to allow access to media rights or other information only through the portal or to channel the availability and delivery of particular services only through the portal. If the cash flows of the portal were to be securitised, the intellectual property rights and the benefit of the agreements would need to be assigned to the SPV or in some other way made available to it.

An attempt to securitise the cash flows made by organisations which have granted licences or generated by the business having the licence would not be possible if the intellectual property rights or such licence agreements could not be assigned to the SPV. A way round this could be to hold the benefits to be received from the exploitation of the intellectual property rights or benefits receivable under the licence agreement in trust for the SPV. The application of the legal principles of contract and trust law would require the agreement to create the trust between the originator and the SPV to be carefully prepared. The law applicable to the relationship between the originator and the SPV and to the trust agreement will determine if the trust can be set up and the terms of the trust agreement. An illustrative example in UK law is the 1998 case of *Don King Productions Inc.* v *Frank Warren and others*[1]. In this case certain boxing promotion and management agreements were the subject of assignments even though the agreements to be assigned had express terms prohibiting assignment. The court ruled the assignments ineffective but that the benefit of the boxing promotion and management agreements including the profits to be derived from them where held on trust by Frank Warren for the benefit of a partnership set up effectively between Frank Warren and Don King.

Future litigation

Even with the most careful due diligence it is not usually possible to guarantee that no litigation will be brought in relation to the securitised assets. In the case of patents, for example, they may be vulnerable to future challenge as to validity which, in the worst case, could result in revocation of the patent. In the case of copyright this may relate to the infringement of existing copyright.

There are clearly ways to protect against inadvertent invalidity where the relevant matters are within the control of the originator or administrator. Ensuring that licences do not lapse and that renewal fees are paid on time are obvious examples.

Intellectual property portfolio valuation

The valuation of intellectual property rights is often intrinsically difficult but is clearly of major importance in the context of a securitisation. The principle methods are explained and discussed in chapter three. It obviously makes sense to have the relevant assets valued by experts in this area.

Intellectual Property Rights as Loan Security

Introduction

Lenders like tangible assets as security for loans. The reasons are not surprising. The physical presence of the security is reassuring, the existence of a building or piece of machinery can be checked by a non specialist and the value of the security can typically be assessed essentially by reference to a ready market for such assets. The

---

1.   [1998] RPC 817.

techniques used by professional valuers are known to lenders and understood by them.

Unfortunately for lenders many businesses derive their revenues not from employing capital equipment but from intellectual property and other intangible assets such as software and know how. The many businesses operating using the internet are a good example and the failure of many of the dot.com businesses left few tangible assets. Lenders have a choice. They can choose to lend primarily against the security of tangible assets and accept that lending to technology based business with few tangible assets is not for them or to find a way of lending to such businesses which constitute a growing sector of the market for finance. Competition for secured lending business is likely to lead lenders to look at increased lending to such sectors.

Intangible assets used to secure a loan might be just intellectual property rights such as a patent or copyright, but it is more likely that a bundle of intellectual property rights will be offered as security. The bundle might be of one type of rights such as a patent portfolio or a combination of, for example, patents, copyright and brands. The intellectual property rights may have been licensed in return for payment, typically of royalties. These licence agreements and any other agreements relating to the use of the intellectual property rights will form an important aspect of the intellectual property rights being offered as security. Lenders need to understand that an evaluation of the intellectual property rights as security should include an evaluation of relevant agreements.

Most of the attributes that made tangible assets reassuring as security are absent from intellectual property. They have little or no physical presence and there is usually no ready market by which to assess the value of the assets and in which to sell them should the security need to be realised.

Legal issues

Intellectual property rights can be charged like any other assets. A fixed or floating charge can be taken over them. They can be the subject of a loan agreement. The nature of the intellectual property rights will determine whether, in practice, the asset is suitable as security. A granted patent can in a legal sense be charged as security as can know how. Each will give legal protection to a concept employed in a business to make money. However the two are really radically different as the section on due diligence and intellectual property rights has shown.

The usual way to take security over a patent is to assign it to the lender on strict terms. The alternative is for the loan agreement or charge to state that the patent will be assigned if the security is to be realised in the event of default. The potential difficulties in putting such a term into effect are obvious. The borrower against whom the security is being enforced is unlikely to be in a co-operative mood! Taking court action to enforce the transfer will be expensive and delay realisation of the asset whilst the legal process grinds on.

Intellectual property rights when assigned to the lender become the property of the lender not the business using it. The business will, therefore, need a licence to use the intellectual property rights from the lender. This will be an exclusive one otherwise the lender could in theory licence a competitor! Of course, in practice, to do so might undermine the business and jeopardise the loan. On default when the lender seeks to maximise the value of the intellectual property rights, the loan agreement must provide that any exclusivity is no longer applicable. The other problem is that the intellectual property rights and related agreements such as licence agreements may prohibit the assignment of the intellectual property rights or the agreements which together constitute the valuable asset offered as security. We have explored this problem and possible solutions to it in the securitisation section of this Chapter under "Potential problems and possible solutions". Other terms of the loan agreement will cover responsibility for keeping the patent in force by paying renewal fees and registering the change of ownership at the relevant Patent Offices. A term of the loan agreement will provide for the patent to be reassigned to the borrower on repayment of the loan. Similar considerations apply to other intellectual property assets such as registered trade marks and designs and for copyright.

These types of intellectual property rights remain in existence for set periods and as such are suitable in legal terms as security for finance. Patents are valid for twenty years and copyrights are for the life of the creator and then 70 years (subject to some exceptions). Registered trade marks last indefinitely in most countries provided renewals are paid. For registered rights like patents and trade marks renewal fees must be paid to keep the rights in force and these type of rights can be found invalid if challenged. The section on due diligence deals with these points in more detail. All these factors make these types of intangible assets more risky as security that traditional tangible assets. The risks can be reduced by undertaking a due diligence investigation and by monitoring the borrower and its activities. The administration burden can be higher as a result than with tangible assets.

In contrast to these rights, secret know how may be of equal value to the business as a patent in protecting the technology of that business but will be of very little value as security. The rights to such know how cannot sensibly be transferred in the way that rights to a patent, for example, can be. Terms to enable the asset to be realised would require the borrower to document the know how and any developments in the future and to ensure that it could be prevented from using the know how if the security was enforced. The lender would very likely need the co-operation of the borrower to transfer or licence the know how to another person to realise the security. The borrower would be unlikely to be in co-operative mood if the security was being enforced.

The distinctive feature about know how is that its existence as an asset with value really depends on secrecy. Once the information is in the public domain, any person can use it. The all-important secrecy can by accident or design easily slip away and with it the value of the asset as security. This is such a weakness as to render know how as an unacceptable asset as security for finance in most cases. A due diligence investigation can establish the position prior to the loan being made but monitoring of the borrower will not in practice reduce the risk significantly of the secret know how coming into the public domain.

Another risk factor in taking intellectual property rights as security is that the rights are often infringed and infringed quite easily. Rights in land and buildings can be infringed but it is a comparatively rare occurrence. Most assets of this tangible type are protected by security measures to prevent unauthorised access or use. However, we have all seen land illegally occupied by "travellers" who seem prepared to occupy even the smallest bit of car park in front of a building. Removing them is possible but usually involves going to court often followed by an eviction process.

Intangible assets like copyright in a computer program, for example, can be easily copied. The copying is difficult to detect and the cost of preventing widespread pirating is expensive. Most businesses where pirating occurs have procedures and even industry bodies to ensure the pirates are wherever possible caught and prosecuted. The costs are acceptable given the revenues produced by the intellectual property rights. The costs might be less acceptable if the revenues from the intangibles were less certain. Any lender taking an intangible asset as security will be faced with the possibility of having to enforce the rights to maintain the value in the event that the borrower defaults.

The lender will need to assess in detail all the potential difficulties in using particular intellectual property rights and any associated agreements as security for a loan and put in place a loan agreement which in all the circumstances will enable the lender to realise the proper value of the intellectual property rights and to have the benefit of any revenues being generated by the use of those rights.

Commercial issues

Two vital aspects to using intangibles as security are the ability to obtain good legal title to the intellectual property rights if the borrower defaults and undertaking a thorough due diligence of the rights and the commercial context in which the borrower uses them. They have a key bearing on the ability to realise the value of the intellectual property rights if the borrower defaults. The lender will be equally concerned with the *value* to place on the intellectual property rights and the *ability to realise* that value to recover the money lent or at least part of it. The value of the intellectual property rights as assets in the business of the borrower is likely to be greater than the value to the lender on their own. If the lender, on default, can effectively offer for sale the intellectual property rights and the business in which they are used, then the value of the intellectual property rights to the lender will be similar to that of the borrower. The lender will need to consider this carefully and possibly take security over the business as a whole not just the intellectual property rights.

The value of certain types of intellectual property rights can be assessed by reference to a given market. A portfolio of book titles or catalogue of musical works by well known artists will have a value which can be ascertained either by known market prices or based on the revenue stream derived from them. These assets are easily separable from rest of the business and can as such have independent value.

Many other types of intellectual property rights have no ready market nor do they produce an income stream which is easily separable from the remainder of the business. Some of these assets may not actually be separable from the business at all. It would, for example, be difficult to do so with secret know how as already mentioned. These assets are difficult to value and difficult to realise in the event of default and lenders are understandably wary about taking them as security.

Separability is a major concern for lenders when considering intellectual property rights as security. Rather like some tangible assets on a break-up of a business, some intellectual property rights will have little value on their own. The potential alternative uses for the asset will be, at best, limited, and may need substantial further investment to exploit the asset to obtain the return. It would need to be a particularly outstanding asset to command a high or even any price if that were the scenario. The value of some intellectual property rights is as a bundle. The administrative burden in taking over such a bundle could be substantial and unacceptable. The due diligence obligation could be equally substantial and unacceptable. Several legal regimes could be involved such as patent copyright and trade mark law, possibly in different jurisdictions.

Intellectual property rights which are generating a substantial revenue stream will generally make those rights more acceptable as security. It is more like the catalogue of recordings referred to above. The revenue stream will give some basis for valuation separate from the business. The asset as a revenue generator is more likely to be saleable separate from the remainder of the business.

Valuation of intellectual property rights is still regarded in general as difficult. The methods which are used or suggested in this book are not well understood by business people and their professional advisors. Consequently, borrowers do not have confidence to offer intellectual property rights as security nor lenders to accept them. The result is that a business with intellectual property rights as its main assets is likely to be given a much reduced value in debt security terms than would a business in a comparable financial position but having substantial tangible assets capable of being realised in the event of default. Lenders are used to assessing the value of land with debtors possibly obtaining a professional valuation but leaders are not used to valuing intellectual property such as software and brands. Many lenders do not know how to obtain a professional valuation of these types of asset.

A report in 1997 by Arthur Anderson on behalf of the Intellectual Property Institute entitled "The use of intellectual property as security for debt finance" provides a thorough investigation into this area and is a useful source of further information. The report identified the concerns of lenders about intangible assets including intellectual property rights as security for debt finance. Some of those concerns were:

- the subjective valuation approaches which have not yet achieved general acceptance and understanding. There has been a suggestion that a professional body be set up to address these matters;

- separating the intellectual property rights and other intangible assets from the business such that the asset can be shown to have independent value;

- lack of market valuation for most intangible assets;

- the potential for obsolescence to seriously undermine the value of the asset particularly in high technology sectors like electronics or software; and

- the uncertainty in many cases of the revenue stream derived from the asset with the exception of some sectors like the music business. However, cash flows offer the most reliable data on which to value an intangible asset.

Intangible assets are not used extensively as security for finance except where substantial and regular cash flows can be demonstrated such as in the music and film industries. As business value comes ever more to be generated from intangible and particularly intellectual property rights, lenders will need to find ways to lend to these businesses and yet have sufficient security in the event of default. The need to maximise value from assets of all types and the shortening of product life cycles in a global economy is leading to more collaboration and more licensing of technology. This trend to exchange or share intangible assets to mutual benefit may lead to a more developed market for intangible assets with businesses actively looking for technology to enhance the value of the business. A growing interest is being expressed in intellectual property rights valuation which is likely to lead to approaches to valuation being better understood.

These two developments might well lead to more loans being secured against intellectual property rights as the circumstances increases where both lenders and potential borrowers have confidence that a reliable value can be placed on such intellectual property rights and that the value of the intellectual property right can be realised if necessary.

CHAPTER 7
SUMMARY

The increasing sums being paid for IP rights in the open market suggest that the values attaching to them are rising. However, there appears to be a pervasive lack of awareness of the inherent value of IP within organisations, and a resultant lack of attention to the management of this important area. Consequently, companies are missing opportunities to realise full returns on the huge investments that are being made in IP development every year. Furthermore, companies are potentially exposing themselves to business risks, for example from their failure to adequately protect these key assets.

- Despite the large sums spent on developing IP, relatively little is spent on managing or enforcing it.

- Over half of all companies surveyed do not have a well-articulated procedure in place to charge other group companies for their use of IP.

- The majority of companies are unable to estimate the value of their IP, or the IP revenue generated from subsidiaries or third parties.

- Only 11% of participants admitted they already use or are considering using their IP as collateral, which demonstrates just how under-valued IP is within most organisations.

- Less than a third of companies surveyed undertake an annual review of royalty rates, which may mean that the remainder of companies are under-valuing or losing out on a valuable income stream.

- Organisations are failing to monitor important developments which may have a fundamental effect on the value of their IP and the operations of their businesses.

UK companies could be more aggressive with regard to IP issues than they are being, and more methodical about their practices when it comes to charging both internal subsidiaries and external third parties, in order to derive greater value from their IP. There is also an argument for them becoming more defensive. Few seem to have the structural solutions in place necessary to defend their IP against infringement.

Businesses should be looking to appoint dedicated IP professionals tasked with understanding thier IP portfolio, or should at least be looking to bring together specialists from all internal disciplines that deal with IP, in order to form a consistent and accurate view of the value of this important asset. Organisations that fail to understand the relative importance of their IP portfolios will find it difficult to make informed, reliable decisions about the business. Many organisations may struggle when they encounter financial reporting, litigation or tax situations which require disclosure of, or negotiation with third parties over, the value of certain items of IP. Finally, organisations should look to monitor more closely any developments that might affect the IP portfolio and the way it is used, and should be taking a more pro-active approach to identify ways to use those developments to their best advantage.

When properly understood and managed, IP rights can create significant competitive advantage and generate direct short, medium and long term benefits for international business in all sectors.[1]

We hope that this book has gone some way to helping readers achieve such advantage.

---

1.   Source: PriceWaterhouseCoopers/Landwell.

APPENDIX 1
MORE ON INTELLECTUAL PROPERTY RIGHTS

Contents

APPENDIX 1
MORE ON INTELLECTUAL PROPERTY RIGHTS

The meaning of "Europe" in this book

The European Commission has over many years been bringing into effect legal measures the effect of which is to harmonise many laws within Europe. The European Commission has been active in recent years producing harmonising measures for trade marks, various aspects of copyright law, databases and rights in designs. The effect of these measures is that national laws of European states are required to be enacted or amended to bring into effect the law as harmonised.

The European Commission produces most of the Europe-wide harmonising laws by using a **EC Directive** covering a particular legal subject. An EC Directive is a type of European legislation which is binding upon Member States with regard to the result to be achieved by the Directive but which usually requires implementation in each Member State through national legislation before it can become fully effective in law.

The **European Union** is the result of co-operation between the 15 member states of the European Union (which at the time of writing are Belgium, France, Luxembourg, Germany, Italy, the Netherlands, Denmark, Ireland, the United Kingdom, Greece, Spain, Portugal, Austria, Finland and Sweden) to promote economic and social progress, assert a European identity, introduce European citizenship, develop an area of freedom, security and justice within the member states and to maintain and build on established European law. The European Union was created by the Treaty on European Union which was signed in Maastricht in December 1991. The **European Economic Area** comprises the European Union together with Norway, Liechtenstein and Iceland. The expression **Member States** is used in this book interchangeably to refer to both the member states of the European Union and the member states of the European Economic Area because some EC Directives will apply just to the European Union countries whereas others have the effect of applying to countries of the European Economic Area.

For completeness, the **European Free Trade Association ("EFTA")** was established in 1960 to eliminate tariffs and other restrictions on trade between members. EFTA is now composed of just Norway, Liechtenstein, Iceland and Switzerland.

Copyright

Introduction

In the UK, the need to prevent the unlawful copying of books lead to the laws which became known as copyright. The need became particularly acute after the printing process had been invented in the fifteenth century and developed. For the first time books could be duplicated quickly by the standards of the time. The need arose to prevent copying and the loss of business for earl book makers. Copyright owners today have the same concerns as the early bookmakers all those hundreds of years ago. Lobbying of governments and interstate bodies to change or amend the law to protect the interests of copyright owners continues most recently in connection with the accessing and use of copyright work over the internet.

The protection against unlawful copying given by copyright has two broad aspects to it. First, the types of creative works qualifying for copyright. Copyright now covers such diverse subjects as sound recordings, works of sculpture, and computer programs. Secondly, the activities that constitute an infringement of the rights given by copyright.

Copyright is not a right arising out of registration. It is a right which arises out of the act of creating and recording in some way the thing created. In copyright parlance the thing is commonly referred to as " the work " or "the copyright work". A book is not the subject of copyright protection until it has been 'recorded', for example, on paper or on a computer. It may be confidential before being 'recorded' which would give the author rights in confidential information which are covered later. A key concept follows from this. *Copyright does not protect ideas but the form in which those ideas have been expressed.* This concept is interpreted differently by the courts of countries round the world.

The law of copyright is a complex subject. The detailed laws of individual countries are different. Earlier, reference was made to some of the international treaties about intellectual property rights. Copyright is subject to a further national variation. The rights given by copyright are enforced by national courts. The rulings of those courts as to the extent of copyright protection depends on three things:

- first, and obviously, on the idiosyncrasies of the national laws;

- secondly, on the extent of the creative effort required for copyright to exist in a work; and

- thirdly, on the interpretation of the similarity required to constitute unlawful copying.

EU Copyright directive

The EU Directive (2001/29/EC) came into effect on 22nd May 2001. The EU states must implement the Directive by 22nd December 2001. The Directive seeks to harmonise aspects of copyright law across Europe with the aim of encouraging the development and exploitation of intellectual property. The other objective of the Directive was to effect changes in the laws of EU states so that the European Community as an independent body and EU states will conform with certain international treaties relating to copyright.

Those treaties were adopted following work done by the World Intellectual Property Organisation (WIPO) in 1996. They are the WIPO Copyright Treaty and the WIPO.

The Copyright Directive is one of the most important legislative developments in the field of copyright. The important provisions are:

- comprehensive rights to enable authors, performers and others to control the reproduction of their work and to enable authors to control distribution of their work;

- a new right for authors, performers and others to control the communication of their work to the public by wire or wireless means;

- an exhaustive set of exemptions to the rights given by copyright, although adoption of these by member states is optional;

- an obligation on member states to give legal protection to technological measures used by rights owners to prevent the unauthorised use of copyright material;

- an obligation on member states to give legal protection to management information attached to copyright works by rights owners for the purpose of controlling the use of their works.

Member states will be required to amend their laws to implement these provisions to the extent that the current laws do not provide the rights and exemptions set out in the Directive and which are expressed to be mandatory.

The new powers given to rights holders must be understood and used to their advantage. The obligations to allow access to legitimate users and exemptions must also be understood so that the extent of such legitimate use and use of the exemptions can be monitored and controlled.

EU Electronic Commerce Directive

The need to harmonise the laws in Europe applying to activities in the electronic network environment concerns not only copyright and related rights (the meaning of both of which are explained later) but also other areas, such as defamation, misleading advertising, or infringement of trademarks. This need has been addressed in Directive 2000/31/EC on certain legal aspects of information society services, in particular electronic commerce (EU

Electronic Commerce Directive). This Directive clarifies and harmonises various legal issues relating to information society services including electronic commerce.

The Copyright Directive and the Electronic Commerce Directive should be implemented within a similar timescale. This is a desired outcome because The Electronic Commerce Directive provides a harmonized framework of principles and provisions relevant to important parts of the Copyright Directive.

These Directives and the national legislation that will follow have been designed specifically to address the concerns of rights holders in relation to copyright works which have arisen through the ease of access and copying of copyright works over the internet. The ease of access and copying has been of particular concern to businesses developing software, in the media and information industry, and those in the music business.

Copyright Works

Copyright works are defined in the UK in the Copyright Designs and Patents Act 1988 as amended by subsequent legislation, and in numerous regulations such as statutory instruments. The categories of copyright works are outlined below. These are taken from UK law and illustrate the breadth of works now capable of being protected as copyright works generally. In each country local nuances will exist but these categories can be taken as general guidance on what copyright can protect. The categories are:

- literary works
- dramatic works
- musical works
- artistic works
- sound recordings
- films
- broadcasts
- cable programmes
- typographical arrangements
- databases.

A work only becomes a copyright work if it meets certain qualifying conditions such as being original and being recorded in writing or otherwise.

For example, a book is a literary work and any illustrations will be artistic works. A computer game or website will have software (a literary work), complex graphics (artistic works), animations (a film), and sounds (musical works and a sound recording).

Subsistence of copyright

If a particular work comes within one of the categories of copyright work under UK law, then copyright will subsist in that work if a number of conditions are satisfied. The relevant conditions are detailed, and only the main two are outlined here. These will also serve to illustrate the complexity which can be involved in assessing whether or not the claimed copyright really exists. In some cases, making this assessment will be easy. For example a work created by a person who is a British national will have copyright protection in the UK and elsewhere. But for a multimedia product such as a computer game or a website, the assessment could be complex involving works created by a number of persons of different nationalities and in different places. The fundamental conditions are:

- whether the work qualifies for copyright by reference to the creator of the work or to its place of first publication (**"the Qualification Condition"**); and

- whether the work has sufficient originality (**"the Originality Condition"**).

The Qualification Condition

No copyright will subsist in a work unless the qualification requirements are met by reference to one of the following:

- the author must be a person who satisfies certain detailed nationality requirements; or

- the publication must be made in a qualifying country. A country will be regarded under UK law as qualifying if that country has signed a relevant international treaty or is named in relevant UK legislation. Publication means the issuing of copies of the work to the general public in quantities which satisfy public demand;

- in the case of a broadcast or cable programme, the country from which the broadcast was made or cable programme sent must be a qualifying country.

The Originality Condition

In UK copyright law, a literary, dramatic, musical or artistic work must be original to be protected by copyright. This is not the same as patent law where novelty and inventiveness are required. The test for originality for copyright to subsist is not so strict. Originality is not defined in UK copyright law except in relation to databases. A good rule of thumb is that a work will be original in the copyright sense if a reasonable amount of skill and effort has been put into the creation of the work.

So in the 1988 case of *Interlego AG v Tyco Industries and others*[1], Lego claimed to be the owners of the copyright in drawings of components which when moulded in plastic were sold as part of the child's toy LEGO. Lego brought an action alleging infringement of copyright. Tyco claimed that the drawings in which Lego were claiming copyright had been copied from earlier drawings. Lego had to show that some elements, at least, in the drawings were original. The court ruled that the drawings in issue were copies of earlier drawings with

---

1.   [1987] F.S.R. 409.

insignificant additions and were not original works attracting copyright protection even though much skill and labour had been used to copy the earlier drawings when making the later ones. But the court did note that relatively small changes, if significant, could convert something essentially a copy of an earlier work with no copyright protection into an original work with copyright protection. In the 1993 case of *Waylite Diaries CC* v *First National Bank*[2], which concerned the layout of a diary, the court ruled that it is the input by the author which must be considered when determining originality. The input by the author cannot be determined merely by the time spent on the work. There must be enough quality of individuality to be able to distinguish the work. In this case the court ruled that there was insufficient distinctiveness and the work lacked originality.

Ownership

This is the fourth of the main areas of investigation about copyright. If the work is (1) one of the defined works, (2) copyright subsists in it, and (3) the work is an original work, then the next verification required is ownership. In UK law, ownership is determined by reference to the author. Therefore, a key concept in relation to copyright is that of authorship. The author is the first owner of copyright in a work. This is subject to an exception. For a literary, dramatic, musical, or artistic work made by an employee during the course of employment, the employer is the first owner of the copyright in the work unless there is an agreement to the contrary. The author of a work is the person who creates it. For literary or artistic works, the person who is the creator will be a matter of fact and is not the subject of further statutory definition. However, with some other copyright works further statutory definition is provided. The author of a sound recording or film, is the person by whom the arrangements necessary for the making of the recording or film are undertaken. For a broadcast, the author is the person making the broadcast. For a cable programme, it is the person providing the cable programme service in which the programme is included.

If a literary, dramatic, musical, or artistic work is computer generated then the author is the person who undertook the arrangements necessary for the creation of the work. A work has joint authors where the work has been produced by a collaboration of two or more persons and where the contribution of each is not distinct. All such persons shall be considered authors for UK copyright purposes.

Works created by Employees?

A work created by an employee will in UK law be owned by the employer if the work was:

- created by the employee;
- during the course of his employment with the employer claiming ownership; and

---

2.   [1995] 1 S.A. 645.

- there is no agreement that some other person should own the copyright.

If the claim to title is that the author was an employee, the due diligence investigation will need to address three points. First, is the author in fact an employee? Secondly, was the work created during the course of author's employment? Thirdly, was there an agreement as to who would own the copyright?

The first two do not usually cause any difficulty in practice. Occasionally, the facts of a particular case make these questions more difficult to answer. Then legal advice will need to be taken based on the body of law – legislation and decided cases – applicable to the case. This is a good example of the need to move from general concepts (here of English law) to the detail of the relevant law which is not necessary for the purpose of this book.

Any agreement about ownership?

The third question of whether any agreement about ownership existed will again depend on the relevant facts.

The existence of an agreement between an employer and employee is often a written agreement or is clear from the circumstances and surrounding documents – such as correspondence – and usually does not cause a problem in practice. It is unusual for such an agreement to give ownership to the employee.

The existence of an agreement about ownership of copyright outside the employment relationship can be more difficult to confirm. A clear written contract dealing with ownership may exist. But often the written agreement does not cover ownership or is unclear about it. Often the agreement is formed by a number of documents or from correspondence.

When undertaking any due diligence, the person doing the work will need to be alive to the possibility of such agreements and investigate accordingly. But like many things in the law, there are times when an agreement about ownership might be implied from the circumstances or an ownership term implied into a contract. In the 1993 case of *John Richardson Computers* v *Flanders*[3], a former employee who had written software for John Richardson Computers, was commissioned and agreed to write enhancements to the software after he had ceased to be an employee. He was given instructions as to the required enhancements. The terms on which he would do this were agreed in writing and included terms about payment. But these terms made no reference to ownership of the copyright in the enhancements. The court ruled in a subsequent dispute that a term was implied into the agreement in all the circumstances that John Richardson Computers owned the copyright.

Equitable ownership

In UK law an asset can be held with a full legal title with all the legal rights of ownership or with a partial or incomplete title. This later title is usually referred to as an "equitable" title. The legal title to the asset will be owned by one person. The person who owns the equitable title has the right to call for

---

3.   [1993] F.S.R. 497.

the transfer of the legal title. This right is enforceable at law if necessary. A reasonable illustration is the position after exchanging contracts to buy a house but before completion. The buyer does not own the legal title until completion. Until then, the buyer has an "equitable" title and the right to require that the legal title be handed over.

It is not uncommon for an equitable title to be claimed in respect of a copyright, often because the parties to a particular relationship have not considered ownership properly or at all. This was the position in the John Richardson Computers case mentioned earlier. Once again each case depends on its own circumstances. Consequently, it will be a matter of judgement as to whether an equitable title has been established.

Transfer of copyright

By agreement

One way of removing doubts about the ownership of copyright is to confirm the ownership in one person by an agreement to which all the relevant persons are made party. It is perhaps a counsel of perfection but if the copyright is to form the basis of a substantial business investment, a risk free title should be the aim.

Of course insurmountable problems may exist to obtaining such a confirmatory agreement. Typical problems are that the person who could have an ownership claim may:

- no longer be willing to co-operate as a result of a dispute;
- demand a substantial sum believing that the other person is over a barrel. The amount based on the "ransom strip" principle. The amount may be too much compared to the risk should the title be defective;
- no longer be contactable;
- have purported to transfer the rights to someone else.

By operation of law

Copyright would form part of a person's estate. Therefore, it would pass by operation of law in the event of say death or bankruptcy.

Duration

The duration of copyright protection under UK law depends on the identity of the author of the work. Copyright in an original literary, dramatic, musical or artistic work will exist for 70 years after the end of the year in which the author dies. This is the case irrespective of ownership of the copyright. Where the author of the work is unknown, the copyright will expire 70 years after the end of the calendar year in which the work was first made available to the public. If authorship to the work is joint (this is often the case in computer programs and websites, and literary works), then providing all the authors are known, protection lasts until 70 years after the last surviving author dies. If all are not known, the right lasts for 70 years after the death of the last known author. The copyright in typographical arrangements only exists for 25 years. A typographical arrangement is the layout of a page, say of a newspaper ready for printing.

Infringement – rights to prevent unlawful copying

The right to prevent unlawful copying is really the fundamental point of copyright. The commercial value of the copyright derives from the ability to prevent others copying a commercially successful work without permission. It is only an infringement of copyright if copying has occurred without permission. This is straightforward with counterfeit goods, but can be more difficult where products are similar but not identical. The copyright owner must prove that copying has occurred to win a copyright case. The copying must be of at least a substantial part. Substantial is assessed by reference to both quantity and quality. If the original work and "copy" are closely similar, a court will often infer that copying took place and require an explanation from the person accused of copying. Such a person, to escape a finding of copying, will need to show a convincing defence of independent creation not copying. As always, the facts believed by the judge in a court will determine who succeeds.

The importance of the infringement rights to a commercial assessment or valuation of the copyright as a business asset are that they define the products that the copyright owner can prevent others copying and selling.

Legitimate Copying

It is not an infringement of copyright to copy a copyright work in certain limited circumstances. These are often referred to as permitted acts. These include so called "fair dealing" exceptions such as copying for private study or for criticism, review and news reporting. Others cover use in education and for libraries and archives.

This subject is also covered in chapter 5 on due diligence starting at page 253.

Databases

Intellectual property rights of two kinds now potentially exist in a database under UK law. First, a database is now specifically categorised as a literary work in which copyright will subsist if the qualifying conditions are met. Secondly, by an intellectual property right called a database right which is more limited than copyright.

Defining a database?

An understanding of UK law about databases will give a good indication of the protection of databases throughout the EU States because the UK law implements EC Directive 96/9 harmonising intellectual property rights for databases in member states. In UK law (and under the Directive) a database means a collection of independent works, data or other materials which have two characteristics. First, they are arranged in a systematic or methodical way. Secondly, they are individually accessible by electronic or other means.

A database normally has a structural part and the part which forms the content of the database. Each of these can be protected by the intellectual property rights in databases either by the database right or by copyright.

A database will include collections of existing independent works and other data such as musical works, texts, sounds, images, financial information collected together as the contents of the database. But to qualify for the database right or copyright, other qualifying conditions set out below must be satisfied.

Certain types of work will not satisfy the definition or qualifying conditions for the database right. These works include the software used to operate the database and recordings of literary and musical works as such or any film as such. Copyright will subsist in these works if the qualifying conditions for copyright are satisfied.

In the 2001 UK case of *British Horseracing Board Limited* v *William Hill Organisation Limited*[4] the database comprised details of horses, their owners, the runners in any given race, the race course, date and time of the races. The Court of Appeal regarded this as a data base within the definition and in which database rights would subsist. However, the Court of Appeal suspended its decision and referred the case to the European Court of Justice for guidance on interpretation of the Database Directive in a EU wide context.

Subsistence of copyright in a database

As with other copyright works, copyright will exist in a database if the database is original. However, there is a important difference from other copyright works. The standard of originality is much stricter for a database than with other copyright works. The stricter standard is that a database will only be original for copyright purposes if the database constitutes the author's own intellectual creation by reason of the author's selection or arrangement of the contents of the database. Whether a particular database qualifies as a copyright work will depend on all the particular circumstances. Eventually, rulings from cases in the courts of England and other member states, and by the European Court of Justice, will establish the standards required.

---

4.   [2001] R.P.C. 31.

Ownership of copyright in a database

The author (for copyright purposes) of a database will be the person who creates it. In practice many databases are produced using computer systems. If this happens, the author will be the person by whom the arrangements, necessary for the creation of the work, are undertaken. Typically, this will be a business or corporate body rather than an individual.

As explained earlier, the key to establishing who owns the copyright in a database is knowing who is the author. The author will own the copyright unless that person is an employee creating the database during the course of employment duties or an agreement provides that someone else will own the copyright.

Subsistence of the database right

The first point to understand is that database rights can exist whether or not the database is a copyright work. The database right will exist if there has been a substantial investment in the obtaining, verifying or presenting of the contents of the database. Investment in this context includes any investment which is financial, human or technical. The practical assessment of the database right as an intellectual property right will need careful application and evaluation. As in other areas of intellectual property, once the courts have made rulings on database rights, the extent of the protection afforded will be clearer.

Ownership of the database right

The maker of a database is the first owner of the database right in it. For these purposes, the maker of the database is the person who puts the effort into organising the information for the database, checking it and investing in it. An employer will be the maker if the person who makes the database is an employee acting in the course of his employment unless an agreement to the contrary exists.

Infringements of the database right

Broadly, a person infringes the database right if, without permission, that person extracts or re-utilises all or a substantial part of the contents of the database. Substantial will be considered taking into account quality and/or quantity. This pretty well speaks for itself. One point worth emphasising is that repeated and systematic extraction or re-utilisation of insubstantial parts of the contents of the database can amount to infringement.

Duration

The database right lasts for 15 years. The trigger point forming the start of that period needs care. The 15 year period can:

* either start from the end of the calendar year in which the making of the database was completed; or

- 15 years from the end of the calendar year in which the database was first made available to the public provided this was done within 15 years from the end of the year in which the database was completed.

Other relevant matters

There are requirements to be met for a database to qualify for database right protection. These are broadly similar to those requirements for qualifications for copyright protection although the detail would always need to be verified. There are also certain things that can be done which would not be regarded as infringements of the database rights. They generally cover non-commercial activities such as accessing public records.

Author's Rights

These rights are separate from rights in copyright works but are related to them. They are sometimes referred to as related rights or, equally ambiguously, as author's rights or even moral rights. In UK law, these rights are known as moral rights and only exist in copyright works. In other words, no copyright, no related rights. The same applies generally in other jurisdictions.

A further complication may arise because the person having these individual rights might not be the person who is the owner of the copyright in the particular work. This has implications for anyone wishing to exploit the particular work commercially. The author's rights are often not assignable (depending on the jurisdiction) whereas the copyright in the particular work can be assigned. However, author's rights can sometimes be waived again in respect of some countries but not all because under some national laws these rights cannot be waived.

This fact is important when it comes to due diligence in relation to using a created work such as a photograph, lyric or some text. If it can be established that no copyright exists, then no author's rights will arise. If these rights do exist, exploiting the copyright can be problematic. The complexity and details of national laws would always need to be checked before using the work in any particular country. This is covered later in Chapter three on due diligence.

The 2002 EU Copyright Directive, referred to earlier, has provided a harmonised set of rights for authors in relation to reproduction and distribution of their works, and a new right to authorise or prohibit the communication of their works to the public whether by wire or wireless means. The Directive must be implemented by EU states by 22nd December 2002.

Author's rights are not the same as the rights of performers of copyright works which will be covered in the next section.

These author's rights and the rights set out in the EU Copyright Directive give individuals some control over the copyright works they have created. In some circumstances, this is so even if the individual does not own or no longer owns the copyright in the copyright work in question. These rights are of crucial importance in the exploitation of literature, music, recordings of music and other literary works, films and in broadcasts. The extent to which author's rights exist and can be enforced depends on a number of factors which interrelate and make this area of copyright law complex. The extent to which authors have these rights varies depending in the nationality of the person who created the rights, the country in which the rights were created and the countries in which the rights are to be exploited.

Case Study

A good practical example involved the exploitation of music and music videos which were recorded by a group of musicians whilst touring throughout Europe and the United States. This was before the EU Copyright Directive and implementing laws came into effect. The recordings were made in several countries using several different recording studios and using many individual session musicians in those different countries. In these circumstances, to make sure that all rights – the copyrights and all related rights of each person – and permissions had been acquired or waived to exploit the recordings of the music and the videos across many national boundaries was difficult and time consuming. In some cases the author's rights could not under local law be acquired or waived so that in relation to these individuals modest compensation arrangements were made to exploit their work. This exercise would have been much easier if the recordings had been organised in a more systematic way using one studio, in one country, with one group of identified musicians to provide background or accompanying music.

There are two primary rights which individuals have in works they have created. First, the right to be identified as the author of a literary, dramatic, musical or artistic work or to be identified as the director of a film in which copyright subsists. This is sometimes referred to as the "paternity right". Secondly, the right of such an author not to have the work subjected to derogatory treatment. This is sometimes referred to as the "integrity right".

Under UK law, the paternity right must be asserted by the individual before it is effective and can be enforced. Assertion must be in writing and can either be part of an assignment of copyright or by some other written notice which comes to the attention to any person contemplating using the work in question. For example, it is common to see in the notices in books about copyright, a statement that the author asserts his or her rights to be identified as the author. The need to have asserted the right is a precondition to the enforcement of the paternity right. In other countries this is not a requirement so that the paternity right in relation to a particular work might not exist in the UK because not asserted but this right is likely to exist in respect of other countries. This needs to be born in mind. The rights of both paternity and integrity can be waived by the relevant individuals as far as the UK is concerned.

Individuals often come under pressure from publishers and recording companies to waive their rights. Many individuals are reluctant to do so. It is important to bear in mind that waivers obtained under the UK moral rights laws may not be effective under the laws of other countries. This means that when the copyright works come to be exploited in those countries, the rights of the individuals will need to be taken into account in a way that was not necessary in the UK because the rights were waived.

What is derogatory treatment?

The Berne Convention[5] is perhaps the best source for a general view of this. It provides that an author of the work shall have the right to object to any distortion, mutilation or other modification of, or other derogatory action, in relation to the work in question which would be prejudicial to his honour or reputation. This is comprehensive but does not help much in identifying what the limits of protection might be or when any person seeking to exploit the work needs to consult with the author about any changes or adaptations which might be seen as derogatory in this sense.

Some cases are illustrative. An objection was successfully made under French law that the conversion of a black and white film into a version in colour was a derogatory treatment of the original work. French law has traditionally given creators and authors of copyright works strong rights to control the way such works are used.

The law in the UK has been traditionally at the other end of the scale. In the 1998 UK case of *Pasterfield* v *Denham*[6], Pasterfield and others had designed two leaflets and a brochure for a public body. Later, the public body asked Denham to update the leaflet which they did. Some features were copied into the new leaflet but other features and colourings were changed. The leaflet also bore the legend "Produced by Denham Designs". Pasterfield sued alleging derogatory treatment of the work being the leaflet as well as for copyright infringement. The copyright claim failed because the court found that ownership of the copyright had transferred to the public body. The derogatory treatment case also failed because the court said derogatory treatment meant distortion or mutilation which prejudiced the honour or reputation of the designer as an artist. This had not been proved. It was insufficient that the designer was aggrieved.

---

5.   International Convention for the Protection of Literary and Artistic Works, signed Berne 1886, and amended since then.

6.   [1999] F.S.R. 168.

Rights in Performances

Rights in performances are rights of individuals. They are distinct from the author's rights. The legal position is again complex. Performer's rights are primarily of concern in the entertainment industry involving the exploitation of recordings of music and literary works, films and making of broadcasts.

An important starting point is a convention signed in Rome in 1961 which commits those countries which have signed the convention to give performers certain rights. These rights relate to unauthorised broadcasting, recording of performances and exploiting those recordings. The WIPO Performance and Phonograms Treaty 1996 is another important treaty for performers. The 2002 EU Copyright Directive, referred to earlier, provides harmonised rights for performers in member states. The rights give performers the right to control the reproduction of "fixations" of their performances and the communication of them to the public by wire or wireless means. The intention is that the issuing of the Copyright Directive and the its implementation by member states will enable the European Community and individual EU states to ratify the WIPO Performance and Phonograms Treaty 1996.

The European Parliament has issued another Directive which impacts on the rights of performers in recordings of their performances. It is the EU Directive 92/100 on Rental and Lending rights. This gives performers the exclusive right to authorise or prohibit certain things in relation to their performances. These can be summarised as including recording of live performances, the distribution of such recordings, the rental and lending of those recordings and the broadcasting of them. The existence of performer's rights in any country will require the laws of that country to assessed.

The effect of performer's rights, where they exist, will be to give to performers some control over the exploitation of recordings of their live performances and to obtain some remuneration from that exploitation. Therefore, when seeking to exploit commercially the recording of a copyright work such as a play or some music, check to what extent the permission of any relevant performers of the work needs to be obtained.

This may not be as difficult as it sounds since many of the rights which exist in a recording of a performance will be administered by organisations set up for this purpose. These are generally referred to as collecting societies. In the UK there are a number of these such as the Mechanical-Copyright Protection Society which represents major UK music publishers. The Performing Rights Society licences works of composers and publishers of music for public performance of these works. The Phonographic Performance Limited licences public performances of commercial recordings.

Typically recording companies will seek to transfer, where this is legally possible, the rights of individuals in their performances so that the recordings can be commercial exploited without the need to consult the performers and seek their agreement to the particular exploitation.

Other issues

Various qualification requirements must be met for the rights of performers to exist. The ownership of the rights depends on who created the work and their relationship with other persons or businesses, particularly those organisations such as music recording companies and broadcasting organisations which might be involved in the commercial exploitation of any recordings. In certain circumstances, a performer is entitled to what is described as equitable remuneration. For example, where a sound recording is broadcast or is otherwise made available to be heard by the public. There are provisions as to how this equitable remuneration will be assessed if it cannot be agreed by those involved. Finally, various rights are given to performers to prevent infringement of their rights and provide for compensation to be payable.

Recording Rights

These are rights accorded to any person having an exclusive recording contract with performers. Typically, record companies and broadcast organisations will have the benefit of such exclusive recording contracts. The recording rights exist for the benefit of the person having exclusivity in relation to the commercial exploitation of such recordings. They are clearly valuable rights. The usual remedies exist for the prevention of infringement of these rights.

Patents

Introduction

Patents can be obtained for inventions if certain criteria are met. There is no definition of an invention. There are requirements for a patentable invention. The general requirements for a patentable invention and for obtaining the grant of a patent are now applicable in most of the important countries in the world. This is the culmination of the effects of the various international conventions. The most important of the conventions in this respect is the Patent Co-operation Treaty. This usually referred to as the "PCT".

The exception is the United States. The basic concepts are the same as the rest of the world. However, there are important differences in law and procedure. A separate section giving an overview of the important conceptual differences appears later in this Appendix.

A patent is a nationally registered right. It is obtained by filing an application. The application is filed at a Patent Office where the administration of the patent granting process takes place. The application can be filed at a national or at a regional Patent Office. The national Patent Office could be that of the United Kingdom. The regional Patent Office might be the European Patent

Office in Munich. An international patent application is filed at a national or regional Patent Office designated for that purpose. In the language of the patent world, you will come across expressions like "a national filing", "an international filing", "a PCT filing" used to describe a patent application as appropriate. The application must comply with certain administrative formalities as well as meeting the requirements for a patentable invention. The administrative formalities are complex and must be met by the application if the application is to proceed through the process to a granted patent. More importantly, if these formalities have not been completed properly, they are difficult and often impossible to correct subsequently and particularly after the patent has been granted. The failure to meet properly these formalities can make the patent eventually granted open to challenge later or to be not as strong as it could have been.

In any detailed due diligence investigation an assessment needs to be made as to whether these requirements have been met and, if not, what likely effect will the omission have on the validity or strength of the patent and can it be corrected.

At the time this book was being completed a proposal was being considered for a regional patent covering all member states. This would be a regional not a national patent.

Basic requirements for a Patent

There are four key legal, rather than administrative, requirements to be satisfied to conclude that a patentable invention exists and before a patent can be granted. An understanding of these is necessary for anyone attempting to understand patent rights and any due diligence investigation about patent rights which might be the subject of an investment decision or as part of the evaluation of those rights so as to put a value on them. The key requirements are that the invention:

- must not be excluded by law from being patented;

- must be new. This is often referred to in patent parlance as "having novelty" or "being novel";

- must involve an inventive step meaning a technical advance over existing technological understanding which is not obvious. Again in patent parlance, this is often referred to by the shorthand expression "the invention is obvious" or "is not obvious" or "is inventive";

- must be capable of industrial application.

Is the innovation patentable?

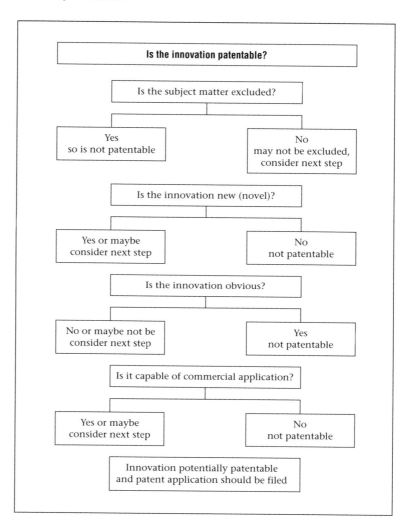

Essential patent terminology

Each of these key requirements will be considered in more detail later in this section. These key requirements cannot be understood without first being aware of three other fundamental concepts in patent law. These are the concepts of:

- the priority date of a patent;

- prior art; and

- the person skilled in the art, sometimes referred to as the "person skilled in the art" or simply as "the skilled person".

A knowledge of these concepts is necessary to understand the process by which patents are granted and to appreciate how a patent might be attacked as being invalid. The classic defence to a patent infringement claim is to show that the patent is invalid. If invalid, no patent. No patent, no infringement. Also without this understanding many of the due diligence points cannot be understood which are covered in chapter five.

Priority Date

This could be, but might not be, the date of filing given to an application for a patent by the Patent Office where it has been filed. However, the priority date might be an earlier date being the filing date of an earlier filed application. This needs explaining! But before that, remember also that the process is quite different in the United States where the date of filing is usually not decisive of priority.

Now the explanation. The international Paris Convention instituted a system whereby the applicant for a patent had a twelve month "priority period" in which to file further applications in the same country as the original patent filing and in respect of other countries. Later applications in that twelve month period and based on the original application can have the filing date of the original application for many purposes under patent law. Only a properly filed first application can be used to claim priority. To be properly filed, the application will usually have to meet the complex formalities under the patent law of the Patent Office where the application is lodged.

Priority date is important in this context because no event or publication of information after the priority date can be used when considering two important concepts in patent law. These are validity and the scope of the patent or application. Validity means determining whether a patent should be granted in respect of an application or once granted to determine whether that patent should have been granted, perhaps when challenged in defending an infringement allegation. The scope of the patent is a complex and technical subject. Suffice to say that it means the extent of protection for the inventive concept disclosed in the patent or application against use without permission.

Prior Art

This is sometimes referred to as the "state of the art". "Art" in the patent context simply means the relevant field of technology in which the invention is claimed to have been made. The European Patent Convention has a definition of prior art in Article 54 (2) which gives a good general indication of the meaning of prior art:

> "(1) The state of the art shall be held to comprise everything made available to the public by means of a written or oral description, by use, or in any other way before the filing date of the European patent application."

This might more helpfully have said "...before the priority date of the European patent application" since that date is the key date to determine what information "has been made available to the public". It is information made available to the public before that date only which can be used when considering the validity and scope of the patent.

The concept of prior art and what constitutes the "state of the art" is important in undertaking a due diligence investigation into a patent or patent application and understanding the result of the investigation. It is the background information against which the two most important determinants of a valid patent are assessed. These are namely whether the patent is novel and whether it constitutes an inventive step. More about this later.

The case of *Biogen* v *Medeva* [7] in the UK illustrates this point well. Biogen filed a UK patent application in 1978 for a ground breaking invention in the biotechnology field. This case study illustrates the importance of the technical aspects of filing a patent application, the priority date and prior art. After filing the first UK patent application, in the twelve month "priority period" Biogen then filed an application for a European patent at the European Patent Office. But between filing the first application and the European application, disclosures had occurred of further developments in the same technical field. These disclosures were prior art against the European application but not the first UK application. Later Biogen sued Medeva for patent infringement. Medeva adopted the classic defensive strategy and claimed the patent was invalid.

Medeva argued that the UK patent did not disclose enough information about the invention to justify stating the invention broadly so that it covered very many possible ways of using the technology which had been developed. One of the requirements validity is that the invention must described in away that is adequate to enable the "skilled person" is put the invention into practice in all those ways. In this case the patent did not adequately describe the invention. The requirement had not been met.

---

7.   [1995] F.S.R. 4.

This allowed Medeva then to argue that:

- the European patent could not be back-dated to the filing date of the first UK application because the information in the first application did not support the extent of protection sought. In other words, the UK application was not a "valid" application giving a "priority date".

- the European patent was not inventive on the actual date that it was filed (rather than the 'priority date') in the light of the information (prior art) disclosed since the filing of the first UK application. Biogen had admitted this.

If the European application could have adopted the earlier "priority date" of the first UK application, it would have been inventive over the prior art at that time which did not include the information disclosed later.

Decision? European patent could not be back-dated and was not inventive on the date when it was filed. It was invalid. So no infringement by Medeva.

The person skilled in the art

This person is a fictional character and the touchstone used by the Patent Office and the courts when applying certain aspects of patent law in the circumstances of individual cases when deciding if the patent should be granted or later if it is valid. The Patent Office or court seeks to take on the persona of this fictional skilled person in a particular case when deciding whether the invention involves an inventive step. Many patent cases over the years have ascribed certain characteristics to this fictional character which apply in many cases. Other characteristics of this person vary with the technical field relevant to the particular case. It is a flexible concept enabling the decision maker whether in a Patent Office or a court to achieve a fair result in all the particular circumstances of each invention. Of course, with flexibility comes uncertainty in that the outcome is often difficult to predict.

This uncertainty equates to risk when investing in "patented" technology. The risk can be reduced considerably by proper intellectual property management but cannot be eliminated.

Exclusions from patentability

Certain types of innovations are excluded and cannot be patented. Article 52 of the European Patent Convention has a good summary of these types of innovation. There is no equivalent provision which has been established at the international level in the Patent Co-operation Treaty. Article 52 states:

"(2) The following in particular shall not be regarded as inventions.......;

- (a) discoveries, scientific theories and mathematical methods;
- (b) aesthetic creations;

(c)   schemes rules and methods for performing mental acts, playing games or *doing business* and *programs for computers*;

(d)   presentations of information.

(3)   The provisions of paragraph 2 shall exclude patentability of the subject matter or activities referred to in that provisions only to the extent to which a European patent application or European patent relates to such subject matter or activities **as such**."

Article 33 of the European Patent Convention contains two other general exceptions to patentability. These relate to inventions the publication or exploitation of which would be contrary to public order or morality and to plant or animal varieties which have a scheme of protection of their own. The prohibition on inventions the publication or exploitation of which would be contrary to public order or morality has in recent years been used to challenge bio-technology patents in particular. This was one of the grounds invoked to object to the grant of a patent under the European Patent Convention for the Oncomouse developed by Harvard University in the United States. The invention related to a genetically engineered mouse and other mammals. The challenge was unsuccessful. The benefits were perceived to outweigh the risks of uncontrolled distribution of modified genes.

The patent law in the United States has no such limitations stating simply:

"Whoever invents or discovers any new and useful process, machine, manufacture, or composition of matter, or any new and useful improvement thereof, may obtain a patent therefor, subject to the conditions and requirements of this title."

This difference has lead to confusion amongst business people and their advisors as to whether software and business method inventions can be patented. In the United States software patents have been granted for many years and business method patents likewise in recent years. These type of patents have been granted because of the absence of the exclusions in the European patent law and because they meet all the other requirements for a valid patent.

In Europe the position in relation to software and business methods is explained in the next section. Software patents are now allowed. But not yet business method patents. Time will tell if this changes.

Software and business method patents

The current position in Europe is stated in this section. Patenting software was thought not to be possible because of the seemingly specific exclusion of software in Article 52. Patents were granted for software when operating a machine or similar since this was not regarded as a patent for software as such. But about fifteen years ago patents in Europe were filed for software. Some have been successful. Complex arguments were adopted to get round the exclusion of software as such. Recently, the European Patent Office has ruled on a software patent application by IBM. The effect of the ruling is that any innovative software which would otherwise meet the requirements for a patent will not be excluded. But simple software will still be excluded.

Software became in the 1980s a important source of technical advance directly and indirectly by allowing processes to be automated. The discovery of the complete human genome could not have been achieved without sophisticated computer systems. Software developers wanted to patent their software innovations. This is now possible as a result of some clever but tortuous interpretation of the exclusions. A United States patent was granted for software that manages libraries of molecular shapes. The patent covers methods of storing, searching and retrieving chemical information and biological assay results as well as structure, chemical name or molecular formula searching. Now, it would be expected that a patent for the same software would be obtained for European countries.

The internet as a new channel for doing business has become another source of technical advances. Some of these are essentially software innovations and can be patented if all the requirements for a patent are present. But other innovations are essentially ways of doing business using the internet. These would appear to be excluded from being patented in Europe just as software "as such" was excluded. But many patent applications have been filed for methods of doing business relating to the internet. Those applying believing the pressure of innovation and the need to give protection for such innovations will lead to arguments being accepted by the courts or patent offices to enable these applications to be granted. After all this is exactly what happened with software patents. Certainly in the United States such business method patents have been granted and are being enforced. An example of this is the 1999 landmark case in the US of *State Street Banking and Trust Co* v *Signature Financial Group Inc*[8]. A more definitive statement about the patenting of these methods in other countries cannot be given at this time. Certainly, at the time of writing, business methods are not regarded as patentable in Europe.

Novelty

Article 54(1) of the European Patent Convention sets out the meaning of novelty which for the purposes of this book can be taken as a universal meaning of novelty. This Article states that:

> "An invention shall be considered to be new if it does not form part of the state of the art."

The date on which an invention shall be assessed as to whether it is new is the priority date. So the state of the art is taken to comprise all matter made available to the public before the priority date of the invention whether by written description or in a conversation or by use or in some other way. Information forming part of the state of the art and which is argued makes

---

8. Federal Circuit Court of Appeals N° 96–1327 (7/23/1998).

an invention not novel, must be information which would enable the skilled person to conclude that the invention being claimed is not novel.

An illustration of this concept in practice is the 1988 UK case of *Gore* v *Kimal*[9]. This case is about the patents protecting the technology behind the well-known GORETEX fabric. A patent granted to Gore claimed a process for the production of a porous polymeric material. The process comprised forming and stretching a shaped article of the polymer under defined conditions. Before the priority date of the claim, Gore had supplied to potential customers in the United Kingdom, samples made in the US using the claimed process. In court proceedings for infringement of the patent, it was held that the patent was invalid. The public distribution of the product in the course of trade before the priority date constituted prior use. The process was in the public domain before the patent was filed. Consequently, the patent could not be novel.

Another important point illustrated by this case is that the process used could not be ascertained from the finished product, samples of which had been supplied. The UK court decided that supplying the samples put the process in the public domain. After more recent cases, the result might have been different. In UK law, and probably in most European countries, the disclosure of information about an invention before the application is filed must "enable" the skilled person to know the invention. Therefore now in a case like *Gore* the process would probably not be prior art and the patent would not have been invalid.

Inventive Step

Article 56 of the European Patent Convention provides a good explanation which for the purposes of this book can be taken as a universal meaning of inventive step stating that:

> "An invention shall be considered as involving an inventive step if, having regard to the state of the art, it is not obvious to a person skilled in the art."

Again understanding the concepts of the state of the art and the person skilled in the art is vital to an understanding of inventive step. The state of the art is broadly the same as that used when assessing novelty although there are some differences in detail.

If an invention is obvious having regard to the state of the art in the eyes of the relevant skilled person, then no patent can be validly granted for it or maintained in place if challenged later as a defence to an infringement claim.

This is one of the most difficult areas in patent law about which to advise. Guidance can be obtained from some decided cases in a particular jurisdiction. These often depend on their own facts and are not precedents as such. But some generally applicable principles have emerged. A good opinion

---

9.   [1988] R.P.C. 137.

on whether the invention is inventive or not for patent law purposes requires knowledge of these principles and lots of experience.

The UK case of *Wndsurfing International* v *Tabur Marine*[10] in 1985 illustrates two points about patents. First, the way in which inventiveness should be assessed in practice. Secondly, that the validity of a patent is never certain. This is an aspect of the risk inherent when investing in "patented" technology.

Windsurfer's patent claimed a wind-propelled vehicle having these features:

- an unstayed spar;

- connected through a universal joint;

- a sail attached along one edge to the spar; and

- held taut between a pair of arcuate booms mounted on the spar at one end and joined together at the other. The unstayed sail was used to steer the vehicle.

In an court action for patent infringement by Windsurfer, Tabur counter-claimed for revocation of the patent on the grounds that the claimed invention lacked novelty over a prior user by a boy and was obvious in view either of the prior user or a printed publication.

The publication was an article entitled "Sailboarding – Exciting New Watersport" which described the same basic concept. The cited prior user had taken place about ten years before the date of patent, when a 12 year old boy had built a sailboard and used it on an inlet near Hayling Island on the south coast of the UK during two consecutive seasons. The user was open and visible. The boy's sailboard differed from what was claimed only in that the sail was held between a pair of booms which were straight rather than arcuate when the vehicle was at rest.

The UK Patents Court found the claims invalid as not novel compared to by the prior user and obvious in view of the cited publication but made no finding of obviousness based on prior user. The patent was revoked. Windsurfer sought to amend by restricting their claims specifically to a surfboard of the "Californian type", but the judge concluded that there was no scope for such an amendment and refused to allow it. Windsurfer's appeal to the Court of Appeal was dismissed.

Industrial Application

This definition from the international Patent Co-operation Treaty is a good guide to this concept. An invention is considered industrially applicable if:

> "...according to its nature, it can be made or used (in the technological sense) in any kind of industry. "Industry" is to be understood in the broadest sense as in the Paris Convention for the Protection of Industrial Property....".

[1985] R.P.C. 59.

This requirement does not, in practice, usually cause a problem. Most inventions will be industrially applicable. The requirement will be interpreted in a broad sense and will cover most technical activities. Various cases that have excluded inventions from patentability on this ground tend to be the extreme ones. For example, patents sought for apparatus aimed at achieving perpetual motion have been rejected.

Validity and Revocation

The grant of a patent is not a guarantee that the patent will continue to be registered. This is often not understood and leads to a common misconception with registered intellectual property rights that once registered the rights given by the registration cannot be challenged.

The examination of the patent application by a Patent Office makes sure that the patent application and the invention disclosed in it meets all the administrative requirements for a patent to be granted. It also searches for prior art. Whilst this search is reasonably extensive, it will include mostly patents which have been granted and possibly other literature. If the invention is apparently valid compared to this prior art, the patent would be granted.

However, subsequently it is open to any person affected by the patent rights to make an application to have the granted patent cancelled. This is referred to as revoking the patent or revocation of the patent. The patent will be revoked if it is found to be invalid. The terms revocation and invalidity are closely related.

The grounds on which a patent can be found invalid are set out for the UK in section 72 of the Patents Act 1977. These mirror the provisions of various relevant international treaties. The most important one is that an invention will be invalid if it is not a patentable invention. This sounds slightly circular but it means if the invention is not new or is obvious or does not involve an industrial application, it will be invalid. The first two are the normal grounds on which a patent is challenged as being invalid.

There are other grounds but they are difficult to understand without a more detailed knowledge of complex areas of patent law and are not necessary for the purposes of this book.

If the patent is invalid, an application to revoke it can be made. The application can be made either to the Patent Office or a court. Many patents are challenged as being invalid and the revocation sought as part of a defence to a patent infringement claim, usually as a counterclaim to revoke a patent.

The patent application process

A patent is a right obtained by registration. After registration the patent owner, called the "proprietor", has a document which defines the rights in the invention which is the subject of the patent. This document is the patent.

The process by which a patent is granted for an invention is now similar whichever Patent Office is handling it. The procedure if an international application is filed under the Patent Co operation Treaty is rather different as will be explained.

The normal process may generally be described like this. The inventor files an application for the patent. This must comply with many administrative requirements. Most inventors would employ a patent agent to assist them to do this. A filing fee is payable. The application will be acknowledged. There are provisions in place to file a patent application by fax and e-mail.

The application will be examined to ensure that it meets all the administrative requirements. Once an application has met the administrative requirements, various events happen in accordance with a set timetable. The timetable provides dates by which certain events must happen. The applicant can request that some of these events happen earlier or ask for some of the time periods to be extended. The nature of the event that must be accomplished by a particular date determines the ease with which an extension can be obtained. In some cases an extension is easily obtained, in others not. Further, most patent application systems allow late completion of activities if done during short periods after the due date. These are referred to as grace periods and are explained in more detail later.

There are two key events in the application process. First, the patent application is examined after a request to do so by the applicant and the payment of a fee. The examination process scrutinises the patent application to ascertain whether it is a patentable invention. In particular the invention, the subject of the application, is scrutinised for novelty, that it involves an inventive step and is capable of industrial application. The examination also seeks to ensure that the application meets various other administrative requirements. Secondly, the application is published in accordance with the procedures of the Patent Office undertaking the examination. Publication does not take place usually earlier than 18 months after the priority date of the application. Publication typically takes place shortly after the end of the 18 month period.

In most cases, the individual at the Patent Office undertaking the examination, known as the examiner, will raise objections on various grounds to the patent application. These will be notified to the applicant or to the patent agent advising the applicant. A dialogue will then take place between the applicant or his patent agent and the examiner seeking to resolve these objections. In most cases objections are overcome either by persuading the examiner that the objections are not correct or by making amendments to the patent application.

Once the application has passed these hurdles it can go forward to grant and the intention to grant the patent will in many Patent Offices be published in an official journal to allow any interested party to oppose the grant of the patent. Such a procedure exists under the European Patent Convention but does not exist in the United Kingdom.

Once the patent has been granted the applicant is sent a document which is the grant of the patent and appropriate entries are made on the register of patents. From the date of grant, the patent establishes legally enforceable rights which date back to the priority date of the application which became the granted patent.

The patent when granted consists of a specification and several claims at the end. The specification essentially describes the invention and the claims are a statement of the features of the invention which cannot be used without the permission of the owner of the patent.

Worldwide and European patents

Framework

Worldwide or European patent rights can be obtained through procedures set up by agreement between countries. The agreement is then recorded in a treaty to which each country adheres. The treaty providing for an international patent application process is called the Patent Co-operation Treaty or PCT for short. There are two treaties for Europe. These are the European Patent Convention and the Community Patent Convention. Respectively shortened to EPC and CPC.

The CPC is not yet in force despite being agreed many years ago. When in force, the CPC will enable one patent to be obtained covering the whole of Europe. It is already possible to obtain a trade mark and design rights for the whole of Europe as well as separate national rights. Recently, discussions have begun to activate the CPC. It is likely that this will happen.

The framework provided by the PCT and the EPC are similar to process described above. The difference is that one patent application is filed for several countries. So a European patent application covers most, but importantly not all, European countries. This is because not all the countries of Europe have adhered to the EPC. An international patent application covers most, but again importantly not all, countries of the world. Not all the countries of the world have adhered to the PCT. An international patent application can include the United States.

Designating countries – every country or only some?

In an International or European patent application, the countries for which a patent is required must be designated when the application is filed. It is important to do this correctly since the opportunities to add countries later are very limited. Countries can be deleted easily later up to a certain stage. This leads to many international and European applications designating all possible countries and deleting those not needed later. For those countries not covered by an international application, individual national applications must be filed.

The international and European patent application process

The process of scrutinising the application is carried out in a central patent office rather than in local national patent offices. The basics of the application through to grant are similar. Once the application has reached a certain stage – either after the international prior art search has been done or for some countries after both that and the international examination have been done – the application "cascades" to each designated country for translations to be filed and other formalities to be attended to. It is these national requirements which make obtaining world wide patent protection expensive.

Grace Periods

An invention, if disclosed and made public, is not new. If not new, a patent cannot be obtained for it. This is a trap for business people and others not familiar with the qualification requirements for obtaining a patent. The effect of falling into the trap will result in a good innovation being denied patent protection and can seem unfair. There are, however, good reasons in support of the strict qualification requirements based around certainty. It is not necessary to set them out in full here. But in essence, if the innovation had been disclosed publicly and was still able to be regarded as new for patent purposes, allowing the inventor or owner of the invention to delay for a even a relatively short time before claiming the right to a patent could be unfair. Other people would now of the innovation but would not be sure of whether the innovation could be used or not. If eventually no patent was claimed, the innovation could have been used. But if a patent was claimed, it could not. The U.S. patent system deals with this in a unique way which is explained later.

A way round this trap is to allow in certain limited circumstances a period from public disclosure in which a patent application can be filed. These are referred to as grace periods. In most countries, there are currently two such circumstances. First, where disclosure has been in breach of confidence or otherwise as a result of being obtained unlawfully. Secondly, where disclosure is at an international exhibition definied by reference to the Convention on International Exhibitions. Effectively, only really large international exhibitions are likely to qualify. The grace period is six months.

Two recent developments in relation to grace periods should be noted. First, discussions have been taking place amongst interested parties and government bodies in Europe about the introduction of a general grace period into the Europe patent systems.

Secondly, a grace period has been introduced in Australia covering disclosure within the 12 month period prior to the filing date of a complete patent application.

Overview of the US Patent system

The basic concepts explained about the patenting of inventions, the application process, and the rights given by a granted patent apply in the United States. However, there are some conceptual differences in the law and procedure which it is important to understand when managing intellectual property.

The essential difference

The most significant difference between the United States patent system and the rest of the world relates to novelty. Novelty in the United States patent system is covered in the next paragraph. The important point to keep in mind is that public disclosure of an invention before filing does not necessarily mean that no patent can be obtained for the United States.

Such a disclosure would effectively prevent a patent being obtained for the publicly disclosed invention anywhere else in the world unless the grace periods apply and the application is filed in the time allowed. This is not a categoric statement because it is just possible that under the local patent laws of a particular country a patent could be obtained despite the public disclosure. However, these countries will not be the main developed economies.

Types of patent

There are three types of patent in the United States patent law namely a utility patent, a plant patent, and a design patent.

Utility patents relate to the invention or discovery of any new and useful process, machine, article of manufacture, or compositions of matters, or any new useful improvement. Design patents are for inventions relating to new, original, and ornamental designs for an article of manufacture. Plant patents may be granted to anyone who invents or discovers and asexually reproduces any distinct and new variety of plants.

Novelty

The United States patent law on novelty states:

"A person shall be entitled to a patent unless–

(a) the invention was known or used by others in this country, or patented or described in a printed publication in this or a foreign country, **before the invention thereof** by the applicant for patent, or

(b) the invention was patented or described in a printed publication in this or a foreign country or in public use or on sale in this country, **more than one year prior to the date of the application for** patent in the United States, ..."

(Section 102. Conditions for patentability; novelty and loss of right to patent)

There are two key concepts here which need to be understood. First, in the United States public disclosure of the invention before the date the invention was made by the person applying for the patent means the invention cannot be novel as required to obtain a patent. It fails at the first hurdle. Secondly, an alternative hurdle in connection with novelty in the United States is that the invention must not have been publicly disclosed more than 12 months before the priority date of the patent application.

So if an invention is made on the 1st June 2001, a public disclosure before that date will prevent a patent being granted or render a granted patent invalid because the invention was not novel.

If the disclosure was on the 30th June after the date of the invention (1st June 2001), an application must be made within 12 months – that is by 29th June 2002 – otherwise the public disclosure will prevent a patent being granted or render a granted patent invalid because the invention was not novel.

Inventive Step

This is essentially the same as in the rest of the world.

Utility

This is another difference of United States patent law compared to the rest of the world although it is akin to the need for industrial application referred to earlier. To be regarded as having "utility" the invention must be "useful." The term "useful" in this connection really means that the invention has a useful purpose and is effective in use. So that a machine which will not operate to perform the intended purpose would not be called useful, and therefore a patent could not be granted for it or if granted was liable to be rendered invalid.

The date of the invention

The date of the invention is important in the US patent system but not in other patent systems. In those other systems, it is the date of filing the patent or patent application or those on which the particular patent is based which is critical. In other words, the priority date. This was explained earlier in this chapter. This has the advantage of certainty and is comparatively easy to administer.

Not so in the United States where the date of the invention can be and often is critical. The date of the invention is the date when the inventor proves that the innovation was conceived by the inventor. The date of the conception of an invention is insufficient on its own to be effective in deciding questions about novelty and ownership. The date of conception will be effective if coupled with the date of reduction to practice by diligence on the part of the inventor. Such diligence must also be shown from the date of actual reduction to practice to the filing date of a patent application.

Reduction to practice is a complex subject but basically has two meanings. Actual reduction to practice is the making of some embodiment of the innovation to show that it works. Constructive reduction to practice is the filing of a patent application completely disclosing the invention.

Inventor must apply

In the United States only the inventor may apply for a patent, with certain exceptions. If a person who is not the inventor should apply for a patent, the patent, if it were obtained, would be invalid. The person applying in such a case who falsely states that he/she is the inventor would also be subject to criminal penalties.

If the invention is owned and so the patent is to be owned by some one else such as an employer of an employee inventor then an assignment of the invention and all rights in it is required and is usually filed with the patent application.

Application for a patent

Another, important difference in the United States is that two types of application are possible. A provisional application and a non-provisional, also known as a "regular" patent application.

The regular patent application is a full application similar to the patent applications filed in other patent offices outside the United States. The provisional application is a device to allow United States patent applicants to rely on the "priority date" and the first to file concept of patent ownership as applies in the rest of the world. The applicant has then 12 months to file a regular application in the United States or designating the United States if part of a PCT international application.

Publication

This is another difference. A patent application for a United States patent used to be kept secret until granted. If not granted, the invention remained secret. If granted, the details of the invention and the application were published. This can still be the case but this right has now been limited.

Publication is now required by the American Inventors Protection Act of 1999. This applies to most plant and utility patent applications filed on or after November 29, 2000. So that after November 29, 2000 an applicant may request that the application not be published, but only if the invention has not been and will not be the subject of an application filed or to be filed in a foreign country that requires publication in 18 months after filing (or earlier claimed priority date) or under the Patent Cooperation Treaty.

If it is to be published, the United States application will be published after the expiration of an 18-month period following the earliest effective filing date or priority date claimed by an application. The application is not held in confidence by the Office after publication of the application and any member of the public may request access to the entire file history of the application.

Publication gives the applicant for the patent provisional rights which may be asserted. These rights provide an opportunity to obtain a reasonable royalty if a published application claim is infringed provided actual notice is given to person alleged to be infringing and a patent issues from the application with a substantially identical claim. Thus, damages for pre-patent grant infringement by another are now available.

Interference

This is the process by which conflicts of ownership are resolved. It is a process by which evidence is exchanged and filed and oral testimony can be taken. Then a decision is given. There is an appeals process.

Patent Term Extension and Adjustment

Yet another important difference. The term of certain patents may be subject to extension or adjustment. Such extension or adjustment results from certain specified types of delays which may occur while an application is pending before the patent office in the United States.

Ownership

The proprietor of a patent or patent application will be the person named on the relevant patent register unless the contrary is proved. A search of the relevant national registers will show who is the registered patent proprietor. The entry on such a register is not a guarantee that the person registered as the proprietor is in fact the true owner.

Three situations typically account for this. First, an assignment of the patent or the patent application from one person to another has not been recorded at the national Patent Office in question. This is usually easy to spot during due diligence. The recording of the relevant assignment will rectify the position unless an intervening transaction has occurred in good faith without any knowledge of the assignment. If this has occurred, the person to whom the patent was originally assigned and where the assignment was not registered might not be able to establish ownership. Secondly, an employee claims ownership against an employer who filed the patent application. Thirdly, where one party has filed a patent application for an invention claimed to be owned by another. For example, a collaboration partner. Collaborations are usually regulated by a proper formal agreement which should make adequate provision for intellectual property rights ownership.

An example of this involved two chemical business which will be called A and B to preserve confidentiality. They were involved in a collaboration where the collaboration agreement was short and made no provision for ownership of intellectual property rights which might arise out of the collaboration. B without informing A filed a domestic and then international patents through the Patent Cooperation Treaty route. When the relationship began to turn sour, A decided to search for patents and found that several had been filed. After a lengthy and expensive court battle, the dispute was resolved whereby both parties would have joint ownership of the invention and the patents which protected it.

Infringement and scope of a patent

The teeth of a patent are the rights to prevent others using the invention without permission. Such unauthorised use is referred to as an infringement of the patent. The extent of the rights given by the patent are broadly similar from country to country, but the details vary. Typically, it is an infringement to do any of the following without the permission or licence of the patent owner:

- if the patent is for a product, making the product, keeping it or advertising, selling or otherwise disposing of it. Importing can be an infringement;

- if the invention protects a process, it would usually be an infringement to operate the process and to deal in product which had been made by the use of the process by advertising, selling or importing them.

These powers to prevent infringements, if necessary by taking court action against an infringer, give the patent its potential value. The patent gives in effect a monopoly as defined by the patent specification and the claims. The patent owner (and in some circumstances an exclusive licensee) has the right to prevent anyone else commercialising a product or a process which falls within the specification and those claims.

The skilled person mentioned earlier has a vital role in the determining if in particular circumstances an infringement of the patent has taken place. The claims will be written to cover the invention claimed as broadly as possible. Words and phrases are used which have broad meanings, as broad as possible in the circumstances but not so broad as to render the patent invalid as happened in the *Biogen* v *Medeva*[11] case mentioned earlier. This inevitably leads to different possible interpretations of the meaning of a particular claim or even part of a claim. The court in deciding which of the possible interpretations is correct relies on the interpretation which the skilled person in the relevant technological field would place on the claims of the patent. This is often referred to as the scope of the patent.

The interpretation by a national court of the specification and claims of a patent determine whether a particular activity or product is an infringement of the patent. The following case clearly illustrates this point. The courts in the United Kingdom and Germany took a different view as to whether the teeth would bite in the particular circumstances. In Germany they did bite, whereas in the United Kingdom they did not. Such an outcome is clearly unsatisfactory for business. In considering the valuation to be put on the patent it is important to know the extent of the protection that is available since that would determine the size of the particular market that the patent owner might be able to retain by keeping competition out using the patent rights.

---

11.   [1995] F.S.R. 4.

Infringement Case Study – Improver and Remington

This case study is based on the reported patent case in the UK of *Improver Corporation v Remington*[12]. Improver had developed a new depilatory device, designed to pluck hairs from the human body. Sold under the name of Epilady, it was the subject of an international patent filing programme. The European patent was filed as part of the programme. The European patent is shown in appendix [   ].

Much of the background information is taken from the case report. The report summarises the background to the invention as follows. Depilation means the removal of hair by the root, as opposed to shaving which leaves the root behind. The advantage of depilation is that the hair takes much longer to regenerate. Various methods have been used in the past for cosmetic depilation, but none was completely satisfactory. An article published in an American marketing journal in 1976 began as follows:

> "...If you were seeking a truly new product that meets a genuine consumer need you might start with the women's depilatory market......It is a huge, waiting market, and the company that comes up with a safe, effective, product will hit the jackpot.....Everyone knows the market is there and some in the field have been searching for the key to unlock the treasure...".

Epilady was invented by in 1982. It consisted of a small electric motor in a hand-held plastic housing to which is attached a helical steel spring held by its ends and stiffened by a guide wire to form a loop. The arcuate form of the spring causes the gaps between the windings to open on its convex side but to be pressed together on the concave side. When the spring is held close the skin and rotated by the motor at high speed, hairs enter the gaps on its convex side and are gripped between the windings as the rotational movement brings them round to the concave side. The effect is to pluck them out of the skin.

Marketing of Epilady began in June 1986. It was an enormous commercial success. In the first two years over 5.8 million devices were made, generating a gross retail turnover in excess of $340,000,000.

---

12.   [1990] F.S.R. 181.

The patent describes a motorised helical spring and a body for encasing the motor and holding the spring so that it can be used against the body. The claims of the patent which define the monopoly were limited to a helical spring. This is clearly depicted in the patent drawings and photographs of an Epilady product clearly shows the use of the helical spring.

Remington produced a depilatory product based on the same principle. It was sold under the trade mark name "Smooth & Silky". It had a housing to contain a motor, the motor to drive a hair plucking device. In this case the hair plucking device was not a helical spring but an elastomeric rod with slits cut in it at intervals. In use, the elastomeric rod was held in a shallow arc.

Both devices plucked hairs from the human body by trapping the hair and pulling it out as the spring or rod rotated. The elastomeric rod operated in almost exactly the same way as the helical spring in the Epilady device. The slits on the outer side of the arc were open but as the rod rotated, and those slits moved to the inner side, the slits were closed. Hairs went into the open slits and were trapped as the slits rotated and closed plucking out the hair.

Improver felt that the "Smooth & Silky" product infringed its patent. Proceedings were issued in a number of jurisdictions but for our purposes in Hong Kong, United Kingdom and Germany. The law about patent infringement in Hong Kong and the UK is very similar. The European Patent Convention established the framework by which a European patent could be obtained. The intention was that national laws would be put in place and that national courts would interpret patents in a common way. It is important for the commercial assessment of a patent since otherwise competitive products could be on the market in one country where they were not regarded as infringing the patent but not in another market where they would be regarded as a infringing the patent. Anybody undertaking the assessment and valuation would need to try to assess those countries where a wider monopoly and therefore less competition was likely to exist compared to those where a narrow monopoly existed and more competition might exist. This case illustrates this point extremely well.

The legal battle in the European arena was conducted in both Germany and UK. The comparison of the products can be summed up by quoting again from the case report:

> "Dr Laming, a distinguished design engineer called as an expert witness by the defendants [Remington] said that [the "Smooth &

Silky " design] contained nothing which distinguishes Smooth &
Silky from Epilady by function. The difference lay in their
respective forms."

Patent infringement can occur when the elements of the rival
product do not fall within the literal meaning of the elements of the
claims of the patent. That was the case here. The claim required a
helical spring but the rival product had a different element namely a
bendy rod with slits in it. Such a difference is often referred to as a
variant. The courts in most countries have developed a body of law
as to whether infringement by use of a variant is an infringement.

In both the United Kingdom and Germany, the courts were asked to
make a preliminary ruling. In UK, the judge concluded that "helical
spring" should not be given a wide construction. The "Smooth &
Silky" product did not infringe the Improver patent in the United
Kingdom. However, the German Court decided that there was an
infringement of the Improver patent in Germany by the "Smooth &
Silky" product. The case subsequently settled.

Transactions in patents

Patents can be transferred by assignment or can be licensed. The licence can
be exclusive or non exclusive. There are some technical requirements when
making an assignment or granting a licence and these would need to be
checked carefully in any due diligence investigation. It is important that
assignments and licences and other dealings such as a charge over a patent
are properly registered at the national Patent Offices.

Supplementary Protection Certificates

A supplementary protection certificate can be granted for a patented
medicinal or plant protection product and is intended to compensate a
patent owner for the loss of the opportunity to exploit the patent invention
by the making and selling of a particular product during the period that
regulatory approval to market such product was being obtained. The power
to grant a supplementary certificate are derived from EC Regulation Numbers
1768/92 and 1610/96. The Regulations have direct effect in all European
Member States. A product for these purposes is the active ingredient or
substance, or a combination of the active ingredients or substances, in a
medicinal or a plant protection product respectively. A supplementary
protection certificate is not itself a patent nor is it an extension of a patent as
such. The certificate extends the protection conferred by a patent but only in
respect of those products covered by regulatory marketing approval – the
seeking of which caused the delay in being able to exploit the invention. The

certificate does not have the effect of extending the statutory term of the patent generally.

A supplementary protection certificate takes effect at the end of the lawful term of a basic patent protecting the product or a process. The duration of the extension in member states is the period from the filing date of the basic patent for the product to the date of approval for use of the product, reduced by five years subject to a maximum extension of five years from the date the certificate has effect. The supplementary protection certificate can be enforced as if it were a patent.

The EC Regulations have different effects in different member states in which the Regulation has effect. If a patent is being considered for valuation and a supplementary protection certificate is in place or is being sought, the applicable national rules of the relevant state must be carefully considered.

Trade Marks

Introduction

The legal rights in trade marks are of two types. Those that derive from a registration of the trade mark and those that are based on laws which might generally be described as unfair trade practice laws. In the UK, the law relating to an unregistered trade mark is called "passing off" and is much more limited in the protection it can give to a trade mark than some of the unfair trade practice laws in, say, Germany. Since passing off is a common law right based on court decisions, the courts have been able to adapt to the operation of modern business when giving protection to established trade marks through the passing off laws.

There is no scheme for obtaining a world wide trade mark registration by a single application for registration. Some international schemes do exist for the registration of trade marks. The Madrid Protocol relating to the International Registration of Trade Marks is one. Another arises in Europe from a European Regulation on trade mark law leading to a registration covering all member states.

At national level each country has its own requirements. Some of these are harmonised, for example in Europe, as a result of an EC Directive (not the same as the Regulation mentioned above) requiring countries in Europe to modify their laws relating to registered trade marks in member states.

This section will consider the registration of trade marks by reference to the law and procedures operating in Europe governed by a European Regulation since this illustrates the sort of considerations which will apply in Europe and generally in countries granting registered trade marks. The detail will vary in different countries and not all the aspects of registration will be relevant. However, the reader will achieve an understanding of the factors likely to be in issue when considering the registration and legal rights in a trade mark.

These rights give the trade mark its *market power* which is closely related to the *value* of the trade mark. Weak legal rights will not enable exclusivity to be enforced easily or at all. Exclusivity is an important factor in building trade mark value.

Registration

General requirements

Any system for the registration of trade marks has to address some key concepts. These are common to many systems around the world, though each country will deal with them differently in the detail.

There are three key concepts.

1.   The trade mark to be registered must be sufficiently distinctive and not descriptive. Descriptiveness should be seen as shorthand for several related grounds on which a trade mark could be refused registration. These are illustrated below.

2.   Rights are given to prevent the unlawful use of the trade mark or one similar to it. This unlawful activity constitutes an infringement of the rights given by the registration of the trade mark.

3.   The need to establish in many cases confusion between trade marks or at least the likelihood of such confusion for infringement.

The aim of any trade mark legal system is, therefore, to balance these competing interests. For registration, the balance is between distinctiveness and descriptiveness. For infringement, the balance is as to whether a rival trade mark is identical or is sufficiently similar to cause confusion, or not. Both are difficult to achieve in practice as the illustrations later will demonstrate.

European Trade Mark Rights

In recent years, two legislative changes have been instigated for the whole of the European Union. One change is effected by a European Directive in respect of trade marks with the intention of harmonising many aspects of national laws about the registration of trade marks and the rights in such trade marks in each member states. The other change is brought about by a European Regulation providing laws and procedures for the registration of trade marks and giving rights in them applicable to all member states as a region, rather than at the national level only. Remember that a European Regulation gives rights directly to people and to businesses and other organisations operating in member states. A Directive does not. A directive requires member states to implement laws at the national level to give rights as required by the Directive.

European Directive[13]

The detail of how the rights required by the Trade Marks Directive are to be achieved at the national level in a particular member state is up to that country at local level.

Many implementation deadlines set in Directives are breached by member states. National laws may or may not have been amended as required to achieve the limited level of harmonisation set out in the Trade Marks Directive. Eventually compliance is achieved if necessary by the European Commission taking action though the European Court of Justice against the country concerned.

European Regulation[14]

This Regulation provides a whole legal regime for obtaining one trade mark registration covering all member states in addition to the rights in trade marks given by national laws. The rights given by the Regulation are now in force.

The EC Directive harmonising trade mark rights in Europe provides essentially the same legal rights for the registration and use of trade marks. This means that an understanding of the legal rights and concepts in relation to trade marks explained here referring to the European Regulation will be applicable across Europe even if some detailed differences at national level exist. Theses legal rights and concepts are also applicable in general terms in many countries across the world.

Community Trade Mark

What is a trade mark?

The European Regulation defines a trade mark in Article 4 as follows

> "... any sign capable of being represented graphically, particularly words including personal names, designs, letters, numerals, the shape of goods or their packaging, provided that such signs are capable of distinguishing the goods or services of one undertaking from those of other undertakings."

It follows the trade mark must be:

* a sign,

* be represented graphically, and

* give some distinction to the goods or services with which it is going to be used.

Traditional trade marks such as names, logos, and some slogans will not pose any particular problem for registration as a trade mark. However the extent to which more elaborate trade marks can be registered in any particular country is still developing. The shape of goods and packaging may in fact be accepted under the trade mark rules operating now in member states if the shape is considered to be distinctive. However, the application in the UK to register as

---

13.   EC Directive 89/104 ("the Trade Marks Directive").
14.   Council Registration No. 40/94.

a trade mark the Dualit toaster shape was rejected in 1999 as not being sufficiently distinctive when compared to the shape of toasters generally. Colours have in the past been registered, for example, in the United Kingdom. A good example are the registrations secured by Smith Kline & French (as it then was) for a series of colour combinations applied to pharmaceutical capsules. However, it failed to obtain registration for a single pale green colour applied to biconvex round or oblong tablets. The conclusion here was that a combinations of colours could be distinctive whereas the single colour could not be. The outcome of an application to register sounds, smells and tastes is more difficult to predict. The provisions of national laws will be need to be considered carefully in deciding whether sounds, smells and tastes are registrable. If a sound, smell or a taste can be represented graphically and is distinctive, there is every reason why it should be registered.

One registered smell mark is represented "graphically" *"The mark is a high impact fresh floral fragrance reminiscent of plumeria blossom"*. This was registered for sewing thread and embroidery yarn. A sound mark is as follows *"The mark consists of the sound of clip, clop, clip, clop, moo"*. This was registered for restaurant services. Another recent example of a trade mark registered on the 11th October 2000 under the European Regulation is the trade mark "THE SMELL OF FRESH CUT GRASS" registered for tennis balls with this description "The mark consists of the smell of fresh cut grass applied to the product"

What is a Community Trade Mark with legal rights?

If the proposed trade mark is a "sign" as defined for trade mark purposes, then the trade mark can be registered if it satisfies the requirements for registration. Some of these are procedural such as completing the correct form with all the necessary information. However, the main requirements are that the trade mark is distinctive and not descriptive. These concepts are important ones in trade mark law generally and discussed next. Once registered, it becomes a Community Trade Mark with associated legal rights.

Distinctiveness and Descriptiveness

The European Regulation requires distinctiveness to be addressed by reference to two categories of grounds for refusing an application to register a trade mark. These are absolute grounds and relative grounds. Some are based on public policy or to protect the rights of others. Some grounds are to prevent descriptive trade marks being registered.

Absolute Grounds for refusing registration

The absolute grounds for refusal will lead to the following types of trade marks being refused:

- trade marks with no distinctive character;

- trade marks which are no more than designations of such things as kind, quality, quantity, geographical origin, or other characteristics of the goods or service;

- signs or indications customary in the trade;

- the shape which results from the nature of the goods themselves.

This is a list indicating in an easily understood way some of the more important grounds of refusal. The full details are set out in Article 7 in the Regulation.

Some of these grounds for refusal can be overcome by establishing that the particular trade mark has become distinctive as a consequence of the use that has been made of the mark. The concept of distinctiveness acquired by use is one of the most important concepts in trade mark law. It impacts not just on the registrability of the trade mark but also on the protection against infringement given by the registration. No hard and fast rule can be laid down as to what amount of use will turn a trade mark which is borderline distinctive into one which is sufficiently distinctive for registration. Some idea of what is required in the UK can be judged from reported cases both about attempts to register trade marks and about cases involving passing off.

Relative grounds for refusing registration

The relative grounds for refusal are set out in Article 8 of the Regulation and will lead to a trade mark being refused registration:

- if it is identical to an earlier trade mark and to be registered for identical goods or services;

- if because of its identity with or similarity to an earlier trade mark and the identity or similarity of the goods or services covered by the trade marks there exists a likelihood of confusion.

Some recent trade mark registration decisions in the UK

These examples illustrate in practice the grounds on which applications for trade marks are considered for registration.

- **POLACLIP** for clip-on sunglasses passed for registration despite opposition from the owners of the registered trade mark **POLAROID** registered also for clip-on sunglasses;

- **BLUE COLOURED BOTTLE WITH OPTICAL EFFECTS** for bottled water refused registration because the mark could have covered any shape and shade of blue, it was not sufficiently specific to be registered;

- **FROOT LOOPS** for cereal preparations containing fruit and fruit flavouring refused registration because it was equivalent to FRUIT LOOPS and, therefore, descriptive of the product for which registration was being sought;

- **SAVILE ROW** for spectacle frames refused registration because to give one person a registered trade mark for SAVILE ROW could interfere with the rights of other businesses in Savile Row to use that name;

- **BONUS GOLD** for investment account services refused registration because the words BONUS and GOLD had acquired descriptive meaning in the banking field and the combination of the two words did not make it distinctive;

- **COFFEEMIX** for coffee preparations was refused because it was descriptive of products being a mixture of coffee and other substances.

Some recent Community Trade Mark applications which have been refused are:

ALWAYS CLEAR ALWAYS SHARP	NOVOLATEX
APPLE-TEA	ONLINE TODAY
BOATGUARD	QUICK-SCRIBE
CABLEFREE	SINGLECARE
CHEEZY CRUST PIZZA	SNAPNUT
CLUBCARD	TASKLINK
CYBERFONE	WHAT YOU WANT,
DIGIFONE	WHEN YOU WANT IT
HANDY-JET	YELLOW PAGES
MEDISYSTEMS	YOGHURTGUMS

Registration procedure

The registration procedure in most countries will follow a general pattern. However, there are many subtle national nuances to the application for the registration of a trade mark. In many cases these will not be relevant but if the trade mark is one which is on the borderline of qualifying for registration, is similar to other trade marks or is part of a portfolio of trade marks, these nuances can be important. These nuances can be exploited in arguing for registration of trade marks to give the registration the best chance of succeeding, and being found valid if challenged.

The application for a Community Trade Mark can be made at a central office or at the equivalent office in a member state. The central office is the Office for Harmonisation in the Internal Market (Trade Marks and Designs) usually referred to by the awkward acronym "OHIM". It was instituted by the Regulation. This office is located in Alicante, Spain. The equivalent office in the UK is the Patent Office which despite its name deals with applications to register patents, trade marks and designs.

The registration procedure is similar to that discussed in relation to patents, although simpler. As explained in relation to patents, the fact that the trade mark has been registered is not conclusive of the validity of the registration. The registration can still be challenged at anytime usually by a person or company with a commercial interest in defeating the registration. This most often happens, again as with patents, when the owner of the trade mark seeks to enforce it by court action. The almost invariable defensive response is to deny infringing the rights in the registered trade mark and to claim that the trade mark registration is invalid.

The procedure is usually simple. Goods and services are divided into 45 classes. Trade marks are registered by reference to these classes. The classification system is international. The application is begun by completing a form and filing it with a trade mark "office" accompanied by a fee. The application must show a graphical representation of the trade mark, state the class of goods or services for which registration is sought and the specification of the goods or services within the class for which registration is sought. The specification of goods is used to assess the infringement rights of the owner and to assess the extent of previous use if necessary to support the registration during the course of the application process, and if there is a revocation or validity challenge. Once filed, the trade mark "office" will in due course scrutinise the application. In some countries, a detailed scrutiny is made together with a search for similar registered trade marks. In others countries, this does not happen. On the basis of the result of the search and scrutiny, the mark will be accepted or rejected. If rejected, usually a dialogue ensues between the examiner at the trade mark "office" and the applicant or the applicant's professional agent. The purpose of the dialogue is to see if there are reasons why the trade mark should be registered perhaps with amendments.

It is not the purpose of the trade mark registry to prevent registration but rather to ensure that trade marks are registered which appear valid.

Once the trade mark has been accepted, perhaps after amendment, the application is published by OHIM for a given period. This is three months. This period is one in which opposition by any person who has trade marks rights which might be adversely affected by the acceptance of the application in question can be lodged to the registration of the trade mark. If an opposition is lodged, then an opposition procedure commences with the exchange of evidence and ultimately a hearing to decide whether the trade mark should be registered or not. If there is no opposition or after an unsuccessful opposition challenge, the trade mark proceeds to be registered as a Community Trade Mark on the OHIM register of trade marks.

Once registered, the rights of the trade mark owner date back to the original date of filing. But no rights to enforce the trade mark come into effect until the trade mark is actually registered. Once granted, the trade mark proprietor receives a trade mark certificate.

Length of protection

Under Article 46 of the regulation "...Community trade marks shall be registered for a period of ten years from the date of filing of the application". Registration may be renewed in accordance with Article 47 for further periods of ten years. Article 47 provides that an owner of a Community Trade Mark can renew the Community Trade Mark for the same types of goods or services for successive periods of tens years until such time as the owner no longer wants to have the Community registration. There is no maximum length of time for which the trade mark can be registered. Where the renewal is submitted or the fees paid in respect of only some of the goods or services for which the Community Trade Mark is registered, registration shall be renewed for those goods or services only.

The renewal is to be paid during the period six months before the end of any such ten period. It can be paid in the six months afterwards as well provided that an additional late renewal fee is also paid. This is an example of a grace period.

Amending the Community Trade Mark

It is not possible to amend a Community Trade Mark once it has been registered. Article 48 of the regulation provides that

> "....The Community trade mark shall not be altered in the register during the period of registration or on renewal thereof. ....Nevertheless, where the Community trade mark includes the name and address of the proprietor, any alteration thereof not substantially affecting the identity of the trade mark as originally registered may be registered at the request of the proprietor."

If a business wants to change the "sign" (as defined widely for trade mark purposes) which is the subject of a Community Trade Mark, a new registration must be obtained unless perhaps if the change is only minor such as a style of script for a word or slogan or a slightly different shade of colour. The registration of the Community Trade Mark can be put at risk if the registration is for one "sign" and another different one is used in practice. Use of the different trade mark may not count as use of the trade mark as registered. Everything depends on the circumstances. As will be explained later, failure to use a trade mark for five years exposes the trade mark as registered to being revoked.

In the UK case of *British Sugar Plc* v *James Robertson & Sons Ltd*[15] in 1996 British Sugar had registered "TREAT" for 'dessert sauces and syrups; all included in Class 30'. British Sugar used its trade mark on a product as part of the expression "Silver Spoon Treat", a sweet syrup in a range of flavours to pour onto ice cream. It did not use the word as a trade mark on its own. Robertson launched a sweet spread labelled, "Robertson's Toffee Treat" which it sold along with its range of jams and preserves. It was held that the mark had not been infringed and was invalid.

Ownership

The person – individual or organisation – making the application is taken to be entitled to the registration of the Community Trade Mark unless it appears from the application that the person is not or may not be so entitled. Processes exist including an opposition procedure by which a person's entitlement to the registration can be challenged later.

Priority

The application to register a trade mark in a country which has signed up to the either of two international conventions gives a right of priority to apply to register the same trade mark as a Community Trade Mark for the same type of goods or services. The two conventions are the Paris Convention and the Agreement to establish the World Intellectual Property Organisation. The right of priority last for six months from the date of filing the first application. A right of priority also arises from the showing of the goods or services under the trade mark at certain classified international exhibitions. The period is six months form the date of disclosure.

Seniority

Rights to seniority are similar to rights to priority in that they are intended to protect individuals or businesses who have existing trade marks rights from being prejudiced by someone else applying to or actually registering a Community Trade Mark for the same trade mark and for the same types of goods or services. Article 34 of the Regulation provides as follows:

"..   The proprietor of an earlier trade mark registered in a Member State ..... or registered under international arrangements having effect in a

---

15.   [1996] R.P.C. 281.

Member State, who applies for an identical trade mark for registration as a Community trade mark for goods or services which are identical with or contained within those for which the earlier trade mark has been registered, may claim for the Community trade mark the seniority of the earlier trade mark in respect of the Member State in or for which it is registered.

2.   Seniority shall have the sole effect under this Regulation that, where the proprietor of the Community trade mark surrenders the earlier trade mark or allows it to lapse, he shall be deemed to continue to have the same rights as he would have had if the earlier trade mark had continued to be registered.

3.   The seniority claimed for the Community trade mark shall lapse if the earlier trade mark the seniority of which is claimed is declared to have been revoked or to be invalid or if it is surrendered prior to the registration of the Community trade mark."

So if a particular business has a French national trade mark already registered, successfully applies for a Community Trade Mark, and allows the French national trade mark registration to lapse by not paying the renewal, the effect of the Community Trade Mark in France will be to give no less rights than the French national trade mark registration would have done had it been continued.

Scope of protection and infringement

Infringement means the right to prevent another person using the registered trade mark without the consent of the owner. The national laws of each country where the trade mark is registered will determine the extent of protection given to a trade mark in that country. This will be a combination of the laws of that country and the interpretation of them by the local courts. The legal rights given by the Community Trade Mark can be enforced in any member state by using the national courts of the country in which the Community trade mark is to be enforced. Article 14 of the Regulation provides as follows:

"The effects of Community trade marks shall be governed solely by the provisions of this Regulation. In other respects, infringement of a Community trade mark shall be governed by the national law relating to infringement of a national trade mark....."

Infringement rights are set out in the Regulation. Member states have implemented the Trade Mark Directive several years ago so that national trade mark laws in member states will be very similar to those set out in the Regulation. This means that the national courts in member states are used to enforcing the type of legal rights given by the Community Trade Mark.

In summary, these trade mark infringement laws in member states allow the owner of a registered trade mark to prevent all third parties not having consent from using in the course of trade:

- any sign which is an **identical** with the registered trade mark and used in relation to **identical** goods or services;

- any sign which is **similar** to the registered trade mark and used in relation to **identical** goods or services and where there exists a likelihood of confusion on the part of the public;

- any sign which is **identical** to the registered trade mark and used in relation to **similar** goods and services and where there exists a likelihood of confusion on the part of the public;

- any sign which is **identical** with or **similar** to the registered trade mark in relation to goods or services which are **not similar** where the use of that sign without due cause takes unfair advantage of, or is detrimental to, the distinctive character or the repute of the registered trade mark.

If a sign was to be used which would be caught by these restrictions, the following will be the types of activity likely to be trade mark infringements:

- affixing the sign to the goods or the packaging thereof;

- offering the goods, putting them on the market or stocking them for these purposes under that sign, or offering or supplying services thereunder;

- importing or exporting the goods under the sign;

- using the sign on business papers and in advertising.

In some cases, to find infringement, the court must be satisfied that there "exists a likelihood of confusion on the part of the public". Confusion is not necessary where the marks in question are identical and used in respect of identical types of goods or services. How important confusion will be to the rights of the trade mark owner depend on the national courts interpretation and application of the trade mark laws. These courts have the ability to refer questions about the understanding and interpretation of such laws to the European Court of Justice. The ability to refer such questions is used regularly by the courts in member states. This process eventually leads to the particular area of law being understood and applied in a particular way consistently across all member states. This is will not happen until such a reference is made and decided, which can take a long time. Of course in the meantime the courts and everybody else have to do their best to interpret the law. This inevitably leads to different interpretations in different legal systems. In jurisdictions like the United Kingdom confusion has historically been important. In other member states, confusion is less important and in some cases irrelevant.

An example of this process of referral in relation to confusion is the case[16] involving MGM and Canon about the proposed registration and use of the

---

16.   [1999] F.S.R. 332.

trade mark CANNON by MGM for videos and distribution of films to cinemas, amongst other things. A court in Germany asked the European Court of Justice to answer a question about the interpretation of the Trade Mark Directive and the German implementing law where two marks might be confusingly similar. The answer by the court involved legal technical considerations. Broadly, the courts of member states when assessing confusion between two trade marks had to look at all the circumstances and not adopt a narrow overly legal interpretation. So a very well known trade mark registered for particular goods or services might lead to a finding of confusion when compared to a similar trade mark even if used for quite different goods or services. But in different circumstances, the same finding of confusion might not occur if the first trade mark is less well known.

You might rightly conclude that this is the trade mark equivalent of the question "how long is a piece of string?" to which the answer given by the court is "It depends on the piece of string"! In other words, it depends on individual circumstances.

Confusion must be amongst people. The relevant people will be those who purchase the type of goods or use the type of services offered using the trade mark in question. For retail goods or services provided generally, the relevant persons will be the general population. However, for specific markets or types of goods, the persons to consider could be a narrower section of the population. All relevant surrounding circumstances are important and will be taken into account in assessing whether or not confusion is likely. These will include:

- the way the way trade marks are used;

- the size of the goods;

- the sort of goods or services in question;

- the market channels through which they are supplied;

- other factors such as the number of other similar trade marks used in the market sector; and

- normal practices in the particular business sector.

Limitation on Community Trade Mark rights

Certain activities cannot be prevented by the legal rights given by a Community Trade Mark. These are set out below and can be taken as a good guide to the sort of commercial activity which Community Trade Mark rights can not stop. Article 12 of the Regulation provides:

Limitation of the effects of a Community trade mark

A Community trade mark shall not entitle the proprietor to prohibit a third party from using in the course of trade:

(a) his own name or address;

(b) indications concerning the kind, quality, quantity, intended purpose, value, geographical origin, the time of production of the goods or of rendering of the service, or other characteristics of the goods or service;

(c) the trade mark where it is necessary to indicate the intended purpose of a product or service, in particular as accessories or spare parts,

provided he uses them in accordance with honest practices in industrial or commercial matters.

Validity and Revocation

The registration of a trade mark is only a good indication that the registration is correctly registered. As with patents, the fact of a trade mark being registered is not a guarantee that the trade mark will continue to be registered. There are two grounds on which the registration of a trade mark can be attacked.

First, that the registration is invalid. Secondly that the registration is liable to be revoked. The difference between these two is broadly as follows. A finding of invalidity means that the registration should never have been granted. A finding of revocation means that because the trade mark has not been used or because of some activity during the life of the registration, the registration should be cancelled.

Dealing with the Community Trade Mark

The rights in the Community Trade Mark may be transferred and otherwise dealt with as a property right and as if a national registered trade mark of the country in which the holder is based. The details are more complex but this is sufficient to understand that ownership of the rights can be transferred.

The ownership of the Community Trade Mark must be transferred "..in its entirety, and for the whole area of the Community": Article 16 of the Regulation.

Article 17 of the Regulation contains important statements about the transfer of a Community Trade Mark. First, that a "... Community trade mark may be transferred, separately from any transfer of the undertaking, in respect of some or all of the goods or services for which it is registered." In other words, the trade mark can be (say) sold separately from the business in which it was used. This is important because in many previous trade mark legal systems a trade mark could only be transferred with the goodwill, usually in a sale, of a business.

Secondly, that a ".... transfer of the whole of the undertaking shall include the transfer of the Community trade mark except where, in accordance with the law governing the transfer, there is agreement to the contrary or circumstances clearly dictate otherwise. This provision shall apply to the contractual obligation to transfer the undertaking." This is a kind of default provision so if a business is to be sold the Community Trade Mark will be deemed sold with it unless the contrary is provided in an agreement or was obviously intended not to be transferred.

Rights in Trade Marks in the UK

Registered trade marks in the UK

There is a separate national registered trade mark law and procedure for the United Kingdom. The law was, in 1994, changed to implement the Trade Mark Directive[17] in respect of trade marks. The law is now effectively the same as for the registered Community Trade Marks in the European Regulation[18] although the rights obtained are only for the United Kingdom.

The application process is again similar in its concept and basic procedural steps to that of OHIM. Differences of detail exist which it is not necessary to explain in this book.

Non-registered rights in trade marks or Passing Off

Many countries give rights to businesses which have used the trade mark in trading activities whether for goods or in respect of services. These laws are often referred to as laws preventing unfair trade practices or rights in passing off. Many European countries have unfair trade practice laws. In the UK there are no unfair trade practice laws as such but instead rights in passing off. Passing off is sometimes referred to as protection of the goodwill in a business or concept. Many countries which have been influenced by the UK system have passing off laws, for example Australia, Canada, New Zealand, Hong Kong, and Singapore.

Rights in passing off arise out of trading or activities akin to trading. For example, charity organisations have been found to have passing off rights although they do not really trade as such.

The three elements required to be established constitute a classic statement of the law. They are that there must be:

- a reputation or goodwill acquired by a business for its goods or services or which relate to a logo, a character or style;

- there must be a false statement not necessarily deliberate in relation to that reputation or goodwill leading to confusion amongst the public or a section of the public;

- there must be damage suffered by the person who has the reputation or goodwill.

There is a mass of case law about passing off and what constitutes a protectable reputation, what constitutes a misrepresentation, whether deliberate or false, and what sort of damage can be recovered. The vast majority of these cases are all unique in the sense that the outcome is dependent upon the facts of the case not on principles of law.

---

17.   EC Directive 89/104***.
18.   EC Directive 89/104***.

Consequently, the only statement of the law which can be used as a guide is that which involves the three elements mentioned above. Everything else depends on the facts of a particular case.

The types of damages which can be claimed are pretty straightforward. They will range from the more certain type of loss such as lost sales to the more speculative such as compensation for loss of the opportunity of expanding into a related market sector.

Assessing whether a particular person or organisation has rights in passing off requires specialist expertise and experience. A distinctive trade mark or character is more likely to be protected by rights in passing off than a descriptive one. A trade mark which has been used for a long time is more likely to have protection than one used for a short period of time. That said, descriptive names or characters can be protectable if used for long enough. They become associated with the person or organisation using them. Similarly, there have been cases where a small amount of use has been sufficient.

The court decisions are often conflicting. This is always likely to happen when cases are decided on their own facts. The law of passing off is flexible allowing the court to do what it regards as fair in all the circumstances of a particular case. So, for example, if the court thought that a person had a trade mark which in all the circumstances ought to be protected but only a small amount of use had taken place, the court may well be prepared to find such use was sufficient to establish a reputation for passing off purposes.

As with other intellectual property rights, the law allows the court flexibility to achieve a fair result but at the expense of some ambiguity as to whether the rights are available or not and in the extent of the rights granted.

Rights in Designs

Introduction

This subject has much in common with copyright but the subject has sufficient differences to merit a section on its own. In fact, it is quite common to hear the expression "design copyright" used as if it were a legal term such as "artistic copyright". In fact, it is not. If the expression has any certain meaning it is as an accepted generic term for the extent to which copyright and similar rights give protection to designs which are more functional than artistic and which are typically manufactured by mass production.

The rights in designs in many countries including in Europe arise out of registered designs and from design rights which do not require registration. Registration gives stronger and longer rights. In some countries other registered rights exist for product designs called "utility models" or "petty patents". The extent to which these give protection depends on the law of the country in respect of which they have been registered. In the United States, designs can be the subject of a design patent to which we referred in the "Overview of the US patent system" on page 402.

In Europe the rights in designs are based on two regimes providing the rights. This is similar to the rights in trade marks where the rights can be acquired for the whole of Europe by a European trade mark registration or nationally by a national trade mark registration in a particular country. However, the rights in designs are yet more complicated than this. First, laws and procedures exist for Europe-wide rights in designs through registered designs *and* design rights not requiring any registration. Then national laws and procedures exist giving national registered rights *and* rights which do not require registration.

European Design Rights

In recent years, two legislative changes have been instigated at the for the whole of the European Union. One change is effected by a European Directive[19] in respect of designs with the intention of harmonising in each member state some aspects of the rights in designs. The other change is brought about by a European Regulation[20] providing laws and procedures for rights in designs applicable to all member states as a region rather than at the national level only. Remember again that a European Regulation gives rights directly to people and to businesses and other organisations operating in member states. A Directive does not. A Directive requires member states to implement laws at the national level to give rights as required by the Directive.

European Directive[19]

The detail of how the rights required by the Design Rights Directive are to be achieved at the national level in a particular member state is up to that country at local level. The Directive required implementation by 28th October 2001. Many implementation deadlines set in Directives are breached by member state. National laws may or may not have been amended as required to achieve the limited level of harmonisation set out in the Design Directive. Eventually compliance is achieved if necessary by the European Commission taking action though the European Court of Justice against the country concerned.

European Regulation[20]

This Regulation provides a whole legal regime for designs for all member states as a region in addition to the rights in designs given by national laws of member states. The rights given by the Regulation came into force on 6th March 2002. There are two separate rights. A registered Community Design and an unregistered Community Design.

Community Design

The definitions and qualifying criteria for the Community Design are the same whether the design is registered as a Community design or not. The

19.   EC Directive 98/71 ("the Design Directive").
20.   Council Regulation No. 6/2002.

rights given by the Community Design are longer, at 25 years, if the design is registered, than if not in which case they last three years only.

The attempts at harmonisation of rights in designs across Europe have lead to expressions being used in stating the law and procedures which are open to interpretation in many different ways. This tends to be a feature of the statements of the law from the European Commission which then relies on interpretation by the national courts of member states. These courts have the ability to refer questions about the understanding and interpretation of such laws to the European Court of Justice. This was covered in relation to trade marks and the samples principles apply. The ability to refer such questions is used regularly by the courts in member states. This process eventually leads to the particular area of law being understood and applied in a particular way consistently across all member states. This is will not happen until such a reference is made and decided which can take a long time. Of course in the mean time the courts and everybody else has to do their best to interpret the law. This inevitably leads to different interpretations in different legal systems.

The rights in designs given by the Designs Directive[21] and European Regulation[22] are recent statements of the law about designs in European context. Court decisions about them are not yet available based on which a commentary could be given to help understand the way in which the new concepts work in practice. Until such time as these laws have been interpreted by courts and some accepted meanings established, they must be read and understood in the particular context based on experience and judgement which comes with that experience.

Meaning of a design

The definition of a design from the Regulation gives a reliable guide to the types of designs for which registration can be obtained for member states. The definitions are from Article 3 of the Regulation:

Article 3

Definitions

For the purposes of this Regulation:

(a) "design" means the appearance of the whole or a part of a product resulting from the features of, in particular, the lines, contours, colours, shape, texture and/or materials of the product itself and/or its ornamentation;

(b) "product" means any industrial or handicraft item, including inter alia parts intended to be assembled into a complex product, packaging, get-up, graphic symbols and typographic typefaces, but excluding computer programs;

---

21.   EC Directive 98/71.
22.   Council Regulation No. 6/2002.

(c) "complex product" means a product which is composed of multiple components which can be replaced permitting disassembly and re-assembly of the product.

Definition of a Community Design with legal rights

The design to qualify for the legal rights given by the Community Design must satisfy several criteria set out in the Regulation. Again these are a reliable guide as to the requirements to register designs for member states. The requirements are complex and detailed. It is not necessary to explain them all for the purpose of this book which is to enable gaining sufficient understanding of the concepts of the registration of designs for effective management of intellectual property. These basic requirements are set out in Article 4 of the Regulation.

Article 4

Requirements for protection

1. A design shall be protected by a Community design to the extent that it is new and has individual character.

2. A design applied to or incorporated in a product which constitutes a component part of a complex product shall only be considered to be new and to have individual character:

    (a) if the component part, once it has been incorporated into the complex product, remains visible during normal use of the latter; and

    (b) to the extent that those visible features of the component part fulfil in themselves the requirements as to novelty and individual character.

3. "Normal use" within the meaning of paragraph (2)(a) shall mean use by the end user, excluding maintenance, servicing or repair work.

Is the design new?

This can be alternatively stated as – does the design have novelty? It is one of the two main requirements for a design to be registered. The concept of "novelty" is one which appears in several guises in intellectual property law and procedure: as originality in copyright law; as distinctiveness in trade mark law; and as a requirement for a patent to be novel. This is a further instance of it. The Regulation has a definition of a new design effectively for all member states purposes in Article 5.

Article 5

Novelty

1. A design shall be considered to be new if no identical design has been made available to the public:

    (a) in the case of an unregistered Community design, before the date on which the design for which protection is claimed has first been made available to the public;

    (b) in the case of a registered Community design, before the date of filing of the application for registration of the design for which protection is claimed, or, if priority is claimed, the date of priority.

2. Designs shall be deemed to be identical if their features differ only in immaterial details.

Does the design have individual character?

The requirement for individual character is the other of the two main requirements for a design to qualify for legal protection as a Community Design. This is in Article 6 of the Regulation:

Article 6

Individual character

1. A design shall be considered to have individual character if the overall impression it produces on the informed user differs from the overall impression produced on such a user by any design which has been made available to the public:

    (a) in the case of an unregistered Community design, before the date on which the design for which protection is claimed has first been made available to the public;

    (b) in the case of a registered Community design, before the date of filing the application for registration or, if a priority is claimed, the date of priority.

2. In assessing individual character, the degree of freedom of the designer in developing the design shall be taken into consideration.

Some excluded designs

This is again a complex part of design law with many details. However, three important aspects of design are excluded which understood in the context of protection for innovative designs in Europe. These exclusions are in Articles 8 and 9.

Article 8

Designs dictated by their technical function and designs of interconnections

1.   A Community design shall not subsist in features of appearance of a product which are solely dictated by its technical function.

2.   A Community design shall not subsist in features of appearance of a product which must necessarily be reproduced in their exact form and dimensions in order to permit the product in which the design is incorporated or to which it is applied to be mechanically connected to or placed in, around or against another product so that either product may perform its function.

3.   Notwithstanding paragraph 2, a Community design shall under the conditions set out in Articles 5 and 6 subsist in a design serving the purpose of allowing the multiple assembly or connection of mutually interchangeable products within a modular system.

Article 9

Designs contrary to public policy or morality

A Community design shall not subsist in a design which is contrary to public policy or to accepted principles of morality.

These exclusions are part of a balancing act performed by the European Commission between the desire for a free and open market within Europe and the need to protect the rights of individuals and businesses. These exclusions are part of the free trade side of the balance.

Scope of protection and infringement

The main legal rights given by a Community Design are the right of the owner to the exclusive right to use the design and to prevent anyone else using the design without the consent of the owner. Use according to the Regulation

> "... shall cover, in particular, the making, offering, putting on the market, importing, exporting or using of a product in which the design is incorporated or to which it is applied, or stocking such a product for those purposes."

The scope of the Community Design, again according to the Regulation ".. shall include any design which does not produce on the informed user a different overall impression." This is one of those expressions capable of being interpreted many different ways. Advising on whether a particular design which is not identical or very closely similar to the Community Design actually comes within the scope of the a Community Design based on this expression will be difficult to do with any certainty. Once this expression has been interpreted by the courts, this task will be easier but not easy.

Infringement is a legal expression meaning that the rights given by the design are being used without the permission of the owner as part of some commercial activity. This activity might be advertising or selling a product made to the design. The activity is usually commercial although this is not a requirement for infringement.

Length of protection

The rights in the Unregistered Community Design last for three years from the date that the design was first made available to the public within the European Community.

The rights in a registered Community Design last for 25 years provided that renewals are paid at five yearly intervals. If a renewal is not paid the rights are lost from that time. The renewal can be paid late within a period of six months after the due date provided an extra fee is paid. This is another example of a grace period.

Ownership

The rights in the Community Design are owned by the designer unless designs are created by an employee "… in the execution of his duties or following the instructions given by his employer, the right to the Community design shall vest in the employer, unless otherwise agreed or specified under national law." A design will be jointly owned if two or more persons have jointly developed the design.

Priority

The application to register a design in a country which has signed up to the either of two international conventions gives a right or priority to apply to register the same design as a Community Design. The two conventions are the Paris Convention and the Agreement to establish the World Intellectual Property Organisation. The right of priority lasts for six months from the date of filing the first application. A right of priority arises from the showing of the design at certain classified international exhibitions. The period is six months from the date of disclosure.

Registration procedure

The application for a registered Community Design can be made at a central office or at the equivalent "Office" in a member state. The central office is the Office for Harmonisation in the Internal Market (Trade Marks and Designs) usually referred to by the awkward acronym "OHIM" and which was instituted by European Regulation (EC) No 40/94 of 20 December 1993 on the Community Trade Mark referred to earlier. This office is located in Alicante, Spain. The equivalent office in the UK is the Patent Office which despite its name deals with applications to registered patents, trade marks and designs.

The registration procedure is similar to that discussed in relation to patents although simpler and trade marks. The procedure is to make an application including representations of the design. The application is examined to ensure that it meets the relevant criteria. It may be necessary to overcome objections raised in the examination process either by successfully arguing the objection is not a correct one or by making amendments. This process normally takes several months. Once any objections are overcome the registration will be granted as a registered Community Design.

As explained in relation to patents and trade marks, the fact that the design has been registered is not conclusive of the validity of the registration. The registration can still be challenged at anytime usually by a person or company with a commercial interest in defeating the registration. This most often happens, again as with patents and trade marks, when the owner of the design seeks to enforce it by court action. The almost invariable defensive response is to deny infringing the rights in the registered design and to claim that the design registration is invalid.

Invalidity

A registered Community Design may be declared invalid either by OHIM or by a national court as a defensive counter claim in court proceedings about infringement of the design. So to invalidate a registered Community Design, an application must be made to OHIM unless infringement proceedings are current in a national court when the national court may decide whether the design is invalid as a counter claim to the infringement claim.

In contrast, an Unregistered Community Design can be declared invalid by a national court either by an application for that purpose or as part of a counterclaim in infringement proceedings in respect of that design.

The grounds for invalidating a Community Design are detailed. The most important grounds mirror the qualification requirements for the subsistence of the design and the obtaining of a registration for it where registered. If these did not or do not exist, then the rights in the design whether registered or not should cease to exist.

A registered Community Design which has been declared invalid on certain grounds maybe maintained in force if amendments are made which correct or overcome the objections which lead to the registration being found to be invalid in its original form.

Dealing with the Community Design

The rights in the Community Design whether registered or unregistered may be transferred and otherwise dealt with as a property right and as if a national design right of the country in which the holder is based. The details are a more complex but this is sufficient to understand that ownership of the rights can be transferred.

The ownership of the Community Design must be transferred "...in its entirety, and for the whole area of the Community": Article 27 of the Regulation.

Rights in designs in the UK

Registered Designs in the UK

There is a separate national registered design law and procedure for the UK as in most other countries. The law has been recently changed to implement the Designs Directive.[23] The law is now effectively the same as for the registered Community Design in the European Regulation[24] although the rights obtained are only for the UK.

The application process is again similar in its concept and basic procedural steps to that of OHIM. Differences of detail exist which it is not necessary to explain in this book.

Design Right in the UK

This right is similar to copyright. It was introduced in the United Kingdom to give product designs protection against copying. It replaces copyright protection for these designs which were perceived in the late 1980s to give too much protection and to stifle competition. The right applies to designs created after 1 August 1989. The design must be original and fall within the relevant definition of a design. Those designs current as at 1 August 1989 retained their copyright protection but the rights were cut down to match equivalent rights given by the Design Right. Copyright protection for these existing designs ended on 1 August 1999.

Definition of a Design Right design

The definition of design covers " any aspect of the shape or configuration (whether internal or external) of the whole or part of an article." This definition will cover most manufactured products. There is no artistic criteria so that purely functional designs will have protection against copying. Some designs are specifically excluded. First, methods or principles of construction and surface decoration are excluded. So in one case the shape of a garment was protected by the unregistered Design Right and the design on the fabric of contrasting colours was copyright protected. Secondly, the so called "must fit" and "must match" exclusions. The "must fit" exemption only excludes those particular features which enable the article to "fit" to other features whereas the "must match" would exclude all those features which enable the article to match the appearance of other parts of an overall design to make the whole complete.

These two exemptions are to prevent owners of the Design Right from using the rights in the design to stop competitors making products to be used with the Design Right owner's products. This again is part of the balancing of free trade with the rights of individuals and businesses. The competitors may be producing accessories or spare parts. For example, a replacement body panel, bumper, or instrument panel "must match" the rest of the design of the car to be of any use. But car seats, steering wheels and road wheels generally do not have to "match" any aspect of the design of the car. Wing mirrors are

---

23.   EC Directive 98/71.
24.   Council Regulation No. 6/2002.

useful to illustrate the boundaries of this exceptions. The design of the wing mirrors of a car may well be an integral part of an aerodynamic shape and so the design would match the overall car design. But in other cases the shape of the wing mirrors have no direct relation to the overall shape of the car.

The shape of a sophisticated alloy car wheel will have features designed to enable the wheel to fit on a car. These features will be covered by the "must fit" exclusion but the remainder of the attractive design of the wheel will have Design Right protection.

Original and not common place

There are two criteria to be met in relation to design if Design Right is to subsist in it. First, the design must be original. Secondly, it must not be "commonplace in the design field in question at the time of its creation". The circumstances of each case will be used by a court to determine if a design is original and not commonplace. The UK Court of Appeal in the 1999 case of *Farmers Build* v Carrier *Bulk Materials Handling*[27] provided some guidance as to the meaning and practical application of "commonplace". *Farmers Build* was a case about an agricultural slurry machine and its various parts. The court found certain parts were not made to a commonplace design including a hopper, bearings in a particular combination, and perforated drum. A distinction had to be made between a type of article, which might be commonplace, and a particular design of the type of article which may not be commonplace. But in the 2001 Court of Appeal case of *Scholes Windows* v *Magnet*[28], a decorative feature forming an integral part of a modern uPVC window design created in the early 1990s was regarded as commonplace since this type of feature was prevalent in Victorian sash windows and some similar but not identical designs were made on such sash windows.

Subsistence of Design Right

For the Design Right to subsist there must be a record of the design. The Design Right will subsist in the record. The design can be recorded in two ways. By making an article to the design or in a design document. In most cases a design document will exist. If not, the fact of making a product to the design will be sufficient to record the design for Design Right to subsist in it. A design document means any record of a design, whether in the form of a drawing, a written description, a photograph, data stored in a computer or otherwise. The protection given to a created work such as a design is normally associated with a visual depiction of the design. For example by a drawing. But here for Design Right protection a "written description" of the design will qualify. Cases in the past have denied copyright protection under the previous law to written descriptions of designs.

In some cases the recording of the design in the finished product will be a life saver because no traditional record was made. This may at first sight seem unlikely. However, when considering if the design qualifies for

---

27.   [1999] R.P.C. 461.
28.   [2002] F.S.R. 172.

protection as a UK unregistered design, the product as the record of the design can be important.

Ownership of a Design Right

The position on ownership is similar to that for copyright with one important difference. The difference is that the unregistered Design Rights in a design which has been commissioned will belong to the person who commissioned the design not the designer. This is not the case with copyright. Nor with the Community Design. UK law states that "the designer is the first owner of any Design Right in a design which is not created in pursuance of a commission or in the course of employment." If there is a commission, the first owner is the person who commissioned the design. If the design was created by an employee during the course of employment, the employer is the first owner of the Design Right There is a fourth type of person who might be the owner. In the next section, we shall consider the qualification requirements in order for the Design Right to subsist in the UK. One of the ways that a design may qualify is by publication. If the design qualifies for Design Right protection through publication, then the person who made the qualifying publication will be the owner of the right.

Qualifying for Design Right

The provisions of UK law relating to the Design Right are similar to those for copyright but not identical. There are four ways that a design may qualify for Design Right protection:

1. If the designer is a qualifying individual unless the design was commissioned or made in the course of employment.

2. If a qualifying person commissions the design.

3. If the design was made in the course of employment by a qualifying person.

4. Where the design does not otherwise qualify, if the first marketing of articles to the design is by a qualifying person exclusively authorised to put such articles on the market and does so in the UK, another country to which these provision have been extended, or another European Member State.

Duration

The rights given by the Design Right continue for either 15 years from the date when the design was recorded or an article was made to the design or 10 years from the date when articles made to the design were first put on the market if that date was within 5 years of the first recording or making to the design. However, any person is entitled during the last 5 years of the Design Right to a licence to do anything which would otherwise be an infringement of the Design Right. If the terms of the licence cannot be agreed a mechanism is provided to settle the terms. The availability of such licences will have a big impact on the value and commercial assessment of designs which are only protected against copying by Design Right. The exclusivity will have been lost and competition can be expected. The level of royalty for the kind of design only given this protection is likely to be low, in the 1–5% bracket.

In an intellectual property management assignment done in 2001, the designs involved were for extruded products. These designs were made by the business but the extruding was outsourced. The extruded products were then sold profitably. However, most of the designs on which the business was based dated from 1991. Any design rights will already had expired or be about to do so. Consequently, any rival business or even a customer could make the extrusions if they realised that the designs no longer had the protection of Design Right in the UK.

Infringement rights

Any person infringes the Design Right who does, or authorises another to do, anything which is the exclusive right of the Design Right owner. The exclusive rights cover almost every commercial activity. Any person who reproduces the design either exactly or substantially by making an article will infringe. So will a person who imports, sells, or has possession of such an article.

It is these exclusive rights that may have substantial value in that other businesses can be prevented from making products to the design.

Know How

Introduction

"Know how" is the riskiest type of intellectual property in which to invest, whether that be to take a licence and gear up for manufacture or to acquire a business whose commercial success is at least partially based on know how. But in many instances, other intellectual property rights will be combined with know how giving more certain protection often making any investment decision less risky.

Know how is the riskiest intellectual property because of its nature. There is no registration to evaluate. It is not like copyright or designs where a particular "thing" is protected which can be seen. Rather know how is information that has value because it is confidential. Confidential means not in the public domain. Not known to everyone. The extent of the know how is often difficult to establish with any certainty. It is common to see know how described as "..financial information about..." or "... the technical specification for ...".

If the know how ceases to be confidential, little or no value can be placed on it as an asset for commercial exploitation. Nobody will pay to acquire information and techniques that are freely and widely available in the public domain. The information may still have immense commercial value to those businesses which use it to derive profit. But any exclusive rights will have been lost.

The protection of know how will be considered under two headings. First, the protection given by the UK common law. The concepts in general will be similar in other jurisdictions. Secondly, contractual obligations to keep information confidential. There is considerable overlap between the two.

UK Common Law of Confidential Information

In the UK it is the law of confidential information which underpins know how as intellectual property protected by rights. The law of confidential information is a common law legal doctrine based on fairness between "persons" – individuals or organisations. The legal doctrine is a set of principles developed over hundreds of years in the UK by its courts. It is the application of those principles in particular circumstances which determines whether information is to be regarded as confidential or not. To achieve fairness the principles allow considerable flexibility. As a necessary consequence, there are no hard and fast rules but instead broad principles. These principles are interpreted and applied by the courts in each set of circumstances.

The fundamental principle on which the UK law of confidence is based is that a person who has received information in confidence from another will not take unfair advantage of it or profit from the wrongful use or publication of it. On this fundamental principle has been built a complex law of confidential information in the UK.

The requirements to be met under UK law for information to be protected as confidential are that a confidential relationship must exist between the owner of the confidential information and the person to whom it has been disclosed, the information must actually be confidential in the sense of not being in the public domain, and is the type of information recognised as protectable. The right in confidential information is broadly the right to prevent the unauthorised disclosure and use of the information.

Type of information

Any information can be protected as confidential if and to the extent that it is not in the public domain. There is no requirement that the information should be inventive as in patent law or original as in copyright law in the sense of having been the result of skill and effort. But information which is of a general or trivial nature is unlikely to be regarded as confidential by a court unless the circumstances are exceptional.

There are many cases which illustrate both the effectiveness and the limitations of rights in confidential information. A good example in a business context is the 1967 UK case of *Seager* v *Copydex*[29]. Mr Seager's business manufactured a patented carpet grip. He approached Copydex to be a distributor of this patented product, but during the negotiations mentioned an idea for a new carpet grip product which was not patented. Mr Seager

---

29.   [1969] 2 All ER 718.

disclosed specific features such as the shape and orientation of spikes to grip the carpet and various alternatives. These were a novel at the time and was confidential. The negotiations came to nothing. Copydex put a carpet gripper rod system on the market which did not infringe Mr Seager's patent but was like the alternative one described to them by Mr Seagar. Copydex also applied for a patent for their product claiming to be the inventor of it. It claimed not to have been influenced by the disclosure to them of Mr Seager's idea. In a court action for breach of confidence, Copydex lost. The court did not make an order preventing Copydex using the information disclosed by Mr Seager. Copydex was ordered to pay compensation to Mr Seagar for use of the information. The amount of compensation was limited to that representing the market advantage that Mr Seager would have had once he had put a product using his idea on to the market.

The *Seagar* case illustrates some important points. Some know how is disclosed as soon as a product is put on the market. This was so with the carpet grip disclosed by Mr Seager and put on the market by Copydex. In a recent case into the assessment of the value of a novel and clever design of a closing for a paper container typically used to hold sweets, the container had been disclosed publicly incorporating the idea so that no patent could be obtained for it. Once the container became more widely known on the market, any rival could copy the idea and produce a competing design being careful not to infringe any copyright or other rights in the particular design. The value of the know how would be based on and limited to the market advantage given by having the product out first.

The know how must be sufficiently detailed and not simply a general concept. The more general the concept, the less likely a court is to find that it has been used in breach of confidence. It is much more likely that several persons could have thought of the general concept. This could not be said of a specific and detailed idea. In the 1995 UK case of *De Maudsley* v *Palumbo*[30] an idea was disclosed at a dinner party about a night club with five new features such as opening all night long, separate areas for dancing and resting, and a VIP lounge. The court concluded the information was too general to be protected as confidential information and that, in the social setting of the dinner party, no confidential obligations arose.

Public Interest Disclosure

In UK law, an obligation to keep information confidential will not extend to prevent disclosure of the information where a serious risk of public harm exists. But the permitted disclosure will only be to the extent necessary to prevent such harm. The harm might be, for example, the commission of crimes, the perpetration of a fraud, or some physical harm to the public. A disclosure in the public interest will only avoid being a breach of the obligation of confidence if the disclosure is limited to those who need to know to prevent the harm. Disclosure, for example, to a national newspaper will not usually be justified. Disclosure to the police or a regulatory body is

---

30.   [1996] FSR 447.

more likely to be meet the requirements of a public interest disclosure. So it would not be in the public interest to prevent the disclosure of confidential information about a product which would reveal that the product was or might be harmful to the public.

A good example is the 1984 UK case of *Lion Laboratories* v *Evans*[31]. Lion Laboratories made a breathalyser product which was approved for use by police forces in the UK. Two technicians left the employment of Lion Laboratories. They approached a national newspaper with internal documents of Lion Laboratories containing information casting doubts on the accuracy and reliability of the breathalyser. Lion Laboratories tried and failed to prevent the publication of the information in these documents. The Court of Appeal accepted that the disclosure was in the public interest. In 1998, a senior employee of British Biotech, a UK biotechnology company, revealed certain confidential information about the results of tests on a cancer treatment to correct public statements published by the company which in his opinion where misleading. The employee would no doubt have relied on the public interest to justify the disclosure if British Biotech had persisted in any court action for breach of confidence.

This UK law common law about public interest disclosure based on the court decisions over the years has know been made a statutory law in the Public Interest Disclosure Act 1998. The application and interpretation by the courts of the rights given in this statute will indicate to what extent, if any, the previous common law position on public interest disclosure has changed.

In 1998 the BBC intended to produce a programme about the workings of the Serious Fraud Office in the UK. In the programme, it planned to publicise information about a Mr Robert Bunn who had admitted in a statement to the police under caution to being involved in a conspiracy to defraud certain banks. No charges ever came to trial. Mr Bunn applied for an injunction. The court held that information given to the police under caution was confidential. The defence that publication of information about wrongdoing given to the police was justified in the public interest was rejected. The injunction was refused because details of the admission had been referred to in open court in connection with the criminal proceedings which never came to trial.

Confidentiality and employees

The extent to which a former employee can and cannot use information gained whilst working for an employer has been the subject of regular legal disputes in the UK over the last hundred years and more. The legal position in the UK of an employer wanting to prevent an employee, whilst still employed, disclosing or using information about the employer's business is strong. The employer's rights are based on the obligations of confidence and good faith owed by an employee to the employer.

The legal position of the employer, however, changes after the employment of an individual ceases. The employer cannot prevent a former employee

---

31.   [1984] 2 All ER 417.

from disclosing and using general skill and knowledge acquired whilst employed by the employer. The type of information which an employer can prevent a former employee from using is limited to information learnt whilst employed that is of a sufficiently high degree of confidentiality as to amount to a trade secret.

This is often frustrating for employers. Assessing in any particular circumstances what is and is not information which an employer can prevent a former employee disclosing and using is difficult. Perhaps a better way to consider this is not by the level of confidentiality but by the level of importance to the business of the confidential information (i.e. the know how). For example, an employer's general organisation and method of business is not likely to be regarded as protectable know how. Chemical formulae, detailed business plans, and new product information will normally be regard as protectable as confidential information. But details of customers and suppliers, prices paid and other similar information fall in a grey area. In some circumstances this type of information may be given protection by the courts but not in others. The practical application in any particular circumstances is difficult.

The position of the employer can be improved by having a contract of employment with an express term dealing with the use of confidential information and terms preventing an ex-employee soliciting and dealing with customers and working in a competing business. The terms of an employment contract to ensure that information is kept confidential during employment are usually not difficult to evaluate. However, evaluating the rights given by express terms to protect know how by preventing an ex-employee soliciting customers and working for a rival business for a period time after the end of that employee's employment requires considerable knowledge and experience when assessing their value.

There is now a great deal of case law about the extent to which such terms are enforceable. Much depends on the circumstances of each case. The need to retain flexibility means that it is not possible to have a detailed check list of points which, if present, will lead to a finding of enforceability. The law is seldom as simple as that. In fact, having considered all relevant factors, the person undertaking the investigation will still have to make a judgement based on knowledge and experience as to whether or not the term will be enforceable. In some circumstances that will be a close call.

European Convention for the Protection of Human Rights and Fundamental Freedoms

The UK ratified the Convention many years ago but no UK government brought it into effect as the law of the UK. The UK Labour Government elected in 1997 decided that it would do so. The Convention became part of UK law on the 2nd October 2000 when the Human Rights Act 1998 came into effect. The Convention has two relevant Articles which are Article 8 giving a right to privacy and Article 10 giving a right to freedom of expression. The Convention was an influence on the law of the UK before the Human Rights Act came into force. The UK appellate courts in various cases involving newspapers have stated that the rights in the Convention should be taken into account as having a persuasive influence on the decisions that the UK courts make.

It remains to be seen how the direct effect of the Convention and the Human Rights Act will affect the law of confidential know how in a business context.

In the public domain

Information, to qualify for protection as confidential information, must not be in the public domain. This means that the information must be not generally accessible by any person who wants to look for it. The qualification that the information must not be generally available is important because information can still be confidential in law yet be known and available to a limited number of individuals. For example, to a research group at a research institute or to certain employees in a company R & D department. So even though one organisation has information, the same information in the hands of a second company could still be regarded as the confidential information of that second company. Information which has been disclosed only in the course of a confidential relationship is clearly not in the public domain. Information which has been widely disclosed publicly is equally clearly in the public domain. But some cases will be in the grey area between these two. The disclosure of an invention to a professional advisor in order that a patent application might be filed is clearly a confidential disclosure. Once the patent application has been published by the relevant patent office, the information in the application is available to the general public and the information in it is clearly no longer confidential.

In the UK in the mid 1980s a series of cases brought by the British Government sought to prevent the serialisation in newspapers of a book by a former spy called Peter Wright. The book had been published in the USA and attempts were made to prevent it being published in the United Kingdom and in Australia unsuccessfully. In the UK, the courts concluded that so much of the information had been disclosed that an order to prevent further publication was pointless. This case illustrates an important point. Once particular confidential information is disclosed, it cannot be made secret again. The extent to which a court will prevent further disclosure and use of confidential information, wrongly disclosed, will depend on the particular circumstances. In commercial negotiations when often parts of the information are disclosed in an iterative process, care must be taken that the point is not crossed accidentally where so much of the information has cumulatively been disclosed that the information will be taken to be no longer confidential. A proper confidentiality agreement put in place before the negotiations begin will help to prevent such circumstances arising.

Information which is publicly available can still form the basis of confidential know how. If a person researches publicly available sources of information to produce useful new information or know how, the results of that work will be protected as confidential information. It is the intellectual effort required to produce this information or know how from publicly available sources that gives rise to the protection against another person taking the know how and avoiding the effort to find the information by the same effort.

Information can still be regarded as confidential even when it has been disclosed to a limited number of persons because it can not be taken that practically the information is generally available so that the information could be said to be in the public domain. There will be a point where the number of persons who know the information is so large that the information will be taken to be in the public domain. In any particular circumstances, it will be ultimately for a court to decide.

Confidential relationship by agreement

Reaching an agreement to keep information confidential is a familiar event in business life. Employees are usually required to keep their employer's business information confidential by a term of the contract of employment. Non-disclosure agreements are sought before sensitive business information is disclosed in any negotiation or if an inventor is seeking backing from a potential business partner or provider of finance. The use of such non disclosure agreements is discussed later. Confidential information is exploited commercially often by a licence from one person or organisation to another using know how agreements which require the information to be kept confidential and that a payment for use is made. Typically, a lump sum and a royalty.

The requirement to keep information confidential is a specific obligation in these contracts. But an obligation to keep information confidential can be implied into any contract if justified by the circumstances. It is not possible to give a checklist of factors which if all or most were present would indicate that such an obligation would be implied. The best guide would be to imagine what one party to an agreement being a reasonable person would think if receiving the confidential information. Did an obligation arise to keep the information confidential?

Confidential relationship by circumstances

An obligation to keep information confidential arises in many relationships without any doubt and this has been recognised by the law. For example, in the relationships between doctor and patient, solicitor and client, and banker and customer. But other relationships can give rise to an obligation to keep information confidential. For example, in a business negotiation where valuable business information is disclosed in trying to reach a deal. The obligation is more likely to arise if the information communicated is either detailed or highly valuable or both. But where the information is communicated in a social setting rather than a business one, the obligation is less likely to arise. The *Seager* and *De Maudsley* cases mentioned earlier illustrate this point well.

This ambiguity makes assessing whether or not a confidential obligation arises (if there is no confidentiality agreement in place) in particular circumstances difficult, at least with any precision. There are no hard and fast rules except in those few types of relationships mentioned above where the law is clear. The best guide that can be given is similar to that in relation to obligations of confidence being implied into a contract. Imagine what one person being a reasonable person would think if receiving the confidential information. Did an obligation arise to keep the information confidential?

The law in relation to confidential information is such that it allows flexibility to do the fairest thing in the circumstances – but this is at the expense of certainty in any particular circumstances. The 1998 UK case of *Drummond Murray* v *Yorkshire Fund Managers*[32] involved a business plan for a management buy-out of a company and the proposed management team. Each team member had contributed to the business plan. The business plan and the price to be paid for the assets of the target company were very important confidential information of the proposed management team. There was no agreement between the team members as to how this confidential information could be used. Yorkshire Fund Managers were interested in backing most of the team but not Mr Murray who was the proposed managing director. One of the investment managers at Yorkshire Fund Managers put himself forward as managing director in place of Mr Murray. Mr Murray did not agree, the rest of the team did. Mr Murray left the proposed management team. Yorkshire Fund Managers then agreed to back the venture. Mr Murray took court action to prevent use of the confidential information. The Court of Appeal decided that the relationship between the team members was not covered by a contract and that there was no reason to impose good faith obligations of uncertain extent. The court also decided that the confidential information ceased to the property of Mr Murray once the relationship between the other team members and Mr Murray was ended. Consequently, he could not prevent the others using the confidential information after he had left the team.

The Non Disclosure Agreement

Disclosing secret information involves a risk that the information escapes the control of the person who owns it and becomes generally available. The chance to exploit commercially that secret information is lost. Yet often if the information is not disclosed, it is not possible to maximise that commercial potential. The aim must be to manage this risk and the non-disclosure agreement is an important part of risk management.

The non-disclosure agreement confirms that information is being disclosed in confidence, identifies the company which, and often individuals who, will have access to the information, and identifies the information. These three essential requirements are not always appreciated by business people keen to negotiate and do a deal. The agreement need not be long or complex. A letter is often perfectly adequate, typically in preliminary discussion. A non-disclosure

---

32.   [1998] F.S.R. 372.

agreement with comprehensive rights and obligations is essential where a substantial amount of confidential information is to be disclosed and evaluated.

A good non-disclosure agreement will be appropriate to the circumstances, be carefully prepared, be succinct, and will properly identify the company or individuals who are signing the agreement and to whom the information is being disclosed. Care should be taken to ensure that the agreement is signed on behalf of a company or organisation by an individual properly authorised to sign. The writer has experience of both companies and research organisations attempting to wriggle out of obligations in non-disclosure agreements covering valuable intellectual property on the basis that the individual who signed was not authorised to do so.

A non-disclosure agreement signed by a company or other organisation identifies and imposes obligations on that entity but such an agreement will not impose those obligations directly on individuals working for the company or other organisation. A wrongful disclosure by an employee would be most likely to put the company in breach of the agreement. But if the information has been disclosed into the public domain, a claim for breach of contract or misuse of confidential information may be of little comfort especially if the person or company disclosing could ill afford to take such court action over such a claim. Prevention of disclosure in the first place is the objective. A decision needs to be taken about whether or not to make particular individuals parties to the non-disclosure agreement. The right to sue these individuals personally for breach or disclosure of the information is a powerful incentive for them to keep the information disclosed to them confidential. An alternative is at least to name the individuals in the agreement to limit the internal disclosure of the information by the company or organisation which is receiving the information. There is value on having such named individuals countersign the agreement even though they are not parties to it. The object would be to use the countersigning of the agreement as evidence later that each knew an obligation of confidence was being created.

The next key element of the non-disclosure agreement is identifying the confidential information being disclosed under the terms of the agreement. This is one of the most important parts of putting a non-disclosure agreement in place and yet typically receives the least attention. It is useless to be able to show that an agreement was in place with certain other parties to keep any information disclosed confidential, if the person or business disclosing cannot, after disclosure, prove what information was disclosed. It is common to see a non-disclosure agreement referring to information about a named certain project, business opportunity, or innovation plus some all encompassing almost unintelligible legal definition of confidential information. Information is then disclosed in a meeting and perhaps in documents too. Soon nobody has an accurate record of what was actually disclosed and what part of the information disclosed is the confidential information. This raises the serious risk that, if a dispute arises, the identity of the confidential information cannot be proven with sufficient certainty.

This is common but a far too relaxed approach to disclosing confidential information if the information is important or valuable or both.

The information deemed confidential should be identified in a dossier of some kind so that the information can be clearly identified later. For example, this might be a business plan or a technical specification. Subsequent discussion should be minuted and kept with the dossier. If no dossier is possible minutes of meetings at which the confidential information was disclosed must be kept. This advice is often seen as impractical. It is certainly tedious to do, particularly as most non-disclosure agreements do not result in a dispute. When a dispute does arises, suddenly the individuals involve have conflicting accounts about dates of meetings, who was present, what was said, and about the meaning of what was said. Then it is too late. The outcome of the dispute cannot be predicted with any certainty. The non-disclosure agreement has not given the protection that it was intended to do. So even with a non-disclosure agreement, the disclosure of the information needs to be managed carefully, even in the midst of urgent and hectic negotiations.

Many non-disclosure agreements have a term stating that the information should be returned in the event of negotiations ceasing. But once the information has been disclosed to an individual, it cannot be removed from that individual's memory by any legal means. The information may be forgotten over time. The agreement should deal with this by controlling to whom the information can be disclosed and how it may be used. The agreement should require that any records of the information and any documents containing the confidential information be kept separate from other records and documents of the recipient of the information. This will enable any such records and documents containing the confidential information to be given back later or destroyed if the purpose for the disclosure comes to an end.

APPENDIX 2
CASE STUDIES ON LEGAL RIGHTS

Contents

CASE STUDY A

Introduction

This case study is based on an actual due diligence investigation. It has been simplified and specific identifying details removed. The fictitious report in appendix [ ] illustrates the result of the investigation and some of the points that were thrown up. The report is simplified and the facts have been changed but the points brought out are the same. It is based on an actual investigation but though the facts bear no relation to the actual facts, the results do. Many of the complex details have been omitted. The report illustrates the process of due diligence reporting.

The case study is about the acquisition of the assets of a business. The seller is "Sellout" and the buyer is "Buyin". The assets included intellectual property rights which were an important part of the business. It was the potential better to exploit these intellectual property rights that was one of the major reasons for why the deal was attractive to Buyin. A due diligence investigation was undertaken to assess the state of the intellectual property rights both as to the title and the strength of those rights. The intellectual property rights included a patent, some registered designs, and some trade marks.

The due diligence investigation relied on information from three sources as follows:

- the searching of databases holding information about patents, trade marks and designs;

- from Sellout's own records to which access was given. Reviewing these records and quizzing personnel of Sellout would be vital but time consuming;

- from investigations into other public sources of relevant information about the market in which these products were operating currently and historically. The historical information will give some idea about the market in general at the time the patents and designs were filed, which in turn would give some indication about the strength of the rights.

Patents

The patent position was not satisfactory. The patent had been owned by a company which had gone into receivership. This company had been owned by the management of Sellout. The management had bought the assets out of the company in receivership into a new company, Sellout, or at least thought they had. That new company was given effectively the same name as the old company.

The search of the register of patents showed the patent remained in the name of the old company. There are three possibilities for this. First, that Sellout now seeking to sell the assets had agreed to acquire the patent rights from the receiver of the old company but no assignment document had been registered at the relevant patent office to record the change. To correct this, it would be necessary to record the details of any existing agreement which showed the assignment.

Secondly, that Sellout had agreed to acquire the patent but no document to complete the transfer of the legal title had been concluded. Therefore, only an equitable title had been transferred to Sellout – which can be likened to an incomplete legal title. A document would need to be prepared and signed by or on behalf of the old company to transfer the legal title. Buyin will need legal title to be able to enforce the rights given by the patent.

Thirdly, that Sellout had never purchased the patent from the old company. For Buyin now wishing to acquire the patent rights, this will mean taking steps to obtain the patent rights by finding who now owns them and see if that person will sell them.

It would be necessary to reinstate the old company that had gone into receivership and which at the time had been struck off the companies register in the UK. It could then sign an assignment to register at the relevant Patent Office. Sellout could then pass good title to Buyin. Alternatively, the assignment could be direct from the old company formerly in receivership to Buyin. The rules about the restoration of companies in the UK are detailed and it is by no means certain that the company could in fact be restored.

The third scenario is the worst one: i.e. if the old company in receivership for some reason never agreed to assign the patent rights to Sellout, now the vendor. In that case, the patent rights since the old company has been struck off would have passed to the control of the UK State. It would be necessary to persuade the relevant official to assign the rights either to Sellout or direct to Buyin. This would undoubtedly involve payment of some consideration for doing so.

The renewal fees were due on the patent during the negotiations. Buyin, as part of an elaborate delayed payment arrangement in the overall transaction, paid the renewal fees to keep the patent in force. The delayed payment arrangements were elaborate to balance payments against the obvious risks that the patent would not or could not later be transferred to the purchaser.

Designs

Many of the designs were held in the name of the old company which had gone into receivership. The same considerations applied as discussed in relation to the patent. These became part of the elaborate arrangements for deferred payment. Again, renewal fees were an issue as can be seen from the report. In fact the renewal fee for the Italian design had not been paid on time but it could still be paid within the six month grace period together with an appropriate penalty payment. This was done by Buyin.

Trade Marks

Many of the trade marks too were still registered in the old company which had gone into receivership. Again these would need to be assigned if possible. The same considerations apply as applied to attempting to transfer the patent rights across.

Another issue arose in relation to the trade marks which illustrates an important point. The scrutiny of the records of Sellout and answers given by its personnel revealed that one of the trade marks had not been used since 1991 and one other trade mark had never been used. In the UK, failure to use a trade mark for more than five years leaves the trade mark vulnerable to be removed from the trade mark register. These trade marks were, therefore, vulnerable to being challenged by a competitor and would remain so until Buyin began to use them.

Conclusion

Sellout from the outside had attractive assets which Buyin wished to buy. Of particular importance were the intellectual property rights. It is clear from the due diligence investigation that the title at least to some of those intellectual property rights was severely impaired. It may be possible to cure the defects but this could be time consuming for management of Buyin and expensive.

All these factors were taken into account in the negotiations and in relation to the price that was ultimately paid for the business.

CASE STUDY – B

Introduction

In this case study, a well established company had developed a new pen. We shall call the company Penelope Pens. The developments were in the ink delivery system. The pen had an attractive design which the company had produced after considerable market research and work with a design house, called Plans-it. The product was obviously aimed at the mass consumer market.

The ink delivery system had been developed partly in-house where the theory had been approved. However, Penelope Pens used an independent laboratory to produce a prototype of a pen with the ink delivery system. This laboratory is called Bestlabs. This work led to significant improvements in the ink delivery system.

The market research and design of the shape of the pen, particularly the part held by the user when writing were undertaken by an independent market research company and by Plans-it. None of the design work or the research was undertaken in-house.

The market research indicated that there was a substantial market for such a pen even though there were many competitors already in the market. The company had good contacts with the range of retailers who were eager to take the pen with its new design and technical development.

Penelope Pens produced a detailed strategy for the development of the business in selling the pen. One obvious accessory would be replacement ink cartridges for the pen. These were specifically designed to fit into the novel ink delivery system. They were adapted for that purpose. Penelope Pens saw the potential to licence the product to other companies around the world and also the need to be able to prevent counterfeit products coming on to the market. The company had experience of its products being copied in the Far East and imported into Europe and the United States.

The company commissioned a due diligence report the objective of which was to ensure that all the rights were transferred and retained by Penelope Pens so that it will have all the available intellectual property rights to licence to other companies and to stop counterfeiters and other infringers of those rights.

Patents

The technical developments relating to the ink delivery system were thought to be patentable. The arrangements with Bestlabs in undertaking the prototype and other development work were such that Penelope Pens owned all the intellectual property rights. A simple assignment document was drawn up and all the rights assigned. The named individuals who had undertaken the work were joined in the assignment for certainty. The investigation led to the conclusion that all the work they had done was during their course of their employment and as such all the rights did belong to their employer, Bestlabs.

Ultimately, three patent applications were filed for the ink delivery system and improvements to it.

Designs

The market research about the designs did not lead to any new designs being created but merely indicated the sort of features that would be desirable. Plans-it, however, created a large number of possible designs which were gradually crystallised into the ultimate design. Many hundreds of drawings and sketches were produced. It was agreed that all rights in these designs belonged to Penelope Pens and an assignment had previously been drawn up to reflect this. During the investigation, it was thought that this assignment could be improved to remove some doubts about the ownership of all the rights in the designs. Consequently, a further assignment was drawn up in which the individuals who created the designs joined in and assigned their rights across to Penelope Pens. Whilst these individuals were employed by Plans-it, investigations revealed some facts which cast doubt on whether all the work had been done during the course of their employment such that all the designs had belonged to the employer, Plans-it. There was some doubt also as to whether the individuals had been commissioned directly by the company or through the design house. The assignment removed all these doubts, identified all the drawings referred to in the assignment. All the drawings and other records of the design history and final designs were handed over to Penelope Pens and kept in a safe place.

The designs for the pen would cover the outside appearance, the part where the writer would grip the pen and features where the ink cartridge fitted into the ink delivery system.

The cartridge designs would cover the overall shape of the cartridge which could be protected by a registered design right and the features for connecting to the delivery system could be protected by the unregistered design.

This last point illustrates well the difference between patents and designs. The patent, if granted, will protect the concept of the novel ink delivery system and protect a multitude of ways in which that concept could be put into practice. Design protects the particular way in which Penelope Pens here has decided to put the novel ink delivery system into practice.

Penelope Pens applied to register many aspects of the designs as registered designs in the UK and undertook an international design registration filing programme. It also filed an international design registration through its non-UK registered subsidiary. (Such an international filing is not at the time this report was produced, available to UK based companies since the United Kingdom has not signed up to the relevant treaties. However, in this case, the company had a subsidiary through which the application could legitimately be made. This undoubtedly saved a considerable amount of relevant time and professional costs.)

The designs therefore are potentially protected by two legal rights in the UK. These are registered design rights and unregistered design rights. Summarising briefly, to be registered the design must have some design features which are more than just functional. Features which make the design attractive to potential buyers. The shape of the pen on the outside and possibly the shape of the cartridge to would qualify for registered design protection. But it is doubtful that the design features of the ink delivery system and the cartridge which enable them to connect together would qualify for registered design protection or if included in the overall design for the pen or the cartridge would be given much protection except as part of the overall design.

Extent of Design Protection – UK

Registered design rights last for 25 years if renewals were paid whereas the unregistered design right has effectively a maximum of 10 years only five years of which give exclusive rights to use the designs. Clearly on this basis registered designs give protection for longer and are more valuable.

The reader will be aware from the section on designs (page 424) that there are exceptions to the protection of designs in the UK. These exceptions are:

* where objects have to fit together referred to as "must fit"; or

* where two parts of an article must match referred to as "must match".

The registered design of the outside of the pen as a whole is unlikely to give legal protection to the functional features of the ink delivery system where the cartridge fits. Similarly, any registered design obtained for the overall shape of the cartridge is not likely to give legal protection to the functional features allowing it to be connected to the ink delivery system of the pen. These features being excluded as either solely functional or excluded by the "must fit" exception. However, the distinctive and particular shape of the pen and cartridge could in combination mean in practice that rival manufacturers could not make cartridges to fit the pen without infringing the design registrations. But again account would need to be taken of any features excluded by the "must match" exception.

If registered design protection does not give protection then the design of all the features, but in particular these functional features, would be protected by an unregistered design right subject to the exceptions.

However the interplay of the "must-fit" and "must match" exceptions is important when the cartridge as an accessory for use in the pen is considered. If there were no exceptions to the design protection, no other manufacturer could copy the new connecting feature to make a cartridge to fit the pen. This would provide a lucrative accessory market for the company. If all the design features are excluded by the exceptions this would deprive Penelope Pens of a lucrative accessory market.

Any person undertaking a valuation of the intellectual property rights in this example would need to be aware of that point and take this into account in making a valuation. Designing of accessories is likely to be an important part of the company's business.

Conclusion

The foresight of Penelope Pens in ensuring that all intellectual property rights would belong to it made the due diligence exercise much easier in that all parties were prepared to co-operate and sign simple assignments of their rights over to Penelope Pens. Without such foresight, the position would have been much more difficult, Penelope Pens would have had to argue that the rights in the designs of the products belonged to it because they were commissioned. UK Design Right law provides that commissioned designs would belong to the commissioner. However, the *copyright* in the drawings would not automatically belong to the commissioner because copyright law in the UK is different. Penelope Pens would need to argue that it was implied into the arrangements that it would own the copyright.

Similarly with the patents. Penelope Pens would have had to argue that it was implied into the arrangements that the invention would be owned by it, would have the right to apply for patents, and to have all rights in the development assigned to it.

Bestlabs and Plans-it could easily have disputed the implied claim to ownership. Such a dispute would have lead either to litigation or to a compromise, probably with further payments being made to the laboratory and the design house to effect the transfer of the rights.

CASE STUDY – C

Introduction

In this case study a UK research institution wished to attempt to exploit the technologies it was developing in a better way. It drew up a strategy after careful consideration. The bare bones of the strategy were that technologies should be taken from its own research departments, combined possibly with emerging research from other institutions and from individuals who wish to exploit their own innovations. These individuals would complete the research at one of the research institution and then start a business based on the technology. Various forms of funding were also available.

The individuals would be carefully selected to be individuals who were likely to be able not only to develop the technology in collaboration with the research institution but also to build a business based on the developed technology. It was envisaged that the individual would not be on his or her own but would have a range of support services such as assistance from individuals with relevant expertise in intellectual property law, business management, and corporate finance. Advice from locally-based government supported agencies for training and other requirements was also envisaged.

The strategy depended upon agreements being reached between the research institution which was developing the strategy, the individuals who would take the projects on, hopefully to be successful businesses, and other research institutions. The organising research institution would provide the funding from various public and private sources at appropriate stages for the businesses and for some of the development work. It was envisaged that the development phase might be undertaken with the organising research institution or with other institutions if that was more appropriate.

The scheme required a rigorous assessment of the emerging technology and of the expected exit for the funds invested in the business, together with careful selection of the individual. The exit could be a licensing of the technology trade sale or a stock market float. Several – up to about 10 – projects were envisaged and that not all of which would be successful. The projects would be carefully monitored and funded through milestone points subject to review at each of these stages.

Intellectual Property Rights

The organisation of the intellectual property rights in such a scheme is complex. The purpose of this case study is simply to illustrate the care with which the organisation of intellectual property rights needs to be undertaken. The structure here is just one of the many structures which could have been set up to implement the scheme. The complexities need to be built into the agreements between the participants to ensure an orderly management of the intellectual property rights. Individual projects could fail as well as succeed. In setting up the structure both potential outcomes had to be considered and suitable provisions made.

The due diligence exercise here was to provide a structure by which those intellectual property rights could be managed both in the case of success and in the case of failure of any individual technology development.

Those bringing potential intellectual property rights to the scheme were as follows:

- the organising research institution;
- other participating research institutions;
- the individuals.

During the development phase at one of the other research institutions, further intellectual property rights might arise. The permutations about ownership of these are as follows:

- by the research institution if the individual was employed to carry out further development work;

- by the individual if not employed by institution; and

- if the individual was not employed and there was a joint development then the intellectual property rights in the developments could be owned by the institution and the individual jointly.

A Possible Scheme

One possible scheme is as follows:

- the institutions or individuals retain ownership of their original intellectual property rights;

- an option is created for the company to be run by the individual to take a licence to use all the intellectual property rights once the research is complete. Those intellectual property rights, the subject of the option, would also include intellectual property rights in the developments either on the basis that they were owned by the institution or the individual, or that they were jointly owned;

- the individual and the institutions providing the funding would have an equity state in the company.

Since only a licence had been granted to the company (assuming the option was exercised) if the company was a failure the licence would terminate, the rights would remain with their original owners. As far as the intellectual property rights were concerned all parties would then be in their original ownership positions. None would need to have a continuing relationship with any of the others. However, it was assumed at the outset that some rights would be owned jointly and this could lead to difficulties later if not planned at the outset. A further agreement would be needed to set out these provisions.

Joint ownership brings two potential causes of disagreement and dispute. Prior planning of the structure can avoid both. The first arises out of the legal implications of joint ownership. Typically in the UK, a joint owner of intellectual property rights has the right to exploit the technology personally but not the right to assign or licence others to do so without the consent of the other joint owners. So for example one joint owner could not licence a manufacturer without the consent of the other.

The second is operational rather than legal. Some of the intellectual property rights might be the subject of applications for registration. These bring with them ongoing obligations particularly about the conduct of the applications for registration which are likely to be pending in many Patent Offices round the world. Decisions will need to be taken – some difficult and needing professional advice – as these various applications proceed. The structure of this scheme sets up an arrangement in the from of an agreement to cover these points and also has provisions as to the payment of renewal fees and the costs of prosecution of those applications to registration. There is clearly a potential for disagreement between the joint owners if arrangements are not put into place.

The agreement put in place at the outset to address these points sets out rights and obligations between the joint owners covering the prosecution of applications, payment of costs and renewals and the rights to exploit the intellectual property rights. This agreement was expressed to be contingent upon the termination of the licence agreements because of the failure of the company seeking to exploit the intellectual property rights.

These provisions cover the event of failure. Provision for success were just as important and should be put in place. If the company was successful exploiting the technology, it may well be that it would be necessary to transfer the intellectual property rights into the company: for example if it was raise venture capital funding or to be listed on a Stock Exchange as a way of raising substantial further funding. In one possible scheme, obligations were included to transfer all the intellectual property rights into the company on one of a number of defined trigger events. These triggers included exchange of contracts for the acquisition of the shares in the company or its assets, an agreement about further funding, or the acceptance of the shares of the company to be listed on a recognised stock exchange. These provisions were difficult to draft into an agreement. Many other permutations in the event of success were possible. In another scheme it was decided that to provide a mechanism to cover them all was far too complicated. If success came, transfer of the intellectual property rights was left to subsequent negotiation as to the terms on which the rights might be transferred.

The licensing arrangements with the company provided for sublicensing which would give the company the right to licence a major partner with whom a deal might be done to develop the technology further. Such partnering arrangements are quite common particularly in pharmaceuticals and bio-technology.

One scheme therefore had a number of agreements in respect of each of the projects set up under the scheme:

- to provide for the pooling of the various intellectual property rights and for the further research;

- for the subscription of shares in the company by the investors;

- to give the company an option to take a licence of all the intellectual property rights together with a licence agreement in agreed form which will include an call option for the company to have those rights assigned to it;

- to provide for the management of any intellectual property rights in joint ownership.

INDEX

In this index the acronym IC means intellectual capital.

patents, and
    generally, 71
    overview, 395–396
Numerals
    due diligence, and, 293
    trade marks, and, 81

Occupational premises
    reasons for valuation, and, 130–131
Open market price
    valuation for tax purposes, and,
        136–137
Open market value
    and see Market approach
    valuation for tax purposes, and,
        133–134
Option pricing
    research and development, and,
        46–47
Originality
    copyright, and
        generally, 64
        overview, 377–378
    unregistered designs, and
        generally, 93
        overview, 433
Owner value
    types of valuation, and, 137
Ownership of IPR
    checklist of issues, 339–341
    copyright, and
        employee works, 64–65
        form of declaration, 337–338
        generally, 64
        overview, 378–380
    database right, and, 68
    design right, and
        generally, 90
        overview, 430
    patents, and
        generally, 77–78
        overview, 405–406
        US system, 77–78
    trade marks, and
        generally, 83
        overview, 418

unregistered designs, and
    generally, 94
    overview, 434

Packaging of goods
    due diligence, and, 293
    trade marks, and, 81
Parallel imports
    case study, 323–324
    legal position, 319–322
    strategy implications, 322–325
Paris Convention 1883
    intellectual property rights, and, 59
Passing off
    due diligence, and, 293
    generally, 85–86
    overview, 423–424
Patent Cooperation Treaty (PCT)
    framework, 73
    generally, 70
    introduction, 60
Patents
    application process
        generally, 72–73
        overview, 398–400
    basic requirements
        generally, 70–71
        overview, 389
    business methods, 394–395
    due diligence, and
        effect of risk, 281–283
        generally, 275–277
        overview, 71
        searches, 277–281
        summary, 283
    European system
        application process, 74
        designating countries, 74
        framework, 73–74
        grace periods, 74–75
        overview, 400–401
    exclusions
        generally, 71
        overview, 393–394
    industrial application
        generally, 71
        overview, 397–398